LUCAN'S IMPERIAL WORLD

Also published by Bloomsbury

ANTICIPATION AND ANACHRONY IN STATIUS' THEBAID
by Robert Simms

LUCAN: BELLO CIVILI I
edited by Robert J. Getty

LUCAN: DE BELLO CIVILI VII
edited by O.A.W. Dilke

THE POET LUCAN
by Mark P.O. Morford

LUCAN'S IMPERIAL WORLD

THE *BELLUM CIVILE* IN ITS CONTEMPORARY CONTEXTS

Edited by Laura Zientek and Mark Thorne

BLOOMSBURY ACADEMIC
LONDON • NEW YORK • OXFORD • NEW DELHI • SYDNEY

BLOOMSBURY ACADEMIC
Bloomsbury Publishing Plc
50 Bedford Square, London, WC1B 3DP, UK
1385 Broadway, New York, NY 10018, USA
29 Earlsfort Terrace, Dublin 2, Ireland

BLOOMSBURY, BLOOMSBURY ACADEMIC and the Diana logo
are trademarks of Bloomsbury Publishing Plc

First published in Great Britain 2020
Paperback edition first published 2021

Copyright © Laura Zientek, Mark Thorne and Contributors, 2020

Laura Zientek and Mark Thorne have asserted their right under the Copyright,
Designs and Patents Act, 1988, to be identified as Editors of this work..

For legal purposes the Acknowledgements on p. x constitute an
extension of this copyright page.

Cover design: Terry Woodley
Cover image © Cubiculum (bedroom) from the Villa of P. Fannius Synistor at Boscoreale,
MET DP170943 247017

All rights reserved. No part of this publication may be reproduced or
transmitted in any form or by any means, electronic or mechanical,
including photocopying, recording, or any information storage or retrieval
system, without prior permission in writing from the publishers.

Bloomsbury Publishing Plc does not have any control over, or responsibility for,
any third-party websites referred to or in this book. All internet addresses given
in this book were correct at the time of going to press. The author and publisher
regret any inconvenience caused if addresses have changed or sites have
ceased to exist, but can accept no responsibility for any such changes.

A catalogue record for this book is available from the British Library.

A catalog record for this book is available from the Library of Congress.

ISBN: HB: 978-1-3500-9741-4
PB: 978-1-3501-9372-7
ePDF: 978-1-3500-9742-1
eBook: 978-1-3500-9743-8

Typeset by RefineCatch Limited, Bungay, Suffolk

To find out more about our authors and books visit
www.bloomsbury.com and sign up for our newsletters.

CONTENTS

Notes on Contributors   vii
Acknowledgments   x
List of Abbreviations   xi

Introduction: Lucan and His World   *Laura Zientek and Mark Thorne*   1

Part I Lucan and Contemporary Authors and Traditions   15

1. Imperial Ethics and the Individual in Lucan and Seneca's *Letters*
   Paul Roche   17

2. *Lucanus Mirabatur Adeo Scripta Flacci*: Lucan and Persius
   Thomas Biggs   33

3. Cicero, Lucan, and Rhetorical Role-play in *Bellum Civile* 7
   Annette M. Baertschi   51

Part II The Natural World and Geography in the Neronian Period   71

4. Mining and Morality in Lucan and Seneca   *Laura Zientek*   73

5. Even *Natura* Nods: Lucan's Alternative Explanations of the Syrtes (9.303–18)   *James Calvin Taylor*   91

6. World Geography, Roman History, and the Failure to Incorporate Parthia in Lucan's *Bellum Civile*   *Mauro Serena*   111

Part III Cato's Neronian *Nachleben*   131

7. Lucan's Cato and Popular (Mis)conceptions of Stoicism
   David H. Kaufman   133

8. Sage, Soldier, Politician, and Benefactor: Cato in Seneca and Lucan
   Francesca D'Alessandro Behr   151

Part IV Back to the Future: Republic and Empire   171

9. Lucan and the Specter of Sulla in Julio-Claudian Rome
   Julia Mebane   173

10. Re-Membering the Palatine in Lucan's *Bellum Civile*   *Jesse Weiner*   191

Contents

11 Lucan's Nostalgia and the Infection of Memory *E. V. Mulhern* 209

12 Lucan's Neronian *Res Publica Restituta* *Andrew M. McClellan* 229

Index Locorum Lucani et Senecae 247

General Index 253

CONTRIBUTORS

Annette M. Baertschi is Associate Professor in the Department of Greek, Latin, and Classical Studies at Bryn Mawr College and Director of the Graduate Group in Archaeology, Classics, and History of Art. Her research interests include Roman imperial poetry, especially epic and tragedy, Greek drama and performance, Neo-Latin literature, and the reception of the ancient world in modern media. She has published a monograph on necromancy in Neronian and Flavian epic and a co-edited volume on the history of classical scholarship as well as articles on Senecan tragedy, Lucan, and ancient Greek women in contemporary European film.

Francesca D'Alessandro Behr, a native of Italy, is a Full Professor of Italian and Classical Studies at the University of Houston where she teaches courses on Italian, Latin literature, and classical reception. Her research is similarly oriented on both fields. Her book on Lucan, *Feeling History: Lucan, Stoicism and the Aesthetics of Passion* appeared in 2007 and a new book of hers titled *Arms and the Woman: Classical Tradition and Women Writers in the Venetian Renaissance* came out in 2018.

Thomas Biggs is Assistant Professor of Classics at the University of Georgia. His book, *Poetics of the First Punic War*, is nearly complete. He has recently published an edited volume with J. Blum, *The Epic Journey in Greek and Roman Literature* (2019). His recent articles and chapters treat various topics in Roman literary studies.

David H. Kaufman is Associate Professor of Classics and Philosophy at Transylvania University (Lexington, KY). His research focuses on Hellenistic philosophy and ancient medicine. His recent publications include articles on Greek tragedy, Stoicism, and Galen. He is currently working on a book on the Stoic theory of emotions and a critical edition of Book One of Chrysippus' *On Providence*.

Andrew M. McClellan is the Stepsay Family Postdoctoral Fellow in Classics at San Diego State University. His research interests range widely across ancient literature and its reception, with a particular focus on the topic of violence (physical, rhetorical, and metapoetic). He has published on Homer, Lucan, and Mary Shelley. His book, *Abused Bodies in Roman Epic*, is forthcoming.

Julia Mebane is an assistant professor of Classical Studies at Indiana University, Bloomington. Her research explores the intersection of Latin literature and Roman political thought, including themes of republicanism, civil war, and the *domus Augusta*. Her current book project explores how Roman thinkers used the metaphor of the body politic to address constitutional change between 63 BCE and 68 CE. Previous publications include "Carlyle the Tragedian: Staging Euripides' *Bacchae* in *The French*

Contributors

Revolution," *Classical Receptions* 11.1 (2019) and "Pompey's Head and the Body Politic in Lucan's *De Bello Civili*," *TAPA* 146.1 (2016).

E. V. Mulhern is Assistant Professor of Instruction at Temple University. In addition to her work on Lucan, she is interested in imperial epic more generally, and the way history interacts with Latin literature. Her research focuses especially on late antique approaches to the Roman past, encompassing both pagan and Christian sources.

Paul Roche is Associate Professor of Latin at The University of Sydney. He has published commentaries on Lucan *De Bello Civili* book 1 (2009) and book 7 (2019), and he has edited books on politics in Roman imperial literature (2009) and Pliny's *Panegyricus* (2011). He is currently editing a collection of essays on Lucan and writing a commentary on the first book of Tacitus' *Annals*.

Mauro Serena is completing a PhD in Classics at the University of Reading (UK) on the perception of Persia in Roman culture and works on Achaemenid Persia and the reception of Persian themes in Italian melodrama in the eighteenth century. His article, "Metastasio and the Persian King. Exemplarity and Senecan Echoes in the *Artaserse* and the *Temistocle*," is forthcoming in R. Rollinger and K. Ruffing (eds.), *Das Weltreich der Perser—Rezeption, Aneignung und Verargumentierung von der Antike bis in die Gegenwart / The Persian Empire—Reception, Appropriation and Argumentation from Antiquity to the Present Day*.

James Calvin Taylor is a PhD candidate in Classical Philology at Harvard University, whose dissertation "Plumbing the depths: geological processes, deep time, and the shaping of landscapes in classical literature," explores how the slow, incremental nature of geological processes is used by Greco-Roman authors to imagine much larger timescales than we typically associate with classical literature, and how this deeper, geologic time often disrupts heuristic models and aesthetics that are more intimately tied to the timescale of an individual human life or a community's existence.

Mark Thorne is Visiting Assistant Professor of Classics at Luther College. His research focuses on the intersection of Roman poetry, history, and memory with an emphasis on narratives of Roman civil war, specializing in Lucan and the evolution of Cato the Younger in Roman cultural memory. Publications include studies on the role of memory in Lucan, the value of reading Lucan alongside literary portrayals of the Rwandan genocide, Neronian satire, and efforts to commemorate the Battle of Pharsalia. A chapter on Cato the Younger's transformation into a productive site of exemplarity is forthcoming.

Jesse Weiner is Assistant Professor of Classics at Hamilton College. He publishes broadly on Greek and Latin literature and its reception, with special interests in monumentality and memory, sexuality and gender, and aesthetics. In public humanities, his work has appeared in *History Today* and *The Atlantic*. He is co-editor of *Frankenstein and Its Classics: The Modern Prometheus from Antiquity to Science Fiction* (2018).

Laura Zientek is Visiting Assistant Professor of Classics at Reed College. Her research focuses on the intersection of landscape representation and natural philosophy in Roman epic poetry, and on poetic treatments of natural and built environments. She has published on the Pharos in Lucan, the auditory sublime in Latin epic, and Lucan's landscapes of dread. She is currently writing on the geography of *Oceanus* and on eco-catastrophe between ancient and modern literature.

ACKNOWLEDGMENTS

Just as Lucan did not compose the *Bellum Civile* in a vacuum, this book on Lucan did not come together without a lot of help and encouragement from multiple quarters. We first and foremost want to thank the Department of Comparative Arts and Letters at Brigham Young University for making the unusual choice of hiring two Lucan specialists for both of their visiting appointments in Classics, as that decision made possible the many fruitful conversations that culminated in the decision to organize a conference on Lucan in 2017. Thanks are due to our colleagues Roger Macfarlane, Stephen Bay, Cecilia Peek, Seth Jeppesen, and Mike Pope for their constant encouragement. We also owe a great debt to our department and the BYU College of Humanities, in particular Carl Sederholm and Scott Miller, for their unstinting generosity in providing funding and logistical support.

Those who attended the conference and shared their ideas deserve special thanks for making the event a success and inspiring us to move forward with the idea of putting together this book. We are grateful that our contributors have shared their work with us and chosen to publish it here. The editorial team at Bloomsbury has been a pleasure to work with and a steady source of clear-headed guidance, for which we are grateful; thanks go out especially to Alice Wright, Publisher for Classical Studies and Archaeology, and to Elena Roberts and Lily Mac Mahon, Editorial Assistants, for always steering us in the right direction. We are grateful for the time and expertise of all the external reviewers who read the chapters of this book and provided advice and insight for its improvement. We also acknowledge the support we have received from our current institutions, Luther College and Reed College, in particular the generous award of a Summer Scholarship Research Fund grant from Reed in support of this volume. Finally, we extend our deepest thanks and gratitude to our families and friends; it is their relationships that continue to make this journey worthwhile.

Mark Thorne would like to thank Jung Eun Kim for her love, patience, and encouragement; William for smiling at his daddy every day and reminding him of what matters most; Laura Zientek for holding the ship steady during the editing process; Joshua Trampier and Laura Berlin for a lifetime of friendship; his Luther colleagues Dan Davis and Anne Bulliung for their hospitality and support; and his parents John and Helen Thorne for helping him follow his dream.

Laura Zientek would like to thank her family for their unwavering support and encouragement; her friends and colleagues at Reed—especially Ellen Millender, Sonia Sabnis, Paul Vădan, and Liz Fretwell—for helping make Reed a productive and enjoyable place to complete this project; Sara Korsmo and Brett Rogers for their humor and advice; and of course, Mark Thorne, as a fellow traveler/co-editor on this voyage.

ABBREVIATIONS

AClass	*Acta Classica*
AIV	*Atti dell'Instituto Veneto di Scienze, Lettere ed Arti, Classe di Scienze morali e Lettere*
AJPh	*American Journal of Philology*
AncPhil	*Ancient Philosophy*
ANRW	*Aufstieg und Niedergang der römischen Welt*
ASNP	*Annali della Scuola Normale Superiore di Pisa, Cl. di Lettere e Filosofia*
BAGB	*Bulletin de l'Association Guillaume Budé*
BICS	*Bulletin of the Institute of Classical Studies at the University of London*
C&M	*Classica et mediaevalia: revue danoise d'histoire et de philologie publiée par la Société danoise pour les études anciennes et médiévales*
CB	*Classical Bulletin*
CFC(L)	*Cuadernos de filología clásica. Estudios latinos.*
CJ	*Classical Journal*
ClAnt	*Classical Antiquity*
CPh	*Classical Philology*
CQ	*Classical Quarterly*
CronErc	*Cronache Ercolanesi*
CW	*The Classical World*
Endt	J. Endt (ed.) *Adnotationes Super Lucanum* (Leipzig 1969)
G&R	*Greece and Rome*
GB	*Grazer Beiträge: Zeitschrift für die klassische Altertumswissenschaft*
HAnt	*Hispania antiqua: revista de historia antigua*
HSPh	*Harvard Studies in Classical Philology*
ICS	*Illinois Classical Studies*
InvLuc	*Invigilata Lucernis: rivista dell'Instituto di Latino*
JHS	*Journal of Hellenic Studies*
JRS	*Journal of Roman Studies*
MAT	*Memorie dell'Accademia delle Scienze di Torino*
MD	*Materiali e discussioni per l'analisi dei testi classici*

Abbreviations

NC	*The Numismatic Chronicle*
OSAP	*Oxford Studies in Ancient Philosophy*
PCPhS	*Proceedings of the Cambridge Philological Society*
PhilosQ	*The Philosophical Quarterly*
REL	*Revue des Études Latines*
RhM	*Rheinisches Museum*
RPhA	*Revue de philosophie ancienne*
SIFC	*Studi Italiani di Filologia Classica*
SJPh	*The Southern Journal of Philosophy*
SVF	*Stoicorum Veterum Fragmenta*
TAPhA	*Transactions of the American Philological Association*
TLL	*Thesaurus Linguae Latinae*

INTRODUCTION: LUCAN AND HIS WORLD
Laura Zientek and Mark Thorne

Artist and Environment

Art, like its creators, never exists in a vacuum. All artistic expression arises from the interaction between artist and environment, and any comprehensive understanding of a work of art must take into account its various contexts of production. The environments—temporal, geographical, cultural—that influence the artist and the production of his or her art are fundamentally relevant to a thorough and nuanced understanding of that art. For this reason, when we come to Lucan's *Bellum Civile*, we must read his epic poem on the century-old civil war between Caesar and Pompey not in isolation as merely a literary work of the Neronian period, but as the product, along with its author, of the numerous contemporary environments that shaped them both.

This idea is at the heart of the following collection of papers, which aims to shed greater light on the inescapable fact that Lucan was a man of his own time. When considering major influences on Lucan's epic, however, modern scholarship tends toward looking backward or forward in time than to Lucan's own Claudian-Neronian age. There is of course good reason to do so; the *Bellum Civile* is the only surviving example of Latin epic poetry between the Augustan and Flavian eras and thus is a principle successor of Vergil and Ovid. The influence of Vergil's *Aeneid* upon all subsequent Latin epic is of course immense, and this scholarly attention to Lucan's relationship with his predecessors is rightly crucial in our understanding of the poem (e.g., Thompson and Bruère [1968] 2010; Hardie 1993; Narducci 2002; Casali 2011; Willis 2011; Gross 2013). At the same time, the rich engagement between Lucan's text and subsequent epics written in the Flavian period or later has also received increasing amounts of attention in recent years (e.g., Lovatt 1999; Trinacty 2012; Stover 2014; Berlincourt et al. 2016). These approaches are useful, necessary, and productive, but it remains important not to limit too much our attention on Lucan's text and context primarily to his points of connection with his literary predecessors and successors. While Lucan's epic can indeed be read as a response to Vergil's vision of a founding myth of the Roman people, a continuation of Ovid's transformative take on the epic genre, or a forerunner of Flavian epic themes, the *Bellum Civile* must also be recognized as reflecting the personal, political, cultural, and literary influences of its own time. Lucan and his *Bellum Civile* simply cannot and should not be disentangled from the Claudian and Neronian periods of Roman culture and history.

Interest in Lucan has continued to increase throughout the past two decades, as a growing number of volumes of essays focused on Lucan and his poem indicates (Esposito and Nicastri 1999; Esposito and Ariemma 2004; Walde 2005, 2009; Hömke and Reitz

2010; Devillers and Franchet d'Espèrey 2010; Tesoriero 2010; Asso 2011; Esposito and Walde 2015; Galtier and Poignault 2016); monographs display a similar trend (e.g., Dinter 2012; Fratantuono 2012; Day 2013; Domenicucci 2013; Manolaraki 2013; Ludwig 2014; Tracy 2014; Ambühl 2015; Blaschka 2015; Kimmerle 2015; Galtier 2018; Nill 2018). The goal of this collection of essays is to join this ongoing exploration of Lucan and his world by directing specific scholarly attention toward poet and poem as products of their own time. The specter of Nero looms large over virtually every arena of activity that took place during his reign, arguably more so than the figure of Augustus over the output of his era. In the memorable formulation of Emily Gowers (1994: 131), "Neronian literature, more than that of any other period in Rome, demands to be read in the shadow, or rather, glare of its ruler. The sun-king always penetrates the dark studies and rural retreats that confine Neronian writing." This observation is especially true for Lucan, who explicitly invokes Nero as his epic muse and only necessary source of inspiration: *tu satis ad vires Romana in carmina dandas* ("You are sufficient for granting strength to this Roman song," 1.66). Thus, this collection of papers seeks to renew focus on the *Bellum Civile* in connection with its own contemporary world.[1]

As influential as Nero undoubtedly was in shaping the *Bellum Civile*, much more must be said about Lucan's lived environment beyond the influence of Nero himself. The emperor occupies much of the scholarly attention devoted toward Lucan's constellation of influences, but too often lost in Nero's glare are the other forces at work upon Lucan's life and poem. These include such potential factors as his family, his geographical background, contemporary political developments, the educational (and thus rhetorical) practices in which he and his peers were trained, his eclectic philosophical influences, the sociocultural impact of his aristocratic environment, and the ubiquitous memory landscape of the Roman past—celebratory and obliterating in turns—that surrounded him and his epic audience of the 60s CE. The sum of these and other environments beyond Nero's influence collectively comprise the contemporary contexts that informed Lucan's composition of the *Bellum Civile*. Some analyses on this topic have been undertaken in the past, focusing on political culture, Stoic thought, and wider trends in Neronian literature (e.g., Bonner [1966] 2010; Ahl 1976: 17–61, 333–53; Rudich 1997; Roller 2001; Schrijvers 2005), but further work needs to be done. This collection of papers seeks to invigorate the dialogue concerning how Lucan's lived environments remain central to a comprehensive understanding of his fascinating, enigmatic, and always rewarding epic.

This volume has its roots in the conference "Lucan in His Contemporary Contexts" held in April 2017 at Brigham Young University, which brought together an international team of scholars with the goal of approaching the *Bellum Civile* in full engagement with the cultural, literary, and historical environments in which Lucan lived and worked. We urged the speakers to adopt what we colloquially termed a "Lucan +" approach to reading the epic by focusing on points of contact between Lucan's work and external realities from Lucan's lifetime. Keeping the entire scope of Lucan's life in view relaxes his typical period classification as an exclusively Neronian poet. He was indeed personally connected to the young emperor and composed his epic during Nero's reign, but before his literary career began, he was born under Caligula and grew up into adolescence under Claudius. These formative years profoundly shaped the worldviews of both Lucan himself and those who raised and taught him. His pre-Neronian environments thus should not be neglected, a point perhaps most clear when considering the potential connections between Lucan and his uncle Seneca, who was active in politics and the literary scene long before Nero came to power. An examination of Lucan's contemporary contexts thus follows the poet's life across roughly a quarter century in the final decades of the Julio-Claudian dynasty. The benefits of such an approach are in welcome evidence in the papers collected in this volume.

Lucan's Contemporary Contexts: A Brief Tour

The Annaei: Lucan's Family

Lucan's career as a poet was shaped, perhaps before all else, by his family and its already-established literary reputation. Lucan's uncle, Seneca the Younger, as well as his grandfather, Seneca the Elder, were writers of some repute in the Roman world and served as bridges between his family and intellectual life.

L. Annaeus Seneca the Elder was part of an equestrian family living in Roman Spain. Born sometime around the year 50 BCE, he spent his youth and completed much of his education in Corduba before coming to Rome, where he heard recitations and may have studied rhetoric with a man named Marullus (Griffin 1972: 6). During his adulthood, he spent time between Rome and Spain, where his family estates were established and his children were born. His eldest son, Novatus, later became involved in politics and was appointed as governor of Achaea (Inwood 1995: 64); his youngest son, Mela, preferred the quiet life (*Controv.* 2 Pref. 3–4) and perhaps is most notable as Lucan's father. Seneca the Elder's middle son shared his name and in later generations became even more well-known than his father in his literary career. The elder Seneca lived to old age, wrote the rhetorical works *Suasoriae* and *Controversiae* as well as a history of the civil wars of the first century BCE, and died sometime around the year of Lucan's birth, 39 CE (Griffin 1972: 5). He cannot have had a great influence on Lucan personally, but his reputation both within the family and in Roman culture, the legacy of his writings, and his interest in the civil wars certainly would have shaped Lucan's life and career.

L. Annaeus Seneca the Younger was born between 4 and 1 BCE in Corduba and was brought to Rome as a child for his education (Griffin 1972: 6). Perhaps driven by an interest in pursuing a philosophical life rather than a political career (Inwood 1995: 64), the younger Seneca participated in Roman politics as an orator but did not hold office until after 37 CE when he was elected quaestor (Habinek 2013: 8). Seneca was a senator in 39 BCE when Caligula, offended by Seneca's oratorical skill (Romm 2014: 10), ordered him to commit suicide. Ultimately, Caligula was dissuaded from his plans because he was told Seneca was seriously ill and soon would die anyway (Habinek 2013: 8; Braund 2015: 24; cf. Cass. Dio 59.19).[2] Later in 41 CE the senate, perhaps influenced by Claudius' new wife Messalina, sentenced Seneca to death for his participation in an alleged conspiracy with Caligula's sister, Livilla. Claudius commuted the sentence and exiled Seneca to Corsica (Osgood 2011: 42; Habinek 2013: 9; Romm 2014: 25–6). He remained there until Agrippina, then married to Claudius, recalled him in 49 to be a tutor and advisor to her son Nero (Osgood 2011: 226–7). Seneca's direct connection to and influence over Nero waned rapidly in 62 after the death of S. Afranius Burrus; Seneca attempted to retire (Tac., *Ann.* 14.53–6) and gradually spent less time in the imperial court. Seneca's literary career spanned many years, though his individual works are often difficult to date precisely. His corpus represents a significant source for Stoic philosophy in antiquity and contains twelve dialogues, two additional essays (*De Clementia* and *De Beneficiis*), a collection of 124 letters on moral philosophy, a treatise on Stoic physics, a satire on Claudius, and at least eight literary tragedies. The younger Seneca's influence on Lucan's intellectual life cannot be underestimated, especially in regards to the elements of Stoic theory that appear throughout Lucan's text.

Roman Education

By the late Republic, elite Roman education consisted of a robust system of training in grammar, literature, and rhetoric (Bloomer 2011; Dominik 2017; Steel 2017), and Lucan had access to the best education an equestrian Roman family could offer. Thus, like his older relatives and his own contemporary elite peers, Lucan was trained in both the Greek and Roman literary traditions, and he spent much of his adolescence honing his rhetorical skills in the art of declamation. These were classroom exercises meant to train students in the preparation and delivery of public speeches, encouraging displays of ethical judgment combined with showy performance techniques. In particular, Lucan and his fellow students competed with each other in the two branches of declamation: *controversiae*, forensic speeches for imaginary court cases, and *suasoriae*, deliberative speeches in which the speaker sought to persuade a historical person to pursue a given course of action (Bloomer 2011: 170–91; cf. Gunderson 2003). Bloomer (2007: 297) reminds us that "declamation is the first major literary movement of the Roman empire," and its vast influence on all modes of cultural output in the principate simply cannot be overlooked.

Accordingly, the profound influence of declamatory rhetoric is everywhere in Lucan's epic (Bonner [1966] 2010), and Lucan's own family background goes a long way toward explaining why. Rhetorical skill was in fact a key element in the rise to prominence of several key members of the Annaeus family (Griffin 1972). As outlined above, the elder Seneca moved in the highest circles of Roman rhetoric during the period of transition from Republic to Empire, and his son Seneca the Younger enjoyed a full rhetorical education (Habinek 2013: 8; Keeline 2018: 197). He too rose to prominence through his skill in public speaking, enough so that his entry into public consciousness is attested by the derisive notice Caligula took of his trendy, refined oratorical style, which was at the time already quite popular (*Senecam tum maxime placentem*, Suet., *Calig.* 53). Lucan in turn displayed enormous rhetorical talent, following in the footsteps of both sides of his family; the *Vita Vaccae* identifies his maternal grandfather Acilius Lucanus as a famous orator. Vacca's brief biography further states that Lucan was trained by the best teachers and soon surpassed all other students as he began to "declaim in both Greek and Latin to the great admiration of his audience" (*declamavit et Graece et Latine cum magna admiratione audientium*, p. 2 line 4–5 Endt; cf. Fantham 2011: 5). Even if we accept some amount of retrojected exaggeration within the biographical tradition, the language of the *Bellum Civile* demonstrates that Lucan commanded a remarkable, even precocious, prowess in rhetoric, a feature of the epic text that eventually led to Quintilian's famous assessment that Lucan was "to be imitated more by orators than poets" (*magis oratoribus quam poetis imitandus*, 10.1.90). Lucan's frequent inclusion of memorable *sententiae* and his nods to the exemplary tradition, both traditional tools of the Roman classroom, showcase his consciously rhetorical style, as do the declamatory elements found in the numerous speeches over the course of the epic. In terms of Lucan's distinctive portrayal of a universe in chaos, a rhetorical frame of mind remains one of his characteristic techniques.

Roman Politics from Caligula to Nero

Lucan was born during the short reign of Caligula, lived through the reign of Claudius, and reached the peak of his literary career under Nero, before the events of the Pisonian Conspiracy led to his death. The decisions, policies, and actions, both domestic and international, of these three emperors defined the time and places in which Lucan lived and wrote.

Caligula's reign lasted merely four years, but had vast repercussions within the Roman state. Political reforms early in his reign (Suet., *Calig.* 16.2) and ambitious construction projects gave way to financial crises (Cass. Dio 59.10) and conflict with the senate (Suet., *Calig.* 26). In 40 CE, Caligula began the expansion of the Roman empire in Mauretania (Plin., *HN* 5.2) and attempted inroads to Britain. Caligula's assassination in January of 41 CE led to a failed attempt by the Senate to restore the Republic (Josephus, *Ant.* 19.2) and subsequently to the reign of Claudius.

Under Claudius, a focus on public works improved and expanded Roman infrastructure in Italy. Claudius oversaw the construction of two new aqueducts—the Aqua Claudia and the Anio Novus—as well as the restoration of the Aqua Virgo, new roads and canals were constructed in both Italy and the provinces, and an attempt was made to increase farmland in Italy by draining the Fucine Lake, though this project failed catastrophically when a flood washed out *ludi* held to celebrate the project's "success," and caused many, including Claudius himself, to flee for their lives (Suet., *Claud.* 20; Tac., *Ann.* 12.57). Claudius also oversaw major expansion of the empire's territory and authority. In addition to annexing or otherwise gaining control over Thrace, Noricum, Pamphylia, Lycia, and Judaea, he completed the annexation of Mauretania—as Mauretania Tingitana and Mauretania Caesariensis—and completed the conquest of Britain, a victory for which Claudius took more imperial salutations than even Augustus had during the entirety of his reign (Griffin 1984: 224). Claudius' reign ended when he was poisoned by his wife Agrippina, Nero's mother (Tac., *Ann.* 12.66–7).

Though Nero's personal foibles and vices became well known in the 60s CE, several international events also define Rome during this period. Nero pursued foreign policy in the manner of his predecessors; under his direction, the governors of Britannia oversaw the consolidation of Roman power in their new province, though expansion of Roman authority into the eastern part of Britain was challenged by the rebellion of the Iceni and other tribes led by Boudicca in 60 CE (Griffin 1984: 225–6; Shotter 2008: 91–5). Elsewhere expansion of power in the manner pursued by Rome since the late Republic had long met the greatest resistance from the Parthians in the east. Under the direction of Domitius Corbulo, Nero's appointed governor of Cappadocia-Galatia, Parthian influence in Armenia eventually subsided after years of conflict, and by the end of 63 CE Rome had gained control over the area (Griffin 1984: 227; Shotter 2008: 96–8). Despite the historical record's often hostile approach to Nero as an individual and to his domestic actions in the later years of his reign, in approaching international politics Nero attempted to uphold the reputation of the *princeps* as "a successful commander and diplomat" (Braund 2013: 85; cf. Thorne 2018).

The Aristocracy and the Emperor

Within the well-established hierarchy of the Roman world, Lucan grew up in a wealthy and well-connected equestrian family, putting him in the top echelons of the Roman sociopolitical order. By the mid-first century CE, however, the *princeps* alone occupied the apex of the Roman hierarchy. "The advent of the emperor in Roman society, and of the imperial regime we call the principate, marked a massive and unprecedented relocation of power and authority in the Roman world" (Roller 2001: 6), and this relocation had a profound impact upon the intellectual, social, and political life of every member of the aristocracy. Ever since Julius Caesar had won his civil war and named himself dictator-for-life, and ever since Octavian had won his civil war, received the name Augustus, and took perpetual control of the tribunician power and the military, Rome had been under the *de facto* rule of a single man. In light of this reality, the Roman elite were always in the process of negotiating their fraught relationship with their *Caesar* and the autocracy he embodied (Roller 2001; Osgood 2017). Each emperor sought to "perpetuat[e his own] power and authority" while at the same time the Roman elite sought to "maximiz[e] honor and social prestige" (Noreña 2017: 59). Despite Claudius' attempts to reconcile with the senate (McAlindon 1957: 280–1) and the *quinquennium Neronis* during which the young *princeps* still heeded his inner circle of advisers (Noreña 2017: 59), conspiracies arose repeatedly against the latter Julio-Claudian emperors (e.g., Suet., *Claud.* 35, *Ner.* 36; Tac., *Ann.* 15.48–74; Cass. Dio 60.15.1–6, 62.24–7). The Pisonian conspiracy of 65 CE led to Lucan's death; later, the rebellion of G. Julius Vindex in 68 brought about Nero's death. The violence and intrigue between *princeps* and aristocracy ensured the awareness of Roman autocracy in contemporary literature. Lucan overtly states the importance of this reality from the beginning of his epic when he declares in his opening dedication to Nero that all the horrors of civil war were worth it "because it was all done for you" (*quod tibi res acta est*, 1.45).

Throughout the *Bellum Civile*, Neronian-era anxiety over autocratic rule is on display. The aristocracy in the early principate had a handful of models for envisioning their relationship with their emperor: he could be approached as society's supreme benefactor, its loftiest father figure, or its slave master. This last role, the *dominus*, generated the most concern among the elite whose traditional sociopolitical prerogatives and *libertas* were threatened. Seneca, living with this fear of the loss of *libertas* his whole career under the capricious eyes of multiple emperors (Romm 2014), found various ways to cope with this anxiety, primarily through a flexible combination of pragmatic politics and philosophical ideals. His nephew Lucan, on the other hand, offers in the *Bellum Civile* a starker, more succinct vision: *omnia Caesar erat* ("everything was Caesar," 3.108).

Philosophy in Rome during the First Century CE

Roman philosophy in the mid-first century CE looked back to Cicero and Lucretius in the first century BCE, and more broadly to the foundation and practice of the major philosophical schools—including the Academics, Peripatetics, Stoics, and Epicureans—in Athens between the fourth and third centuries BCE. Since before the foundation of these schools, Athens had been central to the philosophical world of the ancient Mediterranean, and it was not until the early first century BCE that this changed in a significant way. The "philosophical diaspora" that occurred around the years 88–86 BCE was associated with inactivity in the various schools and physical migration of philosophers and their libraries away from Athens to other major cities, including Rome (Sedley 2003: 24–5; Inwood 1995: 63). Though Athens still had the reputation of a city associated with philosophy— enough that Cicero fondly describes hearing lectures and visiting notable locations in the history of philosophy during a visit to Athens in 79 BCE (*De Fin.* 5.1–6)—the momentum of philosophy in Athens had lapsed.

By Cicero's time, Rome was becoming a new central location for philosophy with the arrival of individual philosophers into Italy. Cicero himself interacted closely with several prominent philosophers including the Stoics Panaetius and Diodotus, and the head of the Academy, Philo of Larissa; their influence on his writings can be seen in Cicero's advocation for philosophy as a means of participating in and benefitting the *res publica* (Atkins 2000: 504). Along with the physical presence of philosophers and philosophical texts came the introduction of a Latin vocabulary for Greek philosophical ideas as introduced by authors such as Cicero and Lucretius. Philosophers soon began to have an increasingly influential role in the politics of Rome, notably demonstrated by the Stoics Athenodorus and Arius Didymus in the court of Augustus (Sedley 2003: 30–2).

The political and social upheaval of the Roman civil wars, the end of the Republic, and the rise of the principate also affected the practice of philosophy in Rome. As opposed to their Hellenistic predecessors, the philosophers in early imperial Rome were more concerned with pedagogy and practicality than in the details of theory and dogma. Seneca, Cornutus, and Musonius Rufus—Stoic philosophers of the Claudian and Neronian periods—were particularly focused on teaching practical ethics (Bryan 2013: 147), thus shifting focus from the ideal sage to the person working to be good. Perhaps in a similar vein, they also showed a willingness to borrow from other schools. This "eclecticism" was relatively limited in scope and as such, was not so much an abandonment of orthodoxy as it was a nod toward the practicality of philosophical education (Gill 2003: 44; Bryan 2013: 134). Both Epicureans and Stoics participated in politics, but among the Stoics, such participation—even in service of a monarch—was characterized as being in accordance with their philosophical ideals (*ex institutione Stoica*, Sen., *Ben.* 2.20.2; Bartsch 2017: 153).

The Julio-Claudian period was, generally speaking, a positive time for philosophy. Seneca the Younger stands out as both the most socially and politically prominent and the most literarily prolific philosopher of the early imperial period. His philosophical corpus represents the most complete source for Stoicism in Rome and is notable for its presentation and practice of philosophy in Latin rather than Greek. Seneca's writings, as well as those of his contemporaries Cornutus (Reydams-Schils 2016: 18–19; Boys-Stones 2018) and Musonius (Dillon 2004; Reydams-Schils 2016: 23–4), are also notable in their influence on poetry; the poet Persius worked closely with Cornutus, just as Lucan did with Seneca. Since philosophy—Stoicism especially—had become by this point a common part of the education of an upper-class Roman, it had a significant effect in shaping the literature of the period in a way that is "without parallel in other eras of antiquity" (Gill 2003: 56). Despite the overlapping values of Stoic philosophy and Roman society more broadly, the mid-first century was also the occasion of notable conflicts between philosophers and the state. Nero oversaw the exile of Helvidius Priscus, L. Annaeus Cornutus, C. Musonius Rufus, Paconius Agrippinus, and Curtius Montanus, and the death sentences of Thrasea Paetus, Barea Soranus, Rubellius Plautus, and both Seneca and Lucan (Bartsch 2017: 154–6; cf. Plin., *Ep.* 3.11; Tac., *Ann.* 16.25 and 34), a series of events that also shaped the perception of philosophy in Rome during the mid-first century.

Cultural Memory in the Early Empire

The Romans were a people particularly aware of the power of the past, and accordingly they embraced a wide range of memorial habits (Walter 2004; Gowing 2005; Corbier 2006) that ranged from physical monuments like statues and tombs to less tangible practices like annual calendar celebrations and religious festivals; in addition to these were works of literature and oral storytelling traditions, including *exempla* (Langlands 2018; Roller 2018). These layers of Rome's cultural memory collectively fostered a set of shared narratives for the Roman people regarding who they had been in the past, were in the present, and by implication could and would be in the future. The past century of research has shown that the act of remembering, rather than being merely a straightforward cognitive act of recall, is much more a creative and selective act of reconstructing the past dependent upon the perceived needs of the present (Erll 2011: 8; Galinsky 2014: 3). Commemoration thus requires a conscious choice to privilege an event or person from the past as *significant* for the present and the identity of the people doing the remembering (Assmann 1995; Erll 2011; Galinsky 2016). The corollary is that commemoration also requires selected forgetting.

These traits of cultural memory are deeply relevant to Lucan's memorial epic project. Like his peers, he grew up steeped in selected episodes of Rome's past through his educational years of training in literature, moral *exempla*, and declamatory exercises. He chose as his theme a turning point in Roman history and identity: the civil war that was fought between Caesar and Pompey. As a historical epic, every event and character included in the narrative is in some way a reworking of previously inherited memories, shaped according to Lucan's own contemporary interests and anxieties. The mechanisms of Roman memory are thus of central importance to Lucan's epic (Thorne 2011; Galtier 2018), whether seen in individual episodes such as the Marius and Sulla flashback in Book 2 and the numerous mentions of tombs and ghosts, or in the larger theme of remembering not just what Rome gained but more importantly what Rome lost as a result of the civil wars that made possible a Roman world ruled by a dynasty of Caesars. The victorious Caesars had established their selected narrative of what the civil wars meant for Rome; Lucan's epic counter-memory gave his Neronian-era reader a different selected narrative to encounter anew.

Overview of Chapters

During the spring of 2017, Brigham Young University's Department of Comparative Arts and Letters and College of Humanities hosted the first conference in North America dedicated solely to Lucan and the *Bellum Civile*, and in particular, to the dialogue between Lucan's poem and the cultural, historical, and literary contexts of his own lifetime. The essays in this volume are revised products of this conference and the weekend of discussion and collegiality that it facilitated.

In Part I, Lucan's poetry is examined in relation to the works of contemporary authors and literary traditions. Lucan's own educational history is central here, as is evidenced by the prominence of Lucan's tutor and uncle, Seneca, Lucan's sometimes peer, Persius, and the topic of the rhetorical tradition, which was not only an unavoidable part of an elite Roman education, but also a key focus of Lucan's own grandfather, Seneca the Elder. To study issues of ethics and autonomy in both Seneca's *Letters* and Lucan's epic, Paul Roche highlights moments of similarity and intertext, as well as addressing the consequences of these moments of dialogue between the writing of uncle and nephew. Thomas Biggs identifies intertexts that exist between Lucan's epic and Persius' satires, demonstrating the changes of tone between genres and establishing an intertextual dialogue between the works of these contemporary poets. In a study focusing on the rhetorical tradition in Rome, Annette M. Baertschi examines the speech of Cicero in Book 7—itself a rhetorical creation rather than a historical record—as evidence for Lucan's knowledge of and interaction with the rhetorical schools.

The natural world's physical topography and classifications, its natural resources and their use, and the cultural and political ramifications of geography are the topic of Part

II. These papers use philological and philosophical methods of analysis informed by Stoic physics and modern ecocritical and geographic theories. Laura Zientek examines Lucan's portrayal of intercausality between people and nature against the model provided by Stoic philosophy by focusing on the ways Lucan and Seneca condemn extravagance and the acquisition of wealth in their portrayal of mines, miners, and the use/abuse of natural resources such as precious metals. James Calvin Taylor focuses on Lucan's treatment of the Syrtes, an area of shoals and shifting coastlines off the northern coast of Africa that was notoriously difficult for the Romans to navigate; he reads Lucan's explanations for the origins and structure of the Syrtes against Stoic ideas of cosmic dissolution in order to study the interrelationship between humanity and the natural world. Political geography, especially on the international stage, is at the heart of Mauro Serena's paper, which argues that Lucan's portrayal of the Parthians reflects contemporary Neronian military action in Armenia and Syria and the concurrent social, cultural, and historical consequences.

Part III presents two approaches to Lucan's engagement with the principles of Stoic philosophy and, in particular, with how authors convey the ideas of Stoicism in the mid-first century CE. Lucan's portrayal of Cato Uticensis, the Roman politician and Stoic who died at Utica in 46 BCE, is at the heart of both papers. David H. Kaufman considers Lucan's Cato in light of the gap between Stoic dogma and the popular conceptions and misconceptions of Stoic ideas during the Neronian period. Francesca D'Alessandro Behr compares the ways Lucan and Seneca express Stoic principles in an analysis of the figure of Cato by engaging with the idea of the benefactor in Roman politics and philosophy.

Part IV focuses on the sociopolitical environment that existed in Neronian Rome during Lucan's career. Much as the politics and culture of the Augustan age influenced Vergil's construction of a Roman identity within the context of the *Aeneid*, the political environment of Nero's time cannot be discounted in understanding Lucan's perspective: Lucan's portrayal of the civil wars is distinctly imperial. Julia Mebane establishes Lucan's use of Sullan imagery and language as the context for a discussion of Sulla's significance to political philosophy in Seneca's dialogues. Jesse Weiner focuses on Lucan's subversive, anachronistic, and even revisionist treatment of monuments and memory by exploring the depiction of the Palatine Temple to Apollo in the *Bellum Civile*. E. V. Mulhern examines the distance between the *exempla* of the late republic and the cultural environments of the Claudian-Neronian world, commenting on the simultaneous appeal and challenge of such nostalgia. Andrew McClellan describes how Lucan co-opts the "body of state" metaphor in interstitial poetic spaces between living and dying, drawing on discussions of necropolitics.

Notes

1 Comparable studies on contexts exist concerning Seneca (Parroni 2000), the *Iliad* (Heiden 1997), and ancient historiography (Kraus et al. 2010). More generally, van Dijk (2008: 5) describes contextualization as "a fundamental part of our understanding of human conduct,

in general, and of literature and other texts and talk, in particular;" Lehtonen (2000: 102) notes that contexts "actively affect the conventions writers have at their disposal," and proposes that we "consider contexts [as] variable and special cultural *resources*" (105).

2 What can be pieced together of Seneca's biography suggests that in fact he did suffer from ill-health in his youth; see Griffin (1976: 42); Braund (2015: 25); cf. Sen., *Ep.* 78.1–2; *Helv.* 19.2.

References

Ahl, F. (1976), *Lucan: An Introduction*, Ithaca, NY: Cornell University Press.
Ambühl, A. (2015), *Krieg und Bürgerkrieg bei Lucan und in der griechischen Literatur: Studien zur Rezeption der attischen Tragödie und der hellenistischen Dichtung im Bellum Civile*, Berlin: De Gruyter.
Assmann, J. (1995), "Collective Memory and Collective Identity," *New German Critique*, 65: 125–33.
Asso, P., ed. (2011), *Brill's Companion to Lucan*, Leiden: Brill.
Atkins, E. M. (2000), "Cicero," in C. Rowe and M. Schofield (eds.), *The Cambridge History of Greek and Roman Political Thought*, 477–516, Cambridge: Cambridge University Press.
Bartsch, S. (2017), "Philosophers and the State under Nero," in S. Bartsch, K. Freudenburg, and C. Littlewood (eds.), *The Cambridge Companion to Nero*, 151–63, Cambridge: Cambridge University Press.
Berlincourt, V., L. G. Milic, and D. Nelis, eds. (2016), *Lucan and Claudian: Context and Intertext*, Heidelberg: Universitatsverlag Winter.
Blaschka, K. (2015), *Fiktion im Historischen: die Bildsprache und die Konzeption der Charaktere in Lucans Bellum Civile*, Rahden: Leidorf.
Bloomer, W. M. (2007), "Roman Declamation: The Elder Seneca and Quintilian," in W. Dominik and J. Hall (eds.), *A Companion to Roman Rhetoric*, 297–306, Malden, MA: Blackwell.
Bloomer, W. M. (2011), *The School of Rome: Latin Studies and the Origins of Liberal Education*, Berkeley: University of California Press.
Bonner, S. F. ([1966] 2010), "Lucan and the Declamation Schools," in C. Tesoriero (ed.), *Lucan*, 69–106, Oxford: Oxford University Press.
Boys-Stones, G. (2018), *L. Annaeus Cornutus: Greek Theology, Fragments, and Testimonia*, Atlanta: SBL Press.
Braund, D. (2013), "Apollo in Arms: Nero at the Frontier," in E. Buckley and M. T. Dinter (eds.), *A Companion to the Neronian Age*, 83–101, Malden, MA: Wiley-Blackwell.
Braund, S. (2015), "Seneca Multiplex: The Phases (and Phrases) of Seneca's Life and Works," in S. Bartsch and A. Schiesaro (eds.), *The Cambridge Companion to Seneca*, 15–28, Cambridge: Cambridge University Press.
Bryan, J. (2013), "Neronian Philosophy," in E. Buckley and M. T. Dinter (eds.), *A Companion to the Neronian Age*, 134–48. Malden, MA: Wiley-Blackwell.
Casali, S. (2011), "The *Bellum Civile* as an Anti-*Aeneid*," in P. Asso (ed.), *Brill's Companion to Lucan*, 56–67, Leiden: Brill.
Corbier, M. (2006), *Donner À Voir, Donner À Lire: Mémoir et communication dans la Rome ancienne*, Paris: CNRS Éditions.
Day, H. J. M. (2013), *Lucan and the Sublime: Power, Representation and Aesthetic Experience*, Cambridge: Cambridge University Press.
Devillers, O. and S. Franchet d'Espèrey, eds. (2010), *Lucain en debat: Rhetorique, poetique et histoire*, Paris: Ausonius.
Dillon, J. T. (2004), *Musonius Rufus and Education in the Good Life: A Model of Teaching and Living Virtue*, Dallas: University Press of America.

Dinter, M. T. (2012), *Anatomizing Civil War: Studies in Lucan's Epic Technique*, Ann Arbor: University of Michigan Press.
Domenicucci, P. (2013), *Il Cielo di Lucano*, Pisa: ETS.
Dominik, W. J. (2017), "The Development of Roman Rhetoric," in M. J. MacDonald (ed.), *The Oxford Handbook of Rhetorical Studies*, 159–171, Oxford: Oxford University Press.
Erll, A. (2011), *Memory in Culture*, trans. S. B. Young, London: Palgrave Macmillan.
Esposito, P. and L. Nicastri, eds. (1999), *Interpretare Lucano*, Naples: D'Auria.
Esposito, P. and E. M. Ariemma, eds. (2004), *Lucano e la tradizione dell'epica latina*, Naples: Guida.
Esposito, P. and C. Walde, eds. (2015), *Letture e lettori di Lucano: Atti del Convegno Internazionale di Studi, Fisciano, 27-29 marzo 2012. Testi e studi di cultura classica*, 62. Pisa: Edizioni ETS.
Fantham, E. (2011), "A Controversial Life," in P. Asso (ed.), *Brill's Companion to Lucan*, 3–20, Leiden: Brill.
Fratantuono, L. M. (2012), *Madness Triumphant: A Reading of Lucan's Pharsalia*, Lanham: Lexington Books.
Galinsky, K. (2014), "Introduction," in K. Galinsky (ed.), *Memoria Romana: Memory in Rome and Rome in Memory*, 1–12, Ann Arbor: University of Michigan Press.
Galinsky, K. (2016), "Introduction," in K. Galinsky (ed.), *Memory in Ancient Rome and Early Christianity*, 1–39, Oxford: Oxford University Press.
Galtier, F. (2018), *L'Empreinte des morts: relations entre mort, mémoire et reconnaissance dans la Pharsale de Lucain*, Paris: Les Belles Lettres.
Galtier, F. and R. Poignault, eds. (2016), *Présence de Lucain*, Clermont-Ferrand: Centre de Recherches A. Piganiol-Présence de l'Antiquité.
Gill, C. (2003), "The School in the Roman Imperial Period," in B. Inwood (ed.), *The Cambridge Companion to the Stoics*, 33–58, Cambridge: Cambridge University Press.
Gowers, E. (1994), "Persius and the Docoction of Nero," in J. Elsner and J. Masters (eds.), *Reflections of Nero*, 131–50, London: Duckworth.
Gowing, A. M. (2005), *Empire and Memory: The Representation of the Roman Republic in Imperial Culture*, Cambridge: Cambridge University Press.
Griffin, M. (1972), "The Elder Seneca and Spain," *JRS*, 62 (1): 1–19.
Griffin, M. (1976), *Seneca: A Philosopher in Politics*, Oxford: Oxford University Press.
Griffin, M. (1984), *Nero: The End of a Dynasty*, New Haven, CT: Yale University Press.
Gross, D. (2013), *Plenus litteris Lucanus: zur Rezeption der horazischen Oden und Epoden in Lucans Bellum Civile*, Rahden: Leidorf.
Gunderson, E. (2003), *Declamation, Paternity, and Roman Identity: Authority and the Rhetorical Self*, Cambridge: Cambridge University Press.
Habinek, T. (2013), "*Imago Suae Vitae*: Seneca's Life and Career," in A. Heil and G. Damschen (eds.), *Brill's Companion to Seneca: Philosopher and Dramatist*, 3–31, Leiden: Brill.
Hardie, P. R. (1993), *The Epic Successors of Virgil: A Study in the Dynamics of a Tradition*, Cambridge: Cambridge University Press.
Heiden, B. (1997), "The *Iliad* and Its Contexts: Introduction," *Arethusa*, 30 (2): 145–50.
Hömke, N. and C. Reitz, eds. (2010), *Lucan's Bellum Civile: Between Epic Tradition and Aesthetic Innovation*, Berlin: De Gruyter.
Horster, M. and C. Reitz, eds. (2003), *Antike Fachschriftsteller: Literarischer Diskurs und sozialer Kontext*, Stuttgart: Franz Steiner.
Inwood, B. (1995), "Seneca in His Philosophical Milieu," *HSCPh*, 97 (1): 63–76.
Keeline, T. J. (2018), *The Reception of Cicero in the Early Roman Empire: The Rhetorical Schoolroom and the Creation of a Cultural Legend*, Cambridge: Cambridge University Press.
Kimmerle, N. (2015), *Lucan und der Prinzipat: Inkonsistenz und unzuverlässiges Erzählen im Bellum Civile*, Berlin: De Gruyter.
Kraus, C. S., J. Marincola, and C. B. R. Pelling, eds. (2010), *Ancient Historiography and Its Contexts: Studies in Honour of A. J. Woodman*, Oxford: Oxford University Press.

Langlands, R. (2018), *Exemplary Ethics in Ancient Rome*, Cambridge: Cambridge University Press.
Lehtonen, M. (2000), *Cultural Analysis of Texts*, trans. A.-L. Ahonen and K. Clarke, London: SAGE Publications.
Lovatt, H. (1999), "Competing Endings: Re-reading the End of the *Thebaid* through Lucan," *Ramus*, 28 (2): 126–51.
Ludwig, K. (2014), *Charakterfokalisation bei Lucan: eine narratologische Analyse*, Berlin: De Gruyter.
Manolaraki, E. (2013), *Noscendi Nilum Cupido: Imagining Egypt from Lucan to Philostratus*, Berlin: De Gruyter.
McAlindon, D. (1957), "Claudius and the Senators," *AJPh*, 78 (3): 279–86.
Narducci, E. (2002), *Lucano: un'epica contro l'impero*. Rome: Laterza.
Nill, H.-P. (2018), *Gewalt und* Unmaking *in Lucans* Bellum Civile, Leiden: Brill.
Noreña, C. F. (2017), "Nero's Imperial Administration," in S. Bartsch, K. Freudenburg, and C. Littleton (eds.), *The Cambridge Companion to the Age of Nero*, 48–62, Cambridge: Cambridge University Press.
Osgood, J. (2011), *Claudius Caesar: Image and Power in the Early Empire*, Cambridge: Cambridge University Press.
Osgood, J. (2017), "Nero and the Senate," in S. Bartsch, K. Freudenburg, and C. Littlewood (eds.), *The Cambridge Companion to the Age of Nero*, 34–47, Cambridge: Cambridge University Press.
Parroni, P., ed. (2000), *Seneca e il suo tempo*, Rome: Salerno Editrice.
Reydams-Schils, G. (2016), "Stoicism in Rome," in J. Sellars (ed.), *The Routledge Handbook of the Stoic Tradition*, 17–28, London: Routledge.
Roller, M. (2001), *Constructing Aristocracy: Aristocrats and Emperors in Julio-Claudian Rome*, Princeton: Princeton University Press.
Roller, M. (2018), *Models from the Past in Roman Culture: A World of Exempla*, Cambridge: Cambridge University Press.
Romm, J. (2014), *Dying Every Day: Seneca at the Court of Nero*, New York: Knopf.
Rudich, V. (1997), *Dissidence and Literature under Nero: The Price of Rhetoricization*, New York: Routledge.
Schrijvers, P. (2005), "The 'Two Cultures' in Lucan. Some remarks on Lucan's Pharsalia and ancient sciences of nature," in C. Walde (ed.), *Lucan im 21. Jahrhundert*, 26–39, Munich: De Gruyter.
Sedley, D. (2003), "The School, from Zeno to Arius Didymus," in B. Inwood (ed.), *The Cambridge Companion to the Stoics*, 7–32, Cambridge: Cambridge University Press.
Shotter, D. (2008), *Nero Caesar Augustus: Emperor of Rome*, Harlow: Pearson.
Steel, C. (2017), "Rhetoric and Pedagogy," in M. J. MacDonald (ed.), *The Oxford Handbook of Rhetorical Studies*, 205–14, Oxford: Oxford University Press.
Stover, T. (2014), "Lucan and Valerius Flaccus: Rerouting the Vessel of Epic Song," in M. Heerink and G. Manuwald (eds.), *Brill's Companion to Valerius Flaccus*, 290–306, Leiden: Brill.
Tesoriero, C., ed. (2010), *Lucan*, Oxford: Oxford University Press.
Thompson, L. and R. T. Bruère ([1968] 2010), "Lucan's Use of Virgilian Reminiscence," in C. Tesoriero (ed.), *Lucan*, 107–48. Oxford: Oxford University Press.
Thorne, M. (2011), "*Memoria Redux*: Memory in Lucan," in P. Asso (ed.), *Brill's Companion to Lucan*, 363–81, Leiden: Brill.
Thorne, M. (2018), "Playing the *Victor*: Triumphal Anxiety in Neronian Satire," in S. W. Bell and L. Holland (eds.), *At the Crossroads of Greco-Roman History, Culture, and Religion: Papers in Memory of Carin M. C. Green*, 155–73, Oxford: Archaeopress.
Tracy, J. (2014), *Lucan's Egyptian Civil War*, Cambridge: Cambridge University Press.
Trinacty, C. (2012), "The Manipulation of Juno's μῆνις: A Note on Lucan's *BC* 9.505 and Silius Italicus' *Pun*. 12.284," *ICS*, 37 (1): 167–73.

van Dijk, T. A. (2008), *Discourse and Context: A Sociocognitive Approach*, Cambridge: Cambridge University Press.
Walde, C., ed. (2005), *Lucan im 21. Jahrhundert,* Munich: De Gruyter.
Walde, C., ed. (2009), *Lucans Bellum Civile: Studien zum Spektrum seiner Rezeption von der Antike bis ins 19. Jahrhundert*, Trier: WVT, Wissenschaftlicher Verlag Trier.
Walter, U. (2004), *Memoria und res publica. Zur Geschichtskultur im republikanischen Rom*, Frankfurt am Main: Verlag Antike.
Willis, I. (2011), *Now and Rome: Lucan and Vergil as Theorists of Politics and Space*, London: Continuum.

PART I
LUCAN AND CONTEMPORARY AUTHORS
AND TRADITIONS

CHAPTER 1
IMPERIAL ETHICS AND THE INDIVIDUAL IN LUCAN AND SENECA'S *LETTERS*
Paul Roche

Seneca's *Epistulae Morales* offer an enticing contemporary context for Lucan's *De Bello Ciuili*.[1] Both texts were written in the same period, within the same specific cultural and political context, and from authors of the same family suffering similarly deteriorating positions relative to the center of power. Seneca was compelled to commit suicide in April 65 CE, within days of the same fate befalling his nephew Lucan. Both men died in the wake of the discovery of the Pisonian conspiracy against the emperor Nero. Lucan was certainly involved; his uncle less clearly so (cf. Tac., *Ann.* 15.48–71, esp. 49.3, 60.2–65, 70.1; Vacca, p.2 line 22–7 Endt; Suet., *Lucan* 23–8; cf. Fantham 2011; Braund 2017). Their deaths both mark the end point of their estrangement from Nero, an emperor with whom they had both been closely associated, and reflect the manner in which Nero alienated, suppressed and eliminated the brightest stars in a literary firmament he had helped establish in the first half of his reign.

In this chapter, I shall attempt to consider Seneca's letters as influencing Lucan's epic on issues to do with personal philosophy, autonomy, resistance and the virtuous death. My methodology will be to consider possible intertextual links between the two texts in terms of vocabulary, theme, and context, and to consider whether the relationship suggested by these can be read as importing plausible meaning into the epic. In pursuit of this goal, I shall consider first the linguistic base of evidence which might suggest a relationship between the two texts and then proceed to three case studies where allusion to the letters can be read as offering commentary upon and supplementary meanings to the text and themes of Lucan's epic. The similarity of the contexts of their production, sketched above, combined with the prominent interaction of Lucan and Seneca within other genres holds out the prospect of a literary relationship of some significance. However, the issue of one work's influence upon the other and of the relationship of either or both with Neronian Rome in the 60s CE is by no means uncomplicated, and requires some preliminary considerations.

Given their near contemporaneity, establishing a comparative timeline for the production of both the letters and the *Civil War* is a prerequisite to considering their interaction. A detailed chronology of production is without certain evidence at many crucial junctures, and beyond verification even in some quite basic aspects. The pertinent details are as follows. Tacitus (*Ann.* 14.53–6) records that in 62 Seneca had requested from Nero that he retire from court and donate his wealth to the emperor. Although the request was denied, Seneca receded from public life. Tacitus writes that he remained at home as if suffering from ill-health or devoted to his studies (14.56.3). After the great fire in July 64 he made a second request to retire. When it too was refused, he feigned ill-health and withdrew to his chamber (Tac., *Ann.* 15.45.3). The composition of the *Epistles* on the earliest model (that of Albertini 1924) falls within the period of his first and second request: 62–4 CE. A modified chronology, proposed by Abel (1967: 168) and endorsed by Griffin (1976: 400) and Marshall (2014: 43), argues for a more compressed timeframe of 63–4, publication of some of the letters in the latter part of 64, and continued composition up to Seneca's death in April 65.

In the case of Lucan, we can say that he was working on his epic poem until the moment of his death on April 30, 65. Statius (*Silv.* 2.7.101–2) writes of Lucan being "ordered to plunge headlong into Lethe while you sang of battles" (*iussus praecipitem subire Lethen, / dum pugnas canis*). On the broadly accepted model of Griffin (1976), *De Bello Ciuili*'s composition had begun only after the Neronia of August 60 and, Griffin suggests, after Lucan's quaestorship, which she assigns to 61. This gives a timeframe of 62 to April 65. The late grammarian Vacca gives a further detail: Lucan had published "three books such as we have them" (Vacca, p.2 line 18 Endt). Fantham (2011: 13) accepted this testimony, and put the publication in the period 62–3; Ahl (1976: 352) had dated it to the middle of 64; Masters (1992) was profoundly skeptical about the credibility of this detail. After his relations with Nero soured, Lucan was banned from reciting or publishing poetry, either in 64 on the chronology of Griffin (1984: 158), or in 62 or 63 on the chronology of Fantham (2011: 14 n. 45).

One issue obstructing the attempt to read Lucan against the backdrop of the letters is whether these respective chronologies allow sufficient time for Lucan to have read them. Some observations are worth making. It is easy to imagine that Lucan had access to the letters of his uncle prior to their publication. As a point of comparison, a number of studies (e.g., Maltby 2002: 56; Heyworth 2007: 275–6) have suggested the influence of the *Aeneid* upon texts that predate its first publication in 16 BCE—most notably Propertius 2.34 (no later than 24 BCE) and Tibullus 2.5 (after 19 BCE). This is on the assumption that their authors encountered the epic in the recitation culture of Augustan Rome. It is less problematic still to imagine that Lucan continued to have access to the works of his kinsman prior to their formal publication. There is, of course, no evidence apart from this comparative model and the *a priori* likelihood of exchange, but it should be sufficient to allay any concerns.

Another potential issue is the publication of the three books of Lucan mentioned by Vacca. This event may impact upon how readily we accept the influence of the letters in the earlier books of Lucan. The earlier we date this publication event (whether in 64, 63, or 62), the less likely it may seem that the letters could have influenced the books appearing in this group, since the point at which Seneca began writing them is dated variously to 62 or 63. Apart from (conveniently) adopting a late date of publication for Lucan and an early date of composition for the letters, there are various grounds on which to disregard the "publication" as a complicating factor in the influence of the letters. Firstly, there are good reasons to question the basic reliability of Vacca's fifth- and possibly sixth-century testimony. Masters (1992: 221–2) has cast doubt on its credibility on the grounds that (a) it looks like a variation on the three books that Vergil is meant to have recited before Augustus in the Suetonian *Life of Virgil* (31–2), and that (b) Vacca's detail may be a corruption of Suetonius' testimony that Lucan recited (some of) the poem before the ban (Suet., *Lucan* 1–4). Even if we do credit the publication story as true, we do not know which books Lucan included in the group of three. The common assumption is Books 1–3 and this may seem a natural choice, but it is not inevitable: we know, for example, that Vergil did not compose the *Aeneid* sequentially (see, e.g., Horsfall 1995: 14–17). I further do not see, as Fantham (1992: 14) did, that this testimony rules out the ongoing revision of the books issued as the poem progressed. Ovid may have continued to revise the *Metamorphoses* after it went into circulation (*Tr.* 1.7.13–40; Tarrant 2004: v–vi); and Martial certainly issued a radically revised edition of Book 10 in 98, three years after its initial publication in 95. In sum there are good grounds, whether the basic fact of the publication story is true or not, for discounting its relevance for what could and could not be included in Lucan's epic.

Further ameliorating the tight chronology outlined above is the phenomenal rate of production that both Seneca and Lucan appear to have maintained. Seneca apparently produced the equivalent of 500 Teubner pages of the letters within 24 months, and Lucan produced eight thousand lines of hexameter in four years (contrast Vergil and Statius, who took eleven and twelve years, respectively, for their epics). Perhaps most instructively, a direct line of influence has been drawn between Seneca's *Natural Questions*, which Seneca began in either 62 or 63, and Lucan's *Civil War*: not only Book 4A's influence upon the Nile excursus in Book 10, but also upon the account of flooding in Spain in Book 4, and even upon Etruscan methods of divination in Book 1 (Setaioli 2017: 260).

A final preliminary issue is the manner in which the two works relate to their contemporary contexts. Seneca's letters in many respects turn away from the details of Neronian Rome and toward the author's inner self. He is so reticent to incorporate specific contemporary details, to offer only one illustration, that writing in August of 64 about the conflagration that had destroyed the city of Lyons (*Ep.* 91), Seneca omits to mention the fire that had devastated the capital one month previously, instead offering up the Lyons narrative as a kind of tacit substitution for its Roman counterpart. Lucan has spectacular, isolated moments of explicit contemporary engagement, the invocation to Nero (1.33–66), most obviously. And there are broadsides against living under the emperors: that Rome was poorer than a Caesar (3.168); that the eternal fight is *Libertas* and Caesar (7.695); that he is living in a period when the world is cast down into servitude (7.640). But these sit against a normative pattern of narrating a highly charged foundation/destruction narrative that is in itself a highly provocative and politicized strategy, and one that sits in profound contrast to any positive ideology of principate, and yet resists being mapped in any detail against contemporary Rome in the 60s.

Contemporary Allusion and Linguistic Correlations

Despite their at times oblique manner of refracting the context that produced them, the two texts can be shown at discrete moments to point their readers to the same specific, contemporary cultural touchstones. For example, at Luc. 9.805–14, the unfortunate death of Tullus from the bite of the haemorrhois snake results in symptoms which are compared to saffron streaming upwards from a statue. This is a visual point of comparison that Lucan's Neronian readers could have recollected from their lived experience, since Seneca (*Ep.* 90.15) states that the process for spraying saffron from hidden pipes to a tremendous height was a contemporary invention. Lucan's epic and Seneca's letters also share a remarkable number of linguistic innovations, idiosyncrasies of expression and unique correlations. Many of these are quite local in scale, but the cumulative effect is to suggest a closer relationship than the independent reproduction of contemporary Latin usage.

Let us consider a representative selection. In the midst of the catalogue of Pompey's forces, Lucan praises the people of India for their willingness to die voluntarily (3.241–3):

pro, quanta est gloria genti
iniecisse manum fatis uitaque repletos
quod superest donasse deis!²

O! How glorious!—for a people to have laid their hands on the fates (*iniecisse manum fatis*) and when sated with life to have given what remains to the gods!

The key phrase in this sentence is the paradox *iniecisse manum fatis* ("to have laid their hands on the fates"). It is a typically Lucanian inversion of an established idiom. Compare Vergil's phrase at *Aen.* 10.419 *iniecere manum Parcae* ("the Fates laid a hand [on Helaesus]"): they "claimed him"; that is, it was his destined time to die. In Lucan, this hypallage—the reversal of the usual relationship of subject and object—makes the Indians paradoxically lay a claim upon the Fates rather than the reverse, as we observe in Vergil. Hypallage is a fundamental strategy in Lucan. It estranges his reader from the normalities of their own world and from that of his narrative. It is frequently the vehicle of linguistic paradoxes which cumulatively underwrite the larger inversions of his world turned upside down.

The reversal of this idiom is only elsewhere found in the letters of Seneca, and it is used in precisely the same context as we find it in Lucan. In *Ep.* 70 Seneca debates the virtues of suicide (this is a letter to which we will return). The moral of the letter is stated at 70.4: *sapiens uiuet quantum debet, non quantum potest* ("the wise man will live as long as he ought to, not as long as he can"). And the pivot of this letter, which takes it from negative examples of the unwise who prolonged life irrationally into Seneca's consideration of the various arguments in favor of a chosen death at the right time, is the question *si altera mors cum tormento, altera simplex et facilis est, quidni huic inicienda sit manus?* ("If one death is accompanied by torture, and the other is simple and easy, why not lay hands upon the latter [i.e., death]?" *Ep.* 70.11). Note the same hypallage within the same technical phrase, in which hands are laid (and claims are made) upon death itself.

The above is typical of the shared linguistic strategies in the *Epistles* and the *Civil War*. To give a very brief sense of the pervasive nature of this correlation, consider the following less elaborated examples.³

1. *acquirere* "to add to one's possessions" takes the object *orbem / regnum* ("the world" / "a kingdom") only at Lucan 9.260 and *Ep.* 17.7 (*TLL* 1.426.43–52).
2. *haerere* "to cling" is used of the soul's connection with god only in Lucan 9.573 and *Ep.* 41.5.
3. Only Lucan (9.527) and Seneca in his final prose works (*QNat.* 2.1.4, 2.53.1, 4.5.4, and *Ep.* 55.2) use *alligare* "to bind" of liquid and loose materials (*TLL* 1.1684.26–45).
4. *destillare* ("to distil; to fall bit by bit") as a graphic substitute for *dissolui* ("to be dissolved") is shared only by Lucan 8.777–8, 9.772, *Ep.* 66.51, and the contemporary Sen. *Thy.* 1061–2.
5. *lymphato . . . metu* "frenzied fear" is a collocation found only in *Ep.* 13.9, 85.27, and 7.186.
6. Lucan 9.438 and Sen. *Ep.* 124.11 are the first texts to use *ex(s)erere* "to thrust out" in the sense "to put forth" of plants (*TLL* 5.2.1856.44–52).
7. Only Lucan 9.8 and *Ep.* 102.23 talk of a soul being able to endure the ether as though it were a potentially harmful environment.
8. At 9.3, the verb *prosilire* "to leap forth" is strikingly used of Pompey's soul; it is used of the soul only elsewhere at *Ep.* 58.35 and 92.34 (*TLL* 10.2.2196.65).

There is thus an *a priori* likelihood of exchange between these two texts. The various models of relative chronology do not rule out the possibility or even probability that Lucan had access to the *Epistulae Morales*, and the linguistic idiosyncrasies shared by the two texts suggest exchanges between them. In the three case studies which comprise the rest of this chapter, I aim to position the *Letters* as interpretative supplements to Lucan's narrative. That is, I read the following scenes in Lucan as reacting to Seneca's letters. It seems to me more convincing in the following examples that Lucan has applied language and imagery used by Seneca in more generalizing contexts as a means of informing, undercutting and enriching the more specific contexts of his epic narrative and its characters. It may be possible in other instances (or even in the examples that follow) to read the direction of influence as flowing the other way with Seneca reading and responding to Lucan and positing Seneca's letters as offering commentary on Lucan's epic narrative. But that is a project whose goals are different to my present purpose of suggesting a significant and yet underappreciated point of reference within Lucan's epic.

The Debate on Fate and Chance

One of the most compelling cases for intertextual exchange between the *Epistles* and the *Civil War* occurs at the beginning of Book 2. It turns not on the ethics of an individual hero, but on the appropriate philosophical disposition to adopt for those experiencing the war. At the beginning of Book 2, the narrator posits the alternative philosophical systems governing the universe of the poem (Luc. 2.7–15):

> siue parens rerum, cum primum informia regna
> materiamque rudem flamma cedente recepit,
> fixit in aeternum causas, qua cuncta coercet
> se quoque lege tenens, et saecula iussa ferentem
> fatorum inmoto diuisit limite mundum,
> siue nihil positum est, sed fors incerta uagatur
> fertque refertque uices et habet mortalia casus,
> sit subitum quodcumque paras; sit caeca futuri
> mens hominum fati; liceat sperare timenti.

Whether the parent of the universe, when he first took charge of the shapeless realms and the raw material while the flames were withdrawing, fixed causality for eternity, binding himself by the law with which he controls all things, and separated off the world bearing the ordained generations, according to the immovable limit of the fates; or nothing is laid down, but random accidence wanders and brings change after change and chance governs human affairs – let it be sudden, whatever you are preparing; let the mind of men be blind to future fate; let the fearful hope.

In vocabulary, context and structure of its presentation, Lucan looks to no text more closely than to *Epistle* 16 (Sen., *Ep.* 16.5):

> quicquid est ex his, Lucili, uel si omnia haec sunt, philosophandum est; siue nos inexorabili lege fata constringunt, siue arbiter deus uniuersi cuncta disposuit, siue casus res humanas sine ordine impellit et iactat, philosophia nos tueri debet.[4]

Whichever one of these issues is true, Lucilius, or even if they all are, we must practice philosophy; whether Fate controls us by an inexorable law, or whether god as overseer of the universe has ordained everything, or whether chance drives and tosses human affairs without any order, philosophy ought to protect us.

The two texts share a very strong correlation in vocabulary and context; moreover, this is the only argument structured as "whether…(a) or…(b) then…(c)" (*siue…siue…*) and weighing the alternate possibilities of chance and predetermination in either Lucan or (perhaps more surprisingly) in Seneca's *Epistles*. We thus have a close correlation in context, in vocabulary and subject matter. The timing in this case might reassure the hesitant and suggest the influence of Seneca upon Lucan and not vice versa: the early publication of *Ep.* 16 (in Book 2 of the *Epistles*), allows ample time for Lucan to be aware of it before the publication of the first three books of the epic (whenever we conceive of this happening—if at all—and whichever books we suppose were published by Lucan).

The correlation between the texts appears to sharpen some important nuances of meaning that are highly relevant in the context of Lucan's narrative. Seneca insists that whether the organizing law of the universe is fate or chance, we must—in either eventuality—subscribe to reason and philosophy. As he expounds immediately before the passage quoted, without philosophy no one can live fearlessly or in peace of mind (*nemo intrepide potest uiuere, nemo secure*, 16.3). Seneca follows our quoted passage with the injunction that Lucilius should not allow what is an *impetus* (an "impulse")—that is, his attraction to philosophical reasoning—to grow cold, and that it should develop into a permanent habit of the mind.

Lucan's text pivots from the consideration of two systems to pray for a sudden revelation of disaster so that human beings may indulge in precisely the kind of prospective emotions—hope and fear—that philosophy guards against in Seneca's letters. These will later become one of the key emotional responses to his partisan retelling of the war (cf. e.g., 7.210-13). If Seneca's central message is "whether fate or chance governs, one must philosophize," Lucan's is "whether fate or chance governs, one must not."

For Seneca, philosophy will teach humanity to obey fate cheerfully and to comply with Fortune defiantly (*contumaciter*, 16.5). It will prepare humanity for precisely the contingency that it is impossible to plan beforehand against a chance occurrence (16.4). *Letter* 16 sharpens the point in Lucan, that the narrator's final prayer in either eventuality is for human ignorance with respect to the evidence of the prodigies with which book one had ended and which pointed directly to a Stoic organization of the universe along the laws of fate. The Stoics believed that prodigies were a gift of god to alleviate the mind of mortal man, whereas Epicureans denied any significance to them whatsoever. The narrator's prayer is not made so that the denizens of his world may obey fortune contumaciously and certainly not so that they might embrace their oncoming fate, but that they might indulge in a false hope until they are swept away by the suddenness of the disaster that chance has in store for them. It allows no place for their disciplined accommodation of what lies in store for them, nor for philosophy as a personal means of enduring tyranny once Caesar's destined victory has been won; compare Seneca's insistence that "it is philosophy that must protect us." Lucan's prayer allows only for a delusive and temporary emotional wellbeing of the kind that Seneca's letter warns against. When Lucan ends with a prayer that the mind of men be blind to future fate so that they might have hope, it is instructive to recall that letter 16 ends with an injunction from Seneca against acting on blind desire (16.9).

The Speech of Cotta to Metellus

In Book 3, the tribune Metellus seeks to prevent the forces of Caesar from plundering the treasury contained within the Temple of Saturn. He is dissuaded from this act of resistance by his colleague, Cotta (Hunink 1992: 81-3 for an overview). The scene is framed by Lucan as a test case orchestrated by *Libertas* herself through the instrument of Metellus, to see whether constitutional authority could challenge the force of Caesar (3.112-14). In a sequence of three speeches, Metellus forbids Caesar from acting (3.123-33); Caesar pours scorn upon his attempt and denigrates his inferior status as would-be protector of the laws (3.134-40); and when an *impasse* is met and Caesar looks for a sword, Cotta convinces Metellus to step down (3.145-52). This was a widely known event from the war, and yet none of the extant historical sources mentions Cotta (Hunink

1992: 82). The natural conclusion is that his part in the scene is Lucan's own invention and was included as a contribution to his poetic design.

Cotta begins with a paradox directing us to Stoic philosophical arguments regarding the preservation of one's personal autonomy (Luc. 3.145–7):

> "Libertas" inquit "populi quem regna coercent
> libertate perit; cuius seruaueris umbram,
> si quidquid iubeare uelis."

> "The Liberty," he said, "of a people whom tyranny controls perishes through liberty; you will preserve its shadow if you want to do whatever it is that you are ordered to do."

Cotta's is a craven argument from convenience. His speech lasts only eight lines and develops thus: (i) we have already submitted to many wrongs (147–8); (ii) nothing can be refused Caesar, a notion offered as an excuse for the *pudor* ("dishonor") and *degener metus* ("degenerate fear") claimed by Cotta for the Roman people more generally or the Roman aristocracy more particularly (148–9); and (iii) let Caesar take the gold because our property is no longer our own and, as slaves, poverty cannot affect us but only our master (150–2). The speech's persuasive effect upon Metellus is immediate: he is led away with no indication of any resistance on his part (*protinus abducto . . . Metello*, 153). Cotta's opening paradox strongly recalls Seneca's eighty-fifth letter, in which he expounds upon various Stoic syllogisms. When Seneca turns to the proposition "the man who is brave is fearless, the man who is without fear is without sadness, the man who is without sadness is blest" (*Ep.* 85.24), what follows can be read as a sweeping demolition of both Cotta's argument and the virtue of Metellus' abortive stand against Caesar. Under the subheading "what is an evil?" we find the definition (Sen., *Ep.* 85.28):

> cedere iis quae mala uocantur et illis libertatem suam dedere, pro qua cuncta patienda sunt: perit libertas nisi illa contemnimus quae nobis iugum imponunt.

> It is to yield to those things that are called evil, and to give one's liberty to them for the sake of whose preservation all things should be endured: liberty perishes unless we despise those things which put the yoke on our neck.

The phrase "*libertas perit*" is exceedingly rare. In the surviving corpus of Latin literature, it is found only in these two passages, and then a century after the death of both Lucan and Seneca, in the *Institutiones* of Gaius (2.7.7.9). It is worth noting that Seneca had other expressions for the death of liberty: at *Ep.* 95.72 she "breathes her last" with the suicide of Cato (*emisit animam*), at *Ep.* 14.13 she has "long since gone to rack and ruin" (*olim pessumdata est*), and she "goes under the yoke" at *Ep.* 88.29 (*sub iugum libertatem*).

If one of the fundamental markers of allusion is repetition of exclusive content (e.g., Wills 1996: 1–41, esp. 18), then this unique correlation in Lucan and Seneca may invite consideration as to what interpretative value the letter may have for our understanding of this scene. Most explicitly and directly, the protasis of the condition "liberty is lost" puts Cotta in the scales and finds him wanting: for it perishes, in Seneca, "unless we despise those things which put the yoke on our necks" (*nisi illa contemnimus quae nobis iugum imponunt*). The yoke of personal servitude is given expression at three points in *De Bello Ciuili*, and all in contexts that establish the superior moral strength of Cato, the need to fight the war on one's own personal terms and not in the service of a leader, and above all that Caesar is to be resisted. In Book 2, Brutus provokes his would-be leader with the notion that Cato, by entering the war and rejecting philosophical retreat is going "under the yoke of Pompey" (*sub iuga Pompei*, 2.280); in Cato's riposte he characterizes the whole generation of men going to war as a people "ready for the yoke and wanting to endure servitude" (*ad iuga . . . faciles populi, . . . uolentes / regna pati*, 2.314–15). The image of the personal yoke of servitude is then kept in abeyance until Book 9, when Cato castigates the fleeing republican forces with the barb that now that their neck is finally devoid of a yoke (because after the defeat at Pharsalus they now fight for their own cause), they are seeking one by not continuing the fight against Caesar (*quaerisque iugum ceruice uacanti*, 9.260).

Moreover, Seneca's explanation immediately proceeds to the appropriate conduct of a brave man: "if men knew what bravery was, they would have no doubt as to what a brave man's conduct should be" (85.28). It is instructive to read Metellus' behavior as well as Cotta's through this Senecan lens. The brave man's conduct is not found in "thoughtless rashness" (*inconsulta temeritas, Ep.* 85.28), love of danger, or the desire for things that inspire fear, writes Seneca, but in the knowledge to distinguish between what is evil and what is not. Bravery protects itself and endures with the greatest patience all things that have the false appearance of being evil. An imaginary interlocutor asks Seneca whether the brave man, if threatened with violence (*si ferrum intentatur ceruicibus*, "if the sword is brandished over his neck," 85.29) or even repeatedly stabbed and tortured, does not feel fear or suffer pain. Seneca admits pain but rules out fear: unconquered he looks down from a lofty height upon his own sufferings.

The counterfeit bravery of Metellus emerges in sharp focus in the thoughtless rashness of his stand. Two of his actions are set in high contrast to Seneca's definition of a bravery that is based in *sapientia* and the steadfast endurance of manifestations of evil. This first is the suddenness with which he obstructs Caesar: *rapit gressus* ("with rapid step," 3.116) speaks to violent movement, and the narrator labels his stand an "excessively daring undertaking" (*audax nimium coeptum*). The second is the immediacy of his dissuasion from action. Metellus is also shown to be indulging a love of danger and an empty provocation of the fear-inspiring Caesar, both ruled out as qualities of the brave man in Seneca. These are clear in his insistence upon his own danger in confronting the dictator: he immediately and repeatedly puts his own death as the stake of the exchange, and even commands Caesar to draw his sword (*detege iam ferrum*, 3.128). Seneca's disqualification of fear from the component virtues of the wise man also points to the very shortcomings that Cotta claims for himself and the whole of the Roman aristocracy ("shameful behavior," *pudor*, 3.148; "degenerate fear," *degener metus*, 3.149).

The narrator had already condemned the stand of Metellus at the beginning of the scene (3.118–21). The despoliation of the state treasury provoked the fight against Caesar that the invasion of Italy and the loss of constitutional rule had not. This slips all too easily for the narrator into an editorial about the power of avarice as a motivating principal ("love of gold alone knows no fear of the sword or death," 3.118-19). If, as Hunink (1992: 85) suggests, Lucan's narrator sees Metellus' motives as being devoid of idealism, the context offered by Seneca's letter allows us multiple angles onto the ethics of what could have been presented as a climactic moment of resistance to the unstoppable encroachment of imminent tyranny.

The Speech of Vulteius

In Book 4 of *De Bello Ciuili*, a raft of Caesarian troops is trapped by underwater chains in the late afternoon off the coast of Salonae on the Adriatic coast. After a brief skirmish with the Pompeian forces on the shore, night falls, and Vulteius, a centurion, urges the raft's occupants to commit suicide rather than to allow themselves to be taken alive in the morning (4.476-520). This scene and Vulteius' speech are often recognized as being influenced generally by the Stoic theme of suicide as an escape from tyranny (see, e.g., Saylor 1990; Gorman 2001: 280-5; Sklenář 2003: 26-34; D'Alessandro Behr 2007: 36-45; full commentary and further references in Esposito 2009). Further nuances can be recovered from a closer comparison of Vulteius' speech and the language and context of Seneca's *Letters* 70 and 76 on the same subject matter, since these shed significant light upon the themes of Lucan's epic and on the motivation of its protagonists.

Vulteius begins his speech (Luc. 4.476-80):

"libera non ultra parua quam nocte iuuentus,
consulite extremis angusto in tempore rebus.
uita breuis nulli superest qui tempus in illa
quaerendae sibi mortis habet; nec gloria leti
inferior, iuuenes, admoto occurrere fato."

"Soldiers, free for no longer than one short night, in this narrow time give thought to your final state. Life which remains is short for no one who finds in it the time to seek death for himself; and the glory of death is not diminished, men, by advancing to meet a fate close at hand."

tr. Braund

The impetus to consider Seneca as something more direct than a broad parallel comes in the form of Vulteius' phrase *occurrere fato* ("to rush towards death"). This phrase occurs in three texts, almost simultaneously, for the first time (*TLL* 9.2.393.42-3) in the speech of Vulteius, in Seneca's *Thyestes*, and in his seventy-sixth letter.

The emerging consensus regarding the date of the *Thyestes* (e.g., Fitch 1981; Nisbet 1990; Davis 2003; Volk 2006) puts it in the same period as the *Epistles*. While the *Thyestes* is often highly relevant to the *De Bello Ciuili*, the letter in this case has a stronger, more immediate claim upon the themes of Vulteius' speech. At lines 336–403, the second chorus of the *Thyestes* dwells on what it means to be a good king. Their definition predominately turns on his absence of fear: neither of the elements nor of any weapon. At lines 365–8, the summative definition of the true king is "one set in a place of safety / who sees all things beneath him / and willingly goes to meet / his fate (*occurritque suo libens / fato*), with no protest at death." One could argue that Vulteius instantiates the chorus' definition of the true king as one who lays aside all fear (*rex est qui posuit metus*, 348) when he proclaims "decide on death and all fear is gone" (*decernite letum / et metus omnis abest*, 486–7). However, Seneca's chorus is plainly not concerned with the king's suicide, but rather his potential for going to meet a brave death inflicted by an enemy. This is made clear by the lines immediately prior to our passage when they describe the king as "one that no soldier's lance, no naked steel has subdued." They are encouraging him rather to move out from the safety of the palace in order to meet his fate against "the threats of war."

The context in which Seneca had used the phrase in letter seventy-six is much closer to the rhetoric and situation encountered in Vulteius' speech. It can further be read as commenting upon and supplementing the themes and characterization at work in Lucan's fourth book. Seneca writes (Sen., *Ep.* 76.20):

> dixi, si forte meministi, et concupita uulgo et formidata inconsulto impetu plerosque calcasse: inuentus est qui diuitias proiceret, inuentus est qui flammis manum imponeret, cuius risum non interrumperet tortor, qui in funere liberorum lacrimam non mitteret, *qui morti non trepidus occurreret.*

> I have said (perhaps you recall) that many men have trampled under foot those things which are generally ardently desired and dreaded in a moment of sudden passion: there have been those who would cast away riches, there have been those who would put their hand in the flames, those whose smile the torturer could not break, those who would not shed tears at their children's funeral, *those who would rush to meet death undaunted.*

If the rarity of the phrase *occurrere fato* prompts us to consider the immediate contexts in which they occur, one can only be struck by how many points of correlation these contexts share; and yet their ultimate effect is to draw a pointed contrast between Vulteius and Seneca's *sapiens*. Seneca's *Ep.* 76 is an essay whose central theme is that reason (*ratio*) is the highest quality in a human being (76.9, 10). Seneca insists that while humans share all other virtues to a greater or lesser degree with plants and animals, perfected *ratio* alone is given the name *uirtus* (76.10). In the context of the passage quoted above Seneca disparages the influence of the emotions in such moments of sudden passion (*inconsultus impetus*, 76.20) as motivating factors to act virtuously. As Seneca develops this line of thought, he posits the key issue of *uirtus*—its most important test case—as being whether one would be willing to die for one's country and buy the safety of one's fellow citizens "not only with patience but freely" (*non tantum patienter sed libenter*, 76.27). The power of *honestum* ("what is honorable") is such that one will die for one's *patria* at a moment's notice when one knows that one ought to do so (27).

In high contrast to the letter, Vulteius explicitly rules out a rational encouragement to death, and instead characterizes his troops as *furentes et morti faciles animos* ("hearts frenzied and ready for death," 505–6); he describes his own response to the proximity of death as an obsession or a madness (*furor est*, 517). Vulteius moreover frames the suicide as a claim on *uirtus* (491) and the narrator endorses his view (581). This claim sits in direct contrast to the Senecan model of long meditation and reason (*ratio*, 70.27) as the only true *uirtus*. Throughout his speech Vulteius invokes the kinds of emotions—for example, styling their suicide as the greatest pledge of their love for Caesar (502)—which for Seneca in *Ep.* 76 would disqualify them as even the authors of their own actions (Sen. *Ep.* 76.20):

> amor enim, ira, cupiditas pericula depoposcerunt. quod potest breuis obstinatio animi, aliquo stimulo excitata, quanto magis uirtus, quae non ex impetu nec subito sed aequaliter ualet, cui perpetuum robur est.

> For it was love and anger and desire that have demanded dangers. If a brief stubbornness of the spirit can do this when provoked by some stimulus, how much more can *uirtus* achieve: this does not act on impulse or suddenly but consistently and its strength is permanent!

The larger opening statement made by Vulteius also bears a strong correlation to *Ep.* 70, in which Seneca had poured scorn upon those who would prolong their lives for a brief time under a sentence of death (70.7–9): note the emphasis there that it makes no difference whether the suicide takes place very close to death or not, and compare Vulteius' programmatic emphasis upon advancing to meet a fate "close at hand" (*admoto . . . fato*, 4.480). In the same letter, Seneca had dilated on the very issue of "whether when a power beyond our control threatens us with death, we should anticipate death or await it" (70.11). Particularly close are Vulteius' *sententia* that "no one is forced to wish to die" (*non cogitur ullus / uelle mori*, 484–5) and Seneca's law at 70.11 "I shall choose my death when about to depart from life." *Epistle* 70 is also relevant to the end of the passage: Seneca had argued (70.12) that the soul ought to choose a means of suicide "and burst the bonds of its slavery." This is a sentiment that Lucan transforms at 4.570–9 from a private liberation into a public and political action in the epilogue to this scene. The broader context of *Epistle* 70 serves to radically undercut the position adopted by Vulteius and praised by the narrator.

We might finally consider Vulteius' overall persuasive strategy and his line of argument. His speech develops through the following points:

1. Life is short for no one who finds time to end it (4.478–9).
2. The glory of death is not less because it is coming soon anyway (4.479–80).
3. In a frightening situation, decide on death and all fear is gone (4.485–7).
4. Desire what is inevitable (4.487, an unfortunate echo of Cotta's reasoning).

5. Death in battle is not preferable, because this death will be more conspicuous (4.488–93).
6. As inadequate as it is, suicide is the greatest available pledge of love for Caesar (4.500–2).
7. It will frighten the Pompeians who watch it (4.505–7).
8. They will deserve the fact that Caesar will call their loss a disaster (4.512–14).
9. Death is a blessing: a fact that one only sees when it is near (4.517–20).

A comparison of this reasoning to the cluster of arguments laid out in quick succession by Seneca in *Epistle* 70 shows what a complete travesty of an argument Vulteius adopts. Seneca's *sapiens* will accept the following arguments:

1. The wise man values the quality not the quantity of his life (70.5).
2. Suicide should always be the result of calm reasoning (70.5).
3. It does not matter whether one's death is suffered or self-inflicted (70.6) . . .
4. . . . or whether it happens sooner or later, but whether one dies well (70.6).
5. No man can lose much when a small portion of life remains (70.5).
6. Life is not to be purchased at any price (70.7).
7. Fortune has no power over the one who knows how to die (70.7).
8. Not committing suicide under a sentence of death is "doing another man's work" (70.13).

The "close calls" that Vulteius makes to some of these arguments are instructive in their points of difference. Although the two texts share a concern with combatting objections to suicide when death is near anyway, Vulteius' concern is not with dying well (as at 70.6), or the relative value of life to the individual (as at 70.7), but with the equal share of glory that will accrue to them whether their remaining time is long or short. Seneca insists at 70.13 that suicide is a matter with which *fama* has no concern. Vulteius, on the other hand, is banking on the renown which will follow (4.492–5), and the narrator declares that *fama* running through the world spoke of no craft with louder voice (4.573–4). For Seneca the goal of suicide is to escape from fortune (70.7), but Lucan's Vulteius sees Fortuna as the architect of their suicide, in her preparation of some great and memorable example (4.496–7).

Part of Vulteius' radical misreading of *Epistle* 70 might be seen as partisan: Seneca lauds the Catos and Scipios who committed suicide in this civil war as inimitable paragons of virtue (70.22). Vulteius and his men, on the other hand, are dying to impress a master, to showcase, in their own belief, *fides* and *pietas*. In the final analysis, Vulteius and his men emerge as worse than Seneca's participant in the naumachia with which *Epistle* 70 concludes (26–7): that man took his own life with the weapon by which he was supposed to fight his adversaries and thus escaped life as a torment and a *ludibrium*. In the context of Lucan's civil war, the Senecan moral that dying is more honorable than killing (70.27) holds out to Vulteius the prospect of a more virtuous motive, from which he pointedly abstains.

Conclusion

This chapter has attempted to bring the *Epistulae Morales* into a more direct relationship with Lucan's epic than is customary. It is important neither to de-problematize some aspects of this reconstruction—the tight chronology, or the habit of the texts of looking away from the specifics of Neronian Rome in the 60s—nor to overstate the degree and nature of the literary relationship. It would be misleading to argue that the letters are fundamental to the understanding of Lucan's project, but they can offer more than merely *comparanda* for Lucan's thought and expression or a backdrop to his Stoicism. In many ways, it would be surprising if they could not be established as a powerful contemporary context for Lucan's epic, since the two works share almost every aspect of their production, including time, socio-political circumstances, and the dispositions of their respective authors. It is against this shared context that I hope to have shown that the letters can also be positioned by their reader as offering relevant exegetical commentary on the characters and scenes contained within the *Civil War*. Just as it is with the earlier works of Seneca's oeuvre, the *Epistulae Morales* ought to be seen as a significant thread in the complex fabric of Lucan's thought and language.

Notes

1. I am very grateful to Mark Thorne and Laura Zientek for their invitation to participate in this volume and for their wonderful hospitality at the conference out of which it grew. I am also very appreciative of their constructive feedback on my chapter and editorial guidance.
2. The text of Lucan used throughout is that of Shackleton Bailey (2009); the translations frequently use or adapt Braund (1992).
3. These are drawn largely but not exclusively from Wick (2004), a detailed philological commentary on Lucan's ninth book, and thus show how a late book of the epic compares to the language used in Seneca's letters. My chapter will attend to examples that occur earlier in Lucan's poem.
4. The text of Seneca's *Epistulae* used throughout is that of Reynolds (1965); the translations draw on or adapt those of Gummere (1917) and (where possible) Fantham (2010).

References

Abel, K. (1967), *Bauformen in Senecas Dialogen*, Heidelberg: Carl Winter.
Ahl, F. (1976), *Lucan: An Introduction*, Ithaca: Cornell University Press.
Albertini, E. (1923), *La composition dans les ouvrages philosophiques de Sénèque*, Paris: de Boccard.
Braund, S., trans. (1992), *Lucan: Civil War*, Oxford: Oxford University Press.
Braund, S. (2017), "Seneca *Multiplex*: The Phases (and Phrases) of Seneca's Life and Works," in S. Bartsch and A. Schiesaro (eds.), *The Cambridge Companion to Seneca*, 15–28, Cambridge: Cambridge University Press.
D'Alessandro Behr, F. (2007), *Feeling History: Lucan, Stoicism, and the Poetics of Passion*, Columbus: The Ohio State University Press.

Davis, P. J. (2003), *Seneca: Thyestes*, London: Duckworth.
Esposito, P. (2009), *M. Anneo Lucano Bellum Civile (Pharsalia) Libro IV*, Naples: Loffredo Editore.
Fantham, E. (1992), *Lucan De Bello Ciuili Book II*, Cambridge: Cambridge University Press.
Fantham, E. (2010), *Seneca: Selected Letters*, Oxford: Oxford University Press.
Fantham, E. (2011), "A Controversial Life," in P. Asso (ed.), *Brill's Companion to Lucan*, 1–20, Leiden: Brill.
Fitch, J. G. (1981), "Sense-Pauses and Relative Dating in Seneca, Sophocles, and Shakespeare," *AJPh*, 102: 289–307.
Gorman, V. B. (2001), "Lucan's Epic *Aristeia* and the Hero of the *Bellum Ciuile*," *CJ*, 96: 263–90.
Griffin, M. T. (1976), *Seneca: A Philosopher in Politics*, Oxford: Oxford University Press.
Griffin, M. T. (1984), *Nero: The End of a Dynasty*, London: B. T. Batsford.
Gummere, R. M., ed., trans. (1917), *Seneca: Ad Lucilium Epistulae Morales*, Cambridge, MA: Harvard University Press.
Harrison, S. J. (1990), *Vergil: Aeneid 10: A Commentary*, Oxford: Oxford University Press.
Heyworth, S. J. (2007), *Cynthia: A Companion to the Text of Propertius*, Oxford: Oxford University Press.
Horsfall, N. (1995), "Virgil: His Life and Times," in N. Horsfall (ed.), *A Companion to the Study of Virgil*, 1–25, Leiden: Brill.
Hunink, V. (1992), *M. Annaeus Lucanus Bellum Civile Book III: A Commentary*, Amsterdam: J. C. Gieben.
Leigh, M. (1997), *Lucan: Spectacle and Engagement*, Oxford: Oxford University Press.
Maltby, R. (2002), *Tibullus: Elegies*, Cambridge: Francis Cairns.
Marshall, C. W. (2014), "The Works of Seneca the Younger and Their Dates," in G. Damschen and A. Heil (eds.), *Brill's Companion to Seneca: Philosopher and Dramatist*, 33–44, Leiden: Brill.
Masters, J. (1992), *Poetry and Civil War in Lucan's Bellum Ciuile*, Cambridge: Cambridge University Press.
Nisbet, R. G. M. (1990), "The Dating of Seneca's Tragedies," *Papers of the Leeds International Latin Seminar*, 6: 95–114.
Reynolds, L. D. (1965), *L. Annaei Senecae Ad Lucilium Epistulae Morales*, Oxford: Oxford University Press.
Saylor, C. (1990), "*Lux Extrema*: Lucan, *Pharsalia* 4.402–581," *TAPhA*, 120: 291–300.
Setaioli, A. (2017), "Seneca in the Ancient World," in S. Bartsch and A. Schiesaro (eds.), *The Cambridge Companion to Seneca*, 255–65, Cambridge: Cambridge University Press.
Shackleton Bailey, D. R., ed. (2009), *M. Annaei Lucani De Bello Ciuili Libri X*, Berlin: Walter de Gruyter.
Sklenář, R. (2003), *The Taste for Nothingness: A Study of Virtus and Related Themes in Lucan's Bellum Ciuile*, Ann Arbor: The University of Michigan Press.
Tarrant, R. J., ed. (2004), *P. Ovidi Nasonis Metamorphoses*, Oxford: Oxford University Press.
Volk, K. (2006), "Cosmic Disruption in Seneca's *Thyestes*: Two Ways of Looking at an Eclipse," in K. Volk and G. D. Williams (eds.), *Seeing Seneca Whole: Perspectives on Philosophy, Poetry and Politics*, 183–200, Leiden: Brill.
Wick, C. (2004), *M. Annaeus Lucanus. Bellum Civile: Liber IX. Einleitung, Text und Übersetzung*, Leipzig: K. G. Saur.
Wills, J. (1996), *Repetition in Latin Poetry: Figures of Allusion*, Oxford: Oxford University Press.

CHAPTER 2
LUCANUS MIRABATUR ADEO SCRIPTA FLACCI: LUCAN AND PERSIUS
Thomas Biggs

Introduction

The "and" in the title links two authors. It delineates a relationship between them, one of proximity and priority.[1] It couples and sequences simultaneously. On these terms, Marcus Annaeus Lucanus and the satirist Aulus Persius Flaccus present a challenge. Lucan and Persius are linked in the biographical tradition. They exist in the same schoolrooms and the same poetic performance spaces; their works emerge from a shared extratextual environment, one defined by Nero, Seneca, and Cornutus.[2] But this deep contextual knowledge only helps readers so much, since we do not know who composed first. Approaching the study of Roman literary history through periodized slices of polygeneric activity (be it Augustan, Neronian, or Flavian) often obscures as much as it illuminates. A principal goal of this chapter is to take seriously considerations of literary interaction between two authors whose works are less than readily amenable to established modes of analysis. By embracing with caution the interpretive potential of attested biographical relationships, and by choosing not to privilege linearity in sketching out instances of literary reference that occur simultaneously within these temporal slices, perhaps we can better appreciate how contemporaneous works of art produce meaning.[3] To this end, the chapter seeks out literary interaction between the poetry of Lucan and Persius through readings of the *Bellum Civile* and Persius' third *Satire*.[4]

In the third *Satire*, Persius' treatment of a drunkard, flagging student features key language and imagery also found in the *Bellum Civile*, a correspondence that appears nowhere else in their *corpora* to such a convincing degree. Since chronological indeterminacy clouds any reading that takes a firm stance on the source and target text, I approach the poems from multiple directions. My readings show how these two poems interact both on larger thematic planes (through engagement with similar issues and topics within their shared metrical forms) and on precise referential terms (through acts of literary reference). Scholars have long remarked upon the "strong bent towards Satire" found in Lucan's epic.[5] The poem not only employs diatribe, moralizing language, and type scenes such as the perverted banquet, but the grotesqueries of Lucan's world also trade in the imagery of the "lower genre": one thinks of the grotesque body (the *corpus* at once textual and physical) and the body dismembered.[6] Critiques of luxury, decline, and Caesarism further lend Lucan's poem a biting edge, wherein caustic castigation of vice and political overreach mingle with the traditional apparatus of epic poetry (gods excluded, of course). Potential critique of Nero himself in the so-called "Praise of Nero" has been a perennial topic of scholarly discussion, if ultimately offering little consensus on the matter of parodic panegyric.[7] On the macro level, aspects of tone, register, meter, imagery, and occasionally diction do allow the *Bellum Civile* to vacillate between epic and what might strike readers as satiric poles.[8] There are, however, intriguing limits to the potential for tracking intertextual engagement between Lucan and the *Satires* of Persius. Analysis of Persius and Lucan through the standard computational tools employed in contemporary philology results in somewhat meager distributions.[9] It does appear there is less referential engagement than there is between other Neronian poets: Lucan and Seneca, for example, betray a larger set of shared words, expressions, and modes of description, which is likely attributable at times to their greater overlap in content (see, e.g., Dinter 2012b: 49). Perhaps generic distinctions account for the gulf between Lucan and Persius, but the lexical and syntactic overlap ultimately seems quite stark in this imperial case when compared with the strong intergeneric links between the Augustans Horace and Vergil.[10]

Interpretations of literary reference based on a linear model of reading betray their unstable foundations in the case of Lucan and Persius, predicated as they are on rigid conceptions of source and target. In this instance of chronological indeterminacy, one marked by minimal points of strong verbal overlap, how should we approach comparative analysis? Recent scholarship on Roman literature has embraced several methodologies that may help. We can consider the papers in *Flavian Epic Interactions* which often work to achieve what editors Gesine Manuwald and Astrid Voigt note is a shift in how scholars gauge textual relationships, generic tradition, and imperial periodization (2012: 1–2). The papers in *Roman Literature under Nerva, Trajan, and Hadrian: Literary Interactions, AD 96–138* (König and Whitton 2018) are similarly concerned with texts defined by murky publication/circulation dates, works that are lacking in explicit intertextual links to their desired *comparanda*. Hence that volume's papers focus, as the editors summarize, on "conversations and silences between texts composed . . . during" a period when

> [many] authors knew each other personally; some collaborated in literary production, attending recitals and exchanging drafts; several mention each other or converse intertextually, whether unilaterally or in dialogue. They are joined by a host of personal acquaintances and public figures who walk off the street and into their pages to mingle with literary characters, past and present, in what thus becomes a complex and multifaceted tangle of socio-literary intercourse. (König and Whitton 2018: 2–3)

While Lucan and Persius do interact on traditional terms of literary reference ("whether unilaterally or in dialogue"), as we will see, the real potential for future work on their relationship is likely to be found "beyond 'allusion'" by readers looking "to set texts in conversation (with or without their authors' conniving)," and by readers attuned to the forces that context, periodization, and *bios* have upon the act of interpretation (König and Whitton 2018: 3). Even for the seemingly most intentional of verbal links between their poems, the potential for non-motivated reference remains real: the idea that they represent moments of interdiscursivity or "synchronic but seemingly independent convergences in theme and content" (König and Whitton 2018: 12).[11] To go beyond the status quo (what our *plus quam* poet would wish of us) future studies will need to embrace "the interface between textual and personal encounters."[12] Lucan and Persius are uniquely suited to these approaches. The contours of their *bioi* are what present scholars with the problems of chronological indeterminacy and they shape any modern expectations that Lucan too merits consideration as a satirist of the Neronian age.

Vita

According to ancient biographies Lucan and Persius were acquaintances and schoolmates, tied together by the house of the Annaei, Lucan's family, notably through their teacher Lucius Annaeus Cornutus, who was likely a freedman of Seneca.[13] The Suetonian *Life of Persius* tells us that Lucan was really into Persius' verse (*Vita Persii* 5):[14]

> When he was sixteen years old Persius became such a close friend of Annaeus Cornutus that he never left his side. From him he gained some knowledge of philosophy. From early in his youth he was friends with the poet Caesius Bassus and Calpurnius Statura, who died young, while Persius was still alive. He respected Servilius Nonianus like a father. He came to know Annaeus Lucanus through Cornutus, who was also Cornutus' student and the same age as Persius. Lucan so admired the writings of Persius that, when he read them, he could hardly keep from crying out that Persius' were real poems, but that he was just playing (*Lucanus mirabatur adeo scripta Flacci, ut vix se retineret recitantem a clamore quae illius essent vera esse poemata, se ludos facere*).

Unsurprisingly, the Persianic *Life* has played a major role in shaping critical appreciation of the *Satires*. The image the *Life* provides of the context for poetic composition offers a seductive framework for mapping the literary interaction between our authors and their peers: Persius and Lucan, learning from Cornutus, shuffling in and out of the same houses, the same private and public spaces, bumping into Seneca and other notables at readings and at table.[15] This vibrant world of elite cultural interaction under Nero is, however, an extra or paratextual account: Lucan's epic only touches explicitly on the present in the "Praise of Nero," and "it remains a fact that one cannot find in Persius' satires clear allusions to the persons and events of contemporary political life in Nero's Rome."[16] Even the less fraught or formulaic dimensions of the life fail to boil down to a useful core of "facts." According to the passage of the *Life* quoted above, Lucan had access to Persius' poetic production at a point in his life when he had already composed some of his own works, those now felt to be mere *ludi*. On the other side, Persius' death in 62 CE makes it unlikely he read late books of Lucan, who died in 65, but we cannot be certain in what order Lucan composed all portions of the epic and presented them for performance and circulation. In fact, Lucan is attested to have written several poems beyond the *Bellum Civile*; hence the content of this passage remains suggestive but inconclusive for mapping Persianic impact on the epic.[17] It only highlights the obvious: for several years, Lucan and Persius composed simultaneously, a facet of their reception that must make intertextual readings, such as that conducted in this chapter, a multidirectional enterprise.[18]

Ancient biographical accounts of Lucan's outright contempt for Nero (resulting in his role in the Pisonian Conspiracy) and his treatment of the emperor's own poetry suggest a persona easily compared with the satirist Persius, whose verse may not touch on contemporary political affairs directly but still has much to say on the matter (Cowan 2011: 301–2). Consider a famous anecdote from the Suetonian *Life of Lucan* (9–19):

> Lucan was recalled from Athens by Nero and added to his entourage of friends, and having even been honored with the office of quaestor, he nonetheless did not long remain in Nero's favor. Lucan was quite enraged since, with a meeting of the senate suddenly called, Nero departed when he was giving a recitation, for no other reason than to put the chill on Lucan's performance. From this point Lucan did not refrain from hostile words and acts against the princeps, which are still well known. Once in a public bathroom, when he had taken a crap accompanied by a quite remarkable rumble-down-under, he recited this half line of Nero's, while those who were sitting beside him took flight: "You might think it thundered beneath the earth" (*Sub terris tonuisse putes*).
>
> He also criticized the emperor and the most powerful of his friends in a notorious poem (*Sed et famoso carmine cum ipsum tum potentissimos amicorum gravissime proscidit*).

Lucan's *Life* here turns to scatological humor in order to showcase his discontent with the emperor on political and, perhaps more importantly, aesthetic and literary critical grounds. This striking moment of remix culture in the loo preserves a "satirist Lucan" for the ages, one whose style of humor incorporates the best of corporeal comedy. We should recall that literary critique under the poet-prince Nero is a political act with potentially fatal consequences. It is perhaps not unrelated that Persius is also believed (by some biographers and scholiasts at least) to have mocked Nero's poetry in a similar fashion by quoting it out of context in his own *Satire* 1.92–102:[19]

> [Interlocutor] sed numeris decor est et iunctura addita crudis.
> cludere sic versum didicit "Berecyntius Attis,"
> et "qui caeruleum dirimebat Nerea delphin,"
> sic "costam longo subduximus Appennino."
> "Arma virum," nonne hoc spumosum et cortice pingui
> ut ramale vetus vegrandi subere coctum?

[Persius] quidnam igitur tenerum et laxa cervice legendum?
"torva Mimalloneis inplerunt cornua bombis,
et raptum vitulo caput ablatura superbo
Bassaris et lyncem Maenas flexura corymbis
euhion ingeminat, reparabilis adsonat echo."

[Interlocutor] But elegance and smoothness have been added to the raw rhythms of old poetry. That's how "Berecynthian Attis" learned how to end the line, and "The dolphin parting azure Nereus," and "We stole a rib from the long Apennines" too. "Arms and the man!" Isn't this frothy stuff, with a thick crust, like an ancient dried-up branch with swollen bark?

[Persius] Would you try something delicate, then, for reciting with a floppy neck? "Their fierce horns they filled with Mimallonian booming, and Bassaris, poised to carry off the head torn from the proud calf, and the Maenad, poised to steer the lynx with ivy clusters, shouts and shouts 'Εὐhoë,' and reverberating Echo chimes in."

When compared with Lucan's potty-poetics, Persius and his interlocutor seem to engage in a related enterprise, fragmenting "Nero's" literary corpus and degrading it through recontextualization. Each poet engages with the emperor as author and, by so doing, each deflates the authority of the office.[20] As we will see later in this chapter, specific points of referential language link Lucan and Persius, but they also interact on an even broader platform: both poets meet in the *princeps* (Dinter 2012: 41).[21]

Conpage Soluta

The opening of the *Bellum Civile* famously depicts an unhinged cosmos cast into disarray by civil war. The poet decries the internal thrust of Rome's weapons, lamenting in traditional moralizing modes the need to return to foreign wars and the glories of the past. At line 70 the Stoic cosmic dissolution well studied by previous scholars comes into focus. One example is the famous description of Rome failing under its own excess weight, no longer able to support itself (*nec se Roma ferens*, 1.72), but even more interesting for the present study is Lucan's novel use of *conpage soluta* ("its structure dissolved") at line 73 which draws from Stoic cosmological (specifically ekpyrotic) language employed already in the famous Vergilian sea-storm (*Aen.* 1.120–3). This collocation, a line-end with real resonance in the *later* epic tradition, is actually quite unique (1.70–82):[22]

invida fatorum series summisque negatum
stare diu nimioque graves sub pondere lapsus
nec se Roma ferens. sic, cum **conpage soluta**
saecula tot mundi suprema coegerit hora

antiquum repetens iterum **chaos**, [omnia mixtis
sidera sideribus concurrent,] ignea pontum
astra petent, tellus extendere litora nolet
excutietque fretum, fratri contraria Phoebe
ibit et obliquum bigas agitare per orbem
indignata diem **poscet** sibi, totaque discors
machina divolsi turbabit foedera mundi.
in se magna ruunt: laetis hunc numina rebus
crescendi posuere modum.

It was the envious chain of destiny, impossibility of the very high
standing long, huge collapses under too much weight,
Rome's inability to bear herself. So, when the final hour
brings to an end the long ages of the universe, its structure dissolved,
reverting to primeval chaos, then fiery stars will plunge
into the sea, the earth will be unwilling to stretch flat her shores
and will shake the water off, Phoebe will confront
her brother and for herself demand the day, resentful
of driving her chariot along its slanting orbit, and the whole
discordant mechanism of universe torn apart will disrupt its own laws.
Mighty structures collapse onto themselves: for prosperity the powers
have set this limit to growth.

Since Lapidge's influential study in 1979, *conpage soluta* has been widely recognized as central to the language of the episode. It renders in Latin the ruined cosmic *desmos*, the bond of the Stoic world's *symploke* ("weaving together of the universe"). As Roche summarizes, "*conpages* used of the universe reflects the Stoic conception (and vocabulary) of cosmic cohesion" (Roche 2009: 152 *ad* 1.72). It is a markedly appropriate phrase for an epic depicting universal destruction, the breakdown of a concordant discord on textual and metatextual levels, drawn from the scientific and philosophical language Vergil and Ovid had both appropriated from the Stoics for the final conflagration of the *ekpyrosis*, by which the Stoics indicate the fiery end to the cosmos that occurs at the conclusion of a Great Year.[23] However, the key grouping of words that has occurred nowhere else in extant Latin until this moment in Neronian Rome also appears simultaneously in Persius' third *Satire*.[24] And it is this reoccurrence that activates more layers of meaning.

In the satire, a hungover slacker student is berated or perhaps berates himself. The breakdown in "voice"—and therefore the potential for internal monologue or dialogue— has paramount implications for interpretation and has even exercised no less a textual critic than Housman (1913: 2–32). Regardless of who speaks, the student is certainly instructed to get to his studies and a less profligate lifestyle. He may indeed be a version of "Persius," as the *Satires* themselves craft a vision of educational progression and biographical depth (Hooley 2017: 132). The philosophical studies to which the student of

Satire 3 should devote himself are largely of Stoic dispensation, and the language of the satire often dabbles in the lexicon of that camp (3.58–66).[25]

> stertis adhuc laxumque caput **conpage soluta**
> **oscitat** hesternum dissutis undique malis.
> est aliquid quo tendis et in quod derigis arcum?
> an passim sequeris corvos testaque lutoque,
> securus quo pes ferat, atque ex tempore vivis?
> Elleborum frustra, cum iam cutis aegra tumebit,
> **poscentis** videas; venienti occurrite morbo,
> et quid opus Cratero magnos promittere montis?
> discite et, o miseri, causas cognoscite rerum . . .

You're still snoring and your lolling head with its joint dissolved is yawning yesterday's yawn, with your jaws completely unstitched. Is there something you're heading for, a target for your bow? Or are you taking pot shots at crows with bricks and clods of mud, not caring where your feet take you? Is your life an improvisation? You can see it's useless to ask for hellebore when the sickly skin is already getting bloated. Face the disease at its approach, and what need will you have to promise the earth to Craterus? Learn, you idiotic creatures, discover the rationale of existence . . .

At 3.58–9 the teacher-figure/friend/internal voice accosts the student. Our sleepyhead is apparently more than hung-over, and his morning-after migraine appears quite severe. It may require a trip to the hospital instead of a few more hours in bed. His *caput* has been loosened, and it yawns and gapes drowsily with its *conpage soluta*. In a local sense, the phrase describes the neck (as most scholars have read it). We should recall *Satire* 1's depiction of the Nero-like poet's neck as he was about to spew out the sort of effeminate verse Persius despises (1.98: *quidnam igitur tenerum et laxa cervice legendum*? "Would you try something delicate, then, for reciting with a floppy neck?"). The dissolute of all sorts seem to have dissolute body parts. But dissolution can take on other dimensions when *conpage soluta* is in play.

The phrase is a marked way to highlight ruination of physical form and structure, in this case that of the body. As Roche notes on the collocation in Lucan, "[t]hrough its more literal definitions . . . *conpage soluta* also echoes the imagery of architectural ruination that pervades the poem" (Roche 2009: 152 *ad* 1.72). Reckford's interpretation of *Satire* 3 views the dissolute student on ruined terms as well (this time focusing on the language of pottery): "[t]he youth has quite regressed, 'gone to pieces'" (Reckford 2009a: 89). Although most commentators have acknowledged the verbal repetition itself, to date no one has really considered the cosmic implications of the phrase in Persius, particularly in light of Lucan's usage.[26] Yet our student's hangover is quite ekpyrotic. The only antidote may be a healthy dose of study. Perhaps it is high time to pick up that Stoic physics textbook? If we read Persius' usage through Lucan, the Stoic universal conflagration, especially as filtered through Latin epic predecessors, becomes a vehicle for conveying just how chaotic the student's body is, while the language of dissolution highlights how broken down. Like the Lucanian world of cosmic, social, civic, and bodily dissolution, the ekpyrotic hangover serves to realize an act of dissolution and dismemberment, one that disjoints the student's *corpus* and that of the text itself (cf. Keane 2012 and Dinter 2013 for Persius' *corpus*).

The *caput* attached to the student's loosed neck "yawns," it "gapes open" (*oscitat*). This verb is evocative of the *chaos* present in line 1.74 of the *BC*. The range of meanings in Latin follow upon the Greek, where *chaos* means abyss, gulf, yawning or gaping void, chasm, infinite cosmic darkness, as well as the gaping jaws of a crocodile (cf. *LSJ* s.v.). In the Stoicizing etymological take on the *Theogony* composed by Cornutus, whose teaching and person link Lucan and Persius, a reader even finds that *chaos* is directly connected to Stoic conflagration and cosmic disorder: "'Chaos' is the moisture that came about before cosmic order, so named from the word for *stream* [*chusis*] of fire, which is, as it were, a *burner* [*kaos*] and itself *streams* [(*ke*)*chu*(*tai*)] because of the fineness of its parts … [e]verything, my child, was once fire and will be again when the cycle comes round [i.e., the *ekpyrosis*]" (Boys-Stones 2018: 85).[27] Hence the word *oscitat* in *Satire* 3 may introduce another cosmic dimension to the satire's characterization of the profligate student via *conpage soluta*.[28]

As payback for his wild night *not* spent burning the midnight oil, the student of *Satire* 3 wakes up with an ekpyrotic hangover that in this scenario derives meaning from Lucan's proem: his head, *caput*, is *kaput*; his *conpages soluta*. This reading becomes stronger when we note the wine at stake. Consider the poem's opening lines (3.1–4):

Nempe haec adsidue. iam clarum mane fenestras
intrat et angustas extendit lumine rimas.
stertimus, **indomitum** quod de**spumare Falernum**
sufficiat, quinta dum linea tangitur umbra.

I suppose this is now routine. Already the bright morning is coming through the shutters, enlarging the narrow cracks with light. We're snoring enough to make the untamed Falernian stop fizzing, while the shadow reaches the fifth line.

At the start of the satire the student relates that he has a bit of a drinking problem. He has slept in to recover from last night's wine, offering a version of the digestion and medical metaphor employed throughout Roman satire (see discussion in Bartsch 2015).[29] Persius' *stertimus*, "we're snoring," is later picked up by the friend/teacher's accusation (*stertis adhuc laxumque caput conpage soluta / oscitat hesternum dissutis undique malis*), driving home the importance of that verb and its imagery in the poem while linking these locations together. The snoring relates to the yawning and gaping of *oscitat* and its "chaotic" undertones. And as noted already, the plural verb *stertimus* makes us wonder with Housman and those who have taken up the matter since: who is speaking? Is this dialogue or monologue? The implications matter: can teacher and student be one and the same (D'Alessandro Behr 2005: 269)? And if such confusion infuses the episode, perhaps the dissolution of the subject under the pressures of ekpyrotic allusion helps activate this breakdown of the boundaries between individuals. At any rate, it is no surprise that "Persius" has been drinking Falernian. Only the best will do! But the words he uses for the wine represent another unique grouping found elsewhere only once, in a marked episode of the *Bellum Civile* deeply influenced by satire and diatribe.

In Book 10 Cleopatra hosts an Alexandrian banquet that recalls not only Trimalchio's spread (Petron., *Sat.* 26–78), but also those of Nasidienus (Hor., *Sat.* 2.8) and, indeed, Nero himself. As Coffey (1996: 90–1) puts it, the "description of the political maneuvering and the love-making of Caesar and Cleopatra followed by the resplendent banquet is an essential part of the narrative … [i]t is also a fine example of declamatory satire in hexameters on moral corruption and extravagance."[30] Luxury, moral decay, seduction, the empire on a plate, all emerge in the build up to the post-dinner performance, which is, perhaps surprisingly, a didactic, scientific, rather "Alexandrian" song, performed in Alexandria, centered on the sources of the Nile. The episode thus plays with genres in a wider metapoetic fashion (cf. Tracy 2014).[31] In Alexandria, Caesar hits a generic wall: "[t]he great mover now shows a new appetite for delay and for luxury" (Williams 2017: 102). Our interest is found primarily in Lucan's table setting (*BC* 10.155–71):

> They served on gold a banquet of every dainty that earth or air, the sea or the Nile affords, all that extravagance, unspurred by hunger and maddened by idle love of display, has sought out over all the earth. Many birds and beasts were served that are divine in Egypt; crystal ewers supplied Nile water for their hands; the wine was poured into great jewelled goblets—no wine of Egyptian grapes, but generous Falernian, to which Meroe brings ripeness in a few years, forcing its stubborn nature to ferment (**indomitum** Meroe cogens **spumare Falernum**). They put on wreaths, twined of blooming nard and ever-flowering roses; they drenched their hair with cinnamon, which had not yet grown faint from foreign air nor lost the scent it had at home, and with cardamom, plucked not far away and freshly imported. Caesar learns to squander the wealth of a plundered world; he is ashamed to have made war against one so poor as Pompey, and desires a pretext for war with the Egyptians.

Persius' *indomitum quod despumare Falernum* (3.3) is easily heard in Lucan's *indomitum Meroe cogens spumare Falernum*. The statistics for the words' occurrences confirm the uniqueness of the lines. If Persius is read through Lucan, I submit that the "poetic Persius," the student figure, has in a sense been drinking at Cleopatra's banquet the night before, engaging in exactly the type of satiric dining the genre (not to mention *Satire 3*'s interlocutor) singles out for critique. Latin poetry's most recent scene of decadent dining would thus provide the drink for Persius' lush. On a metapoetic reading, criticism is leveled at Alexandrianism (that is to say, the dense but fluffy neo-Alexandrianism favored by Nero), which is maligned by Persius in his *Vita* and his verse (recall as well the fragments of Nero/Midas and the ears of an ass in *Sat.* 1), by the Suetonian Lucan in his aesthetic assault (with a different ass), and by the Lucanian narrator in Book 10. The satiric banquet is set in Ptolemaic territory at the heart of the city, and the satiric scene performed by its actors, as well as the poetry performed by Acoreus (to entertain a Caesar!), find their origins in the Hellenistic style. Perhaps the episode and its evocation in Persius present another counter to the Alexandrian aesthetic?

We can even suggest that the student Persius is drunk on Lucan's literary scene itself—that he spent last night enthralled by the Egyptian set piece, an episode worthy of a satirist's admiration. Persius is thus trying, in a sense, to digest Lucan's textual *indomitum Falernum*, to "to dispel the froth off a Falernian hangover" as Keane translates it (2012: 89), which in this reading becomes a "Lucanian" one.[32] As we saw earlier, the foolish interlocutor of Persius' first *Satire* engages "Persius" in literary critical debate and praises the line-ends of three heavily Neo-Alexandrian verses (perhaps fragments of Nero's own works). He also refers disparagingly to the *Aeneid* as "frothy" stuff (*spumosum*), which is the only time the adjective is used in a figurative or metaphorical sense to suggest aesthetic assessment. Most interpretations of the adjective ignore the *spuma* at the root of the word, but Harvey's commentary correctly emphasizes the meaning and its foamy dimensions: "*spumosum*, 'frothy, foaming', uniquely of literary style, seems meant to indicate what is overblown and insubstantial."[33] I suggest *Satire* 3's "Lucanian" *despumare* also activates a meaningful link with its earlier use in the first satire as a literary critical term for epic: *'Arma virum,' nonne hoc spumosum et cortice pingui / ut ramale vetus vegrandi subere coctum*? ("'Arms and the man!' Isn't this frothy stuff, with a thick crust, like an ancient dried-up branch with swollen bark?," 1.96–7). If, as many have shown, the poetic corpus is a body (Keane 2012: 81), the Persianic student's body is dissolute on Stoic cosmic terms *and* it is attempting to de-froth its frothy core, perhaps reflecting his relationships with disjointed, grotesque, and baroque neo-Alexandrian puff and other serious hexametric topics (cast on generic terms as the weighty epic *Aeneid* or its Lucanian successor). What dimensions of the negative assessment apply to Neronian Alexandrianism or weighty epic remains a bit unclear, a fact that allows for further subversion of the interlocutor's judgment and further self-reflection on the part of the Persianic student. As Bramble (1974: 127–8) has it,

> [t]he formal criticisms levelled apply more properly to his own type of poetry, as also the moral features of his charges. For accusations of inflation, *spumosum*, fatness, *pingui*, old age, *vetus*, and rottenness, *coctum*, intended by him [the interlocutor] to denigrate the *Aeneid*, have been directed not only at the literature for which he acts as spokesman, but also at the morality of which that literature is symptomatic: his reproaches rebound on himself.

The act of *despumare* may thus be an act of poetic assessment, and it is frothy wine that provides the unexpected point of contact between Lucan and Persius as the word extends in meaning from fermenting and mellowing, to digestion, to literary critique.

If Persius' poem influences our reading of Lucan, the characterization of the student who drinks and slacks from his studies may implicate Caesar. After consuming the same wine and dining at a banquet that would be quite at home in the genre of satire, Caesar tries to turn to learning. Caesar here becomes a momentary student of natural science and philosophy, but at the table he learns something else (10.169): *discit opes Caesar spoliati perdere mundi* ("Caesar learns to squander the wealth of a plundered world"). This is not exactly what Persius' "friend" meant (3.66–8): "Learn, you idiotic creatures, discover the rationale of existence (*discite et, o miseri, causas cognoscite rerum*): What are we and what sort of life are we born for? What rank is given us at the start? Where and when should we make a smooth turn around the post?" Persius' questions continue into a typical critique of exactly what Caesar gets wrong (3.69–76):

> What should be the limit to money? What is it right to pray for? What are the uses of new-minted coin? How much should be lavished on your country and your nearest and dearest? What role is assigned you by god and where in the human world have you been stationed?

Caesar has learned how to undermine each of Persius' exhortations. Limit to money? None. Role assigned to you by god, human station on earth? For Lucan's Caesar, there is none at all. Indeed, this is all made clear with Caesar and *Italia* at the Rubicon in Book 1, and it is driven home by his plundering of the treasury (3.154–68) and his hubristic sailing trip during the sea-storm (5.540–721). But now, as he thirsts for the source of the Nile and a pretext for Egyptian war, Caesar's megalomania is perhaps given its starkest casting. Viewed in a certain light, Caesar is the bad student of *Satire* 3. He learns luxury, greed, and a new thirst for power from the Alexandrian banquet and its *indomitum Falernum*, but he misses the lessons that follow.

Final Thoughts

In a cultural context defined by literary performance and the informal circulation of work we will never diagnose the genealogy of these apparent points of linguistic connection.[34] Likewise, any act of reference links, and in the end the two-way street it creates inevitably undermines the linear compulsion of chronological evaluation: "Persius and Lucan" or "Lucan and Persius" wind up saying the same thing. While synchronic appreciation of the poems must take into account the potential that either text was aware of the other as it took shape, it remains possible that each author came to at least some of these verbal and thematic correspondences independently. This chapter could thus be reframed as a study in interdiscursivity, not intertextuality or acts of literary reference as conventionally understood by some classicists who have moved toward practical allusion-mapping and away from the formulations of Barthes and Kristeva and some of the more experimental approaches that characterized the "New Latin" of the late nineties and early aughts. This chapter has focused on one satire as a case study. Based on provisional analysis it appears that Lucan and Persius have loosely tapped into the same literary system, a poetic network built of similar sources and preferences. I argue that *conpage soluta* and the near whole line repetition concerning Falernian suggest pointed literary references. One must confess, however, that firm verbal links between the poets are far less pervasive than those observed between many other Latin works forged simultaneously, such as those of the Augustan poets and historians. If this lack surprises, perhaps it is our expectations that should change. The way scholars describe literary interaction must continue to expand in order to account for points of contact that remain in defiance of the drive to treat them schematically on allusive or referential terms. For all its limitations, the idea of "contemporary contexts" and of *vita* without recourse to historicist or intentional fallacies opens up new possibilities in the study of Lucan's epic and its multidimensional interaction with Persius' *Satires*. The chronological indeterminacy with which this chapter began is thus both a limiting factor and one that allows for greater freedom in finding meaning within these texts.

Notes

1. I thank the editors, Mark and Laura, for the opportunity to contribute to this volume and for their brilliant comments on several drafts. I also thank the anonymous readers for numerous improvements to the chapter. More years ago than I care to remember, I wrote up an early version of these arguments for a seminar at Yale University run by Kirk Freudenburg. As always, his comments and critiques were insightful. I presented some of the chapter's ideas during *AMPAL* 2009 at the University of Birmingham and at the annual graduate student conference hosted by Duke University and the University of North Carolina at Chapel Hill in 2011. I thank those audiences. I am especially grateful to the participants of the conference that gave rise to this volume, Paul Roche and Francesca D'Alessandro Behr in particular, whose suggestions after my talk helped direct aspects of the final product, for which I am wholly responsible.
2. The equestrian Persius is a bit mysterious outside of what the ancient *Vita* relates, but he "seems to have been extremely well connected: his address book reads like a Who's Who of the Neronian intelligentsia" (Dinter 2012b: 43).
3. For the provisional and artificial nature of "Neronian" as a marker, see Dinter (2012b: 41–2).
4. The risks of such literary comparison are what Victoria Rimell worries about as she explores the similarly contemporary-yet-distant Tacitus and Martial (2018: 66): "will the pressure to make these texts converse throw up no more than clunky, handbook-style oppositions?" Consider also William Fitzgerald (2018: 110) on Pliny and Martial. For the "Neronian Literary Triad" of Seneca, Lucan, and Petronius, Dinter (2012b: 50) notes they are "connected by common themes, motifs, and imagery all of which find their reflection in Persius' oeuvre." Cf. Dinter (2012b: 57).
5. See Welwood's introduction to Rowe's *Lucan*, ([1718] 1779: 7): "It was in the course of ... [his] studies he [Lucan] contracted an intimate friendship with Aulus Persius, the satirist. It is no wonder that two men, whose geniuses were so much alike, should unite and become agreeable to one another; for if we consider Lucan critically, we shall find in him a strong bent towards Satire. His manner, it is true, is more declamatory and diffuse than Persius: but Satire is still in his view, and the whole *Pharsalia* appears to me a continued invective against ambition and unbounded power." See Grimal ([1960] 2010); Weston (1994); Coffey (1996: esp. 86–92); D'Alessandro Behr (2007: 93). Tracy (2014: 127–8) on the Egyptian banquet Caesar attends in

Book 10: "the banquet of Alexandria, however, belongs not to the genre of the symposium but rather to that of satire and diatribe." Cf. Johnson (2015: xvii, xix); Uden (2015: 18–19).

6. See Dinter 2012a for Lucan's "body." Some of Bartsch (1997) focuses on the abject and often grotesque dimensions of Lucanian physicality. D'Alessandro Behr (2005) digs into bodies (poetic and real) in *Satire* 3. Cf. Nichols (2013: 269).

7. Grimal ([1960] 2010); Dewar (1994); Roche (2009: *ad loc.*); Ripoll (2010); Penwill (2010); Nelis (2011).

8. The very idea of "Lucan the Satirist" has offered up enough fodder for several focused studies, including Coffey (1996) and the substantial dissertation of Weston (1994), which offers satire as a way for understanding Lucan's complicated poetics; see (1994: xxxii–xxxiv) for summary; and (1994: 16) for enumeration of "seven ways in which Lucan's style departs from traditional epic poetry." See analysis of satiric features (especially stylistic) in the poem at Weston (1994: 9–34).

9. These tools include the *PHI Latin Texts* database and the *Tesserae* project.

10. Despite Persius' status as Neronian satirist par excellence (a conception that took shape in the years after his death while Lucan was still composing his epic: cf. *Vita Persii* 42–5, wherein "people immediately began to admire it [Persius' book] and snatch it up," "tear it to pieces" *diripere*) the present goal is not a full assessment of Lucan's use of motifs and language considered satiric at the time by the standards of the ill-defined ancient genre, or even by those of the Persianic corpus. Other near contemporary writings would also merit from renewed comparative assessment in future scholarship, including Seneca's Menippean *Apocolocyntosis* and Petronius' *Satyricon*.

11. I indicate here what Prentice and Barker (2017) note is rather different than the more familiar intertextual toolkit: "A common thread across fields has been to argue against situating linguistic meaning within a clause or isolated interaction, emphasizing instead the contextual basis of meaning, both in terms of the influence of prior speech as well as the social influences of genre, discourse, and ideology." This approach sits alongside *and* is at odds with the focused interpretation of literary reference this chapter also performs. Lucan's epic is always likely to activate numerous points of reference, whether "intentional" or not: it is after all, as Hardie (2013: 237) puts it, "an orgy of extravagance and excess, exaggerating features already present in Roman epic, an inherently grandiose and expansive genre."

12. They will also need to ask if "reconstructions of social networking threaten to overdetermine intertextual readings?" (König and Whitton 2018: 33).

13. Cornutus was the author of numerous works, including an extant Stoic treatise on cosmogony and etymology now called the *Theologia Graeca*. He is perhaps most famous for his appearances in Persius' satires as a mentor and educator. On Cornutus, see esp. introduction in Boys-Stones (2018) as well as Bryan (2013) and treatment throughout the essays in Braund and Osgood (2012). See Persius' fifth *Satire* for Cornutus' poetic presence. Cf. Cucchiarelli (2005: 69) and Hooley (2017: 122–3).

14. Translations of Lucan and Persius throughout are after Braund (1992) and (2004). Translations of the lives are my own. Text of Lucan is Shackleton Bailey (1997); for Persius, Clausen (1992). Lucan may have admired Persius' poetry, but the Persianic life tells us Seneca did not impress Persius (*Vita Persii* 4)!

15. Cf. (Nichols 2013: 264–5). Persius does still craft a complex vision of a person and his daily life in Neronian Rome. Cf. Keane (2012: 83).

16. Cucchiarelli (2005: 76). Of course, as he continues (2005: 77), "[t]he inevitability of certain readers finding an allusion to Nero, the consequent risk of censure, and the necessity of an intervention into the text, work to bring the satires of Persius inside the anti-imperial frame of the opposition." Cf. Dinter (2012b: 42).

17. Other works ascribed to Lucan include *Catacthonion*, *Iliaca*, and *Orpheus*. For summary treatment, see Courtney (1993). On Lucan's life, see Fantham (2011).

18. A similar situation surrounds Silius Italicus and Statius. For treatment, see several relevant chapters in Manuwald and Voigt (2012).

19. Dinter (2012b: 49): "Unlikely to be Nero's lines, these samples might simply be a parody of the 'Neronian' style that demonstrated that Persius, although reclusive, was no cultural hermit with no access to or knowledge of the literary fashion of his time."

20. We should recall that many readers find traces of a critique of Nero in the ass's ears at *Satire* 1.121. Cf. Bramble (1974: 26–7); Reckford (2009b); treatment in Sullivan (1978) and Cucchiarelli (2005). The *Life* suggests the line attributed the ears to King Midas but Cornutus revised it to the present, less "dangerous" shape. If Nero's absent-presences inform a reading of *Satire* 1, we can compare the "Praise of Nero" in Book 1 of the *Bellum Civile*, which also teases the potential for imperial critique at the work's outset. Cassius Dio suggests that Cornutus took up a stance of literary/political critique as it concerns Nero, thus creating a further link between the three figures already bound by the schoolroom: "Nero was making preparations to write an epic narrating all the achievements of the Romans; and even before composing a line of it he began to consider the proper number of books, consulting among others Annaeus Cornutus, who at this time was famed for his learning. This man he came very near putting to death and did deport to an island, because, while some were urging him to write four hundred books, Cornutus said that this was too many and nobody would read them. And when someone objected, 'Yet Chrysippus, whom you praise and imitate, composed many more', the other retorted: 'But they are a help to the conduct of men's lives.' So Cornutus incurred banishment for this. Lucan, on the other hand, was debarred from writing poetry because he was receiving high praise for his work" (Cass. Dio 62.29.2–4, translation is Cary [1925]).

21. Coffey (1996) focuses briefly on points of generic impropriety in Lucan, particularly of the satiric sort (an approach not without issues). In this vein, Dinter approaches the text through thematic groupings that offer a wider intergeneric playing field, such as his treatment of hunger and thirst in the Afranius episode ("at home in comedy or satire") under the rubric of "Food and Drink" (2012a: 131). Dinter (2012b: 53–6) explores the links between Neronian authors that emerge through themes and topoi.

22. Cf. *laxis . . . compagibus*, used for the storm-battered ship at *Aen*. 1.122. For the phrase cf. *Aen*. 1.120–3; *Aen*. 2.50–2; Stat., *Theb*. 8.30–3; Sil., *Pun*.17.605–8; also, Tac., *Hist*. 3.27.13.

23. Stoic physics only appear briefly in Seneca and the scant remains of Cornutus and Musonius Rufus. Cf. Bryan (2013: 136): "If Stoicism is the dominant philosophy under Nero, then ethics is clearly the topic that dominates philosophical writing in this period." See Lapidge (1979) for Stoic physics in Latin epic. On Stoic presences within the cultural climate of Lucan's day, Bryan (2013: 137) notes that "Stoicism in Nero's Rome is perhaps better known for its influence on the literature of the period than in its own right." Cf. Bartsch (2017).

24. For Tacitus' later use of the collocation in the *Histories* as an allusion to Lucan, see the excellent treatment in Joseph (2012: esp. 132–3).

25. Persius is by no means consistent in philosophical outlook, and the various speakers of his world multiply the conflicting perspectives. Cf. Cucchiarelli (2005: 70); D'Alessandro Behr (2005: 287); Nichols (2013: 268–9).

26. Cf., e.g., Watson and Watson (2014: 260), where their note on Juvenal's *fracta conpage* at *Sat*. 6.618 includes citation of Lucan with Roche (2009: *ad loc*) but no explicit mention of Persius, whose relevance for Juvenal's sixth satire is quite high (the exact passage depicts the universe gone cosmically and ethically awry as a response to the misdeeds of Caesonia and Agrippina).

Harvey does flag Lucan and cosmic dissolution as relevant (Harvey 1981: 94). Gildersleeve (1875: *ad loc*) misses the deeper point. On *conpage*, Conington (1874: *ad loc*) notes the use of *conpages* at *BC* 5.119 but makes no mention of the actual collocation's appearance in the epic's first book. Cf. also Lee and Barr (1987: 110 *ad* 58); Nikitinski (2002: 155).

27. For didactic postures, cf. Keane (2012: 84–5) (with treatment of *Satire* 3 at 85).

28. I thank one of the readers for pointing out the potential for *chaos* to contribute to my meaning. The same reader also notes that *posco* offers another verbal link between the passages (*poscet*; *poscentis*).

29. (*de*)*coquere* and its relatives are often key, and they suggest a specific distilled poetics. Indeed, *Satire* 3's student is, in a linguistic sense, the one ageing and mellowing the wine in his body—as suggested by Lucan's usage. Nikitinski (2002: 132 ad *Sat.* 3.3–4): "sensus: 'stertimus tam diu atque tam forte, usque dum fortissimum vinum *despumetur* (i.e., concoquendo dometur).'" Cf. Hooley (1997: 212–14); Cucchiarelli (2005: 68–74); Keane (2012: 89–92).

30. No mention of Perisus is made in his discussion of the banquet. For food in the genre, see Horace *S.* 2.4, and treatment in Gowers (1993) and Bartsch (2015).

31. For Lucan and Egypt, see also Manolaraki (2013: 45–120).

32. Cf. *OLD* sv *despumo* "1 to remove the froth or foam from, skim; to draw foam from. b to cause to stop foaming, settle" as well as "2 to remove surface deposits, etc., from; to remove (scum or other unwanted matter)" and "3 (intr.) a To discharge or deposit foam. b to stop foaming, settle down." 1b is the meaning ascribed to Persius' usage, although it little helps unpack the bizarre image. The meaning is so elusive that it has prompted calls for emendation at various points, all of which fail to convince. Attempts to gloss the word are also misleading: Conington (1874: 51 *ad loc*): "*despumare* = 'coquere,' 'to digest.'" This connection is extremely suggestive since Persianic satire self-depicts as *aliquid decoctius* (1.125), but the equivalence he posits is misleading. That being said, the note does gesture to the essential link between these bodily and literary terms. His note on *Sat.* 1.125 rightly emphasizes the link and the difference in meaning: "decoctius opp. to 'spumosus' v. 96." He then cites Verg., *G.* 1.295, where language we might call metapoetic abounds (e.g., *decoquit* and *despumat*). Cf. Lee and Barr (1987: 101): "Horace's epithets for Falernian wine are *forte* (*S.* 2.4.24), *seuerum* (*O.* 1.27.9), *ardens* (*O.* 2.11.19)." This is essentially Jahn (1843: 144) via Gildersleeve (1875). Cf. Conington (1874: 50). Note that these adjectives all carry literary critical meaning for Horace and his successors.

33. Harvey (1981: 45 *ad loc*). He also notes the relationship between the adjective and the verb *despumare* in *Sat.* 1, though the Lucanian passage only appears as a parallel: "a difficult expression. It may arise from the conflation of 'sufficiat ut despumet Falernum' and 'cogat despumare Falernum' (2.1n), *despumare* being intransitively used to mean 'lose strength', cf. Sen., *de Ira*, 2.20.3, *Ep.* 99.27. Alternatively, P. may mean 'sufficient to cause Falernian to cease fermenting', *despumare* being opposite in sense to Lucan's *spumare*. A comic transference would thus be involved: just as time is needed to quiet down wine as it seethes in the vat, so it is needed for wine as it seethes in P.'s stomach." Cf. Saccone (2009: 157); Keane (2012: 91).

34. See Roller (2018) with bibliography for the role of recitation in the circulation of imperial literature and the effect this has on the tracing of influence. For the recitation of epic in particular, see Markus (2000).

References

Bartsch, S. (1997), *Ideology in Cold Blood: A Reading of Lucan's Civil War*, Cambridge, MA: Harvard University Press.

Bartsch, S. (2015), *Persius: A Study in Food, Philosophy, and the Figural*, Chicago: The University of Chicago Press.
Bartsch, S. (2017), "Philosophers and the State under Nero," in S. Bartsch, K. Freudenburg, and C. Littlewood (eds.), *The Cambridge Companion to the Age of Nero*, 151–63, Cambridge: Cambridge University Press.
Boys-Stones, G. (2018), *L. Annaeus Cornutus: Greek Theology, Fragments, and Testimonia*, Atlanta: SBL Press.
Bramble, J. (1974), *Persius and the Programmatic Satire: A Study in Form and Imagery*, Cambridge: Cambridge University Press.
Braund, S. M. (1992), Lucan. *Civil War*, Oxford: Oxford University Press.
Braund, S. M. (2004), *Juvenal and Persius* (Loeb classical library, 91), Cambridge, MA: Harvard University Press.
Braund, S. M. and J. Osgood, eds. (2012), *A Companion to Persius and Juvenal*, Chichester, West Sussex UK, Oxford, Malden, MA: Wiley-Blackwell.
Bryan, J. (2013), "Neronian Philosophy," in E. Buckley and M. Dinter (eds.), *A Companion to the Neronian Age*, 134–50, Chichester, West Sussex UK, Oxford, Malden, MA: Wiley-Blackwell.
Buckley, E. and M. Dinter, eds. (2013), *A Companion to the Neronian Age*, Malden, MA: Wiley-Blackwell.
Cary, E. and H. B. Foster (1925), *Dio Cassius. Roman History, Volume VIII: Books 61–70*, Cambridge, MA: Harvard University Press.
Clausen, W. (1992), *A. Persi Flacci et D. Iuni Iuvenalis* Saturae (Rev. ed.). Oxford: Clarendon Press.
Coffey, M. (1996), "Generic Impropriety in the High Style: Satirical Themes in Seneca and Lucan," in C. Klodt (ed.), *Satura lanx: Festschrift für Werner A. Krenkel zum 70. Geburtstag*, 81–93, Hildesheim: G. Olms.
Conington, J. and H. Nettleship (1874), *The Satires of A. Persius Flaccus*, Oxford: Clarendon Press.
Courtney, E. (1993), *The Fragmentary Latin Poets*, Oxford: Oxford University Press.
Cowan, R. (2011), "Lucan's Thunder-Box: Scatology, Epic, and Satire in Suetonius' *Vita Lucani*," *HSPh*, 106: 301–14.
D'Alessandro Behr, F. (2005), "Open Bodies and Closed Minds? Persius' *Saturae* in the Light of Bakhtin and Voloshinov," in R. Bracht Branham (ed.), *The Bakhtin Circle and Ancient Narrative: Ancient Narrative Supplementum 3*, 260–96, Groningen: Barkhius Publishing and Groningen University Library.
D'Alessandro Behr, F. (2007), *Feeling History: Lucan, Stoicism, and the Poetics of Passion*, Columbus, OH: Ohio State University Press.
Dewar, M. (1994), "Laying it on with a Trowel: The Proem to Lucan and Related Texts," *CQ*, 44 (1): 199–211.
Dinter, M. T. (2012a), *Anatomizing Civil War: Studies in Lucan's Epic Technique*, Ann Arbor: University of Michigan Press.
Dinter, M. T. (2012b), "The Life and Times of Persius: The Neronian Literary 'Renaissance,'" in S. M. Braund and J. Osgood (eds.), *A Companion to Persius and Juvenal*, 41–58, Chichester, West Sussex, UK, Oxford, Malden, MA: Wiley-Blackwell.
Fantham, E. (2011), "A Controversial Life," in P. Asso (ed.), *Brill's Companion to Lucan*, 3–20, Brill: Leiden.
Fitzgerald, W. (2018), "Pliny and Martial: Dupes and Non-Dupes in the Early Empire," in A. König and C. Whitton (eds.), *Roman Literature under Nerva, Trajan and Hadrian: Literary Interactions, AD 96–138*, 108–25, Cambridge: Cambridge University Press.
Freudenburg, K. (2001), *Satires of Rome: Threatening Poses from Lucilius to Juvenal*, Cambridge: Cambridge University Press.
Gildersleeve, B. L. (1875), *The Satires of A. Persius Flaccus*, New York: Harper & Bros.
Gowers, E. (1993), *The Loaded Table: Representations of Food in Roman Literature*, Oxford: Clarendon Press.

Grimal, P. ([1960] 2010), "Is the Euology of Nero at the Beginning of the Pharsalia Ironic?," trans. L. Holford-Strevens, in C. Tesoriero (ed.), *Lucan: Oxford Reading in Classical Studies*, 59–68, Oxford: Oxford University Press.

Hardie, P. (2013), "Lucan's *Bellum Civile*," in E. Buckley and M. Dinter (eds.), *A Companion to the Neronian Age*, 225–40, Chichester, West Sussex, UK, Oxford, Malden, MA: Wiley-Blackwell.

Harvey, R. A. (1981), *A Commentary on Persius*, Leiden: Brill.

Hooley, D. (2017), "'Ain't Sayin': Persius in Neroland," in S. Bartsch, K. Freudenburg, and C. Littlewood (eds.), *The Cambridge Companion to the Age of Nero*, 121–34, Cambridge: Cambridge University Press.

Housman, A. E. (1913), "Notes on Persius," *CQ*, 7: 2–32.

Jahn, O. (1843), *Auli Persii Flacci* satirarum liber: *Cum scholiis antiquis*, Leipzig: Breitkopf und Härtel.

Johnson, W. R. (2015), "Introduction," in B. Walters trans. *Lucan* Civil War, xv–xxxvi, Indianapolis: Hackett.

Joseph, T. A. (2012), *Tacitus, the Epic Successor: Virgil, Lucan, and the Narrative of Civil War in the* Histories, Leiden: Brill.

König A. and C. Whitton (2018), "Introduction," in A. König and C. Whitton (eds.), *Roman Literature under Nerva, Trajan and Hadrian: Literary Interactions, AD 96–138*, 1–36, Cambridge: Cambridge University Press.

Lapidge, M. (1979), "Lucan's Imagery of Cosmic Dissolution," *Hermes*, 107 (3): 344–70.

Lee, G. and W. Barr (1987), *The* Satires *of Persius: The Latin Text with a Verse Translation*, Wolfeboro, N.H.: F. Cairns.

Leigh, M. (1997), *Lucan: Spectacle and Engagement*, Oxford: Clarendon Press.

Manolaraki, E. (2013), *Noscendi nilum cupido: Imagining Egypt from Lucan to Philostratus* (Trends in classics. supplementary volumes, volume 18), Berlin: De Gruyter.

Manuwald, G. and A. Voigt, eds. (2013), *Flavian Epic Interactions. Trends in Classics Supplemenary Volume 21*, Berlin and Boston: De Gruyter.

Markus, D. D. (2000), "Performing the Book: The Recital of Epic in First-Century C.E. Rome," *ClAnt*, 19 (1): 138–79.

Masters, J. (1992), *Poetry and Civil War in Lucan's* Bellum Civile, Cambridge: Cambridge University Press.

Nelis, D. (2011), "Praising Nero (Lucan, *De Bello Civili*, 1.33–66)," in G. Urso (ed.), *Dicere laudes: Elogio, comunicazione, creazione del consenso*, 253–64, Pisa: ETS.

Nichols, M. F. (2013), "Persius," in E. Buckley and M. Dinter (eds.), *A Companion to the Neronian Age*, 259–74, Chichester, West Sussex, UK, Oxford, Malden, MA: Wiley-Blackwell.

Nikitinski, H. (2002), *A. Persivs Flaccvs*, Satvrae: *Commentario atqve indice rervm notabilivm; accedvnt varia de Persio ivdicia saec. XIV–XX*, Munich: K. G. Saur.

Penwill, J. (2010), "Damn with Great Praise? The Imperial encomia of Lucan and Silius," in A. J. Turner, K. O. Chong-Gossard, F. J. Vervaet (eds.), *Private and Public Lies: The Discourse of Despotism and Deceit in the Graeco-Roman World*, 211–30, Leiden: Brill.

Prentice, M. and M. Barker (2017), "Intertextuality and Interdiscursivity," in *Oxford Bibliographies in Anthropology*. Oxford: Oxford University Press. DOI: 10.1093/OBO/9780199766567-0012.

Reckford, K. J. (2009a), *Recognizing Persius*, Princeton: Princeton University Press.

Reckford, K. J. (2009b), "Studies in Persius," in M. Plaza (ed.), *Oxford Readings in Classical Studies: Persius and Juvenal*, 17–56, Oxford: Oxford University Press.

Rimell, V. (2018), "I Will Survive (You): Martial and Tacitus on Regime Change," in A. König and C. Whitton (eds.), *Roman Literature under Nerva, Trajan and Hadrian: Literary Interactions, AD 96–138*, 63–85, Cambridge: Cambridge University Press.

Ripoll, F. (2010), "L'énigme du prologue et le sens de l'Histoire dans le *Bellum Civile*: une hypothèse interprétative", in O. Devillers and S. Franchet d'Espèrey (eds.), *Lucain en débat: Rhétorique, poétique et histoire*, 149–58, Bordeaux: Ausonius Éditions.

Roche, P. A. (2009), *Lucan. De bello civili. Book 1*, Oxford: Oxford University Press.
Roller, M. (2018), "Amicable and Hostile Exchange in the Culture of Recitation," in A. König and C. Whitton (eds.), *Roman Literature under Nerva, Trajan and Hadrian: Literary Interactions, AD 96–138*, 183–207, Cambridge: Cambridge University Press.
Rowe, N. ([1718] 1779), "Rowe's Lucan," in *The Works of the English Poets with Prefaces, Biographical and Critical by Samuel Johnson. Volume the Twenty-Sixth: The Poems of Rowe and Tickell*, London: H. Baldwin.
Saccone, M. S. (2009), "Techniques of Irony and Comedy in Persius' Satire," in M. Plaza (ed.), *Oxford Readings in Classical Studies: Persius and Juvenal*, 138–72, Oxford: Oxford University Press.
Shackleton Bailey, D. R. (1997), *Marcus Annaeus Lucanus* de bello civili libri X, Berlin: De Gruyter.
Tracy, J. (2014), *Lucan's Egyptian Civil War*, Cambridge: Cambridge University Press.
Uden, J. (2015), *The Invisible Satirist: Juvenal and Second-Century Rome*, New York: Oxford University Press.
Watson, L. and P. A. Watson (2014), *Juvenal*, Satire 6, Cambridge: Cambridge University Press.
Weston, E. T. (1994), "Lucan the Satirist," PhD diss., Bryn Mawr College, Bryn Mawr, PA.
Williams, G. (2017), "Lucan's *Civil War* in Nero's Rome," in S. Bartsch, K. Freudenburg, and C. Littlewood (eds.), *The Cambridge Companion to the Age of Nero*, 93–106, Cambridge: Cambridge University Press.

CHAPTER 3
CICERO, LUCAN, AND RHETORICAL ROLE-PLAY IN *BELLUM CIVILE* 7
Annette M. Baertschi

The complex literary ancestry of the *Bellum Civile* is well established.[1] Lucan drew not only on earlier epic and historiographical traditions, but also on didactic, elegy, satire, epistolography, ethnographic and scientific treatises, natural philosophy, Platonic dialectic, and Stoic ethics, to say nothing of oratory. The amalgamation of sources and intertexts helps explain the frequent digressions, embellishments and exaggerations of his narrative, including some purely fictitious scenes and episodes such as Sextus Pompeius' consultation of the Thessalian witch Erictho (6.413–830), Cicero's speech before the battle of Pharsalus (7.62–85), the heroic death of L. Domitius Ahenobarbus (7.599–616), or Caesar's tour of the ruins of Troy (9.961–99), to name only those involving well-known historical figures.

While it is easy to identify the literary models for the necromancy in Book 6 or Caesar's trampling over Troy in Book 9,[2] Cicero's aggressive speech in Book 7 criticizing Pompey's passivity in the war and urging him to attack Caesar has proven more difficult to put in context. It is not merely the unhistoricity of the event that has puzzled scholars— as is widely attested, the Roman orator did not participate in the battle, but stayed behind at Dyrrhachium because of illness[3]—but also the apparent inconsistency with the role he played in the civil war. As Narducci (2003: 79–84) pointed out, Lucan's portrayal of Cicero as the sole proponent of battle is incompatible with the latter's well-documented efforts as peacemaker and his repeated attempts to convince Pompey to postpone armed combat (cf. *Fam.* 7.3.2).[4] In fact, the speech in Book 7 represents the total negation of everything the historical Cicero stood for according to Narducci. He therefore concluded that Lucan deliberately manipulated the truth in order to remove the responsibility for the catastrophe of Pharsalus from Pompey and put it on Cicero and the senate instead.

Similarly, Holliday (1969: 65–9) in her comparative analysis of the depiction of Pompey in Cicero's *Letters* and the *Bellum Civile* claims that Lucan chose Cicero as the spokesman for the discontented Pompeians because he had voiced similar criticisms in his epistolary correspondence of the early 40s BCE, thus making him an ideal scapegoat.[5] By contrast, Radicke (2004: 379–80) sees the main reason for Lucan's deviation from the historical record, in particular Livy, in his desire to emphasize the hexadic structure of the epic by inserting parallel scenes in Book 1 and Book 7. In his view, Cicero's speech before the battle of Pharsalus serves as a complement to that of Curio at the outset of the war, and Cicero's push for an attack by Pompey corresponds with Curio's exhortation of Caesar to march on Italy. Fucecchi (2011: 239–40, 246–7), finally, examining the diverse group of secondary characters who populate the *Bellum Civile* and aiming to establish "recurring typologies" (2011: 239), reads Cicero as another "tragic counsellor" (2011: 246) whose bellicose attitude is a caricature of the frenzied energy displayed by Caesarians such as Curio, Laelius, Vulteius, and Scaeva, and thus helps underscore the problematic leadership of Pompey, who fails to inspire similar devotion and loyalty among his followers.[6]

What is common to all these interpretations is the assumption that Lucan purposefully distorted the historical reality and included "alternative facts" to further either his ideological or narrative goals. In the following, however, I would like to suggest that Cicero's speech in Book 7 is not primarily a stratagem designed to advance the author's literary or political agenda, but rather an instance of deliberate rhetorical role-play, which the educated audience of the imperial era fully recognized and appreciated as fiction. Specifically, I will show that Cicero's harangue is a *suasoria* in the tradition of the Roman declamatory schools[7] and that Lucan may have drawn on the orator's epistolary correspondence for its composition, in keeping with the habit of declamation to rework and creatively adapt pre-existing material. The exact publication date of Cicero's *Letters to Atticus* and *Letters to Friends* as well as the specific editorial process including the selection and arrangement of the two existing collections remain unclear, but for the purpose of this chapter I will assume that both were in the public domain by, if not before, the early 60s CE.[8]

Furthermore, I will argue that the fictional scene that Lucan constructs can be situated within a larger trend in imperial rhetorical training to re-use and expand literary works in contexts different from the original and, with regard to Cicero, to focus especially on "untold episodes and unexplored possibilities in the biography of the Roman orator" (Peirano 2012: 18), "filling in" the gaps or blank spaces. By analyzing the declamatory features of Cicero's speech in *Bellum Civile* 7 and its embeddedness in the contemporary practices, I aim not only to shed further light on the rich intertextuality of the epic, but also to deepen the understanding of the literary culture of the early empire, which "encouraged and sustained the production of historical and authorial impersonations" (Peirano 2012: 12). At the same time, I hope to illuminate the reception of Cicero in the decades following his death and the ways in which the rhetorical education of the time shaped his image and memory.

Rhetorical Education in the Imperial Period

Declamation was the cornerstone of the Roman aristocratic educational curriculum. Derived from Hellenistic schooling practices, it developed its characteristic form during the Augustan era and became the hallmark of the rhetorical classroom in the first century CE.[9] Students usually engaged in declamatory exercises for several years, starting either at grammar school or under the more advanced teacher of rhetoric, and some continued to declaim as adults (especially recommended for lawyers).[10] Declamation comprised two main types of speech training, the *suasoriae* and the *controversiae*, which formed the apex of the rhetorical instructional sequence and represented the mastery of techniques of composition and delivery that had been studied individually before.[11] The *suasoriae* were deliberative speeches in which the declaimer had to persuade a famous figure from myth or history who was facing a dilemma to adopt a certain course of action. In *Suasoria* 3 in Seneca the Elder's collection, for instance, the speaker must advise Agamemnon who is deliberating whether to sacrifice Iphigenia in order to sail to Troy (*deliberat Agamemnon an Iphigeniam immolet negante Calchante aliter navigari fas esse*), while in *Suasoria* 7, he is tasked with counseling Cicero on whether to burn his writings to earn Antony's clemency (*deliberat Cicero an scripta sua comburat promittente Antonio incolumitatem, si fecisset*). The *controversiae* were imaginary legal cases aimed at preparing the student for the courtroom. Usually, a *thema* (or *materia*) was posited, often featuring rather eccentric particulars, and one or more fictitious laws were cited and the declaimer was then asked to argue for either the prosecution or the defense. Especially popular in imperial times were *themata* focusing on tyranny, paternal authority (*patria potestas*), slavery, and rape, as well as cases involving a poor and a rich man.[12]

Suasoriae were considered the less demanding type of exercise because the practitioner only had to come up with one line of argument and explain why the proposed action was appropriate for the literary or historical character addressed. By contrast, the *controversiae* required the speaker to embrace multiple perspectives, from that of kings or famous politicians to slaves to prostitutes, thus anticipating his later role as a legal advocate (Bloomer 1997b: 135–42; 2007: 298, 301). That said, rhetorical role-play was a central aspect of both *suasoriae* and *controversiae*, since the student had to imagine himself in the situation of either the famous person from myth or history he was advising or a stock figure like the tyrannicide, the injured husband, or the rich man, so as to understand (or empathize with) their point of view and deliver a coherent exhortation or argument. Historical accuracy was not of primary importance and was only relevant insofar as it provided a recognizable setting. In fact, sometimes declamation dealt with events or situations that had never happened, so that the speaker was essentially creating a fiction and inserting this into the known course of history.

The collection of *suasoriae* and *controversiae* compiled by Seneca the Elder toward the end of his life (*c.* 38 CE) does not contain any complete speeches as they might have been given. Rather, he provides a sort of anthology with highlights from performances by professional declaimers, assuming the audience's familiarity not only with this mode of rhetorical training, but also with the specific examples that he discusses (Roller 1997: 111). He focuses in particular on the *sententiae* found in each speech as well as the *divisio* (general structure of the argument) and *color* ("line," tone, twist, or plea) adopted by the various practitioners, thus elucidating key elements of declamatory technique.[13] While this form of presentation makes it difficult for a modern reader to envision what a full declamation may have looked like, it reveals the challenges which the speakers faced in each type of exercise, deliberative and forensic, and showcases the strategies that they used to address them (Roller 1997: 112). Furthermore, Seneca's compilation illustrates the competitive nature of declamation, with each performer "trying to outdo the next in novelty, paradox, and compression of language and argument" (Kraus 2000: 447). This in turn helps explain the immense popularity of the genre, both inside and outside of the classroom, thanks precisely to its character as an imaginative intellectual game that allowed its players continually to push the boundaries.

In terms of modes of argumentation, finally, a common and very effective method was the use of moral justifications, since there typically is a conflict between two (or more) socially accepted values in declamation.[14] In a *suasoria*, these values lead to two competing ethical imperatives, hence the need for deliberation. In a *controversia*, the question usually is whether a specific law can or, in fact, must be applied in a certain case given that the law itself encodes correct morality. As a result, ethical considerations (*rectum, honestum, an oportet*, etc.) figure prominently in the *divisio*, the overall organization of the argument that declaimers employ for any theme or case. There are other criteria which can be utilized when assessing different courses of action, among them expediency (*utile*), feasibility (*an possit*), safety (*tutum*), and necessity (*necesse*), and often several of them are combined to reinforce the main line of reasoning. But as Quintilian points out, the most important evaluative criterion for both types of declamatory speech is morality (*Inst.* 3.8.22–47, 7.4.4), since "ethical appeals are more authoritative and persuasive than appeals on any other ground" (Roller 1997: 113). Even an action advocated or defended principally on account of expediency or necessity is required also to be morally right, or at least indifferent, if the speaker wants to make a compelling case.

Cicero's *Suasoria* in *Bellum Civile* 7

Cicero's speech in Book 7 of the *Bellum Civile*, in which he pushes Pompey to cast aside his doubts and attack Caesar, displays all the characteristics of a *suasoria* as it was practiced in imperial Rome, in particular the theme, the privileging of ethical concerns, and the presence of stylistic elements such as paradox, concision, and verbal puns. Needless to say, Lucan's epic is steeped in rhetoric and includes many speeches, most of which are deliberative or exhortatory in nature. But by having Cicero urge Pompey to start the battle, even though he was fully aware that the Roman orator did not fight at Pharsalus, the poet recalls the specific setup of a *suasoria*, in which the speaker is imagined to advise a famous figure from history or literature who is facing a difficult situation about the right course of action.

Cicero serves as the spokesman for the Pompeian troops who complain about their leader's hesitation and timidity and accuse him of being overly patient with his father-in-law. They claim that he, desirous of world dominion, wants to keep command over his large international army and thus actually fears peace (*segnis pavidusque vocatur / ac nimium patiens soceri Pompeius, et orbis / indulgens regno, qui tot simul undique gentis / iuris habere sui vellet pacemque timeret*, 7.52–5).[15] Likewise, Pompey's allies from the East fret about being involved in a long drawn-out war that keeps them away from their home countries (7.56–7). Cicero personally is angry about Pompey's lack of initiative because the conflict prevents him from exercising his political influence (7.62–7):

cunctorum voces Romani maximus auctor
Tullius eloquii, cuius sub iure togaque
pacificas saevus tremuit Catilina securis,
pertulit iratus bellis, cum rostra forumque
optaret passus tam longa silentia miles.
addidit invalidae robur facundia causae.

These voices of all were conveyed by the greatest master
of Roman eloquence, Tullius—under his civilian authority
fierce Catiline had trembled at the peace-making axes.
He was enraged at warfare, because he longed for Rostra
and for Forum, after enduring silence so long as a soldier.
His eloquence gave strength to their feeble cause.

Cicero's introduction as *Romani maximus auctor eloquii* not only explains why he was chosen as speaker of the dissatisfied Pompeians, but also evokes the Roman declamatory classroom, since it was here that he had been canonized as the definitive model of Latin eloquence. Already during his lifetime, Cicero was regarded by many—and regarded himself—as the pinnacle of Roman oratory, but after his death, the rhetorical curriculum further cemented this status, granting him "a sort of educational monopoly" (Keeline 2018: 79). Cicero was fundamental for both rhetorical theory and practice, and students were expected not only to read all his works, but also to speak—and write—following his example. Lucan's characterization of Cicero as the embodiment of oratorical excellence and persuasiveness, even when bolstering a weak cause (7.67), reflects the crucial role Cicero and his writings played in the Roman school system and firmly places the subsequent harangue within the context of declamation.

In addition, Lucan emphasizes the moral dilemma in which Pompey finds himself as the leader of the Republican forces. He needs to engage in combat because his unwillingness to fight is otherwise "interpreted as a desire to retain power for himself by denying a quick and speedy end to the war" (Ahl 1976: 161; cf. 7.52–5). At the same time, the battle of Pharsalus will bring death to most of his followers and envelop the whole world in guilt, as the apostrophe that the poet inserts after reporting the criticisms of the Pompeian soldiers underscores (7.58–61). Pompey is thus confronted with two conflicting social imperatives, as is typical for a *suasoria*, and has to decide which plan of action to adopt.

Consequently, in his speech Cicero focuses primarily on ethical considerations as prescribed by rhetorical theory (7.68–85):

"hoc pro tot meritis solum te, Magne, precatur
uti se Fortuna velis, proceresque tuorum
castrorum regesque tui cum supplice mundo
adfusi vinci socerum patiare rogamus.
humani generis tam longo tempore bellum
Caesar erit? merito Pompeium vincere lente

gentibus indignum est a transcurrente subactis.
quo tibi fervor abit aut quo fiducia fati?
de superis, ingrate, times causamque senatus
credere dis dubitas? ipsae tua signa revellent
prosilientque acies: pudeat vicisse coactum.
si duce te iusso, si nobis bella geruntur,
sit iuris, quocumque velint, concurrere campo.
quid mundi gladios a sanguine Caesaris arces?
vibrant tela manus, vix signa morantia quisquam
expectat: propera, ne te tua classica linquant.
scire senatus avet, miles te, Magne, sequatur
an comes."

"This alone Fortune asks of you, Magnus, in return for all her many
services—that you be willing to make full use of her; we leaders
of your camp and your kings together with the suppliant world
prostrate ourselves and beg you to allow the conquest
of your father-in-law. Shall Caesar mean war for humankind
for so long a time? Rightly do the nations who were tamed
by Pompey racing past resent that he is slow to conquer.
Where has your enthusiasm gone? Or where your confidence in Fate?
Ungrateful man, are you alarmed about the gods? Do you hesitate to trust
to them the Senate's cause? Of their own accord, the ranks will pluck up
your standards and venture forth: you should feel shame to have won
    under compulsion.
If you are our chosen leader, if the war is waged for *us*,
it is right to let the men fight on whichever field they wish.
Why do you keep from Caesar's blood the swords of all the world?
Hands brandish weapons; hardly anyone can wait for the signal
slow to sound: hurry, or your trumpets may leave you behind.
The Senate longs to know: does it follow you, Magnus, as soldier
or as your entourage?"

Cicero points out Pompey's obligations to Fortuna and the world at large and argues that he owes it (*merito*) to the nations he has conquered in quick succession also to defeat Caesar with equal speed and efficiency (7.68–9, 73–4). Furthermore, he stresses that it would be shameful (*pudeat*) if Pompey's troops launched an attack by themselves and forced him into victory (7.77–8). Finally, Cicero highlights Pompey's moral responsibility as the senate's appointed leader (*sit iuris*) to take charge of the military operations and let his men fight against Caesar (7.79–80). The speech culminates in the polemical question whether he views the accompanying senators as his fellow-soldiers or merely as members of his staff (7.84–5), thus underlining again Pompey's duties as a general who needs to allow his peers to play their part in the war against autocracy.

If theme and mode of argumentation clearly identify Cicero's harangue as a *suasoria*, its particular style provides additional proof. The Roman orator was known for his *copia verborum*, but as Narducci (2003: 84) remarked, his speech in *Bellum Civile* 7 with barely twenty lines is not designed to reproduce this hallmark of Ciceronian eloquence. Rather, it showcases the characteristic features of declamation. Particularly noteworthy is, for instance, the paradoxical formulation *iratus bellis*, "enraged at warfare" (7.65) in the introduction to describe Cicero's pacifism, as epic *ira* usually manifests itself in battle and does not stem from a desire for peace. Similarly, Cicero's suffering as a soldier results from his prolonged public silence (*passus tam longa silentia miles*, 7.66) rather than from excessive fighting or other hardships associated with military life. The opening of the speech is cleverly designed as well by directly addressing Pompey and recalling the many services rendered (*pro tot meritis . . . Magne*, 7.68), which the reader first assumes to be Pompey's to the Republic, only to realize in the next line that they are actually Fortuna's to Pompey, thus transforming the apparent *captatio benevolentiae* into a pointed reminder of Pompey's personal responsibilities (Roche 2019, 86; *pace* Rambaud 1955: 264). Moreover, the paradox that Fortuna is praying to the Roman leader and not the other way around accentuates the seriousness of the situation and heightens the emotional force of Cicero's appeal. In the continuation of the speech, rhetorical figures abound, from hyperbole (the whole world implores Pompey to conquer Caesar, cf. 7.70: *cum supplice mundo* and 7.81: *quid mundi gladios a sanguine Caesaris arces?*) to anaphora and alliteration (7.75: *quo tibi fervor abit aut quo fiducia fati?* and 7.79–80: *si duce te iusso, si nobis bella geruntur, / sit iuris, quocumque velint, concurrere campo*) to paronomasia (*scire senatus auet, miles te, Magne, sequatur / an comes*, 7.84–5), specifically the double meaning of *comes* "which can signify either someone equal in social standing or the member of a provincial governor's retinue" (Ahl 1976: 160). This gives Cicero's final question additional bite, as it suggests that Pompey not only does not respect the authority of the senate, but also acts like a government official in peacetime rather than a general during civil war (Ahl 1976: 160; Fucecchi 2011: 230–40). The speech thus is a prime example of the quintessential style and composition of declamation: "We are looking for a certain tone of voice, hectic, hectoring and melodramatic. The declamatory writer takes pleasure in epigram and point, but also in outrageous paradox, exaggeration, and ingenuity of all kinds. His natural vehicle is not the long period but the short phrase, punchy and hard-baked" (Winterbottom 1980: 60).

Cicero's Epistolary Correspondence in the Early 40s BCE

Despite declamation's striving for novelty, paradox, and even shock value, many critics have objected that Cicero's bellicose attitude as evidenced in *Bellum Civile* 7 directly contradicts what the Roman orator says in his letters after the end of the civil war, in which he describes himself as an advocate of peace, even though his voice was progressively marginalized by the Republicans. In an epistle addressed to M. Marius from spring 46 BCE, he claims that he advised Pompey to broker a peace with Caesar after arriving at his camp in Greece and seeing first-hand not only the insufficient number and lack of proper preparation of the Pompeian troops, but also the bloodthirstiness and desire for booty of the ranking officers, many of whom were heavily in debt. When Pompey rejected the idea of an armistice, Cicero says that he suggested at least postponing a direct confrontation with Caesar's army, but the success of Pompey's soldiers against the enemy lines at Dyrrhachium in summer 48 BCE made him also dismiss this plan (*Fam.* 7.3.2):

> quae cum vidissem, desperans victoriam primum coepi suadere pacem cuius fueram semper auctor; deinde, cum ab ea sententia Pompeius valde abhorreret, suadere institui ut bellum duceret. hoc interdum probabat et in ea sententia videbatur fore et fuisset fortasse, nisi quadam ex pugna coepisset suis militibus confidere. ex eo tempore vir ille summus nullus imperator fuit. signa tirone et collecticio exercitu cum legionibus robustissimis contulit; victus turpissime amissis etiam castris solus fugit.

> With these things before my eyes and despairing of victory, I started by recommending peace, of which I had always been an advocate. When Pompey showed himself strongly averse to that policy, I set myself to recommend delaying tactics. At times he tended to favour this course and seemed likely to make it his policy. Perhaps he would have done so, had not the result of a particular engagement given him confidence in his troops. From then on that great man ceased to be a general. With his raw medley of an army he fought a pitched battle against the hardiest of legions, and was defeated. Even his camp was lost. He fled shamefully, alone.[16]

But as emphatically as Cicero presents himself as a peacemaker here, a somewhat more complex picture emerges from his earlier correspondence in 49 and 48 BCE. Particularly illuminating are his letters to Atticus from this period, with whom he communicated almost daily, thus providing a detailed record of his thoughts and vacillating moods. The exact publication date of the collection is unknown—and the same goes for the *Letters to Friends*—just as it is not clear "who selected, edited and arranged the material" (Beard 2002: 118). However, there are unambiguous references to Cicero's correspondence in the works of several early imperial authors which allow one to establish a *terminus ante quem*. For instance, Seneca the Elder mentions in his compilation of *suasoriae*, assembled around 38 CE, a letter of C. Cassius to Cicero (*Suas.* 1.5.5) which most definitely alludes to a passage in *Fam.* 15.19.4. Furthermore, Seneca the Younger quotes a sentence from a letter to Atticus (*Att.* 1.16.5) in his *Epistle* 97 to Lucilius,[17] which was written in the early to mid 60s CE—that is, roughly contemporaneous with Lucan's epic. This proves that by that time, if not earlier, both collections were available as a published corpus and could be consulted by other writers.[18]

In his *Letters to Atticus*, Cicero frequently mentions his desire—and that of others—for peace as well as his efforts to persuade Pompey to seek reconciliation with Caesar, even before the outbreak of the war (e.g., *Att.* 7.14.1, 7.17.4, 7.21.3, 8.11D.6–7, 9.7.3). That said, he also repeatedly criticizes Pompey's passivity and lack of both vigor and strategy once Caesar had marched into Italy. In a letter in early February 49 BCE, Cicero writes that no recruitment was going on and that Pompey had completely broken down (*Att.* 7.21.1):

> haec Capuae dum fui cognovi: nihil in consulibus, nullum usquam dilectum; nec enim conquisitores φαινοπροσωπεῖν audent, cum ille adsit, contraque noster dux nusquam sit, nihil agat, nec nomina dant. deficit enim non voluntas sed spes. Gnaeus autem noster (o rem miseram et incredibilem!) ut totus iacet! non animus est, non consilium, non copiae, non diligentia.

> While in Capua I learned this much, that the Consuls are worthless and that there is no troop levying anywhere. The recruiting officers dare not show their noses with Caesar in the offing, while our leader by contrast is nowhere and does nothing; and there are no volunteers. It is not loyalty they lack but hope. As for our Gnaeus, it is a lamentable and incredible thing. How utterly down he is! No courage, no plan, no forces, no energy.[19]

Shortly afterwards, he again chastises Pompey's poor handling of things and his imprudent actions, and complains that he refused to listen to him (*Att.* 8.3.3):

> nihil actum est a Pompeio nostro sapienter, nihil fortiter, addo etiam nihil nisi contra consilium auctoritatemque meam.

> Our friend Pompey's proceedings have throughout been destitute alike of wisdom and of courage; and, I may add, contrary throughout to my advice and influence.[20]

In particular, Cicero expresses his dismay over Pompey's decision to leave Rome and then also Italy and sail to Greece, which he considers an open admission of defeat (*Att.* 8.7.2):

> quod enim tu meum laudas et memorandum dicis, malle quod dixerim me cum Pompeio vinci quam cum istis vincere, ego vero malo, sed cum illo Pompeio qui tum erat aut qui mihi esse videbatur; cum hoc vero qui ante fugit quam scit aut quem fugiat aut quo, qui nostra tradidit, qui patriam reliquit, Italiam relinquit, si malui, contigit: victus sum.

> You praise that "memorable" saying of mine, that I prefer defeat with Pompey to victory with those others. Why, so I do, but with Pompey as he then was or as I thought him to be. But *this* Pompey, who takes to his heels before he knows where he is running or whom he is running from, who has surrendered all that is ours, has abandoned Rome, is abandoning Italy—well, if I preferred defeat with him I have my wish, defeated I am.[21]

Two days later, he once more berates Pompey's dishonorable behavior and the total absence of any communication or consultation on his part (*Att.* 8.8.1):

> O rem turpem et ea re miseram! sic enim sentio, id demum aut potius id solum esse miserum quod turpe sit. aluerat Caesarem, eundem repente timere coeperat, condicionem pacis nullam probarat, nihil ad bellum pararat, urbem reliquerat, Picenum <a>miserat culpa, in Apuliam se compegerat, ibat in Graeciam, omnis nos ἀπροσφωνήτους, expertis sui tanti, tam inusitati consili relinquebat.

> What a disgraceful and therefore miserable business! For I hold that misery lies chiefly or rather solely in dishonour. He built Caesar up, then suddenly began to fear him, rejected all terms of peace, made no preparation for war, abandoned Rome, culpably lost Picenum, squeezed himself into Apulia, was off to Greece leaving us all without a word, without any part in so momentous and extraordinary a plan.

But it is not only Pompey's personal shortcomings and his failures as a military leader that Cicero lambastes, but also his blatant ambition for sovereignty despite having temporarily yielded to pressure. In fact, Cicero concludes at the end of February 49 BCE, not hiding his disillusionment, that Pompey and Caesar equally desired to imitate Sulla's example of "kingship" (*Att.* 8.11.2):

> dominatio quaesita ab utroque est, non id actum beata et honesta civitas ut esset. nec vero ille urbem reliquit quod eam tueri non posset nec Italiam quod ea pelleretur, sed hoc a primo cogitavit, omnis terras, omnia maria movere, reges barbaros incitare, gentis feras armatas in Italiam adducere, exercitus conficere maximos. genus illud Sullani regni iam pridem appetitur multis qui una sunt cupientibus. an censes nihil inter eos convenire, nullam pactionem fieri potuisse? hodie potest. sed neutri σκοπὸς est ille ut nos beati simus; uterque regnare vult.

> Both of the pair have aimed at personal domination, not the happiness and virtue of the community. Pompey did not abandon Rome because he could not have defended her, nor Italy because he was driven from her shores. His plan from the first has been to ransack every land and sea, to stir up foreign kings, to bring savage races in arms to Italy, to raise enormous armies. He has been hankering for a long while after despotism on the Sullan model, and many of his companions are eager for it. Or would you maintain that no agreement or settlement between them was possible? It is possible today. But neither sees our happiness as his mark. Both want to reign.[22]

Cicero feared as much for the safety of Italy, which he expected to be starved out, ravaged, and plundered (e.g., *Att.* 8.11.2–4, 9.7.4–5), as for himself, uncertain what the best course of action might be for him (e.g., *Att.* 7.12.4, 7.21.3, 7.22.2, 8.3.1.5–6). After much soul-searching, he eventually decided to join Pompey in Greece, just as a large part of the senate had before him, and sailed from the Campanian coast in June 49 BCE, defying Caesar's orders that nobody was to leave Italy (*Fam.* 14.7).[23] As he explained in a letter to Atticus a few weeks earlier, after meeting with Caesar in March 49 BCE and being unable to promise him *not* to speak in favor of Pompey, he could no longer pretend to be neutral (*Att.* 9.18.1).

As this short glimpse of Cicero's correspondence in the early 40s BCE shows, he was deeply invested in Pompey's campaign and highly critical of his leadership or, rather, lack thereof, even though he continued to plead for peace both in public and in private. His comments stand in sharp contrast to a statement that he made at the end of 50 BCE, when he praised Pompey's "courage, military skill, and supreme influence" (*Att.* 7.8.4: *virum fortem et peritum et plurimum auctoritate valentem*). But in the subsequent months, Cicero changed his mind and repeatedly denounced Pompey's inactivity, fearfulness, and ill-advised military and political strategy.

The clear thematic resonances between Cicero's letters and the scene at the beginning of *Bellum Civile* 7, particularly the charge of Pompey's desire for world supremacy and his hesitancy and indecisiveness in the fight against Caesar, suggest that Lucan may have used Cicero's correspondence as a source and adapted the complaints found therein for the *suasoria* he has the Roman orator's deliver before the battle of Pharsalus. It was common practice in declamation to use earlier texts as a repository of themes and phrases to be reworked and "improved" on. Lucan was well versed in rhetoric and renowned for his talent as a declaimer, and so it is quite probable that he drew on Cicero's letters when composing the speech and potentially also other sections of his epic. Indeed, the fact that Seneca in *Epistle* 21 promises to grant immortality to Lucilius just as Cicero did to Atticus and Epicurus to Idomeneus (*Ep.* 21.4) documents that Cicero's epistolary collections were regarded as a literary classic in the early empire,[24] which makes their inclusion in the rich arsenal of intertexts for the *Bellum Civile* even more likely.

Cicero's Early Reception in Declamation

The educated reader of the imperial era was undoubtedly familiar with Cicero's correspondence as well as his unfavorable assessment of Pompey's generalship and so could appreciate the *suasoria* that Lucan put in the mouth of the Roman orator in *Bellum Civile* 7. As mentioned, Cicero was central to the rhetorical classroom as the paragon of Latin eloquence whom students were supposed to imitate and emulate in their own speaking and writing. Besides, Cicero was among the historical *personae* that declaimers would regularly adopt, as Quintilian attests (*Inst.* 3.8.49). Cicero's popularity as a subject in declamation is further reflected by Seneca the Elder's collection of *suasoriae* and *controversiae*, three of which—*Suasoria* 6 and 7 as well as *Controversia* 7—take their theme from Cicero's biography. This sheds light on a larger tendency of declamatory training in the first century CE not only to draw on pre-existing material in terms of diction and style, but also to use it "as a cue to construct fictional scenarios that . . . serve as platforms for rhetorical exercises" (Peirano 2012: 16). In the following, I will argue that

Cicero's speech in book 7 of the *Bellum Civile* also can be situated within this contemporary practice before discussing briefly in conclusion the function and effect of the harangue for the immediate context and the poem in general.

Both *suasoriae* devoted to Cicero in Seneca's anthology focus on the conflict with Antony at the end of the orator's life and ask the performer to provide advice on the best course of action. In *Suasoria* 6, the declaimer is tasked with counseling Cicero on whether to beg Antony's pardon (*deliberat Cicero an Antonium deprecetur*), whereas in *Suasoria* 7, he must offer guidance on whether Cicero should burn his writings after Antony promised that he would spare his life if he did (*deliberat Cicero an scripta sua comburat promittente Antonio incolumitatem, si fecisset*). Similarly, in *Controversia* 7.2 entitled *Popillius Ciceronis interfector*, Cicero's supposed killer, Popillius, whom he had originally defended against the charge of parricide and for whom he had secured an acquittal, is imagined to be prosecuted for misconduct (*de moribus*) because he had murdered his former lawyer (*de moribus sit actio. Popillium parricidii reum Cicero defendit; absolutus est. proscriptum Ciceronem ab Antonio missus occidit Popillius et caput eius ad Antonium rettulit. accusatur de moribus*). The entire situation is fictional—apart from the fact that a certain Popillius did kill Cicero. But Cicero had never defended him, "nor would he have been liable to a civil action *de moribus* even if all else were true" (Kaster 1998: 251).[25] The *thema* merely uses Cicero's life story as a backdrop for an imaginary legal case that allows practitioners to hone their skills in judicial oratory.

As these examples show, declaimers tended to look for gaps or blank spaces in Cicero's biography and to focus on "untold episodes and unexplored possibilities," since both *suasoriae* "stage the very last moments of his life, which are outside the scope of his speeches" (Peirano 2012: 18). Likewise, Lucan constructs a fictional scene in *Bellum Civile* 7 that places Cicero on the plain of Pharsalus right before the climactic battle, even though he never made it there, but had to stay in Pompey's camp at Dyrrhachium because of illness. There is a gap of several months in the *Letters to Atticus* between Cicero's last communications while he was still in Italy and his first from Greece after joining the Pompeian campaign (*Att.* 11.1–4). As Beard (2002: 125–6) pointed out, this does not mean that there was simply no correspondence between Cicero and Atticus during this period, but rather that any letters that may have been written were not included in the later published collection, whatever the precise editorial criteria may have been. As a result, it is not entirely clear what Cicero's role was and to what degree he was involved in military affairs. According to Plutarch (*Cic.* 38), his presence was largely superfluous, and he did not conceal his displeasure at Pompey's lack of preparation and strategy, spending most of his time making inappropriate jokes. In his epistle to M. Marius from spring 46 BCE, Cicero himself reports that he was acting as an advisor to Pompey, even if he was ultimately unsuccessful in convincing him to follow his recommendations (*Fam.* 7.3.2: *coepi suadere ... suadere institui*). His account may have influenced Lucan's decision to supplement the historical narrative with a *suasoria* by the Roman orator and stage a direct confrontation between the two men in his epic. The speech captures what Cicero could or would have said once it had become manifest that a peaceful resolution of the conflict was no longer an option, voicing the same concerns and frustrations over

Pompey's passivity and diffidence as a general as he had in his letters to Atticus in the early 40s BCE. The scene, however, is not an attempt to distort the truth by incorporating "alternative facts"; rather, the harangue that Lucan has Cicero deliver is an instance of deliberate rhetorical role-play, which the contemporary audience, accustomed to this kind of historical impersonation through their declamatory training, fully recognized and appreciated as fiction. The reader is not a victim of authorial manipulation or trickery, but rather a cognizant and willing participant in Lucan's imaginative game.

The educational context and the specific practices of rhetorical instruction in the first century CE elucidate the nature of Cicero's speech before the battle of Pharsalus, but the question remains what purpose it serves, both for the narrative arc of Book 7 and the *Bellum Civile* as a whole. Scholars have argued that Lucan chose to make Cicero the spokesman for the Pompeian troops because he symbolizes the constitutional authority of the senate (cf. especially the reference to his consulship and the suppression of the Catilinarian conspiracy in 7.63–4).[26] His oration dramatizes Pompey's obligations to the political community, since the command of the Republican forces was bestowed on him by the assembled senators in Epirus (5.45–7; cf. 7.79–80) and he now has to act in accordance with this appointment. In addition, critics have claimed that the fact that Pompey has no choice but to yield to the senate's pressure because of the formal conferral of power exonerates him from the subsequent disaster, and that it is the senatorial leaders, and in particular Cicero, who are to be blamed for rushing the engagement with Caesar.[27]

It cannot be denied that Cicero does not appear in a wholly positive light in *Bellum Civile* 7. This is evident from Lucan's characterization of his speech as sophistry, "the rhetorical bolstering of an inherently weak argument" (Sklenář 2003: 111; cf. 7.67).[28] Cicero's pushing for a pitched battle and a quick end to the war reveals his—and the senate's—lack of martial expertise and tactical skills against an opponent of the stature of Caesar.[29] Moreover, Lucan's comment that Cicero is angry at Pompey's hesitation because he longs for Rostra and Forum suggests that his main motivation for advocating for an immediate attack is his desire to regain his public voice and exercise his influence as a statesman and orator (7.65–6). His advice thus seems doubly misguided, and so it comes as no surprise that his harangue has been said to illustrate that the "strength of senatorial *libertas* in peacetime becomes its critical weakness in time of war" (Ahl 1976: 163).

However, such a reading does not take into account Cicero's reputation as the *princeps eloquentiae*, the authoritative model for oratory, that he had acquired as a result of the educational curriculum of the early empire. As time went on, Cicero's career and political convictions became less important than the legacy of his literary and rhetorical achievements, so much so that Quintilian in the 90s CE writes that Cicero's name does not denote the man anymore, but stands for eloquence personified instead (*Inst.* 10.1.112: *iam non hominis nomen sed eloquentiae*). For the imperial authors, Cicero is first and foremost the perfect orator, the preeminent example to be studied and followed, a symbol of the *vox publica* more than of consular authority. A key factor in this shift of perception was that Cicero was equated with his textual corpus soon after his death and that, as the memory of his life and actions slowly began to fade, his body of writing, canonized as the peak of Latin eloquence by the Roman school system, determined the public opinion of him (Keeline 2018: 83). The focus on Cicero's rhetorical brilliance simplified and reduced the complexities of the historical character, and his accomplishments—and failures—as a politician had little bearing on his general image. In the first century CE, "Cicero was not only identified more with his writings than with his person, but indeed more valued for his writings than for anything else that he had done" (Keeline 2018: 83).

It is this view of Cicero as the embodiment of oratorical excellence that Lucan drew on for his fictional *suasoria* in book 7 of the *Bellum Civile*. Cicero speaks for the collective of the Pompeian troops, the common soldiers as well as the Roman aristocrats and the foreign kings (7.62–5: *cunctorum voces ... Tullius ... pertulit*). Each group has their own particular anxieties, but they are united in their discontent and distrust of their leader, and Cicero as the pinnacle of rhetoric is the ideal person to communicate their concerns. This shows that it was above all Cicero's renown as the *vox publica* that prompted Lucan to use him as the spokesman for the Pompeians, and not one of the other senators or a less famous (or even unidentified) character as he does in other places of his epic.[30] The scene allows him to confront Pompey with the unified voice of his multi-ethnic army, represented by the "greatest master of Roman eloquence" (7.62–3) and champion of the declamatory classroom.

Needless to say, it is deeply ironic—and indeed paradoxical—that Cicero's speech helps pave the way for the catastrophe of Pharsalus rather than promote a more favorable course of action, as would have been appropriate for the self-proclaimed "architect of peace." Pompey's reaction makes clear that he is fully aware of the unsoundness of the advice given (7.85–6):

> ingemuit rector sensitque deorum
> esse dolos et fata suae contraria menti.[31]

> The leader groaned and felt that this was trickery
> of the gods and that the Fates were hostile to his own intention.

He grasps the implication of Cicero's provocative final question (*scire senatus auet, miles te, Magne, sequatur / an comes*, 7.84–5) and understands that he is essentially asked to relinquish his strategic authority and surrender to the demands of his army. This is manifest from his response, which echoes Cicero's words, prominently juxtaposing *milite* and *Magno* at the end of the first line (7.87–90):

> "si placet hoc" inquit "cunctis, si milite Magno,
> non duce tempus eget, nil ultra fata morabor:
> involvat populos una fortuna ruina
> sitque hominum magnae lux ista novissima parti."[32]

> He said: "If you all wish it so, if the moment needs Magnus the soldier,
> not Magnus the general, no more shall I detain the Fates:
> let Fortuna engulf the peoples in a single downfall,
> let this day be the last for a large part of mankind."

Pompey uses his demotion to reject blame, stressing that he has been compelled to consent to a battle that will bring heavy losses (7.91–2):

"testor, Roma, tamen Magnum quo cuncta perirent
accepisse diem."

"But I call on you to witness, Rome, that the day of universal doom
was imposed on Magnus."

In the continuation of his speech, he first justifies his attempt to achieve victory without bloodshed and defends his delaying tactics and war of attrition (7.92–109). He keeps reworking verbal material from Cicero's *suasoria* in an effort to refute the latter's arguments, for instance, when he returns the control over the Roman state to Fortuna (*res mihi Romanas dederas, Fortuna, regendas: / accipe maiores et caeco in Marte tuere*, 7.110–11) whom Cicero had admonished him to use for the benefit of the Republic (*hoc pro tot meritis solum te, Magne, precatur / uti se Fortuna velis*, 7.68–9). Then, addressing Caesar, he declares himself defeated by his rival's prayers and predicts many casualties in the ensuing fight as well as an equally inglorious outcome for both winner and loser (7.113–23).[33]

But Pompey's renunciation of leadership and his formal acceptance of a subordinate position do not exculpate him. As Brisset (1964: 120; cf. Bartsch 1997: 87) pointed out, Pompey does not *have* to yield to Cicero's urgings to engage in battle with Caesar, powerful as his speech may have been. Rather, Pompey's capitulation to pressure can be seen as further proof of his personal weakness and incapacity as a general. That said, Lucan's emphasis on the moral dilemma that Pompey is facing, specifically his inability to push back against Cicero without appearing to avoid open combat—and thus a quick end to the conflict—in order to maintain power for himself, complicates the picture. The very inclusion of a *suasoria* by Cicero highlights that Pompey is trapped in a situation in which there is no good path forward, since neither alternative is desirable. This is reinforced by the simile that the poet inserts after Pompey's response likening him to a sailor who, caught in a storm, leaves control of the ship to the winds and is carried along helplessly, with the phrase *ignavum ... onus*, "useless cargo" (7.126–7),[34] epitomizing Pompey's resignation as *rector* of the Republican troops, while simultaneously foreshadowing his later fate.

The fictional scene that Lucan constructs in the tradition of the Roman declamatory schools thus sheds light on the multitude of factors—and players—that shaped the course of events in the run-up to the decisive battle at Pharsalus. His creative supplementation of the historical narrative reveals that there were "complex, invisible, unintelligible forces which brought [Pompey] to this place and forced him to choose as he did, against his instinct, against his better judgment, with the sure sense that what he was choosing meant his ruin and Rome's" (Johnson 1987: 78). By having Cicero voice the concerns and interests of the Pompeian army, even though he was not present at Pharsalus, Lucan brings this fact to the forefront and enables the reader to gain a better understanding of the paradox of civil war. For who could resist when the greatest orator of Rome advised him on the proper course of action?

Notes

1. A first version of this chapter was delivered at the international conference *Lucan in His Contemporary Contexts* at Brigham Young University in spring 2017, and I would like to thank the organizers, Laura Zientek and Mark Thorne, and all participants for their helpful comments and suggestions. Furthermore, I am grateful to Paul Roche for generously sharing the manuscript of his commentary on *Bellum Civile* 7 with me. Finally, I am indebted to the three readers of the revised text for their constructive criticisms as well as, closer to home, to Russell Scott and Mary Somerville for their advice, help, and support through all the stages of the project.
2. The main model for the Erictho episode in the *Bellum Civile* is of course Vergil, *Aeneid* 6; further important intertexts include Apollonius of Rhodes' *Argonautica*, Ovid's *Metamorphoses*, especially book 7, and—outside of epic—Seneca's *Oedipus*. Caesar's tour of Troy is a (parodying?) imitation of historical accounts of Alexander's visit, see Diod. 17.17.3; Plut., *Alex.* 15.4–5; Arr., *Anab.* 1.11.7–1.12.1; see also Cic., *Arch.* 24 and *Fam.* 5.12.7.
3. See Liv., *Per.* 111 (ed. Rossbach): *Cicero in castris remansit, vir nihil minus quam ad bella natus*; see also Cic., *Fam.* 9.18.2; *Div.* 1.68; Plut., *Cic.* 39.1; *Cat. Min.* 55.1–3.
4. For a similar line of argument, see Rambaud (1955) and Lounsbury (1976).
5. For comparable views, see Malcovati (1953: 289–91) and de Nadaï (2000: 240).
6. On the satirical aspects of the scene, see Narducci (2003: 82).
7. The idea that Cicero's speech is a *suasoria* was first floated by Malcovati (1953: 289) but has not been further developed.
8. For a detailed discussion of Cicero's epistolary collections and their publication, see Setaioli (1976, 2003); Shackleton Bailey (1999, 2001); Beard (2002); White (2010).
9. On the development of the practice of declamation in Rome, see Bonner (1949); Sussmann (1978); Fairweather (1981); see also Bloomer (2007) and (2011). On the Latin term *declamatio* and its related forms, see Stroh (2003).
10. On the curriculum of rhetorical instruction, see Bonner (1977: 250–327) as well as Clark (1953: 213–50). Specifically on *controversiae* and *suasoriae*, see also Bonner (1949: 51–70).
11. The preliminary exercises included, among other things, *ecphraseis*, speeches in character (*prosopopoeiae*), fictitious interrogations, the construction of *sententiae*, and *apostrophe*. See Bloomer (2007: 299).
12. On the ideological implications of declamation, see Imber (1997); Kaster (2001); Gunderson (2003); Corbeill (2007). On the lack of engagement with political concerns, see Tabacco (1985).
13. For a detailed discussion of *divisiones* and *colores*, see Burkard (2016); see also Bonner (1949: 54–7); Sussmann (1978: 34–43); Fairweather (1981: 151–78, 202–7).
14. For this whole section, see Roller (1997: 112–13).
15. Throughout this paper, quotations from the *Bellum Civile* are based on Housman's edition. Translations are taken from Braund with occasional minor modifications.
16. Quotations from Cicero's *Letters* as well as translations are based on Shackleton Bailey's *Loeb* editions with occasional minor modifications.

17. See also Sen., *Ep.* 118.1–2 quoting Cic., *Att.* 1.12.1 and 4.
18. The question how much earlier Cicero's epistolary correspondence was accessible in edited form has been hotly debated; see especially Setaioli (1976). See also Holliday (1969: 84–90) and Beard (2002: 118, n47).
19. For a similar assessment of Pompey, see also Cic., *Att.* 7.13 and 7.15.
20. See also Cic., *Att.* 7.21.3: *Ego quid agam σκέμμα magnum, neque me hercule mihi quidem ullum, nisi omnia essent acta turpissime neque ego ullius consilii particeps—sed tamen, quid me deceat.*
21. For a related sentiment, see Cic., *Att.* 7.23.1: *victi, oppressi, capti plane sumus.* See also Cic., *Att.* 8.1.3 and 9.6.4.
22. On Pompey's Sulla-like disposition, see also Cic., *Att.* 9.7.3; 9.10.6; 9.14.2; 10.7.1. The view of Caesar as a would-be tyrant is reflected in Cic., *Att.* 9.4, in which Cicero rehearses various theses on the theme of autocracy and the ethical responsibility of a citizen in a despotic regime.
23. On Caesar's order, see Cic., *Att.* 10.10.2.
24. See, for instance, Fronto, II, p. 158 (Haines): *epistulis Ciceronis nihil est perfectius.* On the perception of Cicero's epistolary correspondence, see also Thraede (1970: 67). On Seneca's engagement with Cicero in general, see particularly Gambet (1970); Setaioli (2003); Fedeli (2004); Gowing (2013: 240–4); Keeline (2018: 196–222).
25. On the declamatory treatment of Cicero's death more generally, see Winterbottom (1981); Roller (1997); Kaster (1998); Keeline (2018: 102–30).
26. See, for instance, Rambaud (1955: 264–6); Ahl (1976: 160–3); Fantham (1999: 120–1); Narducci (2002: 299–302); Radicke (2004: 379); Roche (2019: 84).
27. Proponents of the view that Cicero's speech serves as an apology for Pompey include Rambaud (1955); Holliday (1969); Lounsbury (1976); Fantham (1999); and Narducci (2003).
28. For the traditional notion of rhetoric as a deceptive art, see Arist., *Rh.* 1402a18–28 and Cic., *De or.* 2.30.
29. On the ambivalent role of the senate, see Jessen-Klingenberg (2009); see also Leigh (1997: 146–7) and Fantham (1999). As an advisor to war, Cicero resembles Curio in book 1; see Radicke (2004: 380) and Roche (2019: 84). In addition, he invokes comparison with Pothinus in book 8, who plays a similar role as a negative counselor. On the latter's *suasoria*, see Winterbottom (1981: 67–9).
30. See, among others, Luc. 1.356–86; 3.303–55; 4.591–660.
31. On the Ciceronian connotation of *rector* see Ahl (1976: 162) and Narducci (2003: 85).
32. On Pompey's speech including its relationship to his first harangue in book 2, see Pichon (1912: 137–8); Tasler (1972: 104–7); Lebek (1976: 224–6); Glaesser (1984: 121–5); Schlonski (1995: 121–9); Narducci (2002: 302–9); Sklenář (2003: 111–14); Rolim de Moura (2010: 76–8). See also Roche (2019: 89–100). An important epic model is the speech of Latinus in *Aeneid* 7, in which the king capitulates to his people who angrily throng around his palace and demand war. For a potential Homeric precedent (Hom., *Il.* 22.296–305), see Narducci (2002: 303–4).
33. His hope to be the first to be killed if this will not negatively affect the course of events as well as his own party (7.117–19) mirrors Cato's wish to die in Book 2, but also reveals a fundamental difference, since Pompey's death would not save his troops or atone for the guilt of civil war, but would only be "a convenient suicide destined to terminate a life that is turning into a burden" (Rolim de Moura 2010: 77). This underscores once again his lack of vigor and resolve and undermines his status as *rector* of the Republican forces. For a Stoic interpretation of Pompey's

speech, see especially Sklenář (2003: 111–14); for Pompey's appropriation of the narrator's viewpoint, see, among others, Rolim de Moura (2010: 77–8) and Glaesser (2018: 64–5).

34. On the use of *onus* and related words in Lucan, see Johnson (1987: 77–8). On Pompey's passivity as a leitmotif in *Bellum Civile* 7, see Glaesser (2018: 65).

References

Ahl, F. M. (1976), *Lucan: An Introduction*, Ithaca: Cornell University Press.
Bartsch, S. (1997), *Ideology in Cold Blood: A Reading of Lucan's Civil War*, Cambridge, MA: Harvard University Press.
Beard, M. (2002), "Ciceronian Correspondences: Making a Book out of Letters," in T. P. Wiseman (ed.), *Classics in Progress: Essays on Ancient Greece and Rome*, 103–44, Oxford: Oxford University Press.
Bloomer, W. M. (1997a), "Schooling in Persona: Imagination and Subordination in Roman Education," *ClAnt*, 16: 57–78.
Bloomer, W. M. (1997b), *Latinity and Literary Society at Rome*, Philadelphia: University of Pennsylvania Press.
Bloomer, W. M. (2007), "Roman Declamation: The Elder Seneca and Quintilian," in W. Dominik and J. Hall (eds.), *A Companion to Roman Rhetoric*, 297–306, Oxford: Blackwell.
Bloomer, W. M. (2011), *The School of Rome: Latin Studies and the Origins of Liberal Education*, Berkeley: University of California Press.
Bonner, S. F. (1949), *Roman Declamation in the Late Republic and Early Empire*, Liverpool: University Press of Liverpool.
Bonner, S. F. (1966), "Lucan and the Declamation Schools," *AJPh*, 87: 257–89.
Bonner, S. F. (1977), *Education in Ancient Rome: From the Elder Cato to the Younger Pliny*, Berkeley: University of California Press.
Braund, S. H., trans. (1992), *Lucan: Civil War*, Oxford: Oxford University Press.
Brisset, J. (1964), *Les idées politiques de Lucain*, Paris: Belles Lettres.
Burkard, T. (2016), "Zu den Begriffen *divisio* und *color* bei Seneca maior," in R. Poignault and C. Schneider (eds.), *Fabrique de la déclamation antique (controverses et suasoires)*, 87–134, Lyons: Maison de l'Orient et de la Méditerranée – Jean Pouilloux.
Clark, M. L. (1953), *Rhetoric at Rome: A Historical Survey*, London: Routledge.
Connolly, J. (2007), *The State of Speech: Rhetoric and Political Thought in Ancient Rome*, Princeton: Princeton University Press.
Corbeill, A. (2007), "Rhetorical Education and Social Reproduction in the Republic and Early Empire," in W. Dominik and J. Hall (eds.), *A Companion to Roman Rhetoric*, 69–82, Oxford: Blackwell.
Degl'Innocenti Pierini, R. (2003), "Cicerone nella prima età imperiale: Luci ed ombre su un martire della repubblica," in E. Narducci (ed.), *Aspetti della fortuna di Cicerone nella cultura latina*. Atti del III Symposium Ciceronianum Arpinas (Arpino 10 maggio 2002), 3–54, Florence: Le Monnier.
Dominik, W. J., ed. (1997), *Roman Eloquence: Rhetoric in Society and Literature*, London: Routledge.
Fairweather, J. (1981), *Seneca the Elder*, Cambridge: Cambridge University Press.
Fairweather, J. (1984), "The Elder Seneca and Declamation," *ANRW*, 2.32 (1): 514–56.
Fantham, E. (1999), "Lucan and the Republican Senate: Ideology, Historical Record and Prosopography," in P. Esposito and L. Nicastri (eds.), *Interpretare Lucano. Miscellanea di studi*, 109–25, Naples: Arte Tipografica s.a.s.

Feddern, D., ed. (2013), *Die Suasorien des älteren Seneca: Einleitung, Text und Kommentar*, Berlin: de Gruyter.
Fedeli, P. (2004), "Cicerone e Seneca," *Ciceroniana*, 12: 217–37.
Fratantuono, L. (2012), *Madness Triumphant: A Reading of Lucan's* Pharsalia, Lanham, MD: Lexington Books.
Fucecchi, M. (2011), "Partisans in Civil War," in P. Asso (ed.), *Brill's Companion to Lucan*, 237–56, Leiden: Brill.
Gambet, D. G. (1970), "Cicero in the Works of Seneca *philosophus*," *TAPhA*, 101: 171–83.
Glaesser, R. (1984) *Verbrechen und Verblendung: Untersuchung zum Furor-Begriff bei Lucan mit Berücksichtigung der Tragödien Senecas*, Frankfurt am Main: Peter Lang.
Glaesser, R. (2018), *Lucan lesen – ein Gang durch das* Bellum civile, Heidelberg: Winter.
Gleason, M. W. (1995), *Making Men: Sophists and Self-Presentation in Ancient Rome*, Princeton: Princeton University Press.
Gowing, A. M. (2013), "Tully's Boat: Responses to Cicero in the Imperial Period," in C. Steel (ed.), *The Cambridge Companion to Cicero*, 233–50, Cambridge: Cambridge University Press.
Gunderson, E. (2003), *Declamation, Paternity and Roman Identity*, Cambridge: Cambridge University Press.
Holliday, V. (1969), *Pompey in Cicero's Correspondence and Lucan's Civil War*, The Hague: Mouton.
Housman, A. E., ed. (1926), *M. Annaei Lucani belli civilis libri decem*, Oxford: Blackwell.
Imber, M. (1997), "Tyrants and Mothers: Roman Education and Ideology," PhD diss., Stanford University, Stanford, CA.
Jessen-Klingenberg, K. (2009), "*Partes in bella togatae*: Die Präsenz des römischen Senats in Lucans *Bellum civile*," *Gymnasium*, 116: 29–55.
Johnson, W. R. (1987), *Momentary Monsters: Lucan and His Heroes*, Ithaca: Cornell University Press.
Kaster, R. A. (1998), "Becoming CICERO," in P. Knox and C. Foss (eds.), *Style and Tradition: Studies in Honor of Wendell Clausen*, 248–63, Stuttgart: Teubner.
Kaster, R. A. (2001), "Controlling Reason: Declamation in Rhetorical Education at Rome," in Y. L. Too (ed.), *Education in Greek and Roman Antiquity*, 317–73, Leiden: Brill.
Keeline, T. J. (2018), *The Reception of Cicero in the Early Roman Empire: The Rhetorical Schoolroom and the Creation of a Cultural Legend*, Cambridge: Cambridge University Press.
Kennedy, G. (1972), *The Art of Rhetoric in the Roman World 300 BC – AD 300*, Princeton: Princeton University Press.
Kraus, C. S. (2000), "The Path between Truculence and Servility: Prose Literature from Augustus to Hadrian," in O. Taplin (ed.), *Literature in the Greek and Roman Worlds: A New Perspective*, 438–67, Oxford: Oxford University Press.
Lebek, W. D. (1976), *Lucans* Pharsalia*: Dichtungsstruktur und Zeitbezug*, Göttingen: Vandenhoeck and Ruprecht.
Leigh, M. (1997), *Lucan: Spectacle and Engagement*, Oxford: Oxford University Press.
Lintott, A. W. (1971), "Lucan and the History of the Civil War," *CQ*, 21: 488–505.
Liong, K. A. (2011), "Cicero *de re militari*: A Civilian Perspective on Military Matters in the Late Republic," PhD diss., University of Edinburgh, Edinburgh.
Lounsbury, R. (1975), "History and Motive in Book Seven of Lucan's *Pharsalia*," *Hermes*, 104: 210–39.
Malcovati, E. (1953), "Lucano e Cicerone," *Athenaeum*, 31: 288–97.
Nadaï, de, J.-C. (2000), *Rhétorique et poétique dans la* Pharsale *de Lucain: La crise de la représentation dans la poésie antique*, Louvain: Peeters.
Narducci, E. (2002), *Lucano: Un'epica contro l'impero*, Rome: Laterza.
Narducci, E. (2003), "Cicerone nella *Pharsalia* di Lucano," in E. Narducci (ed.), *Aspetti della fortuna di Cicerone nella cultura latina*. Atti del III Symposium Ciceronianum Arpinas (Arpino 10 maggio 2002), 78–91, Florence: Le Monnier.

Nehrkorn, H. (1960), "Die Darstellung und Funktion der Nebencharaktere in Lucans *Bellum civile*," PhD diss., Johns Hopkins University, Baltimore, MD.
Oppermann, I. (2000), *Zur Funktion historischer Beispiele in Ciceros Briefen*, Munich: Saur.
Peirano, I. (2012), *The Rhetoric of the Roman Fake: Latin Pseudepigrapha in Context*, Cambridge: Cambridge University Press.
Pichon, R. (1912), *Les sources de Lucain*, Paris: E. Leroux.
Radicke, J. (2004), *Lucans poetische Technik: Studien zum historischen Epos*, Leiden: Brill.
Rambaud, M. (1955), "L'apologie de Pompée par Lucain au livre VII de la *Pharsale*," *REL*, 33: 258–96.
Richter, W. (1968), "Das Cicerobild der römischen Kaiserzeit," in G. Radke (ed.), *Cicero: Ein Mensch seiner Zeit. Acht Vorträge zu einem geistesgeschichtlichen Phänomen*, 161–97, Berlin: de Gruyter.
Roche, P., ed. (2019), *Lucan: De bello civili. Book 7*. Edited with Introduction, Text, and Commentary, Cambridge: Cambridge University Press.
Rolim de Moura, A. (2010), "Lucan 7: Speeches at War," in N. Hömke and C. Reitz (eds.), *Lucan's* Bellum civile: *Between Epic Tradition and Aesthetic Innovation*, 71–90, Berlin: de Gruyter.
Roller, M. B. (1997), "*Color*-Blindness: Cicero's Death, Declamation, and the Production of History," *CPh*, 92, 109–30.
Schlonski, F. (1995), *Studien zum Erzählerstandort bei Lucan*, Trier: Wissenschaftlicher Verlag.
Setaioli, A. (1976), "On the Date of Publication of Cicero's Letters to Atticus," *Symbolae Osloenses*, 51: 105–20.
Setaioli, A. (2003), "Seneca e Cicerone," in E. Narducci (ed.), *Aspetti della fortuna di Cicerone nella cultura latina*. Atti del III Symposium Ciceronianum Arpinas (Arpino 10 maggio 2002), 55–77, Florence: Le Monnier.
Setaioli, A. (2014), "*Epistulae morales*," in G. Damschen and A. Heil (eds.), *Brill's Companion to Seneca: Philosopher and Dramatist*, 191–200, Leiden: Brill.
Shackleton Bailey, D. R., ed. (1999), *Cicero: Letters to Atticus*, 4 vols., Cambridge, MA: Harvard University Press.
Shackleton Bailey, D. R., ed. (2001), *Cicero: Letters to Friends*, 3 vols., Cambridge, MA: Harvard University Press.
Sklenář, R. (2003), *The Taste for Nothingness: A Study of Virtus and Related Themes in Lucan's* Bellum civile, Ann Arbor: University of Michigan Press.
Stroh, W. (2003), "*Declamatio*," in B.-J. Schröder and J.-P. Schröder (eds.), *Studium declamatorium: Untersuchungen zu Schulübungen und Prunkreden von der Antike bis zur Neuzeit*, 5–34, Munich: Saur.
Sussmann, L. A. (1978), *The Elder Seneca*, Leiden: Brill.
Tabacco, R. (1985), "Il tiranno nelle declamazioni di scuola in lingua latina," *Memorie dell'Accademia delle Scienze di Torino*, series 5, 9: 1–141.
Tasler, W. (1972), *Die Reden in Lucans* Pharsalia, Diss. Friedrich-Alexander Universität, Erlangen-Nürnberg.
Thraede, K. (1970), *Grundzüge griechisch-römischer Brieftopik*, Munich: Beck.
White, P. (2010), *Cicero in Letters: Epistolary Relations of the Late Republic*, Oxford: Oxford University Press.
Winterbottom, M., ed. (1974), *Seneca the Elder: Declamations*, 2 vols., Cambridge, MA: Harvard University Press.
Winterbottom, M., ed. (1980), *Roman Declamation*, Bristol: Bristol Classical Press.
Winterbottom, M., ed. (1981), "Cicero and the Silver Age," in W. Ludwig (ed.), *Éloquence et rhétorique chez Cicéron*, 237–74, Geneva: Fondation Hardt.

PART II
THE NATURAL WORLD AND GEOGRAPHY IN THE NERONIAN PERIOD

CHAPTER 4
MINING AND MORALITY IN LUCAN AND SENECA
Laura Zientek

According to Pliny's *Historia Naturalis*, the earth produces a vast array of fantastic objects that humanity can exploit; coming from nature, they are the root of many of humanity's problems. Pliny contrasts these *terrae miracula* with nature's crimes (*scelera naturae*, HN 2.206), thus illustrating one way in which Roman authors of the mid-first century CE addressed issues of humanity's relationship with the world around it. Lucan's landscapes—i.e., representations of nature by or through the poet's own perspective—engage with the same issues. Like other ancient poets before him,[1] Lucan incorporates the thematic, structural, and aesthetic context of his poem into both the people he describes and the world they inhabit. J. Donald Hughes notes that when we study the environmental history of ancient Rome, we are directing our attention to "the history of human thought about the environment and the ways in which patterns of human attitudes have motivated actions that affect the environment" (2006: 3). The reverse is true as well, in that we can also examine the effect of the environment on humanity, especially in the cases of extreme weather, climate, or natural disasters. Broadly, the significance of landscape in classical texts rests on the dual premise that landscape is "mediated by culture" (Mitchell 2002: 5) and that "the landscape-consciousness of every culture is historically distinct and subjective" (Fitter 1995: 2). Landscape is thus representational and defined by the cognitive context of those who represent it. In this chapter, reading depictions of landscapes in the texts of Lucan and Seneca facilitates an analysis of the complex, varying, and sometimes contradictory ways in which these authors thought of their culture, the world around them, and the reciprocal relationship between the two.

As Lucan's narrative traces the battles of 49–48 BCE across the Mediterranean region, Lucan describes both the actions of his characters and the geography and landscapes of Italy (Books 1–2), Gaul and Spain (3–4), Greece (5–7), and Egypt and North Africa (8–10) in pointed detail. Lucan likely drew his information about these places from the same sources available to authors such as the geographers Strabo and Pomponius Mela, the natural historian Pliny the Elder,[2] and Seneca, whose *Natural Questions* was a treatise on natural philosophy composed around the same time as the *Bellum Civile*.[3] These nearly contemporary sources allow us a glimpse into the intellectual world of the mid-first century CE and help contextualize our understanding of Lucan's poetic project. In the dialogue between epic and natural philosophy in particular, we can observe the great influence that Seneca's writings on Stoic physics and ethics had on Lucan.

In general, Lucan's poem depicts a world that is composed with the Stoic principles of natural philosophy in mind, though Lucan often bends or even breaks these rules.[4] The imagined landscapes of the poem reflect the knowledge contained in Seneca's *Natural Questions* and scattered throughout the rest of his philosophical corpus. Within Lucan's quasi-Stoic environments, a virtuous life means living in accordance with Nature or at least not disrupting Nature's rhythms and systems. The *discordia* of civil war is the broadest example of immoral human disruption of the world as a whole, but Lucan fills his poem to overflowing with varied episodic examples as well. One example is the motif of moral corruption as it is associated with the acquisition of precious goods, the pursuit of luxury (*luxus*) and wealth (*divitiae*), and the practice of mining to attain these goods and riches. Mining, which the Romans looked down on as "degrading labor" (Hughes 2014: 133),[5] becomes part of this system of ethics in its portrayal as a delving into the earth and thus, as a transgression of humanity's proper place in nature. By focusing on Lucan's civil war epic and a few of Seneca's texts through the critical idiom of landscape studies, this chapter explores the literary and philosophical depiction of mining and its relevance to the larger poetic and philosophical projects in which Lucan and Seneca were engaged. In doing so, it examines the connections and interactions between humanity and the world in which we live. Mining stands as a literary and philosophical trope that demonstrates the consequences of human action on the environment as part of industry and also, especially in Lucan's text, as part of warfare.

Although Lucan mentions mining only in passing, his text alludes to more detailed accounts of the mining process and its connection to moral depravity as described in Seneca's writing and in the texts of other first-century authors. The way Seneca frames mining in respect to the ethical and physical theories of Stoicism is both a point of comparison for Lucan's use of mining imagery and terminology, and the key to understanding the thematic nexus of *luxuria*, *avaritia*, acquisition, exploitation of natural resources, and moral corruption in Lucan's poem. Likewise, Pliny the Elder gives an account of the processes of obtaining precious metals in *Historia Naturalis* 33 that provides our most significant reference for gold mining in ancient Rome in the context of a broader encyclopedic account of *natura* (Syme 1969: 217–19; Pérez González and Matías Rodríguez 2008: 49–50). Pliny's putative Stoic perspective, moreover, engages with the connections between philosophical physics and ethics—or in the interactions between humanity and the world around us.[6]

Mining in the First Century CE and in Lucan's Poem

Lucan's explicit references to mining practices are rare. The most detailed occurs in Book four during the Caesarian siege of Ilerda in Hispania Citerior, in a simile describing Pompey's soldiers as they search for potable water after a cataclysmic storm. In a landscape altered by floods and the engineering of Caesar's soldiers, the Pompeians seek out any moisture by delving into the earth like gold miners (4.295–304):

>   puteusque cavati
> montis ad irrigui premitur fastigia campi.
> non se tam penitus, tam longe luce relicta
> merserit Astyrici scrutator pallidus auri.
> non tamen aut tectis sonuerunt cursibus amnes
> aut micuere novi percusso pumice fontes,
> antra nec exiguo stillant sudantia rore
> aut impulsa levi turbatur glarea vena.
> sic exhausta super multo sudore iuventus
> extrahitur duris silicum lassata metallis.

A well in the hollowed mountain is pressed down to the depths of the flooded plain. Not so deeply, with daylight far abandoned, would the pale searcher for Asturian gold bury himself. Still, neither did rivers resound in subterranean streams nor did strange springs sparkle from the excavated pumice, nor do caves, dripping, distill into scanty dew, nor is gravel, pushed about, disturbed by a light vein of water. Thus the youth, exhausted by much sweaty labor, are dragged up and out, wearied by harsh mining of rocks.[7]

The geography is convenient, in that the imagined mining of the soldiers at Ilerda (a town in northeast Spain) recalls a metaphorical miner digging for gold near Asturia (in northwest Spain).[8] The image Lucan creates is not subtle: the depth of the digging at Ilerda is emphasized by *penitus*, the fact that the youth must be dragged (*extrahitur*) back to the surface, and the comparison to the Asturian digger, *pallidus* from his time underground, and submerged (*merserit*) so deeply that no daylight can reach him. Lucan adapts the mining practice of excavating ore to the actions of soldiers, who must be "mined" out of the earth when their search for water is unsuccessful (Asso 2010: 174). The style of the tunnel that the soldiers dig also reflects an understanding about real Roman mining practices. In letter 94, Seneca also invokes mining, portraying it as a misguided act that is not in accordance with nature (*nulli nos vitio natura conciliat, Ep.* 94.56) but that demonstrates the value of philosophical advice. Mineral resources buried in the earth (*mersa*, 94.58) are dragged back through the gloom of long mine shafts (*per longissimorum cuniculorum tenebras extrahuntur*, 94.58). Seneca's *extrahuntur* and Lucan's *extrahitur* mirror each other. Seneca's mine shaft is a *cuniculum*, however, and thus evokes underground tunnels used in siege works,[9] while Lucan's *metalla* more specifically indicates the metals sought in mines and well as the mines themselves.

It seems likely that Lucan's knowledge—and Seneca's as well—comes from sources such as Posidonius, the Stoic philosopher and geographer whose works included information about Spanish gold and silver mines.[10] Strabo cites Posidonius on Spanish mining, and Seneca himself cites Posidonius in his texts.[11] Lucan's family geography, however, is also a tempting source for knowledge of the Spanish mining industry. The Annaei had acquired some wealth in Baetica at least two generations prior to Lucan (Griffin 1972: 4; Curchin 1991: 81).[12] Corduba was an administrative center for the mining industry in Spain, though the most active and productive gold mines were located further north in the region of Asturia.[13] The image Lucan creates in his simile lines up quite well with our understanding of Roman deep-vein mining (Duncan 1999), a technique in which miners would dig a vertical shaft into the earth and then expand horizontally to access veins of ore. These tunnels could be dug down to the level of the water table—as Lucan implies is done by the *iuventus* at Ilerda— or sometimes even deeper, if proper drainage systems could be installed.[14] On this method, we can look to Pliny *HN* 33.66 for the technical language: *puteorum scrobibus effoditur* (it is mined from shafts of wells), comparable with Lucan's *puteus* at 4.295. Pliny's description of mining technology has been proven to be quite accurate (Zehnacker 1983: 33; Isager 1991: 65) and thus these descriptions with their accompanying technical vocabulary can represent the reality of these practices in the first century CE more generally. As far as Lucan's simile is concerned, though its scope is limited, it is in dialogue with this more extensive network of technological knowledge. Since it occurs in an episode thoroughly preoccupied by water (excessive abundance or deprivation), Lucan's depiction of the Asturian gold miner appears to draw inspiration from the realities of Roman mining practices especially in their use of water and their environmental impacts.

Roman mines were largely dependent on hydraulic technology,[15] which came into use after Rome's victory in the Cantabrian Wars (19 CE)[16] and the Roman state's subsequent investment in northwest Spanish gold mines.[17] At its most basic level, this technology anthropogenically accelerated natural processes like erosion and thus allowed placer mining to supplement deep-vein mining. Archaeological evidence from northwest Spain—including Asturia—shows that this was a widespread practice that made Spain the primary supplier of mineral resources to Rome during the first century CE (Curchin 1991: 136; Magntorn 2001: 27–8; Wilson 2007: 109, 113). The environmental effects are visible on both large and small scales: at Las Medulas,[18] where hydraulic mining resulted in the total erosion of mountainsides (the *ruina montium* method),[19] and in ice-core samples from Greenland that point to the nearly industrial level of ore smelting pollution from the early Roman imperial period (Hong et al. 1996; Wilson 2002: 25–7; McConnell et al. 2018). When read against Lucan's Spanish episode, however, these realities of Roman mining practices reveal a moment of irony. Although real mining infrastructure in northwest Spain and Lucan's cataclysmic storm at Ilerda in northeast Spain were both possible due to immense quantities of water,[20] by the time Lucan introduces his simile, thirst is the focus and the figurative mines (*metalla*) dug by the Pompeians are totally dry.

The term *metalla* indicates the precious metals acquired from the earth and mining as the Roman proto-industrial practice (Rickard 1928: 134; Lewis and Jones 1970: 174–6; Wilson 2002: 25–7; Hughes 2014: 134). Elsewhere in Lucan's poem, it indicates deep-vein mining once more, in a clear allusion to the difficulty of extracting metals from veins of ore and the technology necessary to obtain them. The labor attached to mining iron for later use in war is read in contrast to Lucan's moralizing statement about *libertas* (4.223–7; Asso 2010: 159):

non chalybem gentes penitus fugiente metallo
eruerent, nulli vallarent oppida muri,
non sonipes in bella ferox, non iret in aequor
turrigeras classis pelago sparsura carinas,
si bene libertas umquam pro pace daretur.

The races (of men) would not dig out iron from the mine fleeing into the depths of the earth, no walls would fortify towns, the fierce horse would not go to war nor would the fleet go to sea, about to scatter turreted ships on the deep, if ever freedom were given up for peace.

Chalybes, iron, alludes metonymically to the geographical tradition of a people famous for their iron mines (Str. 12.3.19–20; cf. Fourgous 1976: 1139; Domergue 1981: 90–1) and reproached by Lucan's narrator for iron's association with war (6.396–9; cf. Val., *Arg.* 5.140–6). The verb *eruere* is a common term for extracting ore from the earth (cf. Plin., *HN* 33.4). Lucan's repeated emphasis on the depth of excavation required for mining metals (cf. 4.297) is also characteristic of Roman textual presentations of gold mining, as Lucan's *penitus* echoes Pomponius Mela's *aurum ... penitus egestum* (2.1; 3.62).[21] *Metallum* is also a technical term here, referring to the excavated tunnels underground. Elsewhere in the *Bellum Civile* it indicates such things as the process of collecting placer-gold[22] from the Lydian Pactolus river (*passaque ab auriferis tellus exire metallis / Pactolon*, 3.209–10),[23] the precious metals in Pompey's camps after the battle of Pharsalus that will become spoils for Caesar's soldiers (7.737–42), and the golden apples of the Hesperides (9.360–4). One more instance diverges slightly by identifying the excavated earth—an old mine or a quarry[24]—from which Caesar obtains stones to build siege works at Dyrrhachium (6.29–39):

hic avidam belli rapuit spes improba mentem
Caesaris, ut vastis diffusum collibus hostem
cingeret ignarum ducto procul aggere valli.
metatur terras oculis, nec caespite tantum
contentus fragili subitos attollere muros
ingentis cautes avulsaque saxa metallis
Graiorumque domos direptaque moenia transfert.
extruitur quod non aries impellere saevus,
quod non ulla queat violenti machina belli.
franguntur montes, planumque per ardua Caesar
ducit opus.

Here wicked hope seized Caesar's mind, greedy for war, to surround his unwitting enemy, spread out over vast hillsides with a ramp's earthwork drawn up at a distance. He measures the landscape with his eyes, and is not content to raise up sudden walls from fragile sod; he transfers huge crags and stones torn away from quarries and the Greeks' homes and pillaged city walls. That which is built no savage ram could bring to ruin, nor any machine of violent war. Mountains are broken, and Caesar constructs his work as a plain through the heights.

Earlier, the only moralistic description applied to the Asturian gold miner is the implication that he is unnaturally pale (*pallidus*) because of his time underground. Lucan's exaggeratedly villainous Caesar is different: his greedy mind (*avidam ... mentem*)[25] transforms the significance of his orders and his soldiers' actions. Rather than simply mirroring the work of miners, Caesar's desires lead to a destructive transformation of the landscape as part of the Roman military-industrial complex. Under Caesar's command, mountains are broken apart (*franguntur montes*) in an eerie mirroring of the Romans' most destructive mining practice, often labeled simply as *ruina montium*. Pliny *HN* 33.73 later uses the same kind of language and terminology: *mons fractus cadit ab sese longe fragore qui concipi humana mente non possit, aeque et flatu incredibili. spectant victores ruinam naturae* (The broken mountain falls away from itself with a lasting crash which it is not possible for the human mind to comprehend, and similarly with an unbelievable wind. As victors, the miners behold the ruin of nature). Lucan's use of words such as *metallum* and images of broken, collapsing mountains does not borrow from Caesar's *commentarii* nor from one of his epic predecessors. Instead, the terms are technical and connected to the context and practice of mining. Even beyond the allusive language and mirrored imagery, Lucan encourages us to interpret Caesar's actions in this scene as a morally troublesome disruption of nature in the Stoic undertones of his poetic *mundus*, especially when read in context with the strong anti-industrial position taken by Seneca toward mining.

Seneca on the Exploitation of Mines and the Possession of Gold

Around the same time Lucan was writing the *Bellum Civile*, Seneca was composing the *Naturales Quaestiones*, his treatise on the theories and principles of natural philosophy as understood in Stoic physics. In his discussion of winds and their ability to move underground, Seneca relates a story about a team of men sent by Philip II of Macedon to explore an old mine (Sen., *QNat.* 5.15.1):[26]

> Asclepiodotus auctor est demissos quam plurimos a Philippo in metallum antiquum olim destitutum, ut explorarent quae ubertas eius esset, quis status, an aliquid futuris reliquisset vetus avaritia.

> Asclepiodotus is the authority on the fact that many men were sent down by Philip into an ancient mine, long deserted, to explore what its richness was, what its condition was, and whether ancient greed had left anything behind for future people.

What follows is Seneca's explanation that one of the constant qualities of human nature is the tendency to exploit natural resources and to destroy the landscape in pursuit of *vitia* and *avaritia* (5.15.2):[27]

intellexi enim saeculum nostrum non novis vitiis sed iam inde antiquitus traditis laborare, nec nostra aetate primum avaritiam venas terrarum lapidumque rimatam in tenebris male abstrusa quaesisse.

For I understood that our age does not labor under new vices but from those handed down long ago, nor in our age did greed first cleave open the veins of the earth and stone to seek out things poorly hidden in darkness.

Seneca's opinions about the morality of mining here are in dialogue with the passing references to mining in Lucan's text. As the anecdote proceeds, Seneca asks what great expectation (*quae tanta spes*, 5.15.3) led human beings to descend into mines and identifies hope as a motivating force (*spe ducti*, 5.15.2); in the *Bellum Civile* Lucan identifies *improba spes* (6.29) as Caesar's motivator in taking stones from old mines/quarries to build his siege works at Dyrrhachium. As a direct result of Caesar's hope and the actions it prompts, mountains crumble (*franguntur montes*, 6.38), echoing Seneca's accusation that with people *spe ducti*, mountains fell (*montes ceciderunt*, QNat. 5.15.2). We can also compare both images to Pliny's later use of the same vocabulary as part of his technical descriptions of mining and its effects. Broken and fallen mountains recall the *ruina montium* method of extracting gold from ore, especially given Seneca's subsequent comment: "they stood on top of their profit, at the base of the ruin" (*supra lucrum sub ruina steterunt*, 5.15.2). Seneca also portrays miners as being buried in the innermost depths of the earth (*in fundum telluris intimae mersit*, 5.15.3), and Lucan's Asturian gold miner is likewise buried (*tam longe luce relicta / merserit*, 4.297–8). Seneca criticizes that these miners dig out gold (*erueret aurum*, QNat. 5.15.3), while Lucan's Petreius sees mining as a means to obtain the resources necessary to fight in the civil war (*chalybem* ... / *eruerent*, 4.223–4). Unlike Petreius, Lucan's narrator does not consider civil war a worthy or moral cause, and thus mining metals such as iron or gold remains a troubling process in the broader context of the poem. Lucan's characters may be thought of as "min[ing] out the causes and instruments" of their own destruction (*nos et causas periculorum nostrorum et instrumenta disiecto terrarum pondere eruimus*, Sen., Ep. 94.57).

In Seneca's conclusion to the story of Philip's exploratory mining expedition, he characterizes mining as breaking open the earth and descending into it in search of riches, a perspective based in Stoic theory, where mining is both a symptom and an expression of moral degeneracy. As Gareth Williams notes, Seneca attaches the mining process to both actual and metaphorical *ruina*, in the excavations and the "subsequent (moral) collapse" (2005: 420). Moreover, Seneca describes the riches to which mines give access as an evil poison (*illud malum virus*, QNat. 5.15.4)[28] and notes that the natural order of things in the world—in accordance to which, incidentally, the good Stoic should aspire to live—gives way underground to something strange (*novam rerum positionem*, 5.15.4). Thus, for Seneca the process of mining is both symbol and byproduct of moral decline and collapse.[29] The story of the miners and Seneca's criticism echo his condemnation of *luxuria* and the means of acquiring its material accoutrements as presented in the first book of the *Natural Questions*. In this consideration of vanity and appearance that contrasts the nobler past with a more corrupt present, Seneca notes (1.17.6, 8, 10):

> postquam deterior populus ipsas subit terras effossurus obruenda, ferrum primum in usu fuit—et id impune homines eruerant, si solum eruissent—tunc deinde alia terrae mala ... postea, iam rerum potiente luxuria, specula totis paria corporibus auro argentoque caelata sunt ... processit enim paulatim in deterius opibus ipsis invitata luxuria et incrementum ingens vitia ceperunt.

> After a worse people went down under the earth itself to dig out buried things, iron was first in use—and people would have mined it out with impunity, if they had mined iron only—then next the earth's other evils ... Afterwards, when luxury held sway over everything, full-length mirrors were engraved with gold and silver ... Luxury, enticed by its very riches advanced bit by bit into something worse and vices have increased greatly.

Seneca's criticism does not merely address ostentatious wealth and its origins but implicitly deplores the technologies used to obtain such wealth and, more broadly, the imperial appetites and economics that made the whole process possible (Hine 2006: 52).[30]

Even earlier, in his consolation to his mother, Seneca used *eruere* of the acquisition of the material goods of *luxuria* and the moral evils that accompany them (Sen. *Helv.* 10.2):

> non est necesse omne perscrutari profundum nec strage animalium ventrem onerare nec conchylia ultimi maris ex ignoto litore eruere: di istos deaeque perdant quorum luxuria tam invidiosi imperii fines transcendit.

> There is no need for searching through every depth, nor is it necessary to burden the stomach with the slaughter of animals nor to dig out shellfish from an unknown shore of the most distant sea: may gods and goddesses bring those men to ruin whose luxury transcends the borders of so envious an empire.

We should also notice the verbal similarity between Seneca's description of the acquisition of luxury foodstuffs and Lucan's metaphorical gold miners, where Lucan's *scrutator* (4.298) echoes Seneca's *perscrutari* (*Helv.* 12.10.2). The kind of penetrating investigation conducted by a *scrutator* also characterizes mining for Manilius (*scrutari caeca metalla*, 4.246; cf. 2.824–5) and Pliny (*imus in viscera et in sede manium opes quaerimus ... scrutamur, HN* 33.2). This linguistic context, shared among authors who wrote about natural philosophy and history, foregrounds questions of how people relate to nature in Lucan's poem.[31]

For Seneca, the story of Roman "progress" is simultaneously and inextricably the story of Rome's moral decline. Often, his discussions of *luxuria* and its accompanying moral turbulence look to the causes of both conditions, so that mining as a means of acquiring *luxuria* is woven into the fabric of Seneca's critique. In his treatise *On Benefits*, Seneca addresses forms of wealth (*Ben*. 7.10.2–3):

> nunc volo tuas opes recognoscere, lamnas utriusque materiae, ad quam cupiditas nostra caligat. at mehercules terra, quae, quidquid utile futurum nobis erat, protulit, ista defodit et mersit et ut noxiosis rebus ac malo gentium in medium proditurus toto pondere incubuit. video ferrum ex isdem tenebris esse prolatum, quibus aurum et argentum, ne aut instrumentum in caedes mutuas deesset aut pretium.

> Now I wish to examine your wealth, plates of both materials [gold and silver], to which our avarice gropes about in darkness. By Hercules, the earth, which put forth whatever would be useful to us, has hidden and buried and reclined on these substances with its whole weight as if they are harmful things—and an evil—to be brought into the middle of humanity. I see that iron has been brought forth from the same shadows from which came gold and silver, so that neither instrument nor prize is lacking for mutual slaughter.

The mining process, taking place beneath the surface of the earth, is inherently gloomy, a fact Seneca makes clear in his descriptions of the locations of gold and silver underground (*terra ... defodit, mersit, incubuit*).[32] The precious metals obtained by mining are portrayed here, as they were in the *Natural Questions*, as a harmful evil to humanity; we can compare *noxiosis rebus ac malo* with *illud malum virus* (*QNat*. 5.15.4) and *alia terrae mala* (1.17.6). But here, more directly than in Seneca's commentary on natural philosophy, the respective cause and result of *luxuria* are clear: greed (*cupiditas*) and civil conflict (*caedes mutuas*).

Likewise in *Letter* 115, the desire for material wealth is again a corrupting force, but also, notably, a topic of agreement amidst civic factionalism. The admiration of gold and silver (*admirationem ... auri argentique*) is again a manifestation of *cupiditas* and remains consistent despite other *discordia* (*Ep*. 115.11). In fact, Seneca goes on to say, this appreciation for gold infects the works of poets and the myths of earlier times to the extent that the so-called Golden Age (*saeculum aureum appellant*, *Ep*. 115.13) has been co-opted as a term to refer to any time being praised rather than the archetypal Golden Age, the mythical time of plentiful paradise. Seneca alludes to the myth that developed from Hesiod to Ovid, though he does not use a metallic metaphor in his narrative of decline. Seneca's ironic naming of the age as "golden" hints at two related trends: the reduction of goldweight in imperial coinage (Isager 1991: 62–3) and the ostentatious use of gold by the imperial family.[33] Gold, Seneca tells us, begets greed.[34] He does, however, renew in his tragedies the idea that this primeval paradise lacked a blind desire for gold (*auri ... / caecus cupido*, *Phaedra* 527–8), and was lost because of an impious madness for profit (*impius lucri furor*, 540).

The spurious play *Octavia*, though most likely composed after the end of the Neronian period proper, provides another relevant point of reference for understanding how authors of the first century incorporated ideas about the possession and acquisition of wealth into expressions of philosophical ethics. In a retelling of the Ages of Man by the dramatic character of Seneca, mining is imagined as visceral violence against a parent driven on by a desire for war and hunger for gold (*Oct.* 416–18; cf. *cupido belli . . . atque auri fames*, *Oct.* 425):[35]

> sed in parentis viscera intravit suae
> deterior aetas; eruit ferrum grave
> aurumque, saevas mox et armavit manus.
>
> But a worse age delved into its own parent's entrails: it mined out heavy iron and gold, and soon armed its savage hands.

The Octavia-poet also employs the same kind of language used by Lucan and Seneca in their parallel approaches to this topic: a worse age (*deterior*), the act of mining (*eruit*) metals (*ferrum . . . aurumque*) from the earth, and the increasing tendency toward violence. This *persona* of Seneca goes on to address the collected vices of previous ages (*collecta vitia*, 429)[36] and conquering luxury (*luxuria victrix*, 433) seizing and ruining (*perdat*, 434; cf. *perdant*, Sen. *Helv.* 10.2) the resources of nature. Civic or familial violence is barely subtextual here: the image of mining natural resources from the earth, Nero's murder of his mother Agrippina,[37] and Lucan's characterization of Rome turning weapons against its own vitals are all close to mind in this evocative image of violence against a parent.[38]

The Moral Implications of Seeking and Possessing Gold

Comparing Lucan's text to Seneca's description of the mining process in the *Natural Questions* and Pliny's explanation of the technology involved reveals a reflection of real Roman mining practices behind Lucan's passing references to mines (*metalla*), the mining of valuable mineral resources (iron, gold, other stones), and the processes by which these materials could be obtained (either placer mining using natural or industrial hydraulics, or deep-vein mining). However, the moral condemnation of mining present in Seneca's texts both as a symbol of decline from a "golden age" and as a process that blatantly went against Nature (i.e., the Stoic natural philosopher's opinion on mining) also informs how we should read Lucan's mining references as part of his broader narrative of civil conflict. It may be effective to reflect on this through an example of negative enumeration in the *Bellum Civile*, a description of the natural resources of Libya and their eventual exploitation by the Romans. Lucan writes (9.424–30):

> in nullas vitiatur opes; non aere nec auro
> excoquitur, nullo glaebarum crimine pura
> et penitus terra est. tantum Maurusia genti
> robora divitiae, quorum non noverat usum,
> sed citri contenta comis vivebat et umbra.

in nemus ignotum nostrae venere secures,
extremoque epulas mensasque petimus ab orbe.

Into no riches is it corrupted; nor is it refined into bronze or gold, and with no fault of soil, it is earth to its depths. The people have only Maurusian timber as wealth, the use of which they did not know, but they used to live content with the leaves and shade of the citrus tree. Our [i.e., Roman] axes have gone into the unknown grove, and we seek feasts and tables at the ends of the earth.

Even from this place without mineral resources—at least according to Lucan's geographical description—we can make two relevant observations. First, knowledge of mining and refining technology is implicit to Lucan's verses. The verb *excoquitur*, used of refining or "cooking" the metal out of ore, is first extant in Latin with this meaning here (Wick 2004: 163). The only real parallels come from Pliny's *Natural History*, though Ovid does use *excoquo* of tempering steel (*Fast.* 4.785–6).[39] We can also see that the habits of Roman consumption turned to other luxury goods when faced with a lack of precious metals (*epulas mensasque petimus*). The Roman habit of commodification even extends to the venom of the asp (*lucri pudor*, Luc. 9.706; cf. Fantham 1992b: 108). In this case, however, the exploitation of natural resources is purely for the sake of *luxuria*. It may also, perhaps, inform our reading of Lucan's subsequent description of the opulence of Alexandria's buildings, food, and fashions (10.110–26).

This identification of Roman avarice—somewhat indirectly, as Lucan never uses *avaritia* or *avarus*—also finds embodiment in Alexandria in the person of Caesar himself, against whom the narrator warns (10.146–9, 155–8):

> pro caecus et amens
> ambitione furor, civilia bella gerenti
> divitias aperire suas, incendere mentem
> hospitis armati.
> ... infudere epulas auro, quod terra, quod aer,
> quod pelagus Nilusque dedit, quod luxus inani
> ambitione furens toto quaesivit in orbe
> non mandante fame.

Oh, madness, blind and mindless with ostentation, to reveal one's wealth to a person waging civil wars, to inflame the mind of an armed guest ... They poured the feasts onto gold: what land, what air, what sea and Nile gave, what luxury, maddened by empty ostentation, sought throughout the whole world without hunger commanding.

As in Seneca's deliberate overlapping of physical and moral issues in his depictions of mining (Williams 2005: 420–2), here in Lucan's text, the physical expression of *luxus* is identified with the moral vice of *fames*, even in the introduction to the causes of civil war.[40] Blindness and madness, the same traits associated with Seneca's miners in the *Phaedra*, are directly connected to an increased likelihood of violence and a continuation or worsening of civil war. In fact, these are the same driving impulses that control Caesar's soldiers after Pharsalus when they raid the defeated Pompeian camp (7.746–9):

> nec plura locutus
> impulit amentes aurique cupidine caecos
> ire super gladios supraque cadavera patrum
> et caesos calcare duces.

[Caesar] would not speak more and impelled [his soldiers], mindless and blinded by desire for gold, to walk over the swords and the bodies of the senators and to tread on the generals who had been cut down.

As is the case with Caesar's later *furor* when confronted with the wealth of Alexandria, the soldiers at Pharsalus are *amentes* and *caeci* and, in Lucan's gloss for *avaritia*, *cupido auri* drives them. This desire for gold also evokes Seneca's criticism of wealth as a superficial blessing and his association of the process of mining and refining precious metals with the moral vices inherent in desiring and displaying them.[41]

The underlying questioning of morality is an ongoing pattern in Lucan's text: greed is shown to be a motivating force that commodifies even the Roman state. In Book 4 in particular, metaphysical corruption frames the description of the Asturian gold miner's physical transgression. Throughout the fourth book, luxury and destruction are inextricably bound. From the beginning of the storm and flood narrative, the poet underscores the moral aspects of the pallor of the metaphorical Asturian miner in his exclamation, "Oh pale hunger for profit! A hungry seller is not lacking with gold on offer" (*pro lucri pallida tabes! / non dest prolato ieiunus venditor auro*, 4.96–7). Toward the end of the book, Lucan condemns Curio, the Caesarian leader of a disastrously unsuccessful campaign against the Numidian king Juba, of being in the thrall of Caesar's gold (*captus . . . Caesaris auro*, 4.820) and makes the accusation that while there are no innocents in the commodification of Rome, Curio is particularly guilty (*emere omnes, hic vendidit urbem*, 4.824). The geographical location in Spain, the use of metaphor, and the concentration on cataclysm, both natural and anthropogenic, adds another touchstone in the Roman literary tradition devoted to the damaging power of extravagance.[42] Lucan's mining simile focuses these varied influences and predicts Pliny's observation that the balance between humanity and nature is most disturbed in the acquisition and use of natural resources (Plin., *HN* 2.157–9; cf. Isager 1991: 52).

Lucan's moralizing condemnation of extravagance and the acquisition of wealth is the product of more than one source. He draws on the Roman literary and philosophical tradition that connected luxury and moral decline, and he alludes to the Myth of the Ages while focusing squarely on the consequences of wealth as framed by Stoic philosophy. His work also reads intertextually with the career-spanning criticisms that Seneca makes about the mining industry and its effects on Roman society. Finally, he incorporates real knowledge of the technologies and practices of the mining industry in a way that both augments his simile at 4.295–304 with vivid realism and also integrates contemporary knowledge into his often hyperbolic depiction of both the civil war between Pompey and Caesar and the consequences of this war for the peoples of the Mediterranean and their environments.

Notes

1. For key studies on space, place, and/or landscape, see, e.g., Leach (1988); Masters (1992); Spencer (2010).
2. Although the *Historia Naturalis* postdates Lucan's *Bellum Civile*, Pliny should be considered a contemporary of Lucan. Pliny included "anecdotes about high society [in] the days of his youth under Caligula" (Syme 1969: 210) in *HN*, he can be placed in Italy in 59 CE (ibid: 208), and he mostly likely knew members of the Pisonian conspiracy in 65 CE, in which Lucan and Seneca were also implicated (ibid: 209). Cf. Plin., *Ep.* 3.5.5: *scripsit sub Nerone novissimis annis, cum omne studiorum genus paulo liberius et erectius periculosum servitus fecisset* ([Pliny the Elder] wrote during the last years under Nero, when slavery made it dangerous [to write] any type of studies even a little more independent or elevated).
3. Marshall (2014: 42) locates the composition of the *Natural Questions* "sometime between AD 61 and early 64."
4. On Lucan's use of Stoic physics, see Sklenár (1999, 2003); Bartsch (2005: 500–1); Lapidge ([1979] 2010); Zientek (2014).
5. Pliny reports that the mining of mineral resources was legally prohibited in Italy; cf. *HN* 3.138, 33.78.
6. On Pliny's writing as representative of Stoic influences, see Isager (1991: 32–3); Beagon (2011: 74); Paparazzo (2011: 103–4). Regarding connections between ethics and physics in Stoicism, see for example Long (1968: 341–3); Annas (2007); cf. Cic., *Fin.* 3.73.
7. All translations are my own; Lucan text from Shackleton Bailey (2009).
8. The extensive evidence for Roman mining in Spain in the first century CE makes the location of Asturia as modern Asturias certain. See Pompon. 2.86 on Spain's natural resources and Strabo 3.2.8–9 on Spanish gold mining; for Mela as a source on Spain—and as a Spanish Roman author—see Syme (1969: 221, 223). Cf. Healy (1999: 275).
9. Compare Caes., *B.G.* 3.21, 7.24; Liv. 5.19.10, 31.17.2, and 38.7.6.
10. As reported by Strabo 3.2.9, who notes that Posidonius himself cited information from Demetrius of Phalerum who reported on Attic silver mines.
11. See Sen., *Ep.* 90.9–13 and *QNat.* 4b.3.1–2, among many other citations. Cf. Rosenmeyer (2000); Williams (2012: 150–3, 247, 288–9, and 299–301).
12. The Annaei were likely descendants of Roman settlers in Iberia, though there is a possibility that they were originally of Spanish descent instead; see text and notes in Veyne (2002: 1) for detailed explanation of the Annaei family's potential origins; cf. Habinek (2013: 7).
13. Hirt (2010: 162–3). See also figs 19–20 on pp. 77–8 for maps of gold mines in northwest Spain and silver, copper, and lead mines near Corduba.
14. Wilson (2002: 19–20). Hughes (2014: 135) mentions a drainage tunnel 2 km long near Coto Fortuna in Spain.

15. Hughes (2014: 13) notes that the Romans were the inventors of this kind of hydraulic mining. On Roman technological innovation and hydraulic mining, see Wilson (2000: 140); Magntorn (2001: 29); Fernándo-Lozano, Gutiérrez-Alonso, and Fernández-Morán (2015: 358); Santos Yanguas (2015: 109).

16. On Augustus' order for the exploitation of gold in northwest Spain, see Curchin (1991: 137) and Santos Yanguas (2015: 106); cf. Flor. 2.33.60. Augustus needed gold to mint the *aureus*: Wilson (2007: 110); Reher et al. (2012: 128).

17. Gold mines in Spain were numerous. The largest and most technologically advanced were under control of the Roman state: Curchin (1991: 132–3); Richardson (1996: 168); Wilson (2000: 142); Reher et al. (2012: 131–2); Santos Yanguas (2015: 119). While enslaved populations often worked in mines and may have done so in northwest Spain as well (Pérez González and Matías Rodríguez 2008: 56), the complexity of the technology and presence of the Roman military make some scholars suspect a free labor force (Citroni Marchetti 1991: 205–6; Magntorn 2001: 32). Wilson (2007: 111) assigns the work to "local labour under compulsion and army supervision."

18. On Las Medulas, see Lewis and Jones (1970: 174–8); Magntorn (2001: 31); Wilson (2002: 19–20); Williams (2007: 111); Reher et al. (2012: 129); Fernández-Lozano, Gutiérrez-Alonso, and Fernández-Morán (2015: 359).

19. Cf. Pliny, *NH* 33.66: *aut in ruina montium quaeritur*. See also Hughes (2014: 144–5) on the environmental effects of the near-industrial scale of Roman mining, and Fernández-Lozano, Gutiérrez-Alonso, and Fernández-Morán (2015) on Roman mining technology in Spanish gold mines. On the *ruina montium* generally see Magntorn (2001) and Reher et al. (2012: 129). Pérez González and Matías Rodríguez (2008: 51 n. 14) argue that *ruina montium* refers not to a specific method of mining, but rather to its results: the *ruina* or tailings (cf. Ritchie and Hooker 1997: 8). Because *ruina* can indicate both the action of becoming ruined and the ruins themselves, however, it seems likely that *ruina montium* has a similar versatility which is also comparable to *metalla*, used for both metals and the mines in which they are found.

20. Lewis and Jones (1970: 177) estimate 34 million liters of water per day flowing through three aqueducts into the mines at Las Medulas; Hirt (2010: 34) notes that at Las Medulas, there were a total of seven aqueducts, each 2–3 m wide, and up to 50 km long, which (in part) filled tanks used for hushing with up to 24,000 m^3 of water. Cf. Luc. 4.50–105 for the flood; Sen. *QNat*. 3.27.1 on deluge as apocalyptic cataclysm.

21. Moreover, Mela's *penitus* echoes those of Cic., *Nat. D.* 2.151, *Off.* 2.13 and Lucr. 6.808–10.

22. Placer-gold indicates the flakes of gold in the water or sediment of a stream. More broadly, placer mining can include the processes of extracting precious metals or gemstones (often in small quantities such as flakes or fragments) from the alluvial deposits of a streambed.

23. Lewis and Jones (1970: 169); Duncan (1999); Wilson (2002: 17). Cf. Pompon. 3.8: *et Tagi ostium, amnis gemmas aurumque generantis*; Plin., *HN* 33.66: *fluminum ramentis, ut in Tago Hispaniae, Pado Italiae, Hebro Thraciae, Pactolo Asiae, Gange Indiae*.

24. Quarrying and mining had similar challenges and often made use of the same equipment and technology (Hughes 2014: 142–4).

25. For other relevant Lucanian uses of *avidus*, compare 1.181–2, *hinc usura vorax avidumque in tempora fenus / et concussa fides et multis utile bellum* (hence voracious usury and interest greedy in its timing and shaken credit and war useful to many); 2.71–2, *stagna avidi texere soli laxaeque paludes / depositum, Fortuna, tuum* (swamps of the greedy earth and wide marshes covered your treasure, Fortune). Fantham (1992: 94 *ad* 2.72) notes that *depositum* is certainly meant to be read as buried treasure and compares Sen., *Tro.* 521, *depositum . . . meum*.

26. See Diod. Sic. 16.8.6-7 on Philip's mining expeditions.
27. Cf. Sen., *QNat.* 3.15.3: *hinc est omnis metallorum humus, ex quibus petit aurum argentumque avaritia, et quae in lapidem ex liquore vertuntur*; and *Dial.* (*De Ira Liber 3*) 5.33.4: *si totam mihi ex omnibus metallis, quae cum maxime deprimimus pecuniam proferas, si in medium proicias quidquid thesauri tegunt, avaritia iterum sub terras referente quae male egesserat, omnem istam congeriem non putem dignam quae frontem viri boni contrahat.* Seneca may be representing knowledge passed down from Posidonius as well, wherein the Romans were "avaricious and brutal exploiters" of Spanish mineral resources; see Strasburger (1965: 47).
28. Cf. Sen., *QNat.* 1.17.6, where products mined from the earth are *alia terrae mala.* Williams (2005: 421) identifies Seneca's allusion to Verg., *G.* 1.129 (*malum virus*) as part of a decline narrative featuring the mythical golden age.
29. See Williams (2005: 421-2) on the "moral implications" of Seneca's language, for example, *lutulenta* (*QNat.* 5.15.4) as both "mud-smeared" and "morally polluted."
30. Cf. Tac., *Ann.* 16.1-3 and Suet., *Ner.* 31 who relay the story of an expedition funded by Nero to find the alleged gold of Dido near Carthage. See also Kragelund (2000: 497).
31. Compare Lucan's use of *scrutator* and *scrutari* elsewhere of prophetic inquiry (Appius at Delphi, 5.122; Sextus Pompey and Erictho in Thessaly, 6.429 and 629; the oracle of Ammon, 9.549; and of a snakebite victim searching for *venae* of water, 9.755).
32. Cf. Sen., *Ben.* 4.6.1: *tot metalla deus defodit, tot flumina emisit terra, super quae decurrunt sola, aurum vehentia; argenti, aeris, ferri immane pondus omnibus locis obrutum; cuius investigandi tibi facultatem dedit, ac latentium divitiarum in summa terra signa disposuit.*
33. On associations between Agrippina and gold as a symbol of *luxuria*, see Plin., *HN* 33.63: *nos vidimus Agrippinam Claudi principis, edente eo navalis proelii spectaculum, adsidentem et indutam paludamento aureo textili sine alia materia* (We have seen Agrippina, the wife of the emperor Claudius, when he was producing the spectacle of a naval battle, sitting near him and clothed in a cloak woven from gold without any other material). On Nero's *domus aurea*, see *HN* 33.54: *huius deinde successor Nero Pompei theatrum operuit auro in unum diem, quo Tiridati Armeniae regi ostenderet. et quota pars ea fuit aureae domus ambientis urbem* ("Afterwards his successor, Nero, covered the theater of Pompey in gold for a single day, on which he would show it off to Tiridates, the king of Armenia. And what fraction was that of the golden house which surrounds the city!").
34. Seneca and Pliny build on an existing idea about moral decline, greed, and precious metals represented by earlier authors, e.g., *amor habendi*: Verg., *Aen.* 8.327; Ov., *Met.* 1.131, *Fast.* 1.189-226. Cf. Plin., *HN* 33.49, 134: *habendi cupido*.
35. Compare Plin., *HN* 33.72: *auri fames durissima est* (greed for gold is the most enduring) as a motivating factor behind the industrial-scale hydraulic gold mining in Spain. Citroni Marchetti (1991: 206) cites this expression as an indication that Spanish gold mining was performed largely by a free—rather than enslaved—labor force.
36. Cf. Lucr. 5.1008: *contra nunc rerum copia mersat.*
37. As one of the readers astutely pointed out, *in parentis viscera intravit suae* (*Oct.* 416) may also allude to Nero's alleged incest with Agrippina; cf. Tac., *Ann.* 14.2.
38. Ginsberg (2016: 81-3): "the play imbues Seneca's Iron Age and its embedded critique of imperial Rome with memories of the civil strife at the Republic's end." See also Hardie (2008: 313), cf. Luc. 3.154-7.
39. Plin., *HN* 33.79, 113 and 121 (of gold), 33.95 (of lead), and 33.119 (of silver). Cf. Ov., *Fast.* 4.785-6: *omnia purgat edax ignis vitiumque metallis / excoquit.*

40. Cf. Luc. 1.160–4: *namque, ut opes nimias mundo Fortuna subacto / intulit et rebus mores cessere secundis / praedaque et hostiles luxum suasere rapinae, / non auro tectisve modus, mensasque priores / aspernata fames.* On insatiable seeking, cf. Sen., *Ep.* 89.22.

41. Cf. Pompon. 2.10: *auri argentique maximarum pestium*; Sen., *Ben.* 7.10.3–4 and 9–10, *Ep.* 115.11.

42. See Kragelund (2000: 505) on the traditional connection between *luxuria* and *perdo*; see also *TLL* 10.1.1264–5.

References

Annas, J. (2007), "Ethics in Stoic Philosophy," *Phronesis*, 52(1): 58–87.
Asso, P., ed. (2010), *A Commentary on Lucan, De bello civili IV: Introduction, Edition, and Translation*, Berlin: De Gruyter.
Bartsch, S. (2005), "Lucan," in J. M. Foley (ed.), *A Companion to Ancient Epic*, Malden, MA: Blackwell Publishing.
Beagon, M. (2011), "The Curious Eye of the Elder Pliny," in R. K. Gibson and R. Morello (eds.), *Pliny the Elder: Themes and Contexts*, 71–88, Leiden: Brill.
Citroni Marchetti, S. (1991), *Plinio il Vecchio e la tradizione del moralismo romano*, Pisa: Giardini.
Corcoran, T. H., ed. (1972), *Seneca, Naturales Quaestiones Books IV–VII*, Cambridge, MA: Harvard University Press.
Curchin, L. A. (1991), *Roman Spain: Conquest and Assimilation*, London: Routledge.
Domergue, C. (1981), "La notion d'espace minier dans l'Antiquité gréco-romaine," *Pallas*, 28: 89–99.
Duncan, L. C. (1999), "Roman Deep-Vein Mining," 9 December. Available online: http://www.unc.edu/~duncan/personal/roman_mining/deep-vein_mining.htm (accessed April 4, 2017).
Esposito, P., ed. (2009), *Marco Anneo Lucano Bellum Civile (Pharsalia) Libro IV*, Naples: Loffredo Editore.
Fantham, E., ed. (1992a), *Lucan De Bello Civili Book II*, Cambridge: Cambridge University Press.
Fantham, E. (1992b), "Lucan's Medusa-Excursus: Its Design and Purpose," *MD*, 29: 95–119.
Fernández-Lozano, J., G. Gutiérrez-Alonso, and M. Á. Fernández-Morán (2015), "Using airborne LiDAR sensing technology and aerial orthoimages to unravel roman water supply systems and gold works in NW Spain (Eria valley, León)," *Journal of Archaeological Science*, 53: 356–73.
Fitter, C. (1995), *Poetry, Space, Landscape: Toward a New Theory*, Cambridge: Cambridge University Press.
Fourgous, D. (1976), "L'invention des armes en grece ancienne," *ASNP*, series 3, 6 (4): 1123–64.
Ginsberg, L. D. (2016), *Staging Memory, Staging Strife: Empire and Civil War in the Octavia*, Oxford: Oxford University Press.
Griffin, M. (1972), "The Elder Seneca and Spain," *JRS*, 62: 1–19.
Habinek, T. (2013), "*Imago Suae Vitae*: Seneca's Life and Career," in A. Heil and G. Damschen (eds.), *Brill's Companion to Seneca: Philosopher and Dramatist*, 3–31, Leiden: Brill.
Hardie, P. (2008), "Lucan's Song of the Earth," in E. Cingano and L. Milano (eds.), *Papers on ancient literatures: Greece, Rome, and the Near East*, 305–30, Padova: S.A.R.G.O.N. Editrice e Libreria.
Healy, J. F. (1978), *Mining and Metallurgy in the Greek and Roman World*, London: Thames and Hudson.
Healy, J. F. (1999), *Pliny the Elder on Science and Technology*, Oxford: Oxford University Press.
Henderson, J. (2011), "The Nature of Man: Pliny, *Historia Naturalis* as Cosmogram," *MD*, 66: 139–71.

Hine, H. M. (2006), "Rome, the Cosmos, and the Emperor in Seneca's *Natural Questions*," *JRS*, 96: 42–72.
Hirt, A. M. (2010), *Imperial Mines and Quarries in the Roman World: Organizational Aspects 27 BC – AD 235*, New York: Oxford University Press.
Hong, S., J.-P. Candelone, C. C. Patterson, and C. F. Boutron (1996), "History of ancient copper smelting production during Roman and medieval times recorded in Greenland ice," *Science*, new series, 272 (5259): 246–9.
Hughes, J. D. (2006), *What Is Environmental History?* Cambridge: Polity.
Hughes, J. D. (2014), *Environmental Problems of the Greeks and Romans: Ecology in the Ancient Mediterranean*, 2nd edn, Baltimore: Johns Hopkins University Press.
Isager, J. (1991), *Pliny on Art and Society: The Elder Pliny's Chapters on the History of Art*, Odense: Odense University Press.
Kragelund, P. (2000), "Nero's *Luxuria*, in Tacitus and in the *Octavia*," *CQ*, 50 (2): 494–515.
Lapidge, M. ([1979] 2010), "Lucan's Imagery of Cosmic Dissolution," in C. Tesoriero (ed.), *Lucan*, 289–323, New York: Oxford University Press.
Leach, E. W. (1988), *The Rhetoric of Space: Literary and Artistic Representations of Landscape in Republican and Augustan Rome*, Princeton: Princeton University Press.
Lewis, P. R. and G. D. B. Jones (1970), "Roman Gold-Mining in North-West Spain," *JRS*, 60: 169–85.
Long, A. A. (1968), "The Stoic Concept of Evil," *PhilosQ*, 18 (73): 329–43.
Magntorn, E. (2001), "*Ruina Montium*: a case study of Roman gold-mining in north-west Spain," *KVHAA Konferenser*, 51: 27–34.
Marshall, C. W. (2014), "The Works of Seneca the Younger and Their Dates," in G. Damschen and A. Heil (eds.), *Brill's Companion to Seneca*, 33–44, Leiden: Brill.
Masters, J. (1992), *Poetry and Civil War in Lucan's Bellum Civile*, Cambridge: Cambridge University Press.
McConnell, J. R., A. I. Wilson, A. Stohl, M. M. Arienzo, N. J. Chellman, S. Eckhardt, E. M. Thompson, A. M. Pollard, and J. P. Steffensen (2018), "Lead pollution recorded in Greenland ice indicates European emissions tracked plagues, wars, and imperial expansion during antiquity," *Proceedings of the National Academy of Sciences*, 115 (22): 5726–31.
Mitchell, W. J. T. (2002), "Imperial Landscape," in W. J. T. Mitchell (ed.), *Landscape and Power*, 2nd edn, 5–34, Chicago: University of Chicago Press.
Paparazzo, E. (2011), "Philosophy and Science in the Elder Pliny's *Naturalis Historia*," in R. K. Gibson and R. Morello (eds.), *Pliny the Elder: Themes and Contexts*, 89–111, Leiden: Brill.
Pérez González, M. and R. Matías Rodríguez (2008), "Plinio y la minería aurífera romana: nueva traducción e interpretación de Plin. *Nat*. 33.66–78," *CFC(L)*, 28 (1): 43–58.
Plácido, D. and F. J. Sánchez-Palencia (2014), "La explicación de la minería de oro romana hispana en la Historia Natural de Plinio El Viejo, párrafos 66 a 78 del libro XXXIII," in F. J. Sánchez-Palencia (ed), *Minería romana en zonas interfronterizas de Castilla y León y Portugal (Asturia y NE de Lusitania)*, 17–34, León: Junta de Castilla y León, Consejería de Cultura y Turismo D. L.
Rackham, H. ed. (1952), *Pliny, Natural History Books 33–35*, Cambridge, MA: Harvard University Press.
Reher, G. S., L. López-Merino, F. J. Sánchez-Palencia, and J. A. López-Sáez (2012), "Configuring the landscape: Roman mining in the *conventus Asturum* (NW *Hispania*)," in S. J. Kluiving and E. B. Guttmann-Bond (eds.), *Landscape Archaeology between Art and Science: From a Multi- to an Interdisciplinary Approach*, 127–36, Amsterdam: University of Amsterdam Press.
Reynolds, L. D. ed. (1965), *L. Annaei Senecae ad Lucilium Epistulae Morales*, Oxford: Oxford University Press.
Reynolds, L. D. ed. (1977), *L. Annaei Senecae Diologorum Libri Duodecim*, Oxford: Oxford University Press.

Richardson, J. S. (1996), *The Romans in Spain*, Oxford: Blackwell Publishers.
Rickard, T. A. (1928), "The Mining of the Romans in Spain," *JRS*, 18: 129–43.
Ritchie, N. A. and R. Hooker (1997), "An Archaeologist's Guide to Mining Terminology," *Australasian Historical Archaeology*, 15: 3–29.
Rosenmeyer, T. G. (2000), "Seneca and Nature," *Arethusa*, 33 (1): 99–119.
Santos Yanguas, N. (2015), "El emperador Claudio y la explotación de las minas de oro romanas del noroeste de la Península Ibérica," *HAnt*, 39: 105–21.
Shackleton Bailey, D. R. (ed) (2009), *Marcus Annaeus Lucanus De Bello Civili Libri X*, Berlin: De Gruyter.
Sklenář, R. (1999), "Nihilistic Cosmology and Catonian Ethics in Lucan's *Bellum Civile*," *AJPh*, 120 (2): 281–96.
Sklenář, R. (2003), *The Taste for Nothingness: A Study of Virtus and Related Themes in Lucan's Bellum Civile*, Ann Arbor: University of Michigan Press.
Spencer, D. (2010), *Roman Landscape: Culture and Identity*, Cambridge: Cambridge University Press.
Strasburger, H. (1965), "Poseidonios on Problems of the Roman Empire," *JRS*, 55 (1): 40–53.
Syme, R. (1969), "Pliny the Procurator," *HSPh*, 73: 201–36.
Veyne, P. (2002), *Seneca: The Life of a Stoic*, trans. D. Sullivan, New York: Routledge.
Wallace-Hadrill, A. (1990), "Pliny the Elder and Man's Unnatural History," *G&R*, 37 (1): 80–96.
Wick, C. ed. (2004), *M. Annaeus Lucanus Bellum Civile Liber IX*, Munich: K. G. Saur.
Williams, G. (2005), "Seneca on Winds: The Art of Anemology in *Natural Questions* 5," *AJPh*, 126 (3): 417–50.
Williams, G. (2012), *The Cosmic Viewpoint: A Study of Seneca's Natural Questions*, New York: Oxford University Press.
Wilson, A. (2000), "Industrial Uses of Water," in Ö. Wikander (ed.), *Handbook of Ancient Water Technology*, 127–49. Leiden: Brill.
Wilson, A. (2002), "Machines, Power and the Ancient Economy," *JRS*, 92: 1–32.
Wilson, A. (2007), "The metal supply of the Roman empire," in E. Papi and M. Bonifay (eds.), *Supplying Rome and the Empire: the proceedings of an international seminar held at Siena-Certosa di Pontignano on May 2–4, 2004, on Rome, the provinces, production and distribution*, 109–25, Portsmouth, R. I.: Journal of Roman Archaeology.
Zehnacker, H. (1983), *Pline l'Ancien, Histoire Naturelle, Livre XXXIII*, Paris: Les Belles Lettres.
Zientek, L. (2014), "Lucan's Natural Questions: Landscape and Geography in the *Bellum Civile*," PhD diss., University of Washington, Seattle.
Zwierlein, O. ed. (1986), *L. Annaei Senecae Tragoediae*, Oxford: Oxford University Press.

CHAPTER 5
EVEN *NATURA* NODS: LUCAN'S ALTERNATIVE EXPLANATIONS OF THE SYRTES (9.303–18)
James Calvin Taylor

Introduction

Upon reaching the ninth book of Lucan's *Bellum Civile*, a reader might ask the same question of the epic's narrative trajectory that a mutinous soldier poses to Cato: *quis erit finis si nec Pharsalia pugnae / nec Pompeius erit?* (What end will there be of fighting if it shall be neither Pharsalus nor Pompey?, 9.232–3).[1] The epic repeatedly portrayed the Battle of Pharsalus as Rome's collective day of doom (Joseph 2017), yet neither the battle nor its aftermath has proved as decisive as advertised, and no *telos* to the poem is within sight (Masters 1992: 251–3). If closure "impos[es] completed form on a segment of formless time" (Hardie 1997: 140), formless time might appear to have gained the upper hand. Proceeding from the assumption that Lucan's environments function as a "narrative mirror" (Dinter 2012: 66), this chapter interprets the two alternative explanations of the Syrtes and their perilous conditions (9.303–18) as meditations upon this crisis of closure.

Lucan's fondness for alternative explanations distances the poetic world as an object of inquiry from its creator (Feeney 1991: 278–81). Within the alternative explanations of the Syrtes, the poet seems to step back from the world of his epic to consider why history failed to achieve complete resolution at Pharsalus. To answer that question, both explanations of the Syrtes critique Lucan's "pseudo-Stoic cosmos in which everything connects" (Masters 1992: 106) and the narrative model of conflagration based upon that cosmic framework. The epic's opening simile (1.72–80), which compares civil war to *ekpyrosis*, the conflagration within Stoic cosmology that periodically destroys the cosmos and provides formless matter for its recreation (Lapidge 1978: 180–4; Long 1985; Long and Sedley 1987: 1.274–9, 2.271–7), implies the existence of a single crisis that will engulf the entirety of the Roman state and destroy its current form. Indeed, the persistent reuse of the language of cosmic dissolution encourages us to interpret Pharsalus as being akin to the conflagration ending this cosmos (Lapidge 1979: 369–70; Joseph 2017: 114–15). Each explanation of the Syrtes revises this earlier vision of the quasi-Stoic cosmos, and, in so doing, accounts for a narrative that does not converge on a single event but whose divergent threads avoid such definitive closure.[2]

The Syrtes are two gulfs in North Africa, the Syrtis Minor (Gulf of Gabès) and Syrtis Maior (Gulf of Sidra), which were proverbially perilous to navigate (Morford 1967a: 48; Nisbet and Hubbard 1970: 265–6 *ad* Hor. *Carm.* 1.22.5). Shortly after setting sail from Cyrene for a rendezvous with King Juba of Mauretania, the Republican fleet under Cato's command is shipwrecked by a sea-storm upon the latter of these two gulfs, the Syrtis

Maior, stretching between Benghazi and Misrata (9.300–2). The alternative explanations function as a prelude to the sea-storm by accounting for this navigational obstacle in cosmic terms: the first explanation begins with creation itself (9.303–4), while the second identifies the sun as the cause (9.313).

These cosmic dimensions are thrown into greater relief when compared with other extended accounts of these gulfs, which describe numerous sandbanks, winds threatening to run ships aground, and unusually strong tides, including a reversal in current direction as the tide falls (Quinn 2011: 11–12). Sallust depicts a region in permanent flux: the remodeling of the seabed by the agitated sea's transportation of sand, mud, and stones means that *facies locorum cum ventis simul mutatur* (the appearance of the locales changes with the winds, *Iug.* 78). Strabo notes the risk of a ship running aground on the shoals as the tide turns (Strabo 17.3.20). Pomponius Mela highlights the frequent shallows and reversing current (Pompon. 1.35). Though these pre-existing accounts resemble Lucan insofar as they treat the two gulfs as virtually identical, barring their size, the principal divergence is that Lucan's two explanations primarily concern themselves with the gulfs' static topography, specifically their shoals, while more dynamic elements, such as wind and current, appear in the sea-storm.

Indeed, the sea-storm not only complements the explanations in geographic terms, but also mirrors their narrative significance, insofar as the shipwreck of Cato's fleet actualizes the simile from Book 1 of a shipwreck upon this same coast (1.498–504). This parallel is all the more striking if the shipwreck of Book 9 is a fictitious addition to the historical reality of a land march (Fehrle 1983: 261–3; Fantham 1992a: 115–19; Leigh 2000: 96–7). The sea-storms of simile and main narrative exhibit similar mechanics: the south wind, *Auster*, rolls back the sea and exposes numerous shoals (1.498–9; 9.321–3). The simile compares those fleeing from Rome at Caesar's approach to those who jump from a ship that has run aground on those shoals: *nondum sparsa compage carinae / naufragium sibi quisque facit* (each man brings shipwreck upon himself, although the hull of the ship has not yet been torn apart, 1.502–3). This premature exposure of oneself to the perilous sea, instead of remaining on the intact hull, parallels the paradox of fleeing *into* war while Rome remains unassailed (*sic urbe relicta / in bellum fugitur*, 1.503–4).

This simile uses the rich tradition of the ship of state (Miura 1981: 222; Roche 2009: 310 *ad* 1.498–503), but it also ties into Book 1's cosmic imagery, particularly the *ekpyrosis* of the opening simile (1.72–80; Dinter 2012: 13; Zientek 2014: 55–7). The use of *compages* to describe both the structure of the ship, which is about to fragment, and the framework of the cosmos, whose dissolution prompts the conflagration (*compage soluta*, 1.72), suggests a fundamental correspondence between the two similes in Book 1. That is reinforced by a further parallel in one of the few details given about this ship: *fracta . . . veliferi sonuerunt pondera mali* (the broken weight of the sail-carrying mast has crashed, 1.500). The vague *pondera* suggests huge, ill-defined remnants crashing onto the ship below and threatening its integrity; it also recalls the framing of the opening simile, where cosmic dissolution is compared to Rome collapsing under its own excessive weight (*nimioque graves sub pondere lapsus*, 1.71). These parallels between similes describing civil war underline the narrative logic that binds the cosmos to the dramas raging within it; macro- and microcosm obey the same law: any large structure must ultimately collapse upon itself (*in se magna ruunt*, 1.81).

Though the later shipwreck in Book 9 expands upon the simile in several ways, two differences merit further consideration. In a detailed account of Auster's effect on the fleet (9.324–47; Morford 1967a: 48–9), Lucan devotes the most attention to those ships that possess no masts (9.330–47). Though the collapse of the mast in the simile is a cause of panic, these masts have been deliberately cut down (*arboribus caesis*, 9.332). The masts' removal has the desired effect of allowing the south wind to blow freely over the ships, but also unintentionally leaves them at the mercy of the current, which causes them to run aground (9.331–6). An extended description of the ship's predicament caught between land and sea (9.336–42) closes with a striking vignette: *stant miseri nautae, terraeque haerente carina / litora nulla vident* (the wretched sailors stand about, and, though the ship clings to the land, see no shores, 9.343–4). The drastic attempt to prevent the ship from being blown off course by removing the mast has failed, but even now the sailors cannot abandon the stranded ship, since they see nowhere suitable to disembark. The simile's impetuous flight is replaced by a futile determination to forge ahead, despite there being no clear path forward. This arresting of narrative progress is particularly suitable for Cato's African march, whose multiple setbacks, interruption by several digressions (Morford 1967b: 123), and limited success in reaching the mere halfway house of Leptis Magna (9.948–9) set a new standard for grueling narrative pace in an epic already deeply invested in the poetics of delay (Masters 1992: 3–10; Henderson 1998:183–5).

Of course, not all of the fleet's ships are mastless. Lucan even notes that most ships reached Lake Tritonis safely (9.345–7). The simple replacement of the simile's single ship with the variety of Cato's fleet demonstrates how facile this imagery is, insofar as the representation of the state by a single ship suggests the entire crew's dependence upon its integrity. Yet Rome is not a single entity engulfed in a momentary catastrophe, but a collective, some of whose parts have perished while others soldier on. The fact that the surviving ships fall under the command of a son of Pompey (9.370–1), regardless of whether it is Gnaeus or Sextus (Wick 2004: 1.8), foreshadows the continuing resistance to Caesar after Cato's death at least as far as Munda, in the same way that Pompey's soul settling in Brutus (9.17–18) gestures to Julius' assassination and Philippi. The sea-storm's expansion of the simile stresses the divergent paths that will lead civil war's participants to their separate fates. Just as the sea-storm critiques the ship of state, so the Syrtes' alternative explanations revise the quasi-Stoic cosmos introduced in the epic's opening simile. In so doing, both explanations open up the possibility of endless civil strife, whose lack of resolution extends to the Neronian present.

The First Explanation (9.303–11)

The cosmic implications of the first explanation are made immediately clear by opening with the beginning of the world (9.303–11):

Syrtes vel, primam mundo natura figuram
cum daret, in dubio pelagi terraeque reliquit
(nam neque subsedit penitus, quo stagna profundi
acciperet, nec se defendit ab aequore tellus,
ambigua sed lege loci iacet invia sedes,
aequora fracta vadis abruptaque terra profundo,
et post multa sonant proiecti litora fluctus:
sic male deseruit nullosque exegit in usus
hanc partem natura sui);

When Nature was giving the world its initial shape, she left the Syrtes to be contested between sea and land; for the land did not sink down so as to admit the waters of the deep, nor did it defend itself from the sea, but the region is pathless owing to the place's uncertain condition—sea broken by shoals and land severed by the deep—and the waves, cast forth past many shores, still roar. In this unkind manner Nature has abandoned this part of her own being and put it to no use at all.

This account casts us back to the moment of creation, when Nature in the guise of providential divinity was shaping the world by creating order in primordial matter.[3] As such, she not only resembles the divine craftsman of Plato's *Timaeus* (33b; cf. Cic., *Tim.* 18), but also recalls Lucan's earlier depiction of the Stoic divinity who creates and governs the cosmos (2.7-11). Seneca demonstrates the sheer multitude of names given to this god when he observes that Jupiter, i.e., the governing divinity, can rightly be called Fate, Providence, Nature, the Universe (*mundus*), or indeed any name (*nomen omne*) depending on which of his aspects you wish to highlight (Sen., *QNat* 2.45; Williams 2012: 329-30; cf. Diog. Laert. 7.135). In the proem to Book 2, Lucan uses yet another moniker for this deity as he despairingly wonders whether the *parens rerum* (parent of the universe) predetermines everything by establishing an incontrovertible sequence of events at the beginning of each cosmic cycle (2.7-11) or whether things happen entirely by chance (2.12-13). The divine parent that establishes the Stoic chain of fate is described as he who *primum informia regna / materiamque rudem flamma cedente recepit* (first received the formless realms and raw matter as the fire withdrew, 2.7-8), in a clear reference to the end of the conflagration and the beginning of a new cosmos (Schötes 1969: 17-18). Though the passage concentrates on the diachronic ordering of the universe as a fixed series of causes, the shapeless (*informia*) and unworked (*rudem*) nature of matter also gestures to the provision of a meaningful shape and design to the cosmos by the governing divinity. In the Syrtes, however, *Natura* does not complete this process. Most similar cosmogonies stress the separating out of the elements and the division of land from sea as an early stage in the creation of order (Wright 1995: 75-86; Wick 2004: 2.114 *ad* 9.303). By contrast, Nature does not make these typical divisions in the Syrtes, thereby rendering them neither sea nor land (*in dubio pelagi terraeque*) and leaving a fragment of primordial chaos within the world.

The explanation then zooms down from this divine viewpoint to the mechanical shaping of the earth on the ground. In an account reminiscent of tectonic activity (Wick 2004: 2.112, 115 *ad* 9.305; Zientek 2014: 218), the Syrtes did not sink down low enough (*neque subsedit penitus*) to function as part of the seabed (*quo stagna profundi / acciperet*). The oxymoronic *stagna profundi* presumably refers to the calmer, albeit still shallow, expanse of sea (Wick 2004: 2.115 *ad* 9.305; cf. 5.422–3; 8.853; 2.571 with Fantham 1992b: 191 *ad loc.*) that could have been expected with a lower elevation. Despite this failure to welcome the sea wholeheartedly, the land's elevation is not high enough to resist its advance either (*nec se defendit ab aequore tellus*). The resulting landscape is a fragmented one, in which the sea is continually interrupted by shoals (*aequora fracta vadis*), and the land by the sudden appearance of deep water (*abruptaque terra profundo*).[4] Both land and sea are unable to form continuous expanses with well-defined boundaries. That lack of boundaries in turn limits the ability of humans to carve any bounded space into the region, even that of a road leading elsewhere (cf. Zientek 2014: 241–5). Instead, the Syrtic coast remains pathless (*invia*). The inclusion of the *multa ... litora* past which the waves advance underlines the fact that this area does not possess a single shoreline acting as a definitive boundary, but instead a series of failed boundaries exhibiting the inability of the land to hold back its rival and that of the sea to make any lasting gains within this no-man's-land.

This slip into military language reflects Lucan's framework of conflict. This is most explicit in the use of *defendit* to describe the land's failure to hold back the sea, consistent with the use of *repugnat* (9.315) in the second explanation. That sense of conflict is reinforced by the violence implicit in the use of *fracta* and *abrupta* to describe the interlacing of the two realms. As such, the use of *in dubio* evokes a never-ending contest whose outcome always lies in the balance. Since the conflict between land and sea regularly reflects the human conflict (Schönberger 1960; Tracy 2014: 35–8), it is hard not to see here a reflection of the civil war and the poem's own narrative progress. The persistent lack of resolution to this elemental conflict mirrors the continuing struggle between Caesar and the Republicans, even after Pharsalus and Pompey's death (Wick 2004: 2.113). Indeed, I would argue that here Lucan is utilizing the deficiency in Nature's ordering of the world and the consequent lack of resolution in this region as a reflection of history's failure to find its own resolution.

That deficiency in Nature's ordering of the world is explicit at the close of the first explanation. *Natura* can refer on the one hand to the sum total of everything that exists (Pellicer 1966: 77, 242–6), and on the other to the underlying cause or divinity that has shaped and continues to shape that totality (Pellicer 1966: 280–1, 299–311). The possible overlap between these two senses was particularly pronounced in Stoicism, where Nature could be imagined as the governing divinity that inhabits and rules the entirety of existence (Pellicer 1966: 313–15). When Pliny the Elder in his near-contemporary and largely Stoic cosmology (Beagon 1992: 26–54) describes the universe (*mundus*) as *idem ... rerum naturae opus et rerum ipsa natura* (at once the work of Nature and nature herself, *HN* 2.1.2), he highlights the co-existence of these two meanings by depicting *natura* as "both the creator and the creation" (Beagon 1992: 26). By contrast, Lucan opens up a conceptual gap between these two connotations. To refer to the Syrtes as *hanc partem ... sui* clearly acknowledges that these locales form a portion of *natura* when conceived as the totality of existence; at the same time, *Natura* as providential creator has culpably abandoned this part of herself (*sic male deseruit*) and has explicitly not made it serve any purpose (*nullosque exegit in usus*). Rather than being a deliberate barrier or area of ambiguity, as the introductory remark of *iter mediis natura vetabat / Syrtibus* (Nature forbade the journey with the obstacle of the Syrtes, 9.301–2) implied, the gulfs are in fact without purpose. In Lucan's formulation, the providence of *Natura* has not shaped the totality of nature in skipping over this fragment of primordial matter and has thus left a gap in her own fabric that compromises the cohesion of the world. Though the Syrtes may be part of *natura*, they are not *Natura*'s work nor part of her plan.

The subsequent ethnography of the coast surrounding the Syrtes reflects this sense that the Syrtes are curiously dislocated from the structures that order the world (9.431–44; Thomas 1982: 108–23). The first half of that ethnography deals primarily with temporal dislocation (9.431–7):

> at, quaecumque vagam Syrtim complectitur ora
> sub nimio proiecta die, vicina perusti
> aetheris, exurit messes et pulvere Bacchum
> enecat et nulla putris radice tenetur.
> temperies vitalis abest, et nulla sub illa
> cura Iovis terra est; natura deside torpet
> orbis et immotis annum non sentit harenis.

> But whatever coast surrounds the shifting Syrtis, exposed to too much sun and bordering on the parched sky, dries up crops, and kills the vine with dust, and is held by no root owing to its crumbling nature. The climate that supports life is absent, and Jupiter has no concern for that land. Nature lazes without stirring, and the country is not conscious of the seasons as its sands remain undisturbed.

Lucan signals the irrelevance of the temporal structures that order existence elsewhere through the fact that the region does not experience seasons (*orbis et ... annum non sentit*) nor the agricultural activities appropriate to each season (*immotis ... harenis*). The emphatic absence of the usual triad of crops (*messes*), vines (*Bacchum*), and pasture (*radice*) drives home the region's barren nature (Thomas 1982: 110). That barrenness is closely tied to the excessive heat of the region (*sub nimio ... die*; *perusti / aetheris*; cf. Zientek 2014: 131–2), which not only dries up crops, but also creates the dusty and crumbling earth friendly to neither vines nor roots. The strange manner in which the region persists in the same condition countenances no further agricultural modifications by humans. It is unchanging and unchanged.

This exclusion from the cycle of seasons is complemented by the Syrtes' absence from larger cultural narratives. The claim that the Syrtic coast is of no concern to Jupiter (*nulla sub illa / cura Iovis terra est*) could simply restate the governing divinity's neglect of this region. However, it could also allude to the causal relationship constructed between the accession of Jupiter and the invention of agriculture, according to which Jupiter denied

Even *Natura* Nods: Lucan's Alternative Explanations of the Syrtes

humans the spontaneous sustenance afforded by the earth in the Golden Age and thus made farming necessary (Verg., *G.* 1.121–46; Ov., *Met.* 1.113–24; Perkell 2002: 18–23; Thomas 2004/5: 122–4; Evans 2008: 89–91). Indeed, Lucan's claim that *natura deside torpet* (nature lazes without stirring, 9.436) even alludes to the motivation ascribed to Jupiter for the transformation of nature in Vergil's *Georgics*, namely that he was *nec torpere gravi passus sua regna veterno* (not allowing his own kingdoms to laze in heavy sloth, Verg., *G.* 1.124). The agricultural inertia of the Syrtes suggests that Jupiter's transformation of nature never occurred here. The area exists neither in the Jovian age of agriculture nor in the Golden Age of spontaneous, bountiful nature. In short, the Syrtes lie outside the temporal structures that shape existence elsewhere.

The other side of the coin, spatial dislocation, is accentuated throughout Lucan's account by descriptions of this pathless or forbidden region (Viarre 1982: 105–8), yet the second half of the ethnography elaborates upon such comments (9.438–45):

> hoc tam segne solum raras tamen exerit herbas,
> quas Nasamon, gens dura, legit, qui proxima ponto
> nudus rura tenet; quem mundi barbara damnis
> Syrtis alit. nam litoreis populator harenis
> imminet et nulla portus tangente carina
> novit opes; sic cum toto commercia mundo
> naufragiis Nasamones habent.

> Though this soil is so barren, it still sends forth scattered blades of grass, which the Nasamonians, a hardy people who inhabit the countryside closest to the sea and wear no clothes, gather. Those people the cruel Syrtis feeds with the world's plunder. For the ravager hangs over the sandy shores and knows wealth, though no ship reaches their harbors. Thus the Nasamonians enjoy trade relations with the whole world by means of shipwrecks.

Lucan's use of *commercia* in the latter half of the passage evokes the trade networks extending across the Mediterranean and beyond (*toto ... mundo*), yet these connotations of mutual connectivity are paradoxical when applied to the Syrtes. The Nasamonians are not exchanging goods and sending ships on their way with new cargo as part of a global network, but are parasitically living off the produce of the world (*mundi ... damnis*) that is accidentally shipwrecked here. Ships that arrive here are not reaching their planned destination (*nulla portus tangente carina*), but are disappearing into the Mediterranean's black hole. The Syrtes are at best a dead end and, at worst, a point at which one falls off the map.

The narrative significance of the Syrtes as a gap in the ordered fabric of nature becomes clearer when considered against the quasi-Stoic cosmos of the epic's opening simile (1.70–80):

> invida fatorum series summisque negatum
> stare diu nimioque graves sub pondere lapsus

> nec se Roma ferens. sic, cum compage soluta
> saecula tot mundi suprema coegerit hora
> antiquum repetens iterum chaos, [omnia mixtis
> sidera sideribus concurrent,] ignea pontum
> astra petent, tellus extendere litora nolet
> excutietque fretum, fratri contraria Phoebe
> ibit et obliquum bigas agitare per orbem
> indignata diem poscet sibi, totaque discors
> machina divolsi turbabit foedera mundi.

> It was the work of the jealous chain of fate, and the fact that it is forbidden to stand on the summit for too long, and the heavy collapse beneath excessive weight, and Rome unable to support itself. In the same way, when the framework of the world is undone and the final hour closes off so many ages of the world, reverting once again to primordial chaos, [all the stars will clash in a confusion of stars] the fiery stars will attack the ocean, the earth will refuse to stretch out her shores and will shake off the strait of the sea, Phoebe will march in opposition to her brother and will demand the day for herself, full of disdain for driving her chariot along the orbit running counter to his, and the whole inharmonious frame of the ruptured world will cast its laws into confusion.

The ordered state of the cosmos prior to *ekpyrosis* as depicted here has two interdependent aspects.[5] First, the *invida fatorum series* evokes the Stoic belief in a chain of causes as mentioned above in connection with Book 2's proem, while adding a note of divine malice. That diachronic order is complemented by a synchronic order, in which each part of the universe at any moment is linked to the wider whole in a cohesive design. That cohesion prior to *ekpyrosis* is referenced in the use of *compages* to denote the structure of the cosmos, since words to which the prefix *con-* has been added are habitually used to render those Greek words beginning with συν- that articulate the unity and coherence of the Stoic cosmos (Lapidge 1979: 348, 350, 360–1). Similarly, the *foedera* that the conflagration will disturb may be a Latin equivalent of the Greek δεσμοί (bonds), which bind the Stoic cosmos together (Lapidge 1979: 359, 361), while the normal sense of *foedus* as treaty suggests the peaceful harmony in which the various parts of the cosmos previously existed. The same legalistic language refers elsewhere to the breakdown in nature's order that accompanies the outbreak of civil war: *leges . . . et foedera rerum / praescia monstrifero vertit natura tumultu* (Nature, knowing in advance, overturned the laws and covenants of the universe in a disturbance pregnant with prodigies, 2.2–3).

The evocation of such cohesion emphasizes that the necessary condition for an all-embracing conflagration is the existence of an immanent providence, whose withdrawal from the universe into solitude (Sen., *Ep.* 9.16) or mere suspension of its sustaining function (Bénatouïl 2009: 28–31) entails the complete collapse of the ordered structures that it maintains throughout the cosmos. In other words, if the untying of the cosmic structure (*compage soluta*) is to bring about a universal catastrophe, that ordered structure must have been extensive and efficient enough that its sudden absence spells cosmic collapse. That odd interplay between the level of order in the cosmos and the severity of the conflagration can also be discerned in the simile's mechanical language. The description of this planned cosmos as the *machina ... mundi* even as it battles against itself (*discors, divolsi*) and wrecks its own prior functioning (*turbabit foedera*) captures the supreme irony that the universe as a contraption is carrying out its final task, self-destruction, with the selfsame efficiency with which it functioned (cf. Johnson 1987: 16–18). The world destroys itself like clockwork. The opening simile, therefore, captures the fact that *ekpyrosis* functions as a remarkably satisfying narrative model. Its all-embracing nature does not admit the possibility of loose ends: every thread converges at this moment of cosmic death, before *palingenesis*, the rebirth of an identical cosmos, occurs (Long 1985).

Or so it should according to standard accounts, but here Lucan notably omits *palingenesis* by having no new cosmos arise from the chaos to which the present universe returns (Roche 2005). Though others have questioned whether chaos coheres with Stoic cosmology, Seneca also uses it in his tragedies to designate the primordial state to which the cosmos is returned by *ekpyrosis* (*Thy.* 832; Tarrant 1985: 209 *ad* 830–5, Boyle 2017: 375 *ad* 827–43; *Ag.* 487; cf. [*Her. O*]. 1134; [*Oct.*] 391).[6] Behind such Neronian instances lurks the influence of Ovidian chaos (*Met.* 1.5–20; Tarrant 2002: 355–60), whose portrayal as the co-existence of warring opposites within a single body must have suggested itself to Lucan as a powerful analogy for civil war (Tarrant 2002: 356–8; cf. Keith 2011: 121–2). Such cosmic strife is inaugurated most obviously by the claim that the moon, Phoebe, will fight the sun, her brother, in a sibling conflict typical of Roman civil war (Fantham 2010: 214–18).

As for the choice to end the simile without *palingenesis*, this is not necessarily pessimistic, but paradoxically a form of consolation. The return to chaos without any new universe offers a definitive closure that may be more comforting than the prospect of civil war repeating itself. The poem even articulates that desire for closure—to escape civil war even by a catastrophe exceeding the everyday limits of nature—when Lucan, intruding upon his own narrative as though unaware of the war's outcome (Hutchinson 1993: 250–3, Asso 2010: 135–6 *ad loc.*), prays to Neptune and Jupiter to augment the flood that already traps Caesar's army at Ilerda (4.110–20) and thus *miseras bellis civilibus eripe terras* (rescue these wretched lands from civil war, 4.120). The request for assistance from such distant rivers as the Rhine (4.116) and Rhone (4.117), as well as snows from the Rhipaean mountains (4.118), suggests a global cataclysm. Lucan "must be begging for the very disaster to end civil war which he elsewhere treats as the equivalent of civil war" (Leigh 1997: 45).

Yet if this simile promises curiously complete closure, the first explanation of the Syrtes upsets the premises upon which this narrative model is based. Firstly, the abandonment of the region by *Natura* points to a failure to create the universal cohesion upon which *ekpyrosis* depends: the Syrtes are a gap in the ordered fabric of the world. Secondly, the opening simile suggests a distinction between the usual order of the universe, whose structures are characterized in such quasi-legal terms as *foedera*, and chaos. Yet the Syrtes remain a fragment of the latter state, insofar as land and sea have been left to wage the same battle from the world's beginning. Finally, the description of the *lex loci* as being itself *ambigua* casts quite a different light on the order evoked by *foedera* in the first simile (Asso 2011: 387): is a *lex* that allows such conflict to reign really a *lex* at all? In short, Lucan's first explanation of the Syrtes undermines the cosmic cohesion that promises such definitive closure and provides the reader with an alternative model of Nature, whose gaps in her own structure account for any narrative resolution swiftly receding into the distance beyond the poem's conclusion. If Pharsalus is the conflagration (Lapidge 1979: 369–70; Joseph 2017: 114–15), then the Syrtes could represent the loose narrative thread along which Cato has escaped absolute defeat.

That sense that the Syrtes are an area in which a narrative can continue indefinitely without achieving closure is provided by the sandstorm (9.445–92), which follows the storm at sea (9.319–47). The description of the south wind, which causes the shipwreck, as *in sua regna furens* (raging against its own domains, 9.321) can be interpreted as a new symbol of civil discord that adopts a tyrannical model of inward violence suitable for the coming autocracy. Yet that violence obviously does not reach its conclusion in the shipwreck nor stop at sea, because the same south wind is even more violent (*violentius*) on and even more harmful to dry land (*terrae magis ille nocens*, 9.447–9). The absence of any obstacles on land to break up the force of the wind means that the south wind wreaks its Aeolian madness (*Aeoliam rabiem*) over the entirety of the sands (9.449–54). Just as the waves in the first explanation roll past a series of beaches, none of which form an effective boundary, so the south wind passes from sea to land, inflicting *aequoreos … metus* (fears belonging to the sea, 9.447) upon these soldiers. The familiar motif of civil war as madness (Hershkowitz 1998: 197–246) suggests that we should see the narrative progress of civil war in the furious momentum (*furens, rabies*) of the south wind: for all that Pharsalus promised resolution, here we find ourselves following the momentum of civil war outside of those bounds.

Moreover, the manner in which the forces of nature simply wear themselves out here without meeting any obstacle to hinder their passage is linked to the specific avoidance of a larger, cosmic crisis. A geographic paradox is presented to the reader, according to which the instability of this region's sandy composition makes it peculiarly stable, since the grains on its surface may move about freely while the underlying fabric of this land remains unmoved (9.469–71; Asso 2011: 391–3). The consequences of this peculiarity are fleshed out by the consideration of a counterfactual landscape (9.466–8):

concuteret terras orbemque a sede moveret,
si solida Libye compage et pondere duro
clauderet exesis Austrum scopulosa cavernis.

It would shake the earth and shift the world from its position, if a craggy Libya with solid frame and sturdy bulk confined the Auster in caverns hollowed out.

(trans. Braund)

This counterfactual topography draws upon the explanation of earthquakes that ascribed their cause to wind becoming trapped within subterranean caverns (Sen., *QNat.* 6.12; Morford 1967a: 49; Asso 2011: 392–3). The earthquake envisaged, however, is not simply a local one, but has global consequences. If Libya had a typical coastal terrain, the winds when trapped therein "would shatter the framework of the world" (Morford 1967a: 49). One could, therefore, interpret the instability of the land as a merciful act of providence on the part of *Natura* that belies the narrative of neglect. Nevertheless, such mercy only spares the soldiers to suffer more of civil war, while the earthquake would free them from its grip. The use of *solida compage* inverts the *compages soluta* of the opening simile: Libya's lack of a normal structure reflects its status as a gap in the cosmic *compages*. If the structured nature of the cosmos means that all its parts converge in a universal conflagration, it is striking that the lack of a similar structure here explicitly prevents a catastrophe of similar proportions from occurring. The status of the region as a gap in the structures of the world marks it as a place where neither human nor cosmic narratives can be brought to a decisive conclusion.

The Second Explanation (9.311–18)

The idea of a narrative conclusion receding into the distance is also pertinent to the second explanation, which focuses on lack of water rather than elevation (9.311–18):

> vel plenior alto
> olim Syrtis erat pelago penitusque natabat,
> sed rapidus Titan ponto sua lumina pascens
> aequora subduxit zonae vicina perustae;
> et nunc pontus adhuc Phoebo siccante repugnat,
> mox, ubi damnosum radios admoverit aevum,
> tellus Syrtis erit; nam iam brevis unda superne
> innatat, et late periturum deficit aequor.

> Alternatively, the Syrtis was once deeply submerged in a fuller measure of the sea, but the grasping sun, in feeding his lights on the ocean, has siphoned off these waters that border on the torrid zone; and now the sea still struggles against the drying action of Apollo, but soon, when destructive time has applied these rays, the Syrtis will be land; for already a shallow wave swims about on top of it and the supply of water, which is about to vanish, is exhausted in many locations.

Whereas the first explanation set up a contest between land and sea, here the battle is between the sun and sea with the land passively benefitting once the sun has done its dirty work (Loupiac 1998: 155). The sun's feeding of itself on water alludes to a preexisting theory adopted by the Stoics (Kidd 1988: 458–9 *ad* fr. 118) and already mentioned by Lucan (1.415–16, 7.5–6), according to which celestial bodies are fueled by evaporated moisture. Of course, this feeding by the sun is entirely unsustainable: soon the Syrtis will be land, since even now it only possesses a *brevis . . . unda* that will shortly be consumed. For all that the sea *repugnat*, it has already lost a great depth of water and will eventually lose it entirely as the passage of time can only bring further losses (*damnosum . . . aevum*). The significance of this explanation for the civil war is not hard to fathom. Not only are all forms of water persistent in their enmity toward Caesar throughout the *Bellum Civile* (Chen 2012: 161–234), but Nero, to say nothing of Augustus (Miller 2009), was closely associated with Apollo (*Phoebo*), particularly in his solar aspects, from at least 59 CE (Champlin 2003: 112–44). Therefore, this explanation frames the Republicans' continuing resistance in the aftermath of Pharsalus as a protracted struggle against the inevitable victory of the *gens Iulia* (Schönberger 1960: 89). As we shall see, the slow rate of this process means the cosmos and the Roman state come to a gradual, rather than sudden, end.

In terms of cosmic significance, the movement of the sun's rays by *damnosum . . . aevum* has been seen as a reference to *ekpyrosis* (Schötes 1969: 21–2; König 1970: 447–8), while its appearance alongside the nourishment of the stars has been interpreted in light of a similar connection made by Balbus, Stoicism's advocate, in Cicero's *De Natura Deorum* (2.118):[7]

> quibus [vaporibus] altae renovataeque stellae atque omnis aether refundunt eadem et rursum trahunt indidem, nihil ut fere intereat aut admodum paululum quod astrorum ignis et aetheris flamma consumat. ex quo eventurum nostri putant . . . ut ad extremum omnis mundus ignesceret, cum umore consumpto neque terra ali posset nec remearet aër, cuius ortus aqua omni exhausta esse non posset.

> When the stars and the whole aether have been fed and renewed by these vapours, they send the same material back and again draw it up from the same place, so that almost nothing, or only a truly tiny amount, perishes which the fire of the stars and the flame of the aether consumes. As a result of which our school thinks . . . that there will be a conflagration of the whole universe extending to its furthest point, because, once the moisture has been used up, neither can the earth be nourished nor will the air continue to flow, whose rising cannot occur once all water has been exhausted.

This extended account clarifies the peculiar spin that Lucan has given to the process. Lucan's sun is a grasping figure (*rapidus*; cf. Dinter 2012: 14–15), interested only in feeding himself (*sua lumina pascens*). Though Balbus mentions the sun's heat as the primary cause of evaporation prior to this extract, all the stars use this moisture. Similarly, while Lucan gives no sense that the sun returns any of the moisture evaporated, Balbus emphasizes that this process is almost sustainable with rainfall redistributing evaporated moisture; the only catch is that the stars have to consume something, even if it is almost nothing (*nihil . . . fere*) or minuscule amounts (*admodum paululum*). As a result, the sum total of terrestrial moisture must decrease very gradually indeed, until some distant moment when it is entirely consumed and the conflagration takes place. By contrast,

Lucan's use of *mox* and *periturum* suggests the imminent exhaustion of moisture. In interpreting the imminence of this desiccation through Cicero, Seewald (2008: 182 *ad* 311–18) even argued that the Syrtes act as a sundial ("Sonnenuhr") for the conflagration, whose occurrence must be at hand. In other words, the exhaustion of water in the Syrtes signals its global exhaustion.

The problem with this interpretation is that the positioning of the Syrtes beside the torrid zone (*aequora ... zonae vicina perustae*) explains why its waters have evaporated faster than those of other areas: the heat of the sun is stronger here. Indeed, the fact that the Syrtes are almost uniquely hazardous to ships means the sun must consume greater quantities of water here than elsewhere. Yet, according to Balbus, the conflagration requires the water supply of the world to have been exhausted, not that of one region. Rather than reading the Syrtes as a typical region functioning as a measure of global water levels and the imminence of conflagration, I propose that the processes that shape cosmic time are moving faster in the Syrtes to produce an ekpyrotic landscape in advance of the conflagration. While the first explanation accounts for the Syrtes' similarities to chaos by positing that they never fully emerged from that state, the same features are explained in the second passage as a premature return to chaos.[8]

That sense of time moving faster in certain areas which are, as a result, out of kilter with the rest of the universe, creates a fragmented view of nature that bears similarities to the first explanation and its depiction of a deficient Providence. If the Syrtes are characterized by the swifter movement of destructive time (*damnosum ... aevum*), then we are left with an image not of the universe converging neatly on a single point of destruction, but of the possibility that distinct and localized narratives of destruction operate separately from any final, all-embracing conflagration. This possibility raises the prospect of regions surviving their own quasi-death.

Yet, even though cosmic time may move faster here, the timescale of this process does not operate in tandem with the much smaller scale of human lives passing through the Syrtes. Had Cato and his troops arrived sufficiently earlier or later, they could have found a navigable sea or surer landfall in the Syrtes, but the process grinds on regardless. Indeed, the use of *nunc*, *mox*, and *iam* in emphatic reference to the present can refer both to the timeframe of the narrative and to the narrator's own lifetime, since the waters of the Syrtes have remained in this state of near-exhaustion for several generations. If even the Syrtes' accelerated version of cosmic destruction reaches such slow resolution, we may be led to see the unfolding of destructive time on a global scale sailing off into the horizon. This sense that the dimensions of cosmic time dwarf our own lifespan suggests that the apparent victories and losses of human life are incidental dramas in the unfolding of the cosmos.

This odd interplay between the operation of localized desiccation and the slow speed at which it is realized suggests another link between the destruction wrought by the south wind and that suffered in civil war. After mentioning that the south wind destroyed walls and carried their fragments a great distance (9.490–1), Lucan remarks that *qui nullas videre domos videre ruinas* (those who saw no houses saw their ruins falling, 9.492).[9] That strange phenomenon captures on a small temporal scale the fact that we never see the region around the Syrtes in any sort of pristine form, but only toward the end of a long decline. A similar point could be made for Rome and Italy in the eyes of Lucan and his generation in Book 1, where Lucan presents a vision of a country in such hyperbolic decline that it lies in depopulated ruins, its remains presumably untouched or having declined further since civil war proper (1.24–32). Only the city of Troy, in which *etiam periere ruinae* (even the ruins have perished, 9.969), has the promise of *palingenesis* under Caesar's rebuilding (9.998–9). The sense that all generations of Romans after these civil wars have only known their country's long decay finds a powerful counterpart in the Syrtes' second explanation. There we find a region that morphs into an ekpyrotic landscape so gradually that multiple generations can see within it an advance screening of the cosmos' end (cf. Schötes 1969: 22). Perhaps the playing out of civil war and its consequences is as painful and gradual at Rome, where the victory of the *gens Iulia* is not so much a resolution of civil war as a modulation of its violence in which an autocrat is forever *in sua regna furens* (9.321).

Conclusion

If both explanations reject the prospect of complete closure once promised to Lucan's contemporary reader, it remains for us to consider how different endings to the epic, both real and hypothetical, would cohere with each explanation's view of the cosmos. Insofar as both explanations encourage one to abandon all hope of grand, cosmic closure, they may reconcile readers to the abrupt ending that we currently possess, whether resulting from Lucan's own artistic choice (Masters 1992: 216–59; Tracy 2011) or his death (Henderson 1998: 170). The lack of cosmic cohesion within each explanation suggests that there is no natural end point for this narrative, when all the loose threads of history will be tied up. In such a context, the muted, unmarked ending of Book 10 could be interpreted as a deliberate avoidance of the almost endless epic that would be required, were Lucan to depict the civil strife stretching from Pharsalus to Actium (1.38–43), and of any false sense of historical closure that might arise from the poet imposing his own grand ending on civil war. Since, however, only a minority of scholars accept the ending we possess, let us close by considering how the explanations condition us to receive the epic's most popular hypothetical ending, the suicide of Cato (e.g., Schönberger 1957; Frank 1970; Ahl 1976: 306–26; Stover 2008).[10]

The explicit purposelessness of the Syrtes in the first explanation undermines moralizing readings of Cato's African march. As hardships crush the spirit of Cato's troops, they assert that they do not blame *Natura*, who clearly had not wished this land to be inhabited by men (9.855–8); they then pray to an unknown god to accept their punishment for trespassing on a region that this divinity had obviously cut off by placing the torrid zone and the Syrtes on either side with death in the middle (9.859–62). The deity's alleged motivation, hatred for Roman trade relations (*commercia nostra perosus*, 9.860), provides a moralizing rationale consistent with the narrator's disapproval of the deforestation of Libya to provide Rome with cedar tables (9.429–30) or the importation of asp poison to Rome (9.706-7; Fantham 1992a: 95-6). The imputation of such moral intent to nature, however, is difficult to reconcile with the fact that the Syrtes are a product of neglect that serve no purpose. In a variation on Hanlon's razor, the first explanation warns Lucan's characters and contemporary readers that they need not invoke amoral, malicious, indifferent, or non-existent gods (Due 1970: 214) to explain the Syrtes and other hardships, but merely divine incompetence or neglect. Within this negligent Nature, we can see a critique of the Principate, whose emperors were capable of doing as much damage by negligence as by malice. A scene of Seneca's *Apocolocyntosis* comes to mind, where the deified Augustus castigates Claudius, a candidate for deification, when he claims ignorance (*nescio*) of Messalina's murder, since such ignorance is more shameful than actually murdering her (*Apocol.* 11.1-2).

The negligence of Nature also complicates interpretations of this region as the perfect environment for testing or realizing Stoic virtue in the person of Cato (Morford 1967b; Thomas 1982: 108-23; Viarre 1982; Fantham 1992a; D'Alessandro Behr 2007: 109-11, 124-8). Without the first explanation, one could reasonably interpret the African march in the same manner that Seneca interprets Cato's entire career in *De Providentia*: the hostile environment of Libya is another proof that Cato is the man *quem sibi rerum natura delegit cum quo metuenda conlideret* (with whom Nature chose to contend in her terrifying aspect) to create the ultimate *exemplum* of the good man's immunity to misfortunes (*Prov.* 3.14). The possibility, however, that the African march begins accidentally with a shipwreck caused by Nature's incompetence casts doubt on whether the ensuing struggle between Cato and this environment fulfils any higher moral or cosmic intent. Indeed, it introduces an irony characteristic of Lucan that we enter the optimal environment for Stoic ethics through a space that contradicts the Stoic belief in an ordered cosmos. In such a context, one could even interpret Cato, previously presented as a Stoic *follower* of nature (*naturam ... sequi*, 2.382), as *outpacing* it. The universality of Cato's *virtus* exceeds the partial ordering of the world achieved by Providence. It is as though the order of the microcosm, i.e., the individual human, exceeds that of the macrocosm upon which its order is supposedly based (Inwood 1985: 182-215). Such an interpretation leaves open the possibility that, even if definitive closure is impossible owing to Nature's incompetence, Cato's suicide could have imposed some form of closure upon history (Stover 2008) in spite, or defiance, of Nature.

A more ambitious reassessment of any individual's, even Cato's, significance in the epic's closural dynamics is provided by the second explanation. Its introduction of deep time, a model of natural and historical change achieved through almost infinitesimal increments, questions the significance of any individual actor or action and thus problematizes the choice of any historical moment as the end point of Lucan's epic. In itself, this is a radical revision of the intimate relationship between individuals and nature imagined earlier in the epic. In Book 5, for instance, Caesar's attempt to sail back across to Italy occasions a storm that almost rips the cosmos apart (Morford 1967a: 43-4; Lapidge 1979: 367-8). Here the individual possesses an incredible ability to disturb nature from its foundations. The second explanation, however, depicts Nature as capable of grand designs whose progress spans countless generations and continues indifferently to the lives of humans consumed in the interim. That expansion of nature beyond the limited frame of human life is mirrored by the Nile's sources and the cosmos in general receding beyond Caesar's power and understanding in Acoreus' account within the following book (Tracy 2014: 181–99, 203–6). A natural world of such vast temporal and spatial dimensions can hardly be as responsive or as vulnerable to the whims of humans. It is as though the final books of the epic begin to release nature from its claustrophobic confinement and, in doing so, accept that history cannot reach any swift or immediate resolution keyed to the lives of individuals. Whether the epic ends where it is meant to or would have continued further, the framework of deep time would always encourage us to look beyond any closural moment manifested in the text, and to accept that the true story of civil strife is that of the Julio-Claudian Principate slowly grinding down opposition to itself until we arrive at the post-apocalyptic Italy of Lucan's Neronian present. Here too there may be a shallow wave of resistance, but it is soon to perish before the might of the sun.

Notes

1. All translations are my own unless noted otherwise. The text of Shackleton Bailey (1997) is used throughout. I am grateful to the organizers of the conference, Mark Thorne and Laura Zientek, and to the other conference attendees, whose comments substantially influenced the development of this chapter; to the anonymous readers for helping me hone my argument and alerting me to numerous important parallels; and to Amy Koenig and Richard Thomas, whose insights have improved this chapter significantly.
2. On Lucan and Stoicism, see Marti (1945); Schötes (1969); Le Bonniec (1970); Due (1970); Lapidge (1979; 1989: 1405–9); Roche (2009: 30–6); Sklenář (2003); D'Alessandro Behr (2007). Zientek (2014) is particularly pertinent to the relationship between Stoicism and Lucan's natural world.
3. Nature is only capitalized in the ensuing paragraphs when referring unambiguously to a divine agent.
4. This underwater topography recalls Sallust's description of the gulf (*Iug.* 78) as extremely deep next to the land (*proxuma terrae praealta sunt*) and then an unstable mixture of depths and shallows further out to sea (*cetera uti fors tulit alta alia, alia in tempestate vadosa*).
5. My own treatment of the opening simile has been influenced principally by Lapidge (1979: 360–3); Johnson (1987: 14–18); Masters (1992: 63–5); Sklenář (2003: 3–11); Roche (2005); and Zientek (2014: 21–31).
6. For the problems that could arise for orthodox Stoic readings from Lucan's inclusion of chaos, see Sklenář (2003: 6). Nevertheless, Lapidge (1978: 165; 1979: 361–2); and Long (1996: 80) demonstrate that chaos *could* be interpreted in Stoic terms.
7. On possible contradictions with Stoic doctrine, see Lapidge (1978: 181); Salles (2005). Seewald (2008: 183 *ad* 9.311–18) rightly observes that this account's similarities to Lucan suggest a genuine feature of Roman Stoicism.
8. For an alternative reading of Libya as a return to chaos following the conflagration of Pharsalus, see Zientek (2014: 231–76).
9. *Pace* Shackleton Bailey, I consider these lines genuine.

10. For discussion of various endings, see Ahl (1976: 306–26); Masters (1992: 234–7). For an extensive bibliography of proposed endings, see Stover (2008: 571n2).

References

Ahl, F. M. (1976), *Lucan: An Introduction*, Ithaca: Cornell University Press.
Asso, P. (2010), *A Commentary on Lucan, De Bello Civili IV: Introduction, Edition, and Translation*, Berlin: De Gruyter.
Asso, P. (2011), "And Then It Rained Shields: Revising Nature and Roman Myth," in Asso (ed.), *Brill's Companion to Lucan*, 383–98, Leiden: Brill.
Beagon, M. (1992), *Roman Nature: The Thought of Pliny the Elder*, Oxford: Clarendon Press.
Bénatouïl, T. (2009), "How Industrious can Zeus be? The Extent and Objects of Divine Activity in Stoicism," in R. Salles (ed.), *God and Cosmos in Stoicism*, 23–45, Oxford: Oxford University Press.
Boyle, A. J. (2017), *Seneca, Thyestes*, Oxford: Oxford University Press.
Braund, S. H. (trans.) (1992), *Lucan: Civil War*, Oxford: Oxford University Press.
Champlin, E. (2003), *Nero*, Cambridge, MA: Belknap Press.
Chen, H. (2012), "Breakthrough and Concealment: The Formulaic Dynamics of Character Behavior in Lucan." PhD Diss., Columbia University, New York, NY.
D'Alessandro Behr, F. (2007), *Feeling History: Lucan, Stoicism, and the Poetics of Passion*, Columbus: Ohio State University Press.
Dinter, M. T. (2012), *Anatomizing Civil War: Studies in Lucan's Epic Technique*, Ann Arbor: The University of Michigan Press.
Due, O. S. (1970), "Lucain et la philosophie," in M. Durry (ed.), *Lucain*, 203–24, Fondation Hardt, entretiens sur l'antiquité Classique 15.
Evans, R. (2008), *Utopia Antiqua: Readings of the Golden Age and Decline at Rome*, London: Routledge.
Fantham, E. (1992a), "Lucan's Medusa-Excursus: Its Design and Purpose," *MD*, 29: 95–119.
Fantham, E. (1992b), *Lucan: De Bello Civili Book 2*. Cambridge: Cambridge University Press.
Fantham, E. (2010), "Discordia Fratrum: Aspects of Lucan's Conception of Civil War," in B. Breed, C. Damon, A. Rossi (eds.), *Citizens of Discord: Rome and its Civil Wars*, 207–22, Oxford: Oxford University Press.
Feeney, D. (1991), *The Gods in Epic: Poets and Critics of the Classical Tradition*, Oxford: Clarendon Press.
Fehrle, R. (1983), *Cato Uticensis*, Darmstadt: Wissenschaftliche Buchgesellschaft.
Frank, E. (1970), "The Structure and Scope of Lucan's *De bello civili*," *CB*, 46: 59–61.
Hardie, P. (1997), "Closure in Latin Epic," in D. H. Roberts, F. M. Dunn, and D. Fowler (eds.) *Classical Closure: Reading the End in Greek and Latin Literature*, 139–62, Princeton, NJ: Princeton University Press.
Henderson, J. (1998), "Lucan: The Word at War," in J. Henderson (ed.), *Fighting for Rome: Poets and Caesars, History and Civil War*, 165–211, Cambridge: Cambridge University Press.
Hershkowitz, D. (1998), *The Madness of Epic: Reading Insanity from Homer to Statius*, Oxford: Clarendon Press.
Hutchinson, G. O. (1993), *Latin Literature from Seneca to Juvenal: A Critical Study*, Oxford: Clarendon Press.
Inwood, B., (1985), *Ethics and Human Action in Early Stoicism*. Oxford: Clarendon Press.
Johnson, W. R. (1987), *Momentary Monsters: Lucan and His Heroes*, Ithaca, NY: Cornell University Press.
Joseph, T. A. (2017), "Pharsalus as Rome's 'Day of Doom' in Lucan," *AJPh*, 138 (1): 107–41.

Keith, A. (2011), "Ovid in Lucan: The Poetics of Instability," in Asso (ed.), *Brill's Companion to Lucan*, 111–32, Leiden: Brill.
Kidd, I. G. (1988), *Posidonius: Volume II: The Commentary. (i) Testimonia and Fragments 1–149*, Cambridge: Cambridge University Press.
König, F. (1957), "Mensch und Welt bei Lucan im Spiegel bildhafter Darstellung," in W. Rutz (ed.) (1970), *Lucan*, 439–76, Darmstadt: Wissenschaftliche Buchgesellschaft.
Lapidge, M. (1978), "Stoic Cosmology," in J. M. Rist (ed.), *The Stoics*, 161–202, Berkeley: University of California Press.
Lapidge, M. (1979), "Lucan's imagery of cosmic dissolution," *Hermes*, 107 (3): 344–70.
Lapidge, M. (1989), "Stoic Cosmology and Roman Literature, First to Third Centuries A.D.," *ANRW*, 2.36.3: 1379–1429.
Le Bonniec, H. (1970), "Lucain et la religion," in M. Durry (ed.) *Lucain*, 161–95, Fondation Hardt, entretiens sur l'antiquité Classique 15.
Leigh, M. (1997), *Spectacle and Engagement*, Oxford: Clarendon Press.
Leigh, M. (2000), "Lucan and the Libyan Tale," *JRS*, 90: 95–109.
Long, A. A. (1985), "The Stoics on World-Conflagration and Everlasting Recurrence," *SJPh*, 23 (supplement): 13–37.
Long, A. A. (1996), "Stoic readings of Homer," in A. A. Long (ed.), *Stoic Studies*, 58–84, Berkeley: University of California Press.
Long, A. A. and D. N. Sedley (1987), *The Hellenistic Philosophers. Volume 1: Translations of the principal sources with philosophical commentary. Volume 2: Greek and Latin Texts with Notes and Bibliography*, Cambridge: Cambridge University Press.
Loupiac, A. (1998), *La poétique des éléments dans la Pharsale de Lucain*, Brussels: Latomus.
Marti, B. (1945), "The Meaning of the Pharsalia," *AJPh*, 66 (4): 352–76.
Masters, J. (1992), *Poetry and Civil War in Lucan's Bellum Civile*, Cambridge: Cambridge University Press.
Miller, J. F. (2009), *Apollo, Augustus, and the Poets*, Cambridge: Cambridge University Press.
Miura, Y. (1981), "Zur Funktion der Gleichnisse im I. und VII. Buch von Lucans Pharsalia," *GB*, 10: 207–232.
Morford, M. P. O. (1967a), *The Poet Lucan: Studies in Rhetorical Epic*, Oxford: Blackwell.
Morford, M. P. O. (1967b), "The Purpose of Lucan's Ninth Book," *Latomus*, 26 (1): 123–9.
Nisbet, R. G. M. and M. Hubbard (1970), *A Commentary on Horace: Odes Book 1*, Oxford: Clarendon Press.
Pellicer, A. (1966), *Natura, Étude sémantique et historique du mot latin*, Paris: Presses Universitaires de France.
Perkell, C. (2002), "The Golden Age and its Contradictions in the Poetry of Virgil," *Vergilius*, 48: 3–39.
Quinn, J. C. (2011), "The Syrtes between East and West," in A. Dowler and E. R. Galvin (eds.), *Money, Trade, and Trade Routes in pre-Islamic North Africa*, 11–20, London: British Museum Press.
Roche, P. (2005), "Righting the reader: Conflagration and civil war in Lucan's De Bello Civili," *Scholia*, 14: 52–71.
Roche, P. (2009), *Lucan: De Bello Civili. Book 1*, Oxford: Oxford University Press.
Salles, R. (2005), "'Ἐκπύρωσις and the goodness of god in Cleanthes," *Phronesis*, 50 (1): 56–78.
Schönberger, O. (1957), "Zur Komposition des Lucan," *Hermes*, 85 (2): 251–4.
Schönberger, O. (1960), "Leitmotivisch wiederholte Bilder bei Lucan," *RhM*, 103 (1): 81–90.
Schötes, H.-A. (1969), *Stoische Physik, Psychologie und Theologie bei Lucan*, Bonn: R. Habelt.
Seewald, M. (2008), *Studien zum 9. Buch von Lucans Bellum Civile mit einem Kommentar zu den Versen 1–733*. Göttinger Forum für Altertumswissenschaft Bd. 2, Berlin: De Gruyter.
Shackleton Bailey, D. R. (ed.) (1997), *M. Annaei Lucani De Bello Civili Libri X. Editio Altera*, Stuttgart and Leipzig: Teubner.

Sklenář, R. (2003), *The Taste for Nothingness. A Study of Virtus and Related Themes in Lucan's Bellum Civile*, Ann Arbor: University of Michigan Press.

Stover, T. (2008), "Cato and the Intended Scope of Lucan's Bellum Civile," *CQ*, 58 (2): 571–80.

Tarrant, R. J. (1985), *Seneca's Thyestes*, Atlanta: Scholars Press.

Tarrant, R. J. (2002), "Chaos in Ovid's Metamorphoses and its Neronian Influence," *Arethusa*, 35 (3): 349–60.

Thomas, R. F. (1982), *Lands and Peoples in Roman Poetry: The Ethnographical Tradition*, Cambridge: Cambridge Philological Society.

Thomas, R. F. (2004/5), "Torn between Jupiter and Saturn: Ideology, Rhetoric and Culture Wars in the Aeneid," *CJ*, 100 (2): 121–47.

Tracy, J. (2011), "Internal Evidence for the Completeness of the Bellum Civile," in Asso (ed.), *Brill's Companion to Lucan*, 33–53, Leiden: Brill.

Tracy, J. (2014), *Lucan's Egyptian Civil War*, Cambridge: Cambridge University Press.

Viarre, S. (1982), "Caton en Libye: L'Histoire et la Métaphore (Lucain, Pharsale, IX, 294–949)," in J.-M. Croisille and P.-M. Fauchère (eds.) *Neronia 1977*, 103–110, Clermont-Ferrand: ADOSA.

Wick, C. (2004), *Marcus Annaeus Lucanus, Bellum Civile, liber IX. I: Einleitung, Text und Übersetzung; II: Kommentar*, München-Leipzig: K.G. Saur.

Williams, G. D. (2012), *The Cosmic Viewpoint: A Study of Seneca's Natural Questions*, Oxford: Oxford University Press.

Wright, M. R. (1995), *Cosmology in Antiquity*, London: Routledge.

Zientek, L. (2014), "Lucan's Natural Questions: Landscape and Geography in the Bellum Civile." PhD Diss., University of Washington, Seattle, WA.

CHAPTER 6
WORLD GEOGRAPHY, ROMAN HISTORY, AND THE FAILURE TO INCORPORATE PARTHIA IN LUCAN'S *BELLUM CIVILE*

Mauro Serena

Introduction

The intersection of geography, history, and politics holds special importance to an imperialistic power that claims world control (Nicolet 1988: 17, 46–85).[1] In Lucan's exploration of Roman imperialism, Parthia's relevance is simple: she should have been conquered. This chapter sets out from the premise that Parthia, from the beginning to the end of the poem, is carefully constructed as a symbol of Rome's inability to do what she should have done if she had stuck to the plan ordained for her by nature; that is, to be the leader of the world. It contends that the treatment of Parthia is part of a historical reflection on the consequences of the actions of the past, on the present, on the position of past and present emperors, and on the relevance of the eastern foe to Nero's Rome. Finally, it suggests that the model adopted by Nero in the Parthian affair is based on the Augustan blueprint, and the exposure of the incongruity of the Augustan settlement—both as a historical and cultural event—only emphasizes the incongruity of Nero's pretense.

I will analyze in detail how Lucan, focusing especially on manipulation of geography and geographical metaphors, constructs an image of Parthia as a symbol of Rome's betrayal of her imperialistic nature and of her inability to reach her maximum potential. I will then examine how, after Pharsalus, he highlights Rome's progressive loss of control by emphasizing Parthia's passivity and by giving her the new geographical status of *aliter mundus*. Subsequently, I will examine how Lucan re-elaborates some poems written by Horace in the decade 30–20 BCE to problematize his conciliatory position on Augustus' policy and the Augustan handling of the Parthian affair, and how this may relate to Nero's Parthian policy. I will finally discuss the contrasting speeches of Pompey and Lentulus in Book 8, where the various strands of Lucan's discourse of imperialism converge to deny the usefulness of the Parthian Wars, a revisionist position in contrast with the current emperor's ambitions.

Lucan's Idea of Roman Imperialism

Right after the proem, in which the subject of the poem is announced—a wicked war that turns a nation against itself—Lucan makes several considerations that have important implications in relation to Rome's position as an imperialistic power (1.8–24).

> quis furor, o ciues, quae tanta licentia ferri?
> gentibus inuisis Latium praebere cruorem
> cumque superba foret Babylon spolianda tropaeis
> Ausoniis umbraque erraret Crassus inulta
> bella geri placuit nullos habitura triumphos?
> heu, quantum terrae potuit pelagique parari
> hoc quem ciuiles hauserunt sanguine dextrae,
> unde uenit Titan et nox ubi sidera condit
> quaque dies medius flagrantibus aestuat oris
> et qua bruma rigens ac nescia uere remitti
> astringit Scythico glacialem frigore pontum!
> sub iuga iam Seres, iam barbarus isset Araxes
> et gens siqua iacet nascenti conscia Nilo.
> tum, si tantus amor belli tibi, Roma, nefandi,
> totum sub Latias leges cum miseris orbem,
> in te uerte manus: nondum tibi defuit hostis.

> What madness was this, O citizens? What this excessive freedom
> with the sword—to offer Latian blood to hated nations?
> and when proud Babylon was there to be stripped of Ausonian
> trophies and when Crassus wandered with his ghost unavenged,
> did you choose to wage wars which would bring no triumphs?
> A bitter thought—how much of earth and sea might have been won
> with this blood shed by the hands of fellow-citizens:
> where Titan rises, where the Night conceals the star,
> where midday blazes with its scorching regions,
> where winter, stiff and never eased by spring,
> binds with Scythian chill the icy Pontus!
> Beneath our yoke already the Seres and barbarian Araxes could
> have come and the race, if it exists, which knows Nile's birth.
> If your love of an abominable war is so great, Rome,
> only when you have brought the entire world beneath the laws of Latium,
> turn your hand against yourself; not yet are you without an enemy.[2]

Firstly, Rome has *furor*. *Furor* is a feature that, like *virtus*, may have positive or negative connotations, depending on whether it is directed outwards or inwards. When properly oriented, *furor* is a "fierce passion for war," but in a civil war it is madness (Narducci 2002: 31, 40n44).[3] Secondly, Rome is a mighty nation accustomed to victory, encapsulated in the expression *populus potens* (1.2–3).[4] Thirdly, Rome's way of relating with the other is through domination. The foreigners pass under the yoke (or should), are triumphed over, and are subject to Roman law (*sub iuga isset*, 1.19; 1.22).⁵ Finally, the narrator offers a glimpse of a hypothetical scenario that contrasts with the reality described in the opening verses. After this example of counter-factual history, the author moves to what he perceives as the consequences of the civil war and describes the utter ruin (physical but also social and moral) of the fatherland (1.24–9). Thus, right at the beginning of his poem, Lucan affirms that Rome is a powerful, imperialistic, and warlike nation accustomed to victory, and that she should have directed her passion for war externally.

There is an ideal (and Stoic) concept of order underpinning Lucan's world in disarray. The cosmos is an ordered, balanced entity and the laws of nature must be obeyed. Any individual or society who defies the natural order opens the door to internecine strife and puts the world at risk of total destruction (Lapidge 1979: 358–9; Bramble 1982: 537). But Lucan pushes the point further and exposes a universal "law," crucial to the understanding of the poem (Narducci 2002: 42): it is in the nature of things that "mighty structures collapse on to themselves: for the powers have set this limit to growth" (*in se magna ruunt: laetis hunc numina rebus / crescendi posuere modum*, 1.81–2). Thus, after having associated Rome's potential peak of might with the conquest of the entire world, Lucan now suggests that Rome had fallen under her own weight before reaching that peak. Civil war—just as cosmic conflagration (1.73–80)—may have been inevitable, but what is dreadful (as against universal law) is to wage civil war before having conquered the entire world.⁶

If fighting a foreign enemy would have prevented Rome from plunging into civil war, or at least delayed the course of events, it is worth emphasizing that in theory any enemy would have served said purpose, and Lucan mentions many, stating that Rome had never been short of rivals (1.8–24). Among the "hated nations" (*gentibus invisis*), however, the Parthians stand out. They are placed in an emphatic position and, while there is no stated reason for hating the Seres or the peoples dwelling along the Nile, Lucan provides a very good motive for loathing the Parthians. How could, Lucan asks, a powerful nation accustomed to victory tolerate Parthian arrogance (*superba*) and not retaliate after the humiliation suffered at Carrhae, which left the shade of Crassus wandering unavenged and the Roman standards in Babylon as trophies? As if shame were not enough, there is also impiety, for it is disgraceful and against religious duties to leave the corpse of Crassus unburied.⁷ It is evident that, at the beginning of the poem, Parthia is the "hated people" par excellence, the one that should have been conquered first and foremost. For Lucan this is a constant, valid during the age of Augustus as much as during the reign of Nero.

Power-politics, Geography, and Identity

Refusing to fight Parthia and waging an untimely civil war is not only disgraceful and against the laws of nature; it is also un-Roman. All the causes of the civil war singled out by Lucan (1.66–182) can be read as a reversal of elements that constitute Roman identity.

Firstly, the Triumvirate is a violation of the laws of the universe in that, by definition, absolute power cannot be shared (1.84–6); it is abhorrent because the division of absolute power between three people contrasts with the idea that Rome is a Republic and that each citizen should, like Cato, be the kind of man who labors "for the common good" (*in commune bonus*, 2.390). Furthermore, that Rome's collapse under her own weight is a consequence of the degeneration of Rome's moral character contrasts with the idea of continuous growth that a powerful nation is supposed to pursue.[8] Even fratricide, the paradigmatic image of civil war (1.95),[9] does not simply allude to the duality of Roman nature. Along with the *concordia discors* (1.98) of the first triumvirate, fratricide frames the period of Roman expansion and power when the Romans had managed, with difficulty (*male concordes*, 1.87), to abide by the universal law. It is rather the premature occurrence of the civil war that is against the nature of Rome and the universe (1.96–7).

These themes are revisited and developed at the predicted (see 1.678–88) climactic point of the poem. At Pharsalus (7.387–459), the potential damages of the civil war become real.[10] In a long passage that marks the definitive change in Rome's destiny and character, the poetic narrator laments the fall of Roman imperialism, with language that resonates with the idea that Rome may fall under her own weight.[11] Then he again contrasts foreign wars with civil war; he evokes violence as part of Roman nature once more and suggests that Pharsalus displaced Rome from the center of the world; he concludes his tirade by saying that freedom is lost, and the yoke is now over the Romans' neck (7.645, cf. 9.261; Bexley 2009: 464–9). The presence of a single tyrant makes madness and freedom mutually exclusive; while there were two, Pompey and Caesar, madness—in the form of struggle for power—and freedom were both possible. The consequence of Pharsalus is a trade-off: tyranny in exchange for peace.[12]

The Battle of Pharsalus also affects the power relationship between Rome and outsiders. First, in two speeches that insist on the opposition Roman/non-Roman (7.251–382), Caesar and Pompey say that Rome has the world at her disposal three times.[13] Then (7.420–5) Lucan's narrator claims that, after an unprecedented expansion, Emathia brought Rome's destiny of world power to an end (or even worse, a step back: *sed retro tua fata tulit*, 7.426). The world is now beyond Rome's control and Parthia is unpunished. Finally, Italy lies in ruins (7.387–419), Rome is empty, and—*horribile visu*—inhabited by foreigners. Thus, when freedom is lost, Rome changes, and so does her relationship with the foreigners. Internal peace and tyranny come with the forgoing of imperialism and *Romanitas*.

This change is detectable not only in the changes to Italy's human geography, but also in the way Romans and foreigners move in the geographical space. Every time Rome's way of relating with others is identified by domination over them, there are references to outwards movement. Of course, this is a platitude, but it is remarkable that each reference to expansion made by Lucan is either in the past or represents a hypothetical scenario that will never occur. For instance, the rather emphatic rhetorical question on the theme of *metus hostilis* that opens up Book 1 (1.8–20) draws attention to the fact that no foreign war will prevent the civil war from happening. In the episode of Caesar's looting of the

World Geography, Roman History, and the Failure to Incorporate Parthia

temple of Saturn, Lucan lists the peoples conquered by Rome from the center to the periphery, from the most ancient to the most recent (3.155–68). Pompey's campaigns are also good examples. To contrast these hypothetical or past movements, Lucan creates a crescendo of converging movements of peoples who, from outside the empire or from its extreme margins, descend from the periphery to the center.[14] Taken together, these movements constitute a four-step process that concludes with a complete reversal of the idea of *metus hostilis*.

In the first such movement (2.45–56), distraught citizens in Rome hope that enemies from areas beyond the limits of the empire could fall upon Rome and distract the generals from civil war (2.48–52).

> coniuret in arma
> mundus, Achaemeniis decurrant Medica Susis
> agmina, Massageten Scythicus non adliget Hister,
> fundat ab extremo flauos Aquilone Suebos
> Albis et indomitum Rheni caput.

> let the world league together
> for war: let the lines of Medes swoop down from Achaemenid
> Susa, let Scythian Danube not confine the Massagetae,
> let the Elbe and Rhine's unconquered head loose
> from furthest north the blond Suebi.

These chaotic, unreal, and ultimately impossible geographical representations, in which the Achaemenids take the place of the Parthians, the Massagetae dwell in the wrong area, and the contiguous Dacians and Getae seem to come from different directions, point to the likely impossibility of this scenario ever occurring (Fantham 1992: 89; Hunink 1992: 104–5).

In the second movement (2.234–325), Cato offers a vision that combines foreign peoples—so peripheral that they are unknown (*ignotae*)—and cosmic disaster.[15] Cato reverses the meteorological analogy of Brutus (2.267–73), who had compared the impassibility of the heavens and the gods with the turmoil of the earth, presenting instead the impassibility of the wise and the "hopes" in remote foreign enemies evoked by the Romans at 2.45–56. As a good Stoic, who conceives the world as a unique entity, and as a good Roman who considers the world as the Roman world, Cato draws a picture of civil war not as battles of citizens against citizens but as unknown people and kings falling onto Rome and as stars falling from the sky (2.289–95).[16]

> sidera quis mundumque uelit spectare cadentem
> expers ipse metus? quis, cum ruat arduus aether,
> terra labet mixto coeuntis pondere mundi,
> complossas tenuisse manus? gentesne furorem
> Hesperium ignotae Romanaque bella sequentur

diductique fretis alio sub sidere reges,
otia solus agam?

Who would wish to watch the stars and the universe collapsing,
free from fear himself? To fold the arms and keep them still
when ether rushes from on high and earth shudders
beneath the weight of the condensing universe? Shall I alone live
in peace if unknown races and kings beneath another sky,
separated by the sea, comply with the frenzy
of Hesperia and with Roman wars?

The two alternative manners in which Roman *furor* manifests compound the geography of heaven and earth, and thus blur the distinction between foreign and civil wars.

In the third movement, Pompey orders his son Gnaeus to "probe the world's remotest parts" (*mundi iubeo temptare recessus*, 2.632) and intends to do exactly what Cato was envisaging and dreading. In fact, Pompey plans to rouse the entire conquered world (*totoque urbes agitabis in orbe / perdomitas*, 2.642–3), stir up Egypt, and even Parthia (*Euphraten Nilumque move*, 2.633). When peoples from all around the eastern part of the empire finally begin to converge on Pharsalus (3.169–297), the idea of foreign wars as a viable way out of the civil war is reversed for good.

To sum up, the whole world, should (and could) have been conquered. Facing the choice between foreign wars and "wars which would bring no triumphs" (1.12), the Romans chose (*placuit*) the second option. The main consequences were tyranny and peace after an immense and pointless bloodshed, a world upside-down, and also the end of expansion and a permanent alteration of the relationship with the foreigner. On the one hand, this creates confusion between the internal and external, symbolized by the movements of foreigners toward Rome; on the other, it brings about cosmic chaos due to Rome's failure to pursue her natural (or necessary) expansion. Moreover, since freedom and the ability to exert influence on other peoples are essential components of the Roman character, the new relationship between Rome and the rest of the world alters Roman identity. A colossal change has happened, of which Rome is both instigator and affected party. How does this momentous change, which involves the whole world, affect Parthia's position and reflect Nero's Parthian politics?

Parthia

Lucan presents Parthia uniquely among the foreign nations as an absent, passive foreign enemy. Parthia plays a part in emphasizing the change that Rome has undergone, amplifying the fading of Rome's might. Lucan suggests as much in several passages. In contrast with the mad frenzy of the Romans, the Parthians, like other nations, will attend the spectacle of Roman bloodshed. When Crassus is defeated, the Parthians are unaware of the consequences that they are provoking.[17] In Book 3, however, when the eastern allies of Pompey gather, Lucan becomes much more explicit. At 3.169–297, peoples from the east leave their lands and move toward Pharsalus. Here, with a list of lands and nations 226 lines long, Lucan gives free rein to his fondness for geographical catalogues. The passage contains various digressions, but I would like to focus on the fact that almost every people mentioned is located alongside a river or the sea. Why this insistence on waters? Epic tradition aside, it creates a parallel between the armies moving toward Thessaly and the waters: peoples run like rivers to Pharsalus. These waters, like the allies of Pompey, eventually meet.[18] In fact, we see rivers joining (Marsya and Maeander, 3.208–9; Hydaspes and Indus, 3.236), rivers entering the sea, rivers exchanging fauna (Strymon and Nile, 3.199–200), and even seas flowing into other seas (Maeotis and Pontus, and the Mediterranean and Ocean, 3.277–9). However, when they meet, these waterbodies refuse to amalgamate. Thus, the Hister does not mix with the sea (3.202–3); the rivers Hydaspes and Indus mix, but the latter "does not realize" (*non sentit*) that; the "straight-descending" (*rectis descendens*) Marsya flows into the Maeander, yet the latter's course is unaffected and keeps "wandering" (*errantes*). And then Lucan reinforces the point: not only do the streams (of water and of people) not mix and combine, but they in fact have a partitioning effect on the land. For instance, Lydia is cleaved by the river Hermus, and Phasis cuts Colchis as it flows through it (*secat*, 3.210 and 3.271). The Tanais separates two continents (*dirimens*, 3.275); eastern lands are variously divided into parts by rivers (e.g., Colchis, 3.271), often more than one; and entire regions are isolated by water.[19] Finally, wide portions of lands are left deserted and empty (3.173, 177, 180, 197, 205, 225, 246). As in another catalogue of rivers (at 6.333–94), the hydrological metaphor may allude to the chaos that civil war represents (Masters 1992: 163–78). There may also be Stoic-cosmologic overtones: by becoming in effect "rivers," foreign peoples become like water and produce a destabilization or *confusio* in the balance of the elements.[20] More interesting is that this hydrological metaphor may symbolize the impossibility not only of Pompey's army to find cohesion (made furthermore explicit by the references to Xerxes, Cyrus, and Agamemnon, and their mixed armies) but also of the two parties (Caesar and Pompey) to blend. In this hydrological confusion, there is one exception: Persia and her rivers (3.256–63):

> quaque caput rapido tollit cum Tigride magnus
> Euphrates, quos non diuersis fontibus edit
> Persis, et incertum, tellus si misceat amnes,
> quod potius sit nomen aquis. sed sparsus in agros
> fertilis Euphrates Phariae uice fungitur undae;
> at Tigrim subito tellus absorbet hiatu
> occultosque tegit cursus rursusque renatum
> fonte nouo flumen pelagi non abnegat undis.

> And where great Euphrates and mighty Tigris raise
> their heads, rivers sent forth by Persia from springs
> not far apart: if the earth mixed them, it is uncertain
> which name the waters would bear. But fertile Euphrates

floods over fields like the Egyptian waters,
while the earth with a sudden chasm swallows up Tigris
and covers his secret course, but does not withhold
from the sea's waves the river, which is born again from a new source.

Important to note here is that the land (*tellus*) of Persia produces the two rivers and, by immediately absorbing the Tigris underground while the Euphrates diffuses over the land, makes sure that they do not mix.[21] The land keeps the rivers separated and is not separated by them. Coming after such an elaborate paradox, in which all the possible variants of obstinate resistance to amalgamation are explored, and after water seems to get the upper hand over dry land, the geographical metaphor with its Stoic-cosmological associations emphasizes Parthia's place as the one land that does not join either Rome or Pompey. Lucan contrasts Roman "fluvial chaos" with the neat separation and order represented by Parthian rivers. Since there is a constant exchange between geography and politics in Lucan, the metaphor therefore becomes an introduction to the point that follows, where the poet himself gives us the key to interpreting the passage: "The warlike Parthians held a neutral position, content to have made the rivals two in number" (*inter Caesareas acies diuersaque signa / pugnaces dubium Parthi tenuere fauorem / contenti fecisse duos*, 3.264–6). This is a conscious and strategic decision: when the Parthians act, they do not know what they are doing; when they do not act, they know well what they are doing.

The non-participation of Parthia contradicts the statement that the whole world was present to be conquered at Pharsalus (3.295). It also emphasizes her difference from the other foreigners,[22] creates a stark contrast between Roman frenzy and Parthian order, and puts all the previous references in perspective. Lucan has modeled Parthia into a very well-defined entity, for she is much more than a foreign nation that deserves to be punished. She can harm Roman interests and still go unpunished, and, even more remarkably, she can be indifferent to a war that is so momentous that it threatens to subvert the world order. Since the only relationship that Rome can have with foreigners is to dominate them, Parthia becomes a symbol of Rome's impotence and loss of expanding momentum. It is no coincidence that Pompey's repeated attempts to involve the Parthians in the war against Caesar did not yield any result.

The first consequence of Rome's impotence is that the East is more difficult to penetrate. For example, when Pompey sends Deiotarus east in Book 8, he gives him an itinerary of remote destinations, often vague in their definition, emphasizing their distance and alterity (8.213–17; 222–5; cf. Mayer 1981: 191):

Eoam temptare fidem populosque bibentis
Euphraten et adhuc securum a Caesare Tigrim.
ne pigeat Magno quaerentem fata remotas
Medorum penetrare domos Scythicosque recessus
et totum mutare diem,

...

> si uos, o Parthi, peterem cum Caspia claustra
> et sequerer duros aeterni Martis Alanos,
> passus Achaemeniis late decurrere campis
> in tutam trepidos numquam Babylona coegi.

> [It remains] to test the loyalty of the east and of the peoples who drink
> Euphrates and Tigris, still untouched by Caesar.
> As you seek success for Magnus, do not be loath to enter
> the distant homes of the Medes and Scythian remoteness,
> to change your clime entirely,
> . . .
> O Parthians, do this if, when I headed for the Caspian Gates and chased
> the hardy ever-warring Alani, I ever let you freely
> race across Achaemenid plains and never drove you
> trembling into Babylon's safety.

Lexical choices produce a strong contrast between the swiftness and easiness with which Pompey has swept through Asia (*petere, sequere, decurrere*) and the difficulties that Deiotarus will encounter (*penetrare, totum mutare*). Note also that here the Euphrates divides the world, while at 2.633 Euphrates was a place that the name and fame of Pompey had reached (and crossed). The Euphrates at 3.259–60 is *sparsos in agros* (diffused over the land), an almost opposite image to the *ingentem gurgite* (8.290, a "great stream" but also a "whirlpool"); Euphrates was less of a limit before (cf. Arnaud 1993; Lerouge 2007: 201–9). Lucan thus portrays Parthia as the most alien of the eastern lands, a concept reiterated in Pompey's speech at Syhedris (8.290–4):

> diuidit Euphrates ingentem gurgite mundum
> Caspiaque inmensos seducunt claustra recessus,
> et polus Assyrias alter noctesque diesque
> uertit, et abruptum est nostro mare discolor unda
> Oceanusque suus.

> Euphrates with his flood cuts off an enormous world;
> the Caspian Gates set apart immensurable retreats;
> a different sky revolves Assyrian nights and days;
> their sea of other-coloured wave is separated from ours;
> they have an Ocean of their own.

Eventually, Lucan will drive this process to extreme consequences, and offer a new division of the world in the two continents of Eurafrica and Asia (9.411–13; cf. Pogorzelski 2011: 164–5).

There is only one actor in all this spectacle: Rome. She has lost her centrality in the universe and has been deprived of her power by her tyrant-generals. Parthia is *aliter mundus*, and the rest of the east is beyond Rome's reach forever. This is not a cold war scenario with two opposing powers, but a very explicit symbol of the loss of a global leadership that was lost the instant Rome decided not to fight Parthia (7.427–31):

> hac luce cruenta
> effectum, ut Latios non horreat India fasces,
> nec uetitos errare Dahas in moenia ducat
> Sarmaticumque premat succinctus consul aratrum,
> quod semper saeuas debet tibi Parthia poenas.

> Thanks to that bloody day
> India does not tremble at the Rods of Latium,
> the girded consul does not lead the Dahae, forbidden to wander,
> inside city-walls or lean on a Sarmatian plough,
> and Parthia owes you a savage retribution still and for ever.

In a poem that is openly hostile to tyranny and the Caesars (Ahl 1976: 35–47; Narducci 2002: 7–14), if Parthia plays such a relevant role, how should the contemporary encroachment of Nero in the east be judged? Was he resolving the situation or increasing the damage? There are various ways to approach this issue. One is to search for allusions to places or events, contextualize them, and draw possible conclusions (Pogorzelski 2011). However, considering Lucan's fondness for re-elaborating previous poetic and historical material, it may be of some interest to explore Nero's relationship with Parthia in the poem through the lens of engagement with Horace, the poet who—more than any other—insisted on the Parthian "problem" between 30 and 20 BCE.[23] In Book 1, when Lucan enumerates the causes and consequences of the civil war, he presents several parallels between *Epodes* 7 and 9 and the early *Odes*, especially 1.2 (Gros 2013: 95–101; cf. Roche 2009: 24–5, 114). He shares the concerns of Horace for the havoc caused by the civil wars, but when he reflects on the effects of Pharsalus (7.385–459), Lucan returns to Horace to make a pessimistic re-evaluation of his later poems (especially the *Roman Odes*), where Horace mitigated his indictment of the civil wars and associated the conquest of Parthia to the renewal of Roman *mores* and *pietas*.[24]

One example should suffice. In 7.405–31, Lucan confronts *Ode* 3.5, the so-called *Regulus Ode*.[25] This *Carmen* is possibly the most representative of the way Horace places Roman identity in relation to the Parthian enemy. In this poem, Horace deplores that the soldiers captured at Carrhae are now serving in the army of the Parthian king, have adopted the customs of the enemy, and have even married barbarian wives (*Carm.* 3.5–12). He suggests that all of this represents a stain not only on the individuals involved but also on Rome in her entirety, offering as a counterpoint the exemplum of Regulus as a model of true Roman behavior with his determination and unbending resoluteness against foreign enemies. If Augustus conquers Parthia and maintains Roman *mores*, the poet argues, he will become a god on earth as Jupiter is a god in the heavens and, it is implied, he will rule the entire world.[26]

World Geography, Roman History, and the Failure to Incorporate Parthia

Lucan flips the point made by the Augustan poet: although Rome had almost conquered the entire world, Pharsalus turned back the clock. He adds that Rome is filled with the filth (*faece*) of the world (7.405), that the enemy does not see examples of Roman behavior (7.427-30), and that Parthia is unpunished (7.431). Surely, Horace is not that crude, and the *Ode* plays on ambiguity generated by the juxtapositions of opposites (Oliensis 1998: 140-5). But Lucan forthrightly undermines the very idea that underpins Horace's poem in two ways. First, he compares the fate of the Romans with that of the Persians, who always had a tyrant, and concludes that they are similar; the latter, however, are more fortunate because they cannot bemoan missing the freedom they never experienced (7.443-4).[27] This consideration defies Horace's assumption that there is a clear degradation in status by being or becoming "Persianized" (*Carm.* 3.5.5-13). Significantly, Lucan also removes Caesar—who according to Horace would have been the rescuer of Rome, the avenger, the godlike ruler of the world—from the picture and instead censures his fellow citizens for making humans into gods and worshiping them.[28]

Lucan's shift from a position in which he shared Horace's concerns (in Book 1) to dissociation (in Book 7), implies that nothing that Horace has urged, praised, or suggested has been accomplished, and that there is no satisfaction with the *pax Augusta*. It is therefore significant that Lucan avoids referring to any of the *Odes* of the fourth book of Horace, the book in which the fear of Parthia disappears (*Carm.* 4.5.25-7), the return of the *insigna* is celebrated (*Carm.* 4.15.6-8), and the Medes and other barbarians are afraid of Augustus (*Carm.* 4.14).[29] By retrojecting to the time of Julius Caesar the alternative offered by Horace to Augustus (be *pius*, conquer Parthia, be a good Roman, and you will become a god) and then dismissing it, Lucan questions Horace's conciliatory position on Augustus' policy and exposes the incongruity of the entire Parthian settlement.[30] This is not simply a confrontation on a literary level in order to intensify an idea, nor is it a critique of the handling of foreign affairs after Carrhae. By ignoring the evolution of Horace's take on Parthia, Lucan ignores the evolution of the *princeps* (from Octavian, the general embroiled in civil war, to Augustus, the man who restored the Republic) and produces a historical analysis of not so much the events as the cultural history of Rome's relationship with the Arsacids. Since the scenario proposed at the beginning of the poem was a moral alternative based on war (civil versus Parthian War, evil versus good war), the choice of the Augustan settlement with Parthia is a foil, against which the poet's choice to judge the degeneration of Rome is de facto a position of strong historical revisionism with important contemporary implications for Lucan's Neronian age.

In fact, the Parthian settlement of 20 BCE was probably the most advertised settlement of Roman early imperial history and established the blueprint for all of Augustus' successors, among whom Nero is surely his most enthusiastic imitator.[31] Despite some fluctuations, Nero's strategy in the east followed the Augustan prototype, avoiding the clash with Parthia and focusing on the control over Armenia by means of a friendly king. In 55-56 CE, when the Parthian king Vologases delivered some hostages, Nero—like Augustus (Dio Cass. 51.20.1-4)—celebrated his second imperial salutation but refused more extravagant honors (Tac., *Ann.* 13.8-9; Champlin 2003: 68-9, 138-40). In 57 CE, around the time he received two more salutations for successes in Armenia (Tac., *Ann.* 41.4), he celebrated a *naumachia* modeled on the sea battle staged by Augustus in 2 CE (Suet., *Nero* 12, Dio Cass. 61.9.6). Finally, the closure of the doors of the temple of Janus (RIC I² Nero 283) and the episode of Tiridates' coronation, the culmination of the *Aurea Aetas* (Champlin 2003: 126–7, 140–1), confirm that like his great-great-grandfather, Nero built an image of prosperity and global supremacy (also) on the skillful manipulation of the idea of a diplomatically subdued Parthia. If Nero's Parthian politics were modeled on the Augustan precedent, then it is natural to think that when he speaks of Augustus Lucan is also nodding to Nero. Unfortunately, there is no hard evidence for this. The only place where Nero is mentioned, his apotheosis (1.33–66), does not explicitly refer to Parthia.[32] There are, however, some details in this passage that point to the historical revisionism mentioned above.

Firstly, Lucan alludes to some areas of the east that are related to Nero's Parthian Wars (1.19–20; cf. Pogorzelski 2011: 150–3). Secondly, Lucan seems to problematize Nero's relationship with Augustus by suggesting, for example, that Nero would ride Apollo's chariot as a new Phaethon without provoking any damage (1.45–50). The choice to place Nero in the unusual solar role of the calamitous Phaethon instead of the god of balance Apollo or his counterpart Helios/Sol introduces an unexpected and ambiguous variation on the Augustan model that resonates sinisterly next to the allusion to the damage Nero could cause by choosing the wrong area of the sky.[33] More interesting is the reinterpretation of Horace's *Carmina* 3.4 and 3.5, an anticipation of the reversal of those poems' themes that will occur in Book 7 (Paschalis 1982: 342–6). At the beginning of the invocation to the emperor, Lucan suggests that Nero (and also Augustus, by associating civil war and Gigantomachy as Horace had done in *Ode* 3.4.37–80) is the consequence of the civil war (1.44–5). Then he hints that the fight between the gods and the Giants is itself a form of civil war (1.34–6, again reversing Horace so that the problematic winner is the evil, fierce one). Subsequently, he suggests that the civil war gave the emperors the possibility of becoming gods (1.45–65, another reversal of Horace's point). Thus, to put it bluntly, Lucan declares that the blood shed by the Romans has not acquired lands but rather emperors who fight civil wars and make themselves gods; "crimes" and "the unspeakable" (*scelera* and *nefas*) are well worth it if their upshot is that there are rulers like Nero, a man of such greatness that he will be (and for some already is) a god (Feeney 1991: 286–301).[34] But a few lines below, when he announces the self-implosion of Rome (1.81–2), Lucan adapts Horace once again (*Carm.* 3.4.65: *vis consili expers mole ruit sua*).[35] The reader, at this point, may be prompted to add what Horace says (*Carm.* 3.4.65–8) and Lucan omits: "might without wisdom" (*vis consili expers*) falls under its weight, but the gods cultivate might tempered by wisdom (*vim temperatam di quoque provehunt*) and hate those who perform "the unspeakable" (*nefas*).[36] Regardless of whether the words on Nero are ironic or sincere, or when the panegyric was written in the composition process, we are still quite far from the criticism of deified emperors of Book 7. At the same time, we are also a far cry from Horace's image of the *princeps* as a way out from the crisis and, by implication, as the ruler of a pacified world. Finally, a compelling suggestion comes from the reading of lines 1.53–7, where Lucan acknowledges the transformation of Rome from a powerful entity into one that reflects the power of the emperor. Rome can be the center only insofar as the emperor hovers over her (Bexley 2009: 460).[37] And yet this center is not the center of the world, because the deified Nero can only move along the meridian (1.53–4), and Parthia is always an eastern land, even when she is *aliter orbis*.

Lucan is surely problematizing Nero's eastern policy. But rather than alluding to possible or faked victories, he more subtly works on two levels. Firstly, by acknowledging the transformation of Rome from a powerful entity into one that reflects the power of the emperor, he anticipates the idea that Rome has changed her identity. By moving Parthia out of the deified Nero's sphere of action, Lucan alludes to her aloofness and to the pointlessness of any attempt to conquer her. Secondly, by engaging with Horace, he anticipates the undermining of the foundation of the Julio-Claudian policy toward Parthia. Lucan instills in the reader's mind the idea that Nero and Augustus were both trying to use Parthia to justify their right to rule and dominate the world. They are not the solution, however, just part of the problem: a theme that he develops in Book 8.

Lentulus and Pompey

The loose strands come together in Book 8 where, once the Roman world has shrunk, Parthia's importance expands and becomes the focus of two lengthy speeches. Pompey, defeated and on the run, calls a meeting where the prerogative is to establish the best course of action. Pompey suggests fleeing to Parthia where (he hopes) he could win the king over to his cause (8.262–327); Lentulus replies (8.331–453) and refutes his general's argument point by point (Ahl 1976: 170–3; Mayer 1981: 118–41; Bartsch 1997: 82–7; Narducci 2002: 329–31).

The episode is a rhetorical exercise, but it is also a meditation on Parthia's position in relation to Rome. The two speeches give a similar and rather commonplace description of Parthians seen from the Roman perspective, although interpreted from two diametrically opposed angles (Lerouge 2007: 37, 344–5). They also reflect the two Augustan and post-Augustan representations of the Arsacids: the barbarian who is weak due to effeminacy and the barbarian who is powerful due to being untouched by civilization. For Pompey, as for Trogus and Strabo, the Parthians are *aliter mundus*, the other extreme of the world, but with a similar destiny (*fatum*) and somewhat similar might to Rome; an alternative, so to speak, similar because opposite.[38] For Lentulus, who represents the official position, they are the "other," totally opposite and different. They are barbarian, weak and effeminate, incestuous and debauched—definitely not an alternative, and therefore incompatible. As such, they can only be enemies who must be crushed.[39]

Lucan's attitude is interesting, however: he evidently cannot approve of Pompey's plan to find an agreement with the Arsacids because in addition to their being unreliable (8.306–12) they go against everything that he has identified as Roman. In fact, Pompey not only motivates his strategy with considerations on Parthians' military power, invincibility

(8.299–302), and favor of the gods (8.308), but he also dares to claim that he bestowed a benefit on the Parthians by saving them from the Romans' rightful revenge after Carrhae (8.233–4). As if this were not blameful enough, he believes that Rome and Babylon can compete for the same goals, that Rome does not exist anymore, and, absurd as it may be, that he can remake Rome with Parthian help. Lastly, he even cites Marius, whom Lucan has already censured at 2.68–133, as a precedent for his planned return to Rome at the head of a barbarian army (8.269–71; Ahl 1976: 103–7). Pompey has lost his points of reference and his Roman identity (Ahl 1976: 170; Narducci 2002: 94–100; Casamento 2016). He can grasp the geographical consequences but not the historical and political meaning of Pharsalus.

If Lucan disapproves of Pompey's opinion, he does not fully agree with his opponent's rebuttal either. Lentulus' *suasoria* ends with the expected admonishment that Parthia should be attacked and annihilated (8.420–30). Then Lentulus restates the ideas exposed by Lucan in the first lines of the poem, where the poet claimed that Crassus should have been avenged immediately after Carrhae (1.11–12), and explicitly reproaches Pompey for failing to do so (8.423–6). The passage deliberately brings the reader back to the argument enunciated at 1.10–30 and to the crucial lines of Book 7 mentioned above (7.407–59). The difference is that, unlike Lucan, Lentulus still urges that a Parthian triumph be celebrated as soon as possible, even if led by the much-hated Caesar. He does not see the difference between attacking the Parthians before or after Pharsalus, and believes triumphs are still possible. He does not see that the ghost of Crassus will (at least in the *Bellum Civile*) remain unavenged, so that it could stand as a testimonial to the "unresolved issues of the past" (Bernstein 2011: 279). He, as Pompey, does not realize that Rome has changed, and that her relationship with the outside world has changed for good (7.389–408; cf. Narducci 2002: 34).

In these paired speeches, Lucan ties together his meditations on imperialism and identity, polemically framing the diatribe in terms analogous to the Julio-Claudian representation of the Parthians. The rigidity of this polarity, seen in the fact that neither Pompey nor Lentulus gets it right in their analysis, demonstrates the futility of all Roman attitudes toward Parthia.[40] Lucan extricates himself from any considerations on how to handle the Parthian issue.

Claiming that a Parthian War is useless challenges the opinions of all those who still believe in the possibility of triumphs and amounts to a rejection of the ambitions of the ruler. To suggest after 63 CE that death is the only way out of the impasse (as the end of Pompey and Cato demonstrate) and that both fighting and making peace with Parthia is pointless indicates more than a critical attitude toward Caesarism. I wonder whether these passages may perhaps be read as a message to the Pisonian conspirators to turn their attention inwards and join a general rebellion.[41]

Conclusion

Before and to a greater extent after Pharsalus, every contact with the foreigner brings about the issue of identity. Cato does not escape the Libyan ordeal unscathed but remains an example of Roman firmness (Seo 2011). Egypt contaminates Rome, but at least is conquered. Parthia is instead a perpetual memento of Rome's failure and a symbol of Rome's change. Her place and role have been carefully crafted by the poet to this end. Moreover, Lucan employs all his geographical expertise to demonstrate that Rome has lost her power to impose her will on the enemy, has lost leadership, and is often impotent in the face of the foreigner; she has lost centrality and control over the world or at least a significant part of it. Thus, the place of the eastern foe transcends simple contemporary discourse, for Parthia encapsulates the consequences of the actions of the past, the incurable laceration that they provoked, and the deadlock into which they led Rome.

Lucan also engages with all the variants of the historical memory of the Parthian settlement and concludes that Rome has changed in moral, religious, and military terms, and there is thus no right way to deal with the Parthians, and that there is no *custode rerum Caesare* (Hor., *Carm.* 4.15.17, "Caesar guardian of human affairs") at the head of the state, but a tyrant.[42] The revisionism of Horace's and Augustus' positions, the difficulty of the protagonists in deciphering the meaning of Pharsalus, and the permanence of the consequences of a choice to fight a civil rather than a foreign war intensify Lucan's scathing critique of the imperial model and expose the futility of any discussion—past and present—on the relationship with Parthia, because whatever foreign policy is adopted will bring about negative consequences. Peace with the enemy can exist only if Rome is an empire ruled by a tyrant. A war against Parthia is not going to bring back the *populus potens* and is only to the benefit of the master (cf. 10.147).

Notes

1. Literature on Roman imperialism is vast: Brunt (1990: 287–323) discusses some imperial ideologies. A short introduction that also touches upon contemporary approaches to empire in Mattingly (2011: 2–42). For a list of recent contributions: Eckstein (2008: 5n5 and n7). Acknowledgments: I am indebted to Prof. Annalisa Marzano, Dr. Luke Houghton, and Dr. Andreas Gavrielatos, whose wise advice and insightful criticism greatly improved this chapter. I would like to express my gratitude to the organizers of the conference and the participants for the comments made on that occasion. I am also grateful to the anonymous reviewers and the editors for many helpful suggestions. I take full responsibility for errors and shortcomings.
2. Lucan's translations are from Braund (1992); the Latin is Housman's (1950) except at 1.16 (*oris* for *horis*; cf. Shackleton-Bailey 1988). Horace's translations are from Rudd (2004).
3. On the power of *furor*, cf. Verg., *Aen.* 1.294–6, 8.219–20, and 8.494. In Lucan, Caesar (7.551, 7.557), Egypt (10.147), and Italy (2.292–3) have *furor*; Pompey comes very close (8.266–7, cf. Ahl 1976: 172–3). On the ambivalence of *virtus*, see 6.147–8 with Ahl (1976: 117) and Sklenář (2003: 101–51).
4. *Populus potens* is repeated four times in Book 1 (1.2, 1.83, 1.109, and 1.159; here we are clearly in the moment of Rome's full power). It always appears in the context of a comment of the narrator and refers to the Roman people at large. Afterwards, the Romans as a "powerful people" tend to fade into the background and are substituted by a servile people, while individuals and foreign nations become more and more prominent (Roche 2009: 103).

5. For the image of the yoke and the language of domination, see Lavan (2013: 73–123). More examples: 2.642–4, 8.229–30, and 7.387–419.

6. Lucan's position in respect to Stoic orthodoxy is elusive, but it is evident that he makes use of Stoic language and imagery to reinforce his points (Lapidge 1979; Most 1989: 2053–7; Sklenář 2003: 1–12).

7. Crassus' unburied body is a symbol of guilt. For more examples of abuse of cadavers, see Erictho (6.624–41), Sulla (2.157–9), and Caesar (7.786–99 *passim*).

8. This is a well-established topos of moralizing history already identified as a threat to Rome's identity and connected with change in the Roman attitudes and *mores* by Sallust (*Cat.* 10–11) and Livy (*praef.* 4, 1.19.4, 30.44.8, and 34.30.3).

9. Jal (1963: 407–8). Cf.: Hor., *Epod.* 7.17–19 with Wagenvoort (1956: 169–83).

10. Parallels between Book 1 and Book 7 are developed in Roche (2009: 17–19) and Lanzarone (2016: 11n28). On the themes of the Book 7 and the significance of Pharsalus, see Lanzarone (2016: 4–7).

11. Luc. 7.419–20: *tibi, Roma, ruentis / ostendat quam magna cadas* (to show you in your fall, Rome, how mighty was your fall), cf. 1.72 and 1.81.

12. Luc. 7.695–6: *par quod semper habemus / libertas et Caesar* ("that pair of rivals always with us—Liberty and Caesar"), cf. 1.670–2. Peace is intended here primarily as absence of civil war. For the notion that civil war and tyranny are mutually exclusive cf. 7.645–6, 1.670, and 1.84–6. See also Narducci (2002: 94, 110–11).

13. Pompey: 7.363; Caesar: 7.250; 7.269–70; 7.278.

14. On Pharsalus as a new center, see Bexley (2009: 464–9); on geography in Lucan as symbol of distortion of the relationship between center and periphery, cf. Myers (2011).

15. On the passage Ahl (1976: 237–47); Narducci (2002: 370–404).

16. See Fantham (1992: 132) with an emphasis on *ekpyrosis*; Salemme (1999: 160) emphasizes Rome as the universe. The position of Cato as a Stoic wise man (e.g., Ahl 1976: 247) is not immune from debate, but coherence may well not be Lucan's main concern; cf. Narducci (2002: 375–83 and 395–404).

17. See Luc. 1.106–7: *plus illa uobis acie, quam creditis, actum est, / Arsacidae* (more by that battle you achieved than you suppose, / sons of Arsaces).

18. On Lucan's interest in intersecting waters, in particular as a symbol of the generals mustering their armies and loss of identity, cf. Walde (2007: 35–7).

19. The river Cephisos surrounds (*ambit*) Boeotia (3.174–5), the Bactros and Hircania enclose (*includit*) the Scythians (3.266–7), the island of Peucen is touched by sea-water on one side and by river-water on the other (3.201–2).

20. Cf. 4.126. Note the use of *linquo* (3.177, 180, 197, 246) which recalls, by assonance, *liquo* and *liqueo*, verbs associated to fluidity. On *confusio* of the order of the cosmos and of waters, see Sen., *QNat.* 3.27–30. On the Stoic flavor of these allusions, see Lapidge (1979).

21. Compare the beneficent effect of the diffused Euphrates with the Tiber (2.214–18).

22. This is especially so considering that among the *clientes* that Pompey wishes to summon, the first to be mentioned are the Parthians (2.632–3).

23. On Lucan as a historian, cf. Servius (on *Aeneid* 1.382); cf. Ahl (1976: 70–1); Gowing (2005: 96). On the Parthians in Horace, see Seager (1980); Sonnabend (1986: 197–227).

24. For example: 7.438, 7.387–419, and 7.419–31. See Lanzarone (2016: 348, 356).

25. Compare Luc. 7.447 *mentimur regnare Iouem* (we lie that Jupiter is king) and Hor., *Carm.* 3.5.1–2 *credidimus Iovem / regnare*. See Feeney (1991: 282n137) and Lanzarone (2016: 368–9). On *Carm.* 3.5 in general, see Nisbet and Rudd (2004: 79–96) with bibliography.
26. On Augustan ideology in Horace's *Odes*, see, e.g., La Penna (1963: 78–104); Putnam (1993). On the divinization of the emperor, see Citroni (2015).
27. On freedom as constituent of *Romanitas* and its meaning when granted to an ally, see Badian (1958: 69–75); Gruen (1984: 176–84); Arena (2012: 73); Lavan (2013: 75–123).
28. A similar set of considerations applies, for example, to *Carm.* 3.3 (Groß 2013: 166–9).
29. On foreigners fearing Augustus, cf. Hor., *Epist.* 2.1.112, *Carm. saec.* 53–6.
30. Probably Augustus' claims of Roman dominance over Parthia were (also) aimed at removing, or at least at taking the edge off, the memory of the civil war he had been the protagonist of (Gowing 2005: 17–20). This adds another layer of significance to Lucan's revisionism.
31. Suet. *Ner.* 10.1, cf. Champlin (2003: 138–44); Braund (2013: 83–101).
32. For a survey on the literature on the passage, see Nelis (2011).
33. On Nero as Apollo or Sol, see Champlin (2003: 112–32); on the worrying character of the simile cf. Hinds (1987: 26–9), contra: Champlin (2003: 133–5).
34. On the internal inconsistencies of the praise of Nero, see Holmes (1999: 76 *passim*).
35. To make sure the reader grasps the idea, he even strategically anticipates the point (*nec se Roma ferens*, 1.72; cf. Hor., *Epod.* 16.2).
36. For more problematization of the Augustan model, cf. Fratantuono (2012: 10–11).
37. Other possible readings in Holmes (1999: 78); Pogorzelski (2011: 152).
38. See the portrayals in Just. 41.1.1, Strabo 11.92, Manilius 4.674–5. This idea—apparently at odds with the official position—may have had the support of Augustus; cf. Sonnabend (1986: 209–10); Lerouge (2007: 122).
39. E.g., Aug., *RG* 29; Verg., *Aen.* 8.727; Hor., *Carm.* 1.38 and 2.8.18–23; Prop. 2.10.13–14; cf. Paratore (1966: 505–58); Sonnabend (1986: 172, 280–2).
40. On the ambiguity of the Roman perception of Parthia, cf. Schneider (2007).
41. On the dates of composition, see Fantham (2013: 13–14), with bibliography. Marti (1945: 375–6) has suggested that a series of passages from Book 6 to Book 9 may be an appeal to insurrection. One may also consider Caesar's (failed) *imitatio Alexandri* in Book 10 as an allusion to Nero (Cresci Marrone 1983: 88–9; Luisi 1983–4: 119; Sullivan 1985: 148). If so, it is very tempting to read the words of Acoreus politically (Manolaraki 2011, 154 and 154n2) as a message to Lucan's fellow conspirators announcing the imminent downfall of the tyrant.
42. On the apotheosis of Caesar in Horace, cf. La Penna (1963: 86–8, 104–6).

References

Ahl, F. (1976), *Lucan: An Introduction*, Ithaca, NY: Cornell University Press.
Arena, V. (2012), *Libertas and the Practice of Politics in the Late Roman Republic*, Cambridge: Cambridge University Press.
Arnaud, P. (1993), "Frontière et Manipulation Géographique: Lucain, les Parthes et les Antipodes," in Y. Roman (ed.), *La Frontière. Séminaire de Recherche sous la Direction d'Yves Roman*, 45–56, Lyon: Maison de l'Orient et de la Méditerranée Jean Pouilloux.

Badian, E. (1958), *Foreign Clientelae (264–70 B.C.)*, Oxford: Clarendon Press.
Bartsch, S. (1997), *Ideology in Cold Blood: A Reading of Lucan's Civil War*, Cambridge, MA: Harvard University Press.
Bernstein, N. W. (2011), "The Dead and Their Ghosts in the *Bellum Civile*," in P. Asso (ed.), *Brill's Companion to Lucan*, 257–79, Leiden: Brill.
Bexley, E. M. (2009), "Replacing Rome: Geographic and Political Centrality in Lucan's *Pharsalia*," *CPh*, 104 (4): 459–75.
Bramble, J. (1982), "Lucan," in E. Kenney and W. Clausen (eds.), *The Cambridge History of Classical Literature,* 533–57, Cambridge: Cambridge University Press.
Braund D. (2013), "Apollo in Arms: Nero at the Frontier," in E. Buckley and M. Dinter (eds.) *A Companion to the Neronian Age,* Chichester: John Wiley & Sons, 83–101.
Braund, S. M. (1992), *Lucanus. Civil War*, Oxford: Clarendon Press.
Brunt, P. A. (1990), *Roman Imperial Themes*, Oxford: Clarendon Press.
Casamento, A. (2016), "Ripensare lo Straniero. Lesbii e Parti nell'Ottavo Libro del *Bellum Ciuile* di Lucano," in F. Galtier and R. Poignault (eds.), *Présence de Lucain*, 33–54, Clermont-Ferrand: Centre de Recherches A. Piganiol.
Champlin, E. (2003), *Nero,* Cambridge, MA: Belknap Press.
Citroni, M. (2015), "Autocrazia e Divinità: la Rappresentazione di Augusto e degli Imperatori del Primo Secolo nella Letteratura Contemporanea," in J.-L. Ferrary and J. Scheid (eds.), *Il Princeps Romano: Autocrate o Magistrato? Fattori Giuridici e Fattori Sociali del Potere Imperiale da Augusto a Commodo*, 239–91, Pavia: IUSS Press.
Cresci-Marrone, G. (1983), "Alessandro in Età Neroniana *Victor* o *Praedo*?," *AIV,* 142, 75–93.
Eckstein, A. M. (2008), *Rome Enters the Greek East: From Anarchy to Hierarchy in the Hellenistic Mediterranean, 230–170 BC*, Malden, MA: Blackwell.
Fantham, E. (1992), *Lucanus De Bello Civili Book II*, Cambridge: Cambridge University Press.
Fantham, E. (2013), "A Controversial Life," in P. Asso (ed.) *Brill's Companion to Lucan*, 3–20, Leiden: Brill.
Feeney, D. C. (1991), *The Gods in Epic. Poets and Critics of the Classical Tradition*, Oxford: Clarendon Press.
Fratantuono, L. (2012), *Madness Triumphant: A Reading of Lucan's* Pharsalia, Lanham, MD: Lexington Books.
Gowing, A. (2005), *Empire and Memory: The Representation of the Roman Republic in Imperial Culture,* Cambridge: Cambridge University Press.
Groß, D. (2013), *Plenus Litteris Lucanus: zur Rezeption der Horazischen Oden und Epoden in Lucans Bellum Civile*, Rahden/Westfalen: VML Verlag Marie Leidorf.
Gruen, E. S. (1984), *The Hellenistic World and the Coming of Rome*, Berkeley: University of California Press.
Hinds, S. (1987), "Generalizing about Ovid," *Ramus*, 16, 4–31.
Holmes, N. (1999), "Nero and Caesar: Lucan 1.33–66," *CPh*, 94 (1): 75–81.
Housman, A. E. (1950), *M. Annaei Lvcani Belli Civilis Libri Decem*, Oxford: Blackwell.
Hunink, V. (1992), *M. Annaeus Lucanus Bellum Civile Book III: A Commentary*, Amsterdam: J.C. Gieben.
Jal, P. (1963), *La Guerre Civile à Rome: Étude Littéraire et Morale*, Paris: Presses Universitaires de France.
Lanzarone, N. (2016), *M. Annaei Lucani Belli Civilis Liber VII*, Florence: Le Monnier.
La Penna, A. (1963), *Orazio e l'Ideologia del Principato*, Torino: Einaudi.
Lapidge, M. (1979), "Lucan's Imagery of Cosmic Dissolution," *Hermes*, 107 (3): 344–70.
Lavan, M. (2013), *Slaves to Rome: Paradigms of Empire in Roman Culture*, Cambridge: Cambridge University Press.
Lerouge, C. (2007), *L'Image des Parthes dans le Monde Gréco-Romain*, Stuttgart: Steiner.

Luisi, A. (1983-4), "Il Mito di Alessandro Magno nell'Opera di Lucano," *InvLuc*, 5-6: 105-22.
Manolaraki, E. (2011), "*Noscendi Nilum Cupido*: The Nile Digression in Book 10," in P. Asso (ed.), *Brill's Companion to Lucan*, 153-82, Leiden: Brill.
Marti, B. M. (1945), "The Meaning of the *Pharsalia*," *AJPh*, 66 (4): 352-76.
Masters, J. (1992), *Poetry and Civil War in Lucan's Bellum Civile*, Cambridge: Cambridge University Press.
Mattingly, D. J. (2011), *Imperialism, Power, and Identity: Experiencing the Roman Empire*, Princeton, NJ: Princeton University Press.
Mayer, R. (1981), *Lucan Civil War VIII*, Westminster: Aris & Phillips.
Most, G. W. (1989), "Cornutus and Stoic Allegoresis: a Preliminary Report," *ANRW*, 2.36.3: 2014-65.
Myers, M. Y. (2011), "Center and Periphery in Civil War Epic," in P. Asso (ed.), *Brill's Companion to Lucan*, 399-415, Leiden: Brill.
Narducci, E. (2002), *Lucano: un'Epica Contro l'Impero. Interpretazione della 'Pharsalia'*, Rome-Bari: Laterza.
Nelis, D. (2011), "Praising Nero (Lucan, *De Bello Civili* 1.33-66)," in G. Urso (ed.), *Dicere Laudes: Elogio, Comunicazione, Creazione del Consenso: Atti del Convegno Internazionale, Cividale del Friuli, 23-25 Settembre 2010*, 253-64, Pisa: ETS.
Nicolet, C. (1988), *L'Inventaire du Monde: Géographie et Politique aux Origines de l'Empire Romain*, Paris: Fayard.
Nisbet, R. G. M. and N. Rudd eds. (2004), *A Commentary on Horace: Odes Book III*, Oxford: Oxford University Press.
Oliensis, E. (2009), *Horace and the Rhetoric of Authority*, Cambridge: Cambridge University Press.
Paratore, E. (1966), "La Persia nella Letteratura Latina," in *Atti del Convegno sul Tema: La Persia e il Mondo Greco-Romano, Roma, 11-14 Aprile 1965*, 505-58, Rome: Academia Nazionale dei Lincei.
Paschalis (1982), "Two Horatian Reminiscences in the Proem of Lucan," *Mnemosyne,* Fourth Series, 35 (3/4): 342-6.
Pogorzelski, R. J. (2011), "Lucan and the Limits of the Roman World," *TAPhA,* 141: 143-70.
Putnam M. C. (1993), "Horace *Carm.* 2.9: Augustus and the Ambiguities of the Encomium," in K. A. Raaflaub, M. Toher and G. W. Bowersock (eds.), *Between Republic and Empire: Interpretations of Augustus and his Principate*, 212-38, Berkeley: University of California Press.
Roche, P. (2009), *Lucan De Bello Ciuili Book 1*, Oxford: Oxford University Press.
Rudd, N. ed. (2004), *Horace Odes and Epodes*, Cambridge, MA: Harvard Univ. Press.
Salemme, C. (1999), "*Mundi Ruina* e *Funus* nel II Libro della Pharsalia," in P. Esposito and L. Nicastri (eds.), *Interpretare Lucano: Miscellanea di studi,* 157-66, Napoli: Arte Tipografica.
Schneider, R. M. (2007), "Friend and Foe: the Orient in Rome," in V. S. Curtis and S. Stewart (eds.), *The Age of the Parthians*, 50-86, London: Tauris.
Seager, R. (1980), "*Neu sinas Medos equitare inultos*: Horace, the Parthians and Augustan Foreign Policy," *Athenaeum*, 58: 103-18.
Seo J. M. (2011), "Lucan's Cato and the Poetic of Exemplarity," in P. Asso (ed.), *Brill's Companion to Lucan*, 199-221, Leiden: Brill.
Shackleton Bailey, D. R. (1988), *Lucanus. De Bello Civili*, Stuttgart: Teubner.
Sklenář, R. (2003), *The Taste for Nothingness: A Study of Virtus and Related Themes in Lucan's Bellum Civile*, Ann Arbor, MI: The University of Michigan Press.
Sonnabend H. (1986), *Fremdenbild und Politik: Vorstellungen der Römer von Ägypten und dem Partherreich in der späten Republik und frühen Kaiserzeit,* Frankfurt am Main: Peter Lang.

Sullivan, J. P. (1985), *Literature and Politics in the Age of Nero*, Ithaca NY: Cornell University Press.
Wagenvoort, H. (1956), *Studies in Roman Literature, Culture, and Religion*, Leiden: Brill.
Walde, C. (2007), "Per un'Idrologia Poetica: Fiumi e Acque nella *Pharsalia* di Lucano," in L. Landolfi and P. Monella (eds.), Doctus Lucanus *Aspetti dell'Erudizione nella* Pharsalia *di Lucano*, 13–47, Bologna: Pàtron.

PART III
CATO'S NERONIAN *NACHLEBEN*

CHAPTER 7
LUCAN'S CATO AND POPULAR (MIS)CONCEPTIONS OF STOICISM
David H. Kaufman

Commentators have long recognized that Lucan's portrayal of Cato makes a great deal of Cato's relationship to Stoicism; however, in recent scholarship there has been wide disagreement over what exactly that relationship is and what its implications are for his role in the poem.[1] In this chapter, I revisit Cato's relationship to Stoicism in light of the different conceptions of Stoicism that were current at the time, both within the school and especially in popular (and often polemical) conceptions of it.[2] As we will see, Lucan's portrayal of Cato includes both important and fundamental aspects of Stoic theory, but also some rather striking misrepresentations of it.[3] For instance, although Lucan's Cato holds the distinctive Stoic view that virtue is not merely a greater good than things such as pleasure or life but a different kind of good altogether, he also has a far more restrictive theory of value and a far more circumscribed emotional life than the Stoic wise man, both of which are features of contemporary, popular conceptions of Stoicism. Since the features of Lucan's portrayal of Cato that are more faithful to Stoic theory are *also* well represented in popular representations of Stoicism, I propose that his portrayal of Cato is better understood as exploring the Stoicism of popular Roman imagination and polemic than of orthodox Stoic theory.[4] To be sure, it is hardly objectionable if in composing his *Bellum Civile* Lucan focuses on popular rather than more strictly philosophical representations of Stoicism. Nevertheless, I hope to show that appreciating the complex relationship of Lucan's Cato to Stoic theory, and especially his indebtedness to popular and often polemical contemporary representations of Stoicism, is both helpful for understanding Cato's portrayal in the poem and for arbitrating between some of the different critical views of him.

My argument is divided into four parts. I begin by considering some popular representations of Stoic theory. In the second section, I turn to Lucan's *Bellum Civile* and consider how closely and in what respects Lucan's Cato follows popular representations of Stoicism. Next, I examine some implications that Lucan's debt to popular conceptions of Stoicism have for arbitrating between the wildly different scholarly interpretations of Cato's role in the poem. Finally, in the fourth section, I turn to the death of Aulus in Book 9, which, I argue, engages most directly not with the Stoic notion of suicide, as it has often been understood, but instead with two well-known *topoi* from anti-Stoic polemics, thus providing further reason for taking Lucan's representation of Cato as engaging more closely with popular and polemical interpretations of Stoicism than with Stoic theory itself.

Stoic Axiology and its Critics

Near the beginning of Epictetus' *Discourses*, composed in the early second century CE, Epictetus briefly alludes to a debate among the Stoics over whether a wise person should *prefer* more painful and difficult circumstances to less difficult ones and even, perhaps, to pleasant and comfortable circumstances. As he writes (1.1.26–7):[5]

Θρασέας εἰώθει λέγειν "Σήμερον ἀναιρεθῆναι θέλω μᾶλλον ἢ αὔριον φυγαδευθῆναι." Τί οὖν αὐτῷ Ῥοῦφος εἶπεν; "Εἰ μὲν ὡς βαρύτερον ἐκλέγῃ, τίς ἡ μωρία τῆς ἐκλογῆς;"

Thrasea was accustomed to say: "I would prefer to be killed today than banished tomorrow." What, then, did Rufus say to him? "If you choose death as the heavier misfortune, what folly of choice!"

While this debate might seem rather perverse to non-Stoics, the surprising view that Musonius Rufus considers attributing to Thrasea Paetus here, namely that he *wishes* to experience the more difficult of two misfortunes, is worth considering more closely.[6] Presumably, Thrasea's idea, if this is indeed the right way to understand his phrase, is that he would prefer to experience the heavier misfortune *because* it offers a more compelling test of his virtue, as we also find maintained elsewhere in Stoic sources.[7] For instance, a painful illness presents a greater test of one's fortitude and virtue than a mild cold, let alone continued good health. While the details of Thrasea's view are rather complex, if we take it to imply that a Stoic wise person should in general *prefer* to undergo difficult circumstances in preference to more favorable ones, then it conflicts with one of the fundamental commitments of standard Stoic axiology.

In their axiology, the Stoics made two crucial distinctions. First, they distinguished sharply between virtue and vice, which they took to be the only real good and bad, and other merely conventional goods and bads, such as life, death, pleasure, and pain, which they described as "indifferents" (ἀδιάφορα). Secondly, among such indifferents they made a further distinction between those that are, in their terminology, "preferred" (προηγμένα) and those that are "dispreferred" (ἀποπροηγμένα).[8] As the terms suggest, the Stoics held that we ought, *ceteris paribus*, to pursue and enjoy preferred indifferents and to avoid dispreferred indifferents, without, of course, ever mistaking them for goods or bads. Thus, a good Stoic will energetically aim to maximize preferred indifferents and to minimize dispreferred indifferents when possible, but he will not be troubled at all if, despite his best efforts, he should fail to get the former and should suffer the latter. For instance, should a Stoic sage be faced with an onrushing scythe-bearing chariot, he will, ordinarily, do everything in his power to avoid it; however, if despite his most acrobatic efforts he should fail to do so, then as he crawls off, leaving his legs behind him, he will not be upset in the least. For, as he recognizes, the loss of his legs is not bad, but rather a matter of complete indifference for his virtue, and so too for his overall wellbeing.[9]

Perhaps unsurprisingly, ancient critics objected that the Stoics, in effect, conceived of preferred and dispreferred indifferents as goods or bads, while making a merely terminological distinction between the status of such things and virtue and vice.[10] For instance, in Book 4 of *De Finibus*, Cicero complains that the Stoics' terminological innovations in axiology do not do any real work: "For what is the difference whether you say that wealth, power, and health are 'good' (*bona*) or 'indifferent' (*praeposita*), when that man who says that these are goods, assigns no more value to them than you who call the very same things preferred" (*quid enim interest, divitias, opes, valitudinem bona dicas anne praeposita, cum ille, qui ista bona dicit, nihilo plus iis tribuat quam tu, qui eadem illa praeposita nominas, Fin*. 4.23)? The popular reception of Stoicism seems to have downplayed this aspect of Stoic axiology further still, or even to have disregarded it entirely. For instance, in his *De Vita Beata*, Seneca replies to some unnamed critics who argue that the wealth and opulent lifestyle of many Stoic philosophers, including Seneca himself, contradict their commitment to Stoicism. Seneca outlines their complaint as follows (*Vit. Beat.* 21.1):

> Quare ille philosophiae studiosus est et tam dives vitam agit? Quare opes contemnendas dicit et habet, vitam contemnendam putat et tamen vivit, valetudinem contemnendam, et tamen illam diligentissime tuetur atque optimam mavult? Et exilium vanum nomen putat et ait: "Quid enim est mali mutare regiones?" et tamen, si licet, senescit in patria?

> Why is that man devoted to philosophy, and why does he live a life of such wealth? Why does he say that wealth is to be despised, and has it? Why does he think that life should be despised, and nevertheless lives? Why does he think that health should be despised, and nevertheless watches over it very diligently and prefers it to be as good as possible? And why does he think that exile is an empty word and says, "For what harm is there in changing places?" and nevertheless, if it is permitted, grows old in his homeland?

According to these critics, since the Stoic sage does not believe that merely conventional goods such as health, life, pleasure, and wealth are good at all, he ought not to give *any* attention to acquiring or preserving them.[11] Of course, such a conception of Stoicism simply obliterates the Stoics' distinction between preferred and dispreferred indifferents. Indeed, as Seneca replies, whatever *his own* motives may be in pursuit of wealth, there is nothing in the least contradictory, from a Stoic perspective, between taking health, pleasure, and other merely apparent goods to be indifferents and, at the same time, giving considerable attention to acquiring and preserving them.[12]

By contrast to Seneca, Lucan's Cato fits the popular presentation of the Stoic sage very well, since he seems to be largely insensitive to the Stoics' distinction between merely preferred and dispreferred indifferents and, if anything, seems to prefer dispreferred to preferred indifferents. Nevertheless, while, as we will see, Lucan's portrayal of Cato omits crucial aspects of Stoic axiology, it also emphasizes several key and distinctive elements of Stoic theory, especially regarding the superlative value of virtue and the proper cosmopolitan stance toward other people.

Cato, Stoic Theory, and Popular Stoicism

Lucan represents Cato as being especially concerned with two things: virtue and virtuous action on the one hand, which he takes to be far more important than merely conventional goods such as pleasure and health, and the wellbeing of the Roman Republic and its members on the other, which he tends to assimilate with the entire world and humankind more generally. For example, when we first encounter Cato in Book 2, Brutus finds him brooding on the fate of Rome and, in Lucan's phrase, "alarmed for all, free of care for himself" (*cunctisque timentem / securumque sui*, 2.240–1).[13] In this passage, as elsewhere, Cato's concern for Rome and, more generally, mankind far exceeds his concern for his own physical wellbeing.[14]

However, if Cato is consistently represented as caring more for the citizens of the Roman Republic and, indeed, for mankind at large than for himself, his concern for those closest to him is rather distant and impersonal. In W. R. Johnson's memorable phrase (1987: 43–4): "He [sc. Cato] loves the common good, but, as we shall soon see, if we had not already guessed it, he seems to dislike people intensely." This aspect of Cato's characterization emerges particularly clearly in his gloomy remarriage to Marcia. When Marcia arrives at his house, still wearing her funereal clothing from her late husband's pyre, Cato agrees to remarry her, but insists, with her blessing, on having the wedding immediately, without inviting anyone beyond present company or without her even changing out of her mourning robes. Indeed, in describing their ceremony, the narrator focuses exclusively on what their wedding is missing, including, among other things, the customary torches, festal crowns and garlands, and the matrimonial couch (2.354–7).[15] In effect, their wedding is, in Elaine Fantham's description, an "anti-wedding" that resembles a funeral more closely than a wedding ceremony.[16]

Moreover, not only do the setting and celebration resemble a funeral, but so too does the demeanor of the bride and groom. Indeed, there is no indication that either Marcia or Cato enjoy their wedding at all. As Lucan writes, describing Marcia, "no saffron veil, intended lightly to screen the bride's shy blushes, hid the downcast countenance" (*demissos voltus*, 2.360–1).[17] Cato is, if anything, even less upbeat; not only does he refuse to change his clothes or even to shave, but, in Lucan's phrase, "he did not admit joy to his hard countenance" (*nec ... duroque admisit gaudia voltu*, 2.372–3).[18] Unsurprisingly, we learn a couple of lines later that Cato's "firmness" (*robur*, 2.379) rather ironically masters any inclination he might have to renew their sexual relationship.[19]

Although, to be sure, Cato and Marcia's exceptionally drab wedding is motivated at least partly by the bride's and groom's concern for the imminent threat facing the Roman Republic, there is good reason to think that the spirit of the wedding accurately reflects Cato's more general stance toward his family members and friends. For instance, after describing the wedding, the narrator gives a more general character portrait of

Cato, emphasizing his limited interest in physical goods and familial relationships (2.384–91):

> huic epulae vicisse famem, magnique penates
> summovisse hiemem tecto, pretiosaque vestis
> hirtam membra super Romani more Quiritis
> induxisse togam, Venerisque hic maximus[20] usus,
> progenies: urbi pater est urbique maritus,
> iustitiae cultor, rigidi servator honesti,
> in commune bonus; nullosque Catonis in actus
> subrepsit partemque tulit sibi nata voluptas.

> In his eyes to have conquered hunger was a feast, to have warded off winter with a roof was a mighty palace, to have drawn across his limbs the rough toga in the manner of the Roman citizen of old was a precious robe, and the greatest value of sex was offspring: for Rome he is father and for Rome he is husband, keeper of justice and guardian of strict virtue, his goodness was for the state; into none of Cato's acts did self-centered pleasure creep in and take a share.

As a Stoic *sapiens*, Cato ought to be perfectly content with rough clothing, simple food and shelter, and the rest of it; however, in context, the strong implication is that he is not only capable of enduring such things, but, if both alternatives were available, he would prefer the less pleasant and meaner option to the more pleasant and more refined. In other words, either Cato takes the sort of food he receives and lodging he finds to be a matter of complete indifference or perhaps he even prefers, when he has the choice, conventionally dispreferred to preferred indifferents. Thus, with respect to physical goods and familial relationships, he is at least insensitive to differences in quality. As we have seen, this is quite a departure from standard Stoic theory, which holds that the wise person should both recognize the absolute gulf between goods and indifferents, and also be attentive to the difference between preferred and dispreferred indifferents.

However, if Cato's radical indifference to pleasure and to conventional goods sits uneasily with Stoic theory, it fits very well with Lucan's more general portrayal of Cato as leading a life that does not include *any* positive emotions at all but at most involves negative feelings or emotions expressing either his concern for the state of the Republic or for his virtue.[21] For instance, when we first meet Cato he is, in Lucan's phrase, "pondering the nation's fate in sleepless worry" (*insomnia volventem publica cura / fata*, 2.239–40). Again, in Book 9, Cato is enraged (*concitus ira*) when, during his long march across the deserts of Libya, a soldier offers him the first drink from a small stream the army has come across, implicitly, Cato believes, challenging his claim to virtue (9.509).[22] By contrast, while the Stoics famously denied that the wise man will ever experience ordinary "emotions" (πάθη) such as "pleasure" (ἡδονή) or "distress" (λύπη), they held that he will experience a full range of "good-emotions" (εὐπάθειαι), including "joy" (χαρά) and "rational desire" (βούλησις).²³ Indeed, the life of the Stoic wise man does not merely include episodes of joy, but is rather characterized by constant joy. As Seneca describes it: "the result of wisdom is steadiness of joy. The mind of the wise man is like the superlunary world: it is always serene" (*hunc esse sapientiae effectum, gaudii aequalitatem. talis est sapientis animus qualis mundus super lunam: semper illic serenum est*, *Ep*. 59.16).²⁴ Moreover, according to Stoic theory, the wise man will also experience "pre-emotions" (προπάθειαι), which are emotion-like movements of body and mind that arise without the agent's assent.²⁵ For instance, to use an example from Seneca, even the wise man will shed tears by "natural necessity" (*naturalis necessitas*) when he first learns of the death of a friend, despite not assenting to the impression that his friend's death is something bad and worth being upset over (*Ep*. 99.18). The Stoic wise man thus has a quite rich emotional life, despite never forming ordinary emotions. However, if Lucan's portrayal of Cato's emotional life is rather distant from that of the Stoic sage, it does resemble the more restricted popular account of the Stoic ideal. Indeed, Seneca finds it necessary in *Ep*. 9, as elsewhere, to distinguish the wise man's *apatheia* from the more radical notion of impassivity he ascribes to Stilpo the Megarian and other likeminded philosophers, such as the Cynics. As Seneca comments, "Our position is different from theirs in that our wise person conquers all adversities, but still feels them; theirs does not even feel them" (*hoc inter nos et illos interest: noster sapiens vincit quidem incommodum omne sed sentit, illorum ne sentit quidem*, *Ep*. 9.3).²⁶

Lucan's Cato thus stands in a rather complex relationship to Stoicism. While his love of virtue and his selfless concern for the people of Rome and, indeed, for mankind more generally find ample parallels in Stoic theory, other aspects of his portrayal depart quite radically from Stoic theory, in line with popular contemporary representations of Stoicism. Moreover, while I have focused mostly on the ways in which popular representations of Stoicism misrepresent Stoic theory, the aspects of Lucan's portrayal of Cato that more accurately reflect Stoic theory are present in the popular representation of Stoicism as well. For instance, as we have seen, the popular representation of Stoicism captures the Stoic distinction between virtue and vice, on the one hand, and mere indifferents, on the other, very well. I submit, then, that we would do better to understand Lucan's portrayal of Cato as being based on and exploring contemporary and often polemical popular representations of the Stoic wise man rather than the account described by the Stoic philosophers themselves.²⁷

It remains to consider the significance of Lucan's complex portrayal of Cato's Stoicism for arbitrating between the radically different critical approaches to him. I will argue that Lucan's use of popular representations of the Stoic wise man in his portrayal of Cato helps both to highlight the features of the Stoic wise man in which he and the popular tradition are most interested, and also to focus on some potential difficulties with these aspects of the Stoic ideal, as they are popularly understood. The latter line of interpretation is supported in particular by Lucan's account of Aulus, the first snakebite victim in Cato's march across the Libyan desert, whose death, I argue, alludes to two famous lines of criticism marshaled against the Stoics.

Scholarly Perspectives on Lucan's Cato: Hero or Villain?

Perhaps unsurprisingly, scholarship on Lucan's Cato has disagreed widely on his function in the poem. For my purposes, it will be sufficient to divide scholarship on Cato into three camps: those such as Emanuele Narducci (1979, 2001, 2002; cf. Friedrich 1938; D'Alessandro Behr 2007) who think Lucan portrays Cato as a hero; those such as Robert Sklenář (1999, 2003; cf. Johnson 1987) who think that Lucan's portrayal is ironic and intended to reveal the absurdity of the Stoic ideal; and those such as Shadi Bartsch (1997) and Chris Caterine (2014, 2015) who take Lucan's portrayal to suggest a more ambivalent position. One way to arbitrate between these quite different interpretive strategies is to consider how Lucan's use of popular representations of Stoicism in his characterization of Cato bears on Cato's valence in the poem.

I think that such representations have two key implications for the portrayal of Cato in the poem. First and foremost, they highlight the aspects of Cato and, indeed, of the Stoic ideal in which Lucan and the popular tradition more generally were most interested, namely, his single-minded commitment to virtue and his impartial concern for other people. To see this, it is worth considering for a moment what the Stoic sage, accurately described, might look like. For one thing, while the Stoic sage could not care less, to use Lucan's examples, if he actually had better or worse shelter or food, he would nevertheless consistently select the best food and shelter available to him.[28] Again, although he would value all humans equally, independently of their proximity to him, he would take particular pleasure in his family and friends.[29] The challenge in portraying these aspects of the Stoic sage is that they might obscure the aspects of Cato that Lucan means to emphasize. For instance, Cato's commitment to virtue over other merely apparent goods might seem less marked if, say, he celebrated his remarriage to Marcia with a feast, music, and dancing, while remaining aware that all such things are merely preferred indifferents. So too, it might seem to compromise Cato's disinterested concern for humankind more generally, if he was especially affectionate in his interactions with his family and friends. By leaving these aspects of the Stoic sage out of his portrayal of Cato, Lucan thus emphasizes the features of the Stoic sage which have the most significance for his poem and which are, as we have seen, of greatest interest in contemporary popular culture.[30]

Secondly, Lucan's use of popular representations of Stoicism in his portrayal of Cato also affects the valence of Cato as a character. Cato's exaggerated disinterest in ordinary goods such as pleasure, life, food, and health makes his interest in virtue seem not only more pointed but also, to many readers, less attractive than it might otherwise. For instance, his sharp and even abusive rebuke to a soldier who offers him the first drink of water at a meager stream in the Libyan desert (9.505–9) has seemed to many commentators rather absurdly overblown (e.g., Johnson 1987: 62–3; Sklenář 2003: 90; *pace* D'Alessandro Behr 2007: 133–4).[31] So too, while Cato's cosmopolitan identification of himself with all of humankind is held up for praise in the poem, his apparent disinterest in the people he actually interacts and lives with, as portrayed most strikingly in his gloomy remarriage to Marcia, makes him seem a rather solitary character, which could not be further removed from the Stoic conception of the sage as the most social and loving of people.[32] By including popular misrepresentations of Stoicism in his portrayal of Cato, Lucan thus emphasizes Cato's commitment both to virtue and to a cosmopolitan outlook on mankind while also making these positions seem more alien and less integrated into ordinary life than Stoic theory had conceived of them.

While these considerations are in principle compatible with any of the three dominant strategies of interpretation of Cato described above, on balance I think they militate strongly against heroizing interpretations. This impression is reinforced by Lucan's account of the death of Aulus, the first snakebite victim on Cato's long march across Libya, which provides strong evidence that Lucan intentionally employed several *topoi* from anti-Stoic polemical works, a fact which supports some version of the "ironic" or "ambivalent" reading.

Autocannibalism, the Limits of Self-Control, and Aulus' Death

While it would go beyond the scope of this chapter to consider the sequence of gruesome deaths during Cato's march across the Libyan desert in any detail, I wish to focus briefly on some aspects of the death of Aulus that have, to my knowledge, escaped critical attention and help to elucidate Lucan's portrayal of Stoicism and, implicitly, of Cato.[33] Aulus, one of Cato's standard bearers, is bitten by a *dipsas* snake, causing him to grow red-hot and to be consumed with an unquenchable thirst. Unable to control himself, he throws down his standard and searches for liquid wherever he can find it, ultimately cutting open his own veins and attempting to quench his thirst with his own blood (9.737–60). For my present purposes, there are two especially significant moments here: first, Aulus' decision to throw down the Republic's standard under the influence of his insatiable thirst; and secondly, his turn to autocannibalism at which point Cato and the army desert him. Both of these features of Aulus' death scene find close parallels in anti-Stoic polemical works and, I think, highlight some awkward difficulties for Cato, from which he hurriedly escapes in Lucan's account.

When Aulus is first consumed with the burning pain of the *dipsas*' venom and experiences a violent and unquenchable feeling of thirst, he abandons his previous values and norms of behavior altogether. As the narrator describes (9.747–50):

> non decus imperii, non maesti iura Catonis
> ardentem tenuere virum, ne spargere signa
> auderet totisque furens exquireret arvis
> quas poscebat aquas sitiens in corde venenum.

> Not the glory of the state, nor the authority of saddened Cato stopped the burning man from daring to scatter the standards and in his frenzy to seek far and wide the waters which the thirsty poison in his heart demanded.

In Stoic terms, when Aulus is consumed by extreme thirst, he takes satisfying his desire to be more valuable than his duty either to the Roman Republic or to Cato. Aulus' response to the snake bite and the conflict between his desire to assuage his thirst and the demands of duty recall a *topos* in anti-Stoic polemic, which holds that while the Stoic view that extreme pain, death, and other such conventional bads are merely dispreferred indifferents might seem plausible enough in the lecture hall, not even the Stoics themselves would maintain it were they actually in the grip of such things. In support of this argument, critics often appealed to the case of the prominent Early Stoic Dionysius of Heracleia, who is reported to have abandoned Stoicism for Cyrenaic hedonism after suffering a painful bout of ophthalmia, and coming, thereby, to appreciate the real significance of pleasure and pain. As Cicero reports in *Tusc.* 2.60, Dionysius "in the midst of his very cries of agony, kept shouting that his previous beliefs about pain were false" (*ipso in eiulatu clamitabat falsa esse illa, quae antea de dolore ipse sensisset*). We also hear of Dionysius' defection in polemical contexts not only in the works of more philosophical authors such as Diogenes Laertius and Philodemus, but also in the works of Lucian, Athenaeus, and Timon, attesting to the popularity of the story.[34] More generally, beyond the peculiar case of Dionysius of Heracleia, both philosophical and more popularizing accounts of Stoicism are often skeptical of the Stoics' claim that someone who masters and lives on the basis of Stoic theory could really view intense physical suffering as a mere indifferent. For instance, in his *On Freedom from Distress*, Galen, an author hardly known for his humility,[35] sharply contrasts the limits of his own remarkable self-control in conventionally distressing situations with the Stoics' incredible claim that a virtuous person would be perfectly content and self-controlled even within the infamous Bull of Phalaris.[36] Again, in his *On the Constancy of the Wise Man*, Seneca imagines his addressee objecting that the Stoics' promise to make their audience invulnerable to all harm is simply impossible to believe (*Constant.* 3.1–2; cf. *Ep.* 66.18). I suggest, then, that when Aulus throws down his standards and madly searches for liquid, in spite of, in Lucan's description, "the authority of Cato" (*iura Catonis*), in effect he disregards his previous values under the influence of his burning thirst, thus recalling the popular anti-Stoic *topos* that even the most committed Stoics would abandon their view that severe pain and physical discomfort are mere indifferents were they in the grip of them.[37]

Along similar lines, anti-Stoic works also seem to have given a surprising amount of attention to certain rather unconventional social and political theses proposed by the early Stoics, including, for instance, holding wives and children in common, the abolition of the *agora* and religious institutions, and, should circumstances demand it, even autocannibalism.[38] To take up the case of autocannibalism, the thought seems to be that should part of a person's body—say, their left arm—be separated from them while they are short of food, it would be prudent, and perhaps even rationally obligatory, for them to consume it.[39] While it is hard to imagine that discussion of incest and autocannibalism played an especially large role in Zeno's and Chrysippus' respective *Politeiai*, discussion of such cases makes up, together with a few other similarly unconventional theses, a great deal of our evidence for early Stoic political theory.[40] Indeed, according to Diogenes

Laertius (7.43), such cases were so prominent a topic in interschool polemic that the first century BCE Stoic Athenodorus Cordylion, while chief librarian at Pergamon, attempted to delete the offending passages in Zeno's and Chrysippus' respective *Politeiai* in order to silence the Stoics' critics.[41] The popularity of such "disturbing theses" in both intraschool debate and interschool polemic is also attested in the first century BCE Epicurean Philodemus' *On the Stoics*, which focuses on the attempts of later Stoics to explain away, and defend, the less conventional aspects of early Stoic theory.[42] Accordingly, while autocannibalism played at most a minor part in early Stoic political theory, it seems to have had an outsized role in the reception of Stoic theory and to have been a popular topic of anti-Stoic polemic.[43]

Although recent scholarship on Aulus' death has mostly viewed his attempt to quench his thirst by drinking his own blood in relationship to Stoic models of suicide (Leigh 1997: 267–73; Tipping 2011: 213; Seo 2013: 92), I believe that his behavior is likely to owe more to Stoic models of autocannibalism than of suicide. For one thing, although Aulus hastens his own death by opening his veins, Lucan is quite clear that he does so with the aim not of killing himself, but rather of satisfying his thirst. As Lucan writes, Aulus "does not perceive" (*nec sentit*) the poison and his impending death but instead simply "thinks that it is thirst" (*sed putat esse sitim*), and thus he opens his veins not in pursuit of a quicker death but in order to more readily satisfy this thirst (9.758–60). That is, like the Stoic sage whose arm has been cut off and who happens to need food, Aulus finds himself with an overwhelming need for liquid and cannot find any in his surroundings, and so turns to himself instead.[44]

In his description of Aulus' death, Lucan thus seems to engage with two prominent anti-Stoic *topoi*, focusing in turn on the alleged inability of even the Stoics themselves to manage successfully intense episodes of physical pain and the so-called "disturbing theses" of early Stoic political theory, including the permissibility of autocannibalism. Accordingly, when, at the end of the episode, Cato orders his army to hurry away from the dying man with the aim, the narrator tells us, that "no one might learn that thirst has so much power" (*discere nulli / permissum est hoc posse sitim*, 9.761–2), it is difficult to resist the suspicion that he is fleeing these anti-Stoic *topoi* every bit as much as Aulus himself.

Conclusion

In this chapter I have argued that Lucan's portrayal of Cato incorporates important elements of contemporary popular representations of Stoicism. Appreciating this point is helpful both for resisting idealizing interpretations of Lucan's Cato and also for raising a methodological suggestion for future inquiries into the relationship of Lucan's Cato to Stoicism. In particular, if, as I have argued, Lucan's portrayal of Cato as a Stoic sage is more deeply indebted to popular representations of Stoicism than to Stoic theory, then it is perhaps better approached as an exploration and critique not of the Stoics' own ideal of the wise man, as scholarship has generally conceived of it, but of more popular and polemical conceptions of the Stoic sage, which presumably had a greater impact on Roman popular culture.

Notes

1. For representative examples of differing views in the scholarship, see Bartsch (1997: 101–30); Narducci (2001); Sklenář (2003: 59–100); D'Alessandro Behr (2007: 113–61); Seo (2013: 66–93); Caterine (2015). For a helpful overview of scholarship on Lucan's Cato, see Thorne (2010: 14–27). I presented earlier versions of this chapter at the conference "Lucan in his Contemporary Contexts" at BYU and at the Midwest Classical Literature Conference at the University of Cincinnati. I want to thank the organizers of each conference for their invitation, and the other participants for their comments and suggestions. I also want to thank Yelena Baraz, Chris Caterine, Jackie Murray, Mark Thorne, and Laura Zientek, as well as the anonymous readers for the press, for their very helpful written comments.

2. For discussion of popular philosophy at the time, see, e.g., Billerbeck (1979); Döring (1979); Rawson (1985); Manning (1994). By "popular conceptions" of philosophy, I mean conceptions of it that are popular both in the sense that they are widely held and that they are not based on expert knowledge. Although such conceptions need not misrepresent the theories they describe, they often will—consider, for instance, the common and deeply mistaken portrayal of the Epicureans as selfish, sex and food-obsessed hedonists (see, e.g., Epict. 2.20.6, 3.24.38–9, Sen., *Vit Beat.* 12.4–13.3, *Ep.* 21.9–10). It is worth emphasizing that not all misleading or polemical representations of a philosophical school are "popular" in my sense of the term. For instance, philosophical polemic is often quite sophisticated, even in cases where it misdescribes the view or theory it criticizes: see, e.g., Aristotle's criticism of Plato's notion of the form of the good in Arist., *Eth. Nic* 1.6 and *Eth. Eud.* 1.8.

3. Although there was substantial disagreement among Stoic philosophers over many aspects of Stoic theory, there were also widely shared Stoic tenets, which nearly all Stoic philosophers maintained. For instance, there was wide agreement among Stoic philosophers that conventional goods such as pleasure, life, and so on, are not in fact good at all, but are rather mere "indifferents" (ἀδιάφορα). Throughout this paper, I use the term "Stoic theory" to refer to such fundamental and widely shared Stoic positions. For overviews of Roman Stoicism, see Reydams-Schils (2005); Bryan (2013); Salles (2013).

4. The premise that Lucan's portrayal of Cato is based on Lucan's considered understanding of Stoic theory seems to be common to many commentators, whether or not they take Lucan to present Cato and Stoicism favorably or negatively. Two particularly good examples are Sklenář (2003) and D'Alessandro Behr (2007), who argue for radically different interpretations of Lucan's Cato, but agree that his Cato reflects his view of Stoic theory.

5. Translations from Greek and Latin are my own unless otherwise noted.

6. The first-century CE Roman senator Thrasea Paetus was an important member of the so-called Stoic resistance and famously committed suicide under compulsion by Nero. He also wrote a well-known biography of Cato, which was an important source for, among other works, Plutarch's *Cat. Min*. Musonius Rufus was a first century CE Stoic, who was both an important philosopher in his own right and an influential teacher, whose students included Epictetus and Dio Chrysostom, as well as Thrasea Paetus and other Roman senators. For recent discussion of Musonius Rufus, see Laurand (2014) and Inwood (2017). For a quick survey of Thrasea Paetus' political career, see Griffin (1976: 100–3); for the Stoic resistance with particular reference to him, see Griffin (1984: 171–7); and for his biography of Cato, see Geiger (1979).

7. As Musonius Rufus comments in the following line, Thrasea Paetus might also mean that death really is a "lighter" (κουφότερον) misfortune than exile, which sentiment Musonius also rejects, albeit on different grounds. However that may be, there is strong evidence that the former interpretation, according to which he prefers death because it is the heavier of two misfortunes, presents a view that was expounded as well in other Stoic texts. See, for instance, Sen., *Ep.* 66.49-53, 82.1-2, *Prov.* 3-4, and Muson. 1.5.

8. For the Stoics' distinction between things that really are good and bad and those that are, in fact, "indifferents" see, e.g., Diog. Laert. 7.102; Cic., *Fin.* 3.50-1; Sen., *Ep.* 82.10-14; Epict. 1.30.3, 2.9.15, 2.19.13; M. Aur., *Med.* 5.20, 6.32. For their distinction between "preferred" and "dispreferred" indifferents, see Stob., *Ecl.* 2.7.7, p. 79 Wachsmuth; Diog. Laert. 7.104; Cic., *Fin.* 3.56-7, *Acad.* 1.36-7; Sen., *Ep.* 71.33, 74.17, 92.11-13, *Vit. Beat.* 22.4-5. For a good and accessible discussion of Stoic axiology, see Brennan (2005: 119-68). For the development of the theory in later Stoicism, see the perceptive comments of Reydams-Schils (2005: 59-69).

9. This attitude is well represented by Seneca's account of the "constancy" (*constantia*) of the wise man: see, e.g., Sen., *Const.* 3-4 and *passim*; cf. Epict. 2.5.19-20. The example is adapted from Lucr. 3.642-6.

10. Cic., *Fin.* 4.23; cf. *Acad.* 1.37, *Fin.* 3.41, 4.69-73, 5.22, 5.89-94, Plut. *De Virt. Mor.* 449a-b. It is worth noting that a controversy centering on the role of such indifferents in Stoic axiology seems to have motivated the schism between the early Stoic Aristo of Chios, who denied the significance of a distinction among indifferents, and more mainstream Stoics such as Zeno, Cleanthes, and Chrysippus. For discussion of Aristo's position, see especially Ioppollo (1980).

11. Seneca considers a similar objection in *Ep.* 92.11, where he imagines someone wondering why the Stoics continue to pursue conventional goods such as good health and the absence of pain, if, as they argue, such things are not in fact good at all. Similarly to *De Vita Beata*, Seneca replies that he will continue to pursue such things because they are "in accordance with nature" (*secundum naturam* = κατὰ φύσιν) and so worth pursuing, absent special reason. For the close connection in Stoic axiology between items that are "in accordance with nature" and "preferred indifferents" see, e.g., Diog. Laert. 7.105; Stob., *Ecl.* 2.7.7, pp. 82-4 Wachsmuth; Plut., *De Comm. Not.* 1060b-c.

12. This is not to deny that there may be real tensions between Seneca's own pursuit of wealth and his profession of Stoicism, or even that such tensions may be present in his philosophical views; on the latter point, see especially Jones (2014). However that may be, Seneca is certainly right that, according to Stoic theory, there is no difficulty at all in someone's being *both* an astute and wealthy businessman or woman *and* also, at the same time, a Stoic sage.

13. I print the Latin text of Housman (1926), unless otherwise noted. Translations of Lucan are from Braund (1992), with modifications.

14. For discussion, see Fantham (1992a: 125); cf. Luc. 2.380-3. Along similar lines, in Book 9, when Cato leads the remnants of Pompey's army across the deserts of Libya, he seems to be completely indifferent to the physical hardships of the environment: see, e.g., 9.394-406, 498-510, 587-93.

15. For the broader list of features missing from the wedding, see 2.354-71. For discussion of Lucan's use of so-called "negative enumeration" here and elsewhere, see Henderson (1987: 137); Bartsch (1997: 123-7); and Caterine (2014: 18-24).

16. Fantham (1992a: 144); cf. Ahl (1976: 27-52); Bartsch (1997: 125-6); and Sklenář (2003: 73-4).

17. 2.360-1: *non timidum nuptae leviter tectura pudorem / lutea demissos velarunt flammea voltus.*

18. Cato is frequently described as *durus* in Lucan's text, indeed together with the adjective *securus* it is perhaps his main epithet in the poem—see, for instance, 2.380, 9.385, 444-5, 734, and 889. For discussion, see Sklenář (2003: 87-9); Tipping (2011: 229-32); Seo (2013: 91-2).

19. As has often been noted, Cato's disinterest in further sex and procreation sits uneasily with Stoic theory: see, e.g., Fantham (1992: 149–50) and Sklenář (2003: 75–6). For the Stoic evidence, see, e.g., Cic., *Fin.* 3.68, where Cato himself, in providing an overview of Stoic ethical theory, argues that the wise man will marry and wish to have children, and moreover, that "not even sexual passion, if it is pure, is considered to be alien to the wise man" (*ne amores quidem sanctos a sapiente alienos esse arbitrantur*); cf. *SVF* 3 Antipater 63. For discussion of the sexual passion of the wise, see Schofield (1993) and Nussbaum (1995).

20. I follow Shackleton Bailey (1988) and Fantham (1992a) in printing *maximus*, which is the reading of all of the manuscripts, instead of *unicus*, an emendation printed by Housman (1926). For further argument in favor of reading *maximus* here, see Gotoff (1971: 95) and Håkanson (1979: 29–30).

21. For a possible exception, see Luc. 9.291–2, which in the course of a simile, describes a shepherd as "rejoicing" (*gaudet*) after he has gathered a swarm of runaway bees, perhaps suggesting that Cato to whom the shepherd is compared also rejoices when he successfully regroups his troops after they learn of Pompey's death; for discussion, see especially D'Alessandro Behr (2007: 145–7). However, in context, it seems as likely that the emphasis of the analogy is on the cause of the shepherd's emotion—namely, successfully gathering the swarm of bees—rather than the emotion itself, and thus serves to emphasize Cato's success in preventing his soldiers from sailing away rather than to describe his emotional state in doing so.

22. For the literary background to this passage, see especially Rutz (1970); Leigh (2000: 100); and Narducci (2002: 407–9).

23. For ancient evidence regarding the good-emotions, see, e.g., Cic., *Tusc.* 4.12–14; Diog. Laert. 7.115–16; Andronic.Rhod. 6; Sen., *Ep.* 59.2. For discussion, see Inwood (1985: 173–5) and especially Cooper (2005: 176–218).

24. Sen., *Ep.* 59.16, translated by Graver and Long (2015), with modifications. For the comparison of the wise person's soul to the superlunary heavens, see too Brutus' speech at Luc. 2.266–73.

25. For critical discussion of the Stoic theory of "pre-emotions" see Abel (1983); Graver (2007: 85–108); and D'Jeranian (2014). Graver (1999) argues persuasively that the early Stoics already operated with a notion of non-voluntary, emotion-like movements and feelings.

26. Sen. *Ep.* 9.3, translated by Graver and Long 2015. Seneca expresses this same idea in strikingly similar terms in several different texts: see, e.g., Sen., *Prov.* 2.2, *Const.* 10.3–4, *Brev. Vit.* 14.2, *QNat.* 2.59.3. In addition to Stilpo, Seneca seems to have in mind particularly the Cynics. For a collection of *testimonia* of Stilpo's life and philosophy, see Giannantoni (1983: 1.109–28).

27. To be sure, popular representations of Stoicism are by no means the only important background to Lucan's portrayal of Cato. For a good discussion of other influences and, especially, literary representations of Cato himself, see Seo (2013: 66–93).

28. To be sure, since the Stoic wise man will not be influenced by conventional opinion, he will likely grade the food, shelter, and clothing options available to him quite differently from most people. But there is little reason to think that he will, like Lucan's Cato, consistently choose the least elegant or pleasant option. Indeed, in *Ep.* 5.1–6, Seneca finds it necessary to warn his addressee, Lucilius, against adopting uncouth and ostentatious habits, such as wearing rough clothes, growing out his hair and beard, using earthenware rather than silver plates, and so on, as part of his philosophical conversion. See too, M. Aur., *Med.* 5.28, focusing on appropriate personal hygiene.

29. For instance, Epictetus writes: "I should not be unfeeling (ἀπαθής) like a statue, but should preserve my relations both natural and acquired as a pious man, as a son, as a brother, as a

father, and as a citizen" (3.2.4). For our natural affection for our children, see e.g., Cic., *Fin.* 62–3; Diog. Laert. 7.120; Epict. 1.11 and 1.23.3; Plut., *St. Rep.* 1038b; and for its fundamental importance for the Stoic theory of social *oikeiosis*, see Blundell (1990) and Inwood (1993). For the wise man's affection for his friends and family more generally, see Graver (2007: 173–90) and Reydams-Schils (2005: 115–76).

30. Lucan's Cato thus shares some features with Cynics who provide a vivid example of the ultimate indifference to merely conventional goods and bads, precisely by ignoring luxuries and making do with the bare minimum of physical goods. For scholarly discussion of the popular Roman conception of Cynics, see, e.g., Billerbeck (1993) and Griffin (1996).

31. Moreover, beyond the reaction of modern readers, Lucan's portrayal of Cato's severity also seems to reinforce the popular ancient conception of Stoicism as excessively "harsh" (*asper*), "hard" (*durus*), and "inflexible" (*rigidus*): see, e.g., Cic., *Mur.* 60; Sen., *Clem.* 2.5.2; Tac., *Ann.* 16.22.2.

32. See, e.g., Diog. Laert. 7.123–4; Sen., *Clem.* 2.5.3; Epict. 1.11; Stob., *Ecl.* 2.7, 11, p. 108–9 Wachsmuth.

33. For background to the series of snakebites in Book 9 see Morford (1967); Aumont (1968); Thomas (1982); Fantham (1992b); Bartsch (1997: 29–35); Leigh (1997: 265–82); Eldred (2000); Leigh (2000); Gorman (2001); Saylor (2002); Wick (2004); Bexley (2010); and de Moura (2010).

34. See, e.g., Diog. Laert. 7.166; Cic., *Fin.* 5.94; Athen. 7.281d–e = *SH* 791 = *AP* 10.38; Phld. *Acad. Ind.* col. 20; and Lucian *BisAcc* 21. For discussion of Dionysius of Heracleia, see Lampe (2015: 19–20).

35. For discussion of Galen's frequent use of self-promoting autobiographical episodes throughout his works, see, e.g., Nutton (1972) and Boudon-Millot (2009).

36. See, esp., Gal., *Indol.* 70–6, with the discussions of Boudon-Millot and Jouanna (2010), *ad loc.* and Kaufman (2015).

37. Along similar lines, in discussing Aulus' death, Bartsch (1998: 35) writes: "But perhaps the constraints applied by Stoicism are not, in the end, enough: such philosophy does nothing for poor Aulus, who slurps down his own blood to slake his thirst despite Cato's disapproving presence." Cf. Leigh (1997: 269–72); de Moura (2010: 48).

38. For discussion of the role of the so-called "disturbing theses" in early Stoic political theory, see especially Schofield (1991) and Vogt (2008). While later Stoics seem to have downplayed these positions, there is strong evidence that authors in the imperial period continued to be aware of them. For instance, Epictetus finds it necessary to explain the sense in which, according to Stoic theory, women and children are held in common (Epict. 2.4.8–11).

39. See, e.g., S.E., *M.* 11.189–94 with the excellent discussion of Vogt (2008: 38–9).

40. The sources are collected, with discussion, in Baldry (1959) and, more fully, in Goulet-Cazé (2003).

41. I follow Schofield's identification of the Athenodorus mentioned by Diogenes Laertius with Athenodorus Cordylion; for the details, see Schofield (1991: 8–13, esp. 9).

42. I take the term "disturbing theses" from Vogt (2008: 8). For Philodemus' *On the Stoics*, see the edition of Dorandi 1982, which also includes a short, but helpful, overview of the text and its themes.

43. The Cynic and early Stoic view of the permissibility of cannibalism in certain conditions also seems to have influenced other works of Imperial Roman literature. For instance, as H. D. Rankin (1969) has argued, Petronius' account of Eumolpus' macabre will, which requires his inheritors to publicly eat his dead body before they can collect their inheritance, likely refers to the Cynic-Stoic tradition (Pet., *Sat.* 141). For other instances of autocannibalism in

Imperial Roman Literature, see, e.g., Ov., *Met.* 8.871–8 and Juv., *Sat.* 15.97–103. For more discussion of cannibalism in Roman literature, focusing especially on Juvenal, see Keane (2015: 192–205). For discussion of the prevalence of dismemberment in Neronian literature more generally, and especially in Seneca and Lucan, see Most (1992: esp. 404–8).

44. It is worth emphasizing that from a Stoic perspective there is a world of difference between the behavior of Aulus and the Stoic sage. Most importantly, while the sage consumes his amputated arm on the basis of cool reasoning, Aulus slices his veins open and consumes himself under the influence of his passionate and overpowering desire for liquid. Indeed, it is a *topos* in postclassical accounts of the emotions that impassioned people often fail to consider their own wellbeing or even self-preservation in their mad and myopic pursuit of their emotional goal: see, e.g., Sen., *De Ira* 1.1.1 and 3.2.6; Phld., *Ir.* 23.20–40 and 33.1–7.

References

Abel, K. (1983), "Das Propatheia-Theorem: Ein Beitrag zur stoischen Affektenlehre," *Hermes*, 111: 78–97.
Ahl, F. (1976), *Lucan: An Introduction*, Ithaca: Cornell University Press.
Aumont, J. (1968), "Sur l'épisode des reptiles dans le Pharsale de Lucain (9.587–937)," *BAGB*, 1: 103–19.
Baldry, H. (1959), "Zeno's Ideal State," *JHS*, 79: 3–15.
Bartsch, S. (1997), *Ideology in Cold Blood. A Reading of Lucan's Civil War*, Cambridge: Cambridge University Press.
Bexley, E. (2010), "The Myth of the Republic: Medusa and Cato in Lucan *Pharsalia* 9," in N. Hömke and C. Reitz (eds.), *Lucan's Bellum Civile: Between Epic Tradition and Aesthetic Innovation*, 135–53, Berlin: De Gruyter.
Billerbeck, M. (1979), *Der Kyniker Demetrius. Ein Beitrag zur Geschichte der frühkaiserzeitlichen Popularphilosophie*, Leiden: Brill.
Billerbeck, M. (1993), "Le Cynisme idéalisé d' Épictète à Julien," in M. Goulet-Cazé and R. Goulet (eds.), *Le cynisme ancient et ses prolongements*, 319–38, Paris: Presses Universitaires de France.
Blundell, M. (1990), "Parental Nature and Stoic οἰκείωσις," *AncPhil*, 10: 221–42.
Boudon-Millot, V. (2009), "Galen's *Bios* and *Methodos*: From Ways of Life to Path of Knowledge," in C. Gill, T. Whitmarsh, and J. Wilkins (eds.), *Galen and the World of Knowledge*, 175–89, Cambridge: Cambridge University Press.
Boudon-Millot V., J. Jouanna, and A. Pietrobelli, eds. (2010), *Galien: Ne pas se chagriner*, Paris: Les Belles Lettres.
Braund, S., trans. (1992), *Lucan: Civil War*, Oxford: Clarendon Press.
Brennan, T. (2005), *The Stoic Life: Emotions, Duties, and Fate*, Oxford: Oxford University Press.
Bryan, J. (2013), "Neronian Philosophy," in E. Buckley and M. Dinter (eds.), *A Companion to the Neronian Age*, 134–48, Malden, MA: Wiley-Blackwell.
Caterine, C. (2014), "A Crisis of Interpretation: Contradiction, Ambiguity, and the Reader of Lucan's *Bellum Civile*," PhD diss., University of Virginia, Charlottesville.
Caterine, C. (2015), "*Si Credere Velis*: Lucan's Cato and the Reader of the *Bellum Civile*," *Arethusa*, 48: 339–67.
Cooper, J. M. (2005), "The Emotional Life of the Wise," *SJPh*, supplement 43:176–218.
D'Alessandro Behr, F. (2007), *Feeling History. Lucan, Stoicism, and the Poetics of Passion*, Columbus: Ohio State University Press.
D'Jeranian, O. (2014), "Deux théories stoïciennes des affections préliminaires," *RphA*, 32: 225–57.
de Moura, A. R. (2010), "Cato in Libya (Book 9)," *Letras Classical* 14: 63–91.
Dorandi, T., ed. (1982), "Filodemo. Gli Stoici (*PHerc.* 155 e 339)," *CronErc*, 12: 91–133.

Döring, K. (1979), *Exemplum Socratis. Studien zur Sokratesnachwirkung in der kynisch-stoischen Popularphilosophie der frühen Kaiserzeit und im frühen Christentum*, Wiesbaden: Steiner.
Eldred, K. O. (2000), "Poetry in Motion: The Snakes of Lucan," *Helios*, 27, 63–74.
Fantham, E., ed. (1992a), *Lucan. De Bello Civili. Book II*, Cambridge: Cambridge University Press.
Fantham, E. (1992b), "Lucan's Medusa Excursus: Its Design and Purpose," *MD*, 29: 95–119.
Friedrich, W. H. (1938), "Cato, Caesar und Fortuna bei Lucan," *Hermes*, 73: 391–423.
Geiger, J. (1979), "Munatius Rufus and Thrasea Paetus on Cato the Younger," *Athenaeum*, 57: 48–72.
Giannantoni, G., ed. (1983), *Socraticorum reliquiae*, 4 vols., Naples: Bibliopolis.
Gorman, V. (2001), "Lucan's Epic *Aristeia* and the Hero of the *Bellum Civile*", *CJ*, 96 (3): 263–90.
Gotoff, H. C. (1971), *The Transmission of the Text of Lucan in the Ninth Century*, Cambridge, MA: Harvard University Press.
Goulet-Cazé, M. O. (2003), *Les Kynika du stoïcisme*, Stuttgart: Franz Steiner Verlag.
Graver, M. (1999), "Philo of Alexandria and the Origins of the Stoic προπάθειαι," *Phronesis*, 44: 300–25.
Graver, M. (2007), *Stoicism and Emotion*, Chicago: University of Chicago Press.
Graver, M. and A. A. Long, trans. (2015), *Seneca: Letters on Ethics*, Chicago: University of Chicago Press.
Griffin, M. (1976), *Seneca: A Philosopher in Politics*, Oxford: Oxford University Press.
Griffin, M. (1984), *Nero: The End of a Dynasty*, London: Routledge.
Griffin, M. (1996), "Cynicism and the Romans: Attraction and Repulsion," in R. Bracht Branham and M. O. Goulet-Cazé (eds.), *The Cynics: The Cynic Movement in Antiquity and its Legacy*, 190–203, Berkeley: University of California Press.
Håkanson, L. (1979), "Problems of Textual Criticism in Lucan's *De Bello Civili*," *PCPhS*, 25: 26–51.
Henderson, J. (2004), *Moral and Villas in Seneca's Letters: Places to Dwell*, Cambridge: Cambridge University Press.
Housman, A. E., ed. (1926), *M. Annaei Lucani Belli civilis libri decem*, Oxford: Blackwell.
Inwood, B. (1983), "Comments on Professor Görgemanns' Paper: The Two Forms of *Oikeiosis* in Arius and the Stoa," in W. W. Fortenbaugh (ed.), *On Stoic and Peripatetic Ethics: The Work of Arius Didymus*, 190–201, New Brunswick: Transaction Books.
Inwood, B. (1985), *Ethics and Human Action in Early Stoicism*, Oxford: Oxford University Press.
Inwood, B. (2017), "The Legacy of Musonius Rufus," in T. Engberg-Pedersen (ed.), *From Stoicism to Platonism: The Development of Philosophy, 100 BCE–100 CE*, 254–76, Cambridge: Cambridge University Press.
Ioppolo, A. M. (1980), *Aristone di Chio e lo stoicismo antico,* Naples: Bibliopolis.
Johnson, W. R. (1987), *Momentary Monsters: Lucan and His Heroes*, Ithaca: Cornell University Press.
Jones, M. (2014), "Seneca's Letters to Lucilius: Hypocrisy as a Way of Life," in M. Colish and J. Wildberger (eds.), *Seneca Philosophus*, 393–430, Berlin: De Gruyter.
Kaufman, D. H. (2014), "Galen on the Therapy of Distress and the Limits of Emotional Therapy," *OSAP*, 47: 275–96.
Keane, C. (2015), *Juvenal and the Satiric Emotions*, Oxford: Oxford University Press.
Lampe, K. (2015), *The Birth of Hedonism: The Cyrenaic Philosophers and Pleasure as a Way of Life*, Princeton: Princeton University Press.
Laurand, V. (2014), *Stoïcisme et lien social: enquête autour de Musonius Rufus*, Paris: Classiques Garnier.
Leigh, M. (1997), *Lucan: Spectacle and Engagement*, Oxford: Oxford University Press.
Leigh, M. (2000), "Lucan and the Libyan Tale," *JRS*, 90: 95–109.
Manning, C. E. (1994), "Philosophy and Popular Philosophy in the Roman Empire," *ANRW*, 2.36.7: 4995–5026.

Morford, M. (1967), "The Purpose of Lucan's Ninth Book," *Latomus*, 26: 123–9.
Most, G. (1992), "*Disiecti membra poetae*: The Rhetoric of Dismemberment in Neronian Poetry," in R. Hexter and D. Shelden (eds.), *Innovations of Antiquity*, 391–419, New York: Routledge.
Narducci, E. (1979), *La provvidenza crudele: Lucano e la distruzione dei miti augustei,* Pisa: Giardini.
Narducci, E. (2001), "Catone in Lucano (e alcuni interpretazioni recenti)," *Athenaeum*, 89: 171–86.
Narducci, E. (2002), *Lucano. Un'epica contro l'impero*, Rome: Laterza.
Nussbaum, M. (1995), "Eros and the Wise: The Stoic Response to a Cultural Dilemma," *OSAP*, 13: 231–67.
Nutton, V. (1972), "Galen and Medical Autobiography," *PCPhS*, 198: 50–62.
Rankin, H. D. (1969), "'Eating People is Right': Petronius 141 and a ΤΟΠΟΣ," *Hermes*, 97: 381–4.
Rawson, E. (1985), *Intellectual Life in the Late Roman Republic*, Baltimore: Johns Hopkins University Press.
Reydams-Schils, G. (2005), *The Roman Stoics: Self, Responsibilty, and Affection*, Chicago: University of Chicago Press.
Rutz, W. (1970), "Lucan und die Rhetorik," in M. Durry (ed.), *Lucian*, 235–65, Geneva: Fondation Hardt.
Salles, R. (2013), "Roman Stoicism," in F. Sheffield and J. Warren (eds.), *The Routledge Companion to Ancient Philosophy*, 541–53, London: Routledge.
Saylor, C. (2002), "*Vana species leti*: Cato's March in Lucan, Pharsalia IX," in P. Defosse (ed.), *Hommage à C. Deroux*, 458–63, Brussles: Latomus.
Schofield, M. (1991), *The Stoic Idea of the City*, Cambridge: Cambridge University Press.
Seewald, M. (2008), *Studien zum 9. Buch von Lucans* Bellum Civile. *Mit einem Kommentar zu den Versen 1–733*, Berlin: De Gruyter.
Seo, J. M. (2013), *Exemplary Traits: Reading Characterization in Roman Poetry*, Oxford: Oxford University Press.
Shackleton Bailey, D. R., ed. (1988), *M. Annaei Lucani* de Bello Civili, Stuttgart: Teubner.
Sklenář, R. (1999), "Nihilistic Cosmology and Catonian Ethics in Lucan's *Bellum Civile*," *AJPh*, 120: 281–96.
Sklenář, R. (2003), *The Taste for Nothingness. A Study of Virtus and Related Themes in Lucan's* Bellum Civile, Michigan: University of Michigan Press.
Thomas, R. (1982), *Land and Peoples in Roman Poetry: The Ethnographic Tradition*, Cambridge: Cambridge Philological Society.
Thorne, M. (2010), "Lucan's Cato, The Defeat of Victory, The Triumph of Memory," PhD diss., University of Iowa, Iowa City.
Tipping, B. (2011), "Terrible Manliness?: Lucan's Cato," in P. Asso (ed.), *Brill's Companion to Lucan*, 223–36, Leiden: Brill.
Vogt, K. (2008), *Law, Reason, and the Cosmic City: Political Philosophy in the Early Stoa*, Oxford: Oxford University Press.
Wick, C. (2004), *M. Annaeus Lucans: Bellum Civile Liber* IX, 2 vols., Munich: K.G. Saur.

CHAPTER 8
SAGE, SOLDIER, POLITICIAN, AND BENEFACTOR: CATO IN SENECA AND LUCAN
Francesca D'Alessandro Behr

Introduction

In this chapter, I will consider the relationship between Seneca's characterization of Cato in his prose work and Lucan's depiction of Cato in the *Bellum Civile*. Lucan grew up in Rome where Seneca, his uncle, also resided. Both orbited around Nero's imperial court before distancing themselves from it. They shared an anticlassical style and interest in philosophy and politics. Central ideas and images at the heart of Lucan's *Bellum Civile* (e.g., storms, divinations, meditations on Fate, *sapiens* as superior to god, etc.) are also fundamental in Seneca's writings. Cato Uticensis towers in the minds and works of both authors.

If overall Seneca prefers to highlight the intrinsic moral value of Cato's example (*Ep.* 14 and 24), in some cases he represents the sage as an eminently political figure and the best kind of soldier (e.g., *Ep.* 67.7–9, 95.69–70; 104.30–32). While on the surface, and for reasons tied to his Neronian present, Seneca draws attention to Cato as an exemplar of the Stoic sage principally concerned with his own spiritual freedom, in other ways he reveals a Republican warrior and politically engaged hero. Lucan elaborates on this composite image at *Bellum Civile* 2.286–325 and 9.283–293 by portraying in Cato a conscientious leader able to convince his audiences of the right way to fight which preserves *virtus* and *libertas*. Lucan's rendering of Cato as a philosophically inspired leader resolved to do what he perceives to be his duty for the community will be contextualized through Seneca's view of society in his *De Beneficiis* and *De Clementia*.[1]

Finally, the portrayal of Cato in Lucan's poem should be measured not against his presumed Stoic orthodoxy, but with regard to the poet's dynamic employment of "exemplary traits" which mobilize the literary (especially epic) and philosophical tradition of Rome in a rather political direction. How "Cato fulfills or contradicts the expectations of his mytho-historical persona ... illuminate[s] how we read Lucan's enigmatic protagonist in a Neronian context" (Seo 2013: 67).

Seneca's Cato

In the Roman world, the juxtaposition of philosophy to military terminology was to a degree unavoidable. Roman discourse employs the word *vir-tus* as an equivalent of the Greek *arête* and, as its etymology suggests, it is also linked to the masculine display of bravery in battle. *Virtus* entails moral steadfastness gained through philosophical training as well as assertive courage.[2] When Seneca in his writings suggests that during imperial times the proper—or at least only possible—arena for the exercise of *virtus* is "not warfare, but the endurance of ill fortune" (Roller 2001: 104), he resorts to battle imagery and traditional Roman ethical discourse. For instance, Roman military practices and moral victory are associated by Seneca when he notices "the equality of goods between the returning general in his victory parade, and the mentally unconquered captive that is trundled along in front of his chariot" (*paria bona esse eius, qui triumphat, et eius, qui ante currum vehitur invictus animo, Ep.* 71.22).[3] Lucan alludes to this formulation when he frames Cato's disastrous crossing of the Libyan desert as a triumph greater than those celebrated by Pompey on the Capitoline hill (9.597–600).

About Seneca's representation of Cato, R. Innocenti Pierini remarks that "Seneca did his best to convert Cato from a politician into a sage" (2014: 274; cf. Syme 1985: 557n5).[4] For Innocenti Pierini, the Senecan wise man is above fortune in his being self-mastered and because of that, he does not fear either men or gods. Significantly, the freedom of the sage is acquired after he has liberated himself from the daily *negotia* of political life or, in extreme cases, through suicide (Innocenti Pierini 2014: 174). Widening this horizon, A. Gowing suggests that in Seneca's letters we see a deflation of the Roman Republican past to which Lucan will react with his representation of Cato in the *Bellum Civile* (Gowing 2005: 69). Indeed, for Gowing, during the Neronian regime, Lucan's concerns with memory are "an attempt to counter a political agenda that sought to devalue the past" and that "Seneca, ironically, had a hand in setting" (2005: 100).[5]

Political involvement of the sage in the civil war seems to be criticized by Seneca at *Ep.* 14. In the first part of the letter, he lists poverty, diseases, and the violence of powerful men (*inopia, morbi, vis potentioris*, 3–4) among "things to fear" (*timenda*) and to be avoided. Later he illustrates "the supremacy of the powerful" by introducing Cato in the midst of the civil war, trapped between the aggression of Caesar and Pompey (12–13). Seneca really wonders if in that situation the sage should have become involved (*aliquis disputare an illo tempore capessenda fuerit sapienti res publica*, 13). The sentence *potest melior vincere, non potest non peior esse qui vicerit* (13) vividly recaps the paradoxical situation of a perverted melee in which "the man who prevails is morally the worst," and for which the narrator is perhaps suggesting not to bother (*quid tibi vis?*, 13). Even the political situation of the previous years is described as off-limits to the sage (*ne priores quidem anni fuerunt qui sapientem in illam rapinam rei publicae admitterent*, 13). In another letter, we apprehend that in the end, Seneca's Cato can choose intervention only with the awareness that, if Caesar wins, he will kill himself (*moriturum*), and if Pompey prevails, he will go into exile (*Ep.* 104.32). He can subtract himself from a corrupted environment, opting to die (Bartsch 1997: 106–29).[6] The attitude echoes *Ad Marciam* 20.6 where death is viewed as an "an invention of nature" (*inventum naturae*) against evils.

It follows that in *Ep.* 14 as in *Ep.* 24.6–8, Cato's death is praised as a viable response to irremediable circumstances. While Seneca is hard-pressed to explain the reasons for Cato's participation in civil war, which indeed are not given,[7] he emphasizes Cato's *constantia* and *virtus* and provides a model for proper dying which resonates with the exemplary tradition developed around Cato Uticensis. In addition, Seneca's attitude toward suicide would be consistent with his widespread pessimism about action which cannot, as it does for Cicero, be the expression of internal virtue: for Seneca, Stoic *homologia*—the correspondence between the self and his acts—has become a chimera because virtue is only substantiated and apparent in resistance (Hill 2004: 153). For Hill, Seneca "advances a new model of exemplarity, the message of which is not political but cognitive" and whose purpose is, above all, to deny "the authority of externals over actions" (Hill 2004: 156–7 and 159).

While the moral significance of Cato's death is emphasized in the above-mentioned passages, in others his socially oriented activism is brought into light. At *De Prov.* 2.10, Seneca declares that even during the civil war, Cato's "sword, pure and innocent," manages noble deeds and gives Cato the liberty he could not give to his country. For the ancient Romans, dying remained a "fundamentally active rather than a passive process" and "an act of communication with the living" (Edwards 2007: 5). Genuine *mors voluntaria* "as an assertion of one's autonomy ... was uniquely suitable for conveying reverse political meaning under the Principate by deflating the emperor's guise of absolute power" (Plass 1995: 102). In Lucan's epic, Cato's military engagement and suicide are paramount even if he is not shown fighting in the war or dying in Utica. At *BC* 2, his decision to die is framed not simply as an arena for the exercise of virtue but, as I will argue below, as beneficial for the living.

Cato as a Benefactor in *BC* 2

In *BC* 2.234–325, the dialogue between Brutus and Cato is reminiscent of Seneca's *Ep.* 14.11–14 and *Ep.* 24.6, while other texts are also brought into play. Cato may have historically fought on the side of Pompey, but in *BC* 2 he fights for *his own cause*. He represents what M. Thorne tags a "new option": the opportunity to fight for a different ideal, for Roman freedom especially once it has been violently dragged away by the victor (Thorne 2010: 139). The novelty of Cato's political position defending the integrity of the Roman Republic against Caesar and Pompey had been clearly drawn out by Seneca (cf. *Ep.* 95.70; *Cato fecit aliquas et rei publicae partes*, *Ep.* 104.30),[8] perhaps under the influence of his father Seneca the Elder. In his letters and treatises, Seneca utilized not only his father's *Suasoriae* but also his *History from the beginning of the civil wars* (*Historiae ab initio bellorum civilium*), whose goal was to preserve the truth about the civil wars in the Julio-Claudian political environment, hostile to Republican memory. The Elder Seneca was working on this history at the end of his life and his son published it during Caligula's reign.[9]

Seneca the Elder was interested not only in analyzing how, little by little, *libertas* was being eroded in the city of Rome, but also in showing the underground "civil wars" fought in the city after the establishment of the empire. The younger Seneca could have inherited his father's Republican leaning which would emerge in his praise of Marcia and

Cremutius Cordus ("free in thought, in purpose, and in act" and example of true *Romanitas*, *Ad Marc.* 1.3–4) as well as in that of Cato (Canfora 2000: 170). Canfora's insights on this point are important to restore a dimension of Seneca's socio-historical and pro-Republican stance which he necessarily had to conceal through specific textual strategies (e.g., dissimulation and moralizing discourse on the self) in response to the reduced freedom of speech of his environment (Ker 2009: 255–56; cf. Rudich 1993, 1997). Seneca indeed might have privileged the moral sphere and deflated a more traditional appreciation of the public external manifestation of *virtus* as a tactic to avoid censure while at the same time preserving some authority for the individual (Roller 2001: 103–12).

Returning to Lucan's presentation of Cato in Book 2, we can see that the three elements pointed out by Brutus in his speech to him—the importance of tranquil inactivity (*tranquilla otia*, 266–7), avoidance of violence (*sine armis*, 266), and the necessary isolation of the decent person (*solus*, 267)—echo Seneca's *Ep.* 14 and 24.[10] Eventually, Brutus rejects political disengagement once he has heard Cato's position in favor of intervention.[11] It is particularly significant that, in his response to Brutus, Cato refers to the civil conflict as *Romana bella* (293) and draws attention to what lies at the heart of this confrontation and his involvement: *Roma* herself and *libertas* move him into action. Cato admits to Brutus that his *virtus* can enter the world of civil war and remain *secura* (287), but he himself cannot enter this war and remain *securus* (297).[12] He reminds Brutus that freedom is at stake and that the perverted conflict can be taken away from the hands of both Pompey and Caesar and righted. By following Cato's standards, Roman citizens can fight in an honorable conflict. As we have seen, Seneca depicts Cato's exemplary suicide several times in his work. It is suggestive that the very first time Lucan depicts him in his *BC*, the poet responds to those representations by reshaping Cato's suicide more clearly in political terms and "raises the possibility that ... Cato may afford a consistent and coherent attitude toward the conflict as well as a justification for fighting therein" (Tipping 2011: 226). Besides representing the party of liberty, the importance of Cato's character in the *Bellum Civile* rests upon his ability to persuade Brutus and his audience about the legitimacy of the war. Cato is capable "of bringing the ideal into tangible, living dimensions" by caring like a father for his fellow citizens, and he is presented as "the regenerative force that inspires [them] to follow in his footsteps" (Ahl 1976: 251).

In Book 2, Lucan corroborates the image of the sage's dutiful and beneficial involvement in the war with a multi-layered image in which Cato is presented as a father taking part in his son's funeral (2.297–305):

> Ceu morte parentem
> natorum orbatum longum producere funus
> ad tumulos iubet ipse dolor, iuvat ignibus atris
> inseruisse manus constructoque aggere busti
> ipse atras tenuisse faces; non ante revellar
> exanimem quam te complectar, Roma, tuumque

nomen, Libertas, et inanem persequar umbram.
Sic eat: inmites Romana piacula divi
plena ferant, nullo fraudemus sanguine bellum.

> Anguish orders a parent
> bereaved by the death of sons to prolong the cortège
> to the tomb; it soothes him to thrust his hands
> into the bleak fires and, once the pyre-mound is raised, to hold
> the bleak torch himself; likewise, I will not be hauled back before
> I embrace you, lifeless Rome! I will pursue you,
> Liberty, mourn your name, your insubstantial shade.
> Let the heartless divinities have Roman atonements in full;
> let us not cheat the war of its blood!

The description calls to mind specific moments of a Roman funeral (cortège, construction of the pyre, lighting of the torches) required of the male next of kin and alludes to well-known personages of the Roman Republican past (Mucius Scaevola, the Decii). The cluster *inseruisse manus* brings to mind Mucius Scaevola, who in 508 BCE fought against king Porsenna and was ready to sacrifice himself for the Republic (Liv. 2.12–3). Scaevola was captured and, after having placed his hand into the fire to display to the king his indifference to personal safety, declared that there were many Romans prepared to attack him.[13]

The description is remarkable for its emotional intensity as well as its socio-political overtones detectable in the verbs *iubet* /*iuvat* and in the allegory of the father, a figure laden with political implication. In 63 BCE, after Cicero's repression of the Catilinarian conspiracy, some of his supporters hailed him as *pater patriae*, while others called him a tyrant. The Romans employed "the Greek conception of the 'tyrant' as a figure opposite to the ideal benefactor" (Stevenson 1992: 423). "*Iuvat*," according to E. Fantham, "is the *vox propria* for passionate desire or its expressions in speech" (Fantham 1992: 134); nevertheless, *iuvare* and *gaudere* are also verbs strongly resonant with the terminology of benefaction in Seneca's *De beneficiis*: "To help (*iuvare*) ... is the part of a noble and chivalrous soul; he who gives benefits (*qui dat beneficia*) imitates the gods, he who seeks a return, lenders" (*Ben.* 3.15.4) or "what then is a benefit (*beneficium*)? It is the act of a well-wisher who bestows joy and derives joy for the bestowal of it" (*quid est ergo beneficium? benevola actio tribuens gaudium capiensque tribuendo in id*, *Ben.* 1.6.1).[14] Elsewhere I have highlighted how much Cato's mourning is presented by Lucan with a language that links it with dissenting women in Vergil's *Aeneid* and puts him at odds with *Fatum* (Behr 2007: 150–61). Here, I would like to emphasize Cato as a paternal figure with specific masculine traits and social obligations, fully immersed in the Roman environment and committed to benefitting the collectivity.

Lucan focuses on the funeral procession with the verb *persequar* (I follow into death) preferred over the weaker *prosequar* (I escort) (Fantham 1992: 135). In the cluster "*non ante revellar ... persequar umbram*" (301–3), "Cato draws the analogy between a parent's mourning that persists after death and his own love for the free republican state presented in a hendiadys of Rome and liberty" (Fantham 1992: 135). Cato, unable to be torn away from the dying Republic, walks to its grave and embraces its corpse (*exanimen quam te complectar, Roma*, 302). The syntax and word choice tie Cato so strongly to the dying Republic that the scene can be read as an anticipation of Cato's own death. There is more: in his previous description, the word *umbra* alludes to Pompey being called "shadow of a great name" (*magni nominis umbra*, 1.135) in the programmatic introduction of *BC* 1. Cato is therefore redrawing the profile of the *umbra* in order to correct Brutus's mistaken judgment about his conduct in the civil war. He is following not Pompey, but rather the falling Republic; since it is a father's duty to bury a dead son, Cato will not return until he has done his duty to *libertas* (George 1991: 253). The verbs *iuvat* and *iubet*, when viewed in the context of funeral rights fulfilled by a parent as an obligation but also as a benefit conferred to the state, do not any longer appear as inappropriate or extreme. Instead they invite comparison with some of Seneca's reflections in *De Beneficiis* because Cato behaves like "a good man unable to fail to do what he does" (*vir bonus non potest non facere quod facit*) and like a benefactor who "gives a benefit (*beneficium dat*), not because he does what he ought to do, but because it is not possible for him not to do what he ought to do (*non potest autem non facere quod debet*)" (*Ben.* 6.21.2).[15]

Profile of the Benefactor in Seneca's *De Beneficiis*

The importance and functioning of "how to give, receive, and return benefits correctly" (*Ben.* 1.4.2) are explored in this treatise.[16] In his exposition, Seneca attributes almost every public good to the logic of *beneficium*. At *Ben.* 4.18.1, even peace and security are elucidated not as the result of the good conduct of an emperor or an army, but as a product of the mutual exchange of benefits. The giving of a benefit is characterized as an act of selflessness since the benefactor is concerned not with reimbursement for his gift, but with the welfare of the person who receives it (4.29.3). For Seneca, it is only through this kind of generosity that life becomes in some measure protected and fortified against sudden disaster (4.18.1–2).

According to ancient social norms, outward expressions of grief were rightful acts (*Ep.* 99.16). Cato's *dolor* at *BC* 2.299 is justified in this logic, and the obsequies he performs represent a *iustum* but also the last *beneficium* he can grant. Cicero in his *De officiis* "links beneficence to the obligations imposed by pre-existing social relationship, including those of kinship" (*Off.* 1.50–8; cf. Griffin 2013: 22).[17] For Seneca, instead, a *beneficium* is different from an *officium* because it is not tied to prior obligations and can be withheld (*Ben.* 3.18.1).[18] In Roman culture the father is viewed as the benefactor par excellence for having given the *beneficium* of life to one who is not aware of receiving it (Quint., *Decl.* 368.1). At *Ben.* 4.29.3, Seneca underlines the attitude and intentions of a true benefactor: he must take into consideration the interest of the one for whom the benefit is destined, must deem him worthy, willingly undertake the burden and receive pleasure from the act of giving (*ut eius causa faciam, ad quem volam pervenire beneficium, dignumque eum iudicem et libens id tribuam percipiensque ex munere meo gaudium*). All these qualifications apply to Lucan's Cato when he, like a generous benefactor, by his own will gladly decides to die for the Republic deemed worthy of such a gift.

For Seneca, only philosophy can teach how "to owe and to repay benefits well" (*Ep.* 73.9), and for the Stoics, a sage's perfect knowledge (*oikeiôsis*) of the various layers constituting his identity and how it relates with the larger human social network makes him the perfect benefactor.[19] Lucan shows that Cato views his political commitment to Rome as an obligation and that his commemoration of freedom and death are his last acts of benevolence toward the falling Republic. In *BC* 2.297–305, he contentedly bestows benefits onto the citizens of Rome even when they are not aware of receiving them. Cato keeps giving to Rome with the hope that, at one point, the cycle of dynamic magnanimity necessary for the proper functioning of a state may begin again. Caesar appropriated what Seneca calls *ius dandi beneficii* (*Ben.* 2.20.3) and Florus perceptively recasts as *potentia beneficiorum* (*Epit.* 2.13.92). Emperors, as false benefactors, altered the logic of gift giving (e.g., *Ben.* 2.12; 5.25.2; 2.27.2) and usurped as their own the life of Roman citizens.[20] Only Cato is shown by Lucan as able to offer correctly the most precious thing he has, his own life.[21] In so doing, he embodies the altruistic conferral of benefits depicted by Seneca in the *De Beneficiis*.

Fighting to Benefit the Self and the Collectivity: *BC* 2 vs. *Ep.* 67, 104, and 95

At *BC* 2.297–316 Cato's outwardly oriented *virtus* is reiterated when he frames his death as a sacrifice (*piaculum*, 304) through which he wishes that Rome may be redeemed and restored in character. While the fierce gods demand atonement from the Romans, he remembers Decius' sacrifice of his life (*devotum Decium*, 308) and expresses the hope he could restore peace by offering his head to expiate all faults (*hoc caput in cunctas damnatum exponere poenas*, 306–7). According to Livy, during the Republic, the Decii tried to alter impending doom in battle with a self-sacrifice called *devotio* in which they vowed to give up their lives to the gods of the underworld in exchange for the victory of the group.[22] In *Ep.* 67.7–9, Seneca mentions Regulus, Cato, Rutilius, and Socrates as men who died for their ethical choices (67.7), and he describes the *devotio* of the Decii as an example of how desiring to live a virtuous life obliges the good man to embrace dangers and sometimes death (67.7–9):

> Ita cum optavi mihi vitam honestam, et haec optavi sine quibus interdum honesta non potest esse ... Decius se pro republica devovit et in medios hostes concitato equo mortem petens inruit. Alter post hunc, paternae virtutis aemulus ... in aciem confertissimam incucurrit, de hoc sollicitus tantum, ut litaret, optabilem rem putans bonam mortem.

> So when I wanted an honorable life for myself, I also wanted these things without which, sometimes, life cannot be honorable ... Decius sacrificed himself for his

country: he rushed at full gallop into the midst of the enemy, seeking death. Another Decius after him, emulating his father's virtue ... dashed into the thick of the fray. He was anxious only that his offering be propitious, for the thought that a good death was something worth wishing for.

Illustrating an argument advanced in the *De Beneficiis*—the good that comes to a city from the mutual conferral of benefits between children and parents—Seneca depicts the Decii father and son as protagonists of a praiseworthy competition which sees them engaged in surpassing each other in *virtus* and benefitting the community through this private challenge. Livy's episode "represents the greatest paradigm in Roman history of someone destined for defeat who used that defeat as the means to ensure victory" (Thorne 2010: 174). In *Ep.* 67, Seneca's emphasis is on a *virtus* which aids the community and is demonstrated in external action. Thus, at *BC* 2.297–305, Lucan's Cato resembles that of the Decii, although in contrast with the second Decius, he is no longer concerned with gods who have willed the civil war but only with the fate of the Republic.[23] Under the sign of *devotio*, Cato announces his death as a self-sacrifice that confers its benefits upon others and wants to convince his internal and external audiences to fight. The spectators of a *devotio* play an important role since the sacrificial ride of the devoted men is supposed to inspire them to fight more intensely against the enemy (Feldherr 1998: 84; Edwards 2007: 26). In this logic, Lucan's Cato is summoning Brutus and the Romans to do something about their imminent loss. The vow he formulates will be fulfilled by his suicide in Utica, which cannot be evaluated solely as a private "victory of virtue" but must be considered a beneficial and inspirational act. As M. Thorne observes, not only is Cato's participation in the war dictated by proper reasons, but Cato's *devotio* has the essential goal to memorialize the ideal of a free Rome and as such is a true work of *pietas* (Thorne 2010: 149 and 163).

Beyond *Ep.* 67, Lucan alludes to Seneca's *Ep.* 104.29–34 and 95.67–71 in which we find comparisons of Cato to Achilles and to a horse of good stock. In both letters, Cato's motives for fighting during the civil war emerge much more clearly than in *Ep.* 14 or 24 and it is impossible not to notice that in *Ep.* 104, Seneca focuses exactly on the two main events which Lucan will portray in his extant epic: Cato's decision to involve himself in the war and his desert march.

In *Ep.* 104.31, Seneca elevates Cato to a symbol of political rebellion against Caesar and Pompey, comparing him to Achilles who opposes himself to Priam and Agamemnon. The letter features men who did not let external forces change their disposition and discusses Cato who, among multiple trials and in tremendous turmoil, remained the same (*eundem se in omni statu praestitit*, 30). In the letter, Seneca defends political involvement in general and specific terms. He affirms that nature endows men with a magnanimous spirit which seeks not a quiet but an honorable existence (23) and describes Cato's behavior. During the civil war, while everybody else sides with Pompey or Caesar, Cato by himself sustains the Republic (*cum alii ad Caesarem inclinarent, alii ad Pompeium, solus Cato facit aliquas et rei publicae partes*, 30).[24] Right after this assessment, Cato is compared to Achilles (*Ep.* 104.31–2):

Miraberis, inquam, cum animadverteris
   Atriden Priamumque et saevum ambobus Achillen. [*Aen.* 1.458]
utrumque enim improbat, utrumque exarmat.

You will be amazed, I tell you, when you catch sight of "Atreus's son and Priam, and the scourge of both, Achilles." He [Cato] similarly condemns both [Pompey and Caesar], both he would like to strip of their weapons.

tr. Graver and Long adapted

Seneca cites the *Aeneid* in which Vergil conjures up the dispute of *Iliad* 1. In *Iliad* 9, Achilles, offended by Agamemnon's abduction of his war prize Briseis, is begged to return to the war but rejects the proposal and the compensatory gifts presented to him. Achilles desires renown that he can obtain only by fighting, and he cannot easily withdraw from a war he has chosen nor renege on his alliance with the son of Atreus. However, his acceptance of Agamemnon's gifts would be equally troublesome because as Agamemnon himself spells out at 9.158–61, his real goal is not to acknowledge Achilles' value and admit his own mistake but to establish his prestige as a giver. The offerings reassert his superiority over Achilles.[25] Agamemnon's gifts are enslaving and the reciprocity they construct is intrinsically warped.

During the civil war, Cato finds himself in a situation not so different from that faced by Achilles who joined the war as a free man and voluntarily endangered his life for the Atreides but realized that the war has developed in a way which undermines his generosity, freedom, and position of equality with respect to the same Agamemnon. For this reason, Achilles in the *Iliad* is not simply fighting against the Trojans but is also involved in a civil strife with Agamemnon. In the civil wars when, according to Seneca, men were fighting to decide "not whether, but to which of the two masters, they would be slaves" (*non an servirent, se utri, Ben.* 2.20.2), Cato, like Achilles, risks remaining trapped between Pompey and Caesar, enslaved to their logics and arrogance. However, as I have highlighted above, in Lucan's narrative, unlike Achilles, Cato finds a way out of the dilemma.

Another letter that gives us insights about Cato as a fighter is *Ep.* 95.68–70. Here Seneca compares the virtuous soul (and Cato) to a well-bred horse[26] and underlines the militant dimension of Cato's opposition to Pompey and Caesar:

You'll know at once the foal (*pullus*) of noble stock ... He is the first who dares advance, / risks the threatening floods (*primus et ire viam et fluvios temptare minantis*), entrusts himself / to the unknown bridge, not flinching at mere sound (*ignoto sese committere ponti, / nec vanos horret strepitus*). / Long in the neck and with a shapely head / ... his chest abundant in courage / is richly muscled (*luxuriatque toris animosum pectus*) [*G.* 3.75–81]. If a distant clash of arms / should reach him, he is on the move, his ears / prick up, his limbs are quivering, and he snorts / his nostrils, gathering his inward fire (*Tum, si qua sonum procul arma dederunt / stare loco nescit, micat auribus et tremit artus, / conlectumque premens volvit sub naribus ignem)*" [*G*. 3.83–5]. Our poet Virgil, while treating something else, has delineated the courageous man. I myself would employ no other image for a hero. If I had to describe Cato, fearless amid the clash of civil wars, the first to confront the armies already positioned at the Alps, and braving the perils of civil war himself, this is precisely the expression and demeanor I would give him. No one, in fact, "could have marched with more spirited step" (*altius certe nemo ingredi potuit*), simultaneously facing Caesar and Pompey, with everyone else supporting one side or the other, he challenged both leaders and showed that the Republic too had someone to back it.

tr. Graver and Long adapted

Cato is explicitly compared to a horse which is not afraid to face dangers, and whose *pectus* is *animosus* (spirited, brave) because virtue is described by Seneca as *animosa* (*Ep.* 71.18; cf. *Herc. F.* 20). Spiritedness is a precious trait, indeed indispensable, for one who is about to fight. Seneca's description suggests Plato's *Phaed.* 253d and *Rep.* 439d–441c, in which *thumos* (spiritedness/righteous anger) is proper to the white horse and lowly appetites to the black horse. In Plato's tripartite soul, both the black and the white horse must be led and restrained by the charioteer who represents reason. Whether Seneca accepted (or not) Plato's tripartite structure of the soul, it is clear that he endorses the idea that a well-trained *thumos* is a warrior's greatest ally toward honorable actions.[27]

Seneca relishes the equestrian analogy. He compares those who are being educated in virtue to horses in training (Torre 1995: 371–5). For instance, he elucidates that while some individuals whose nature is fierce and impatient must avoid incitements (*ferox impatiensque natura irritamenta ... evitet, Tranq.* 9.6.2), others, similar to slow and lazy horses, necessitate fire and spurs (*sicut tarde consurgentis ad cursum equos stimulis facibusque ... excitamus, Ira* 2.14.1). In *Ep.* 34, he envisions Lucilius as a horse that he has trained for a race, applying the goad lest he marched lazily (*addidi stimulos nec lente ire passus sum,* 34.2). In *Ben.* 5.25.4–6, the importance of advice in the formation of the soul is discussed employing terms that come from the language of horse training (5.25.4–5, my translation):

> Moneri velle ac posse secunda virtus est. Equus obsequens facile et parens huc illuc frenis leniter motis flectendus est. Paucis animus sui rector optimus.

> The second best form of virtue is to be willing and able to take advice. The horse that is docile and obedient can be guided this or that way by the slightest movement of the reins. Few men follow reason as their best horseman.

At this point, we can understand why in *Ep.* 95 Cato is visualized by Seneca as a splendidly trained horse and in *BC* 2 Lucan's Cato, similar to a good trainer, stirs Brutus to fight (2.323–5):

                        sic fatur et acris
irarum movit stimulus iuvenisque calorem
excitat in nimios belli civilis amores.

                        So speaking, he [Cato] plied
indignation's stinging lash, and the young man's fervor
he roused all too successfully to love for civil war.

Cato's speech is so successful that Brutus changes his opinion and is fired by love for the civil war. The indignation of the adviser now belongs to Brutus who is like Seneca's obedient steed (*Ben.* 5.25.5) or the horse returning to action once the spur has been applied (*Ep.* 34.2–3). The "excess" implied by *nimios* (325) is justifiable when contextualized according to Seneca's citations, for not only does the word spur (*stimulus*) evoke horses and charioteers, but the heat and anger (*irarum . . . calorem*, 324) felt by the youth remind us of "the compressed fire" (*conlectum . . . ignem*, *Ep.* 95.68) which for too long the good horse-Cato has kept compressed inside himself. C. Torre writes about a kind of "metaphorical sympathy" between Cato as a steed and the other *proficientes*-horses, an "overlap" between *sapiens* and *proficiens* in discourse that details the *iter virtutis* (Torre 1995: 376). In Seneca, the language of cavalry and competition intersects with philosophical discourse. The good stallion is able to stir himself and leads others on the path of virtue. This vocabulary is employed by Lucan to highlight Cato's political allegiance and his desire to transmit that devotion to other individuals. In *BC* 2.323–5, Brutus begins to resemble the well-bred steed eager to proceed in his path toward virtue and freedom.

In discussing *Ep.* 95, F. Berno highlights that Seneca's employment of Vergil's horse gives Cato a non-ataraxic and non-apathetic quality necessary to a character who rationally ponders his decision to enter the war, but is also shown as equipped with qualities that will make him successful in that war (Berno 2011: 241–2). Cicero in his *Pro Murena* had criticized Tubero and Cato for their Stoic intransigency that, in the lawyer's mind, made them ineffective political leaders, unable to serve adequately the shifting necessities of the political arena.[28] Seneca in *Ep.* 95 indirectly replies to that accusation: it is thanks to his philosophical resoluteness that Cato can effectively fight the battle against extreme corruption since the progress of vice necessitates a parallel progress in fighting (*Ep.* 95.29–35) and in extreme circumstances, "philosophers cannot remain moderate. On the contrary . . . they must take any measure for the sake of virtue" (Berno 2014: 376).

Engagement, *Parenesis*, and Animal Metaphors at *BC* 9 in the Light of *De Clementia*

The language of the well-bred horse eager to cross places never trampled before (*G.* 3.76–8) returns in Lucan's description of Cato ready to face the inaccessible paths of the Libyan route (*inreducemque viam*, 9.408; *invia*, 9.387); like Seneca's stallion, Lucan's Cato wants to be the first to confront dangers (*primus harenas / ingredia*, 9.394–5;

cf. *primus*, *G.* 3.76). In this ordeal, his sense of obligation and virtue are in evidence (*hac ire Catonem / dura iubet virtus*, 9.444–5) together with his eagerness to persuade his men to gladly welcome (*o quibus...placuit*, 9.379) the "hard path towards law" (*durum iter ad leges*, 9.385) and "die with a neck unyoked" (*indomita cervice mori*, 9.380). Ultimately Cato's persuasion is successful, since he is able to "fire their fearful spirits with virtue and love of toil" (*paventes / incendit virtute animos et amore laborum*, 9.406–7) so that they persist on the desert path. In terms of content, the sequence mimics what we saw at *BC* 2 (Brutus' unwillingness to participate in the war followed by his change of mind after Cato's speech) and stylistically adopts Seneca's "heated" hortatory terminology through which the trainer rouses the sluggish horse toward the right path.[29]

Even earlier, at *BC* 9.255–93, we found Cato's reproach to soldiers reluctant to fight and their reaction to it.[30] Cato's words after Pompey's death emphasize that the disintegration of the Republic is accelerated by the tendency of Roman legionnaires to value individual commanders above the state. In his powerful oration (256–83), he reminds the mutineers that now they have the opportunity to fight as Roman soldiers not for a master but for themselves (257–60) and that they should be ready to offer their lives for the fatherland now that freedom is near (264–65). *Parenesis* to solicit engagement and another animal metaphor from Seneca are employed at 283–93 when the soldiers are compared to bees driven back to their toils by the sound of Phrygian cymbals shaken by a beekeeper (9.283–93):

> dixit et omnes
> haud aliter medio revocavit ab aequore puppes
> quam, simul effetas linquunt examina ceras
> atque oblita favi non miscent nexibus alas,
> sed sibi quaeque volat nec iam degustat amarum
> desidiosa thymum, Phrygii sonus increpat aeris,
> attonitae posuere fugam studiumque laboris
> floriferi repetunt et sparsi mellis amorem:
> gaudet in Hybleo securus gramine pastor
> divitias servasse casae. Sic voce Catonis
> inculcata viris iusti patientia Martis.

> His words summoned
> all ships back from water—the way, once their eggs
> hatch, files of bees abandon their waxen nurseries and,
> heedless of the comb, cease to cluster in swarms, wing on wing;
> each flies off on her own and, indolent, no longer sucks
> pungent thyme. But let clashing Phrygian brass rebuke them:
> thunderstruck, the bees dawdle no more but resume with zeal
> their bloom-born labor, their love of far-flung honey.
> The shepherd in meadows on Monte Ibleo, eased of cares,
> rejoices: he has assured the wealth of his cottage.
> Cato drummed into his men courage to face a just war.

The language fittingly describes bees and soldiers: *examina* (285) designates swarms of bees as well as ranks of soldiers, and the expression *miscent alas* (286) evokes the act of joining battle (cf. 1.682; 3.569, etc.). The army embraces civil war, which under the leadership of Cato has become just (*iusti* . . . *Martis*, 293). Their newly acquired desire to fight is described as a productive enterprise thanks to the mention of the honey (289–90). Lucan's comparison of the soldiers to bees and of Cato to a beekeeper allude to *Clem.* 1.4.1. In this passage, Seneca envisions the supreme leader of the state as the bond which unites the commonwealth (*ille est enim uinculum per quod res publica cohaeret*) and the breath of life (*spiritus uitalis*) which ensures the wellbeing of all subjects; by citing *Georgics* 4.212–13, Seneca compares them to bees which stay safe only if their king is safe.[31] In this treatise, the philosopher building on *G.* 4 elaborates the similarity between the King Bee and the emperor, and establishes an analogy between a well-functioning society and the hive. The *princeps* is believed to be so structurally essential for the state that his subjects are "most ready to expose themselves to the swords of aggressors in his defense" (*obicere se pro illo mucronibus insidiantium paratissimi, Clem.* 1.3.3) and protect his sleep by nightly watches (*somnium eius nocturnis excubiis muniunt, Clem.* 1.3.3). By defending their king, the bees are defending themselves (Braund 2009: 212–13).

Lucan's above-cited passage is also connected to *G.* 4.103–5 featuring a beekeeper who strives to contain the bees swarming away and neglecting their work because of their *instabilis animos* (105). Vergil had described the bees' nature and developed an elaborate comparison between bees and human society.[32] At *G.* 4.153–227, he portrays the bees as sharing offspring (*natos*) and a city (*tecta urbis*), "regulat[ing] their life with mighty laws" (*magnisque agitant sub legibus aeuum*, 154). The bees can work themselves to death (204), are absolutely devoted to their leader (215), and can sacrifice their life in battle (*petunt per vulnera mortem*, 218). Thus they exhibit the patriotism of the old Roman people, but their virtues are not in the service of a Republican society. Vergil's bees fight for a king (*G.* 4.210–18) (Miles 1980: 250; Barton 2001: 113).

At *Clem.* 1.19.2, Seneca legitimizes monarchy using the beehive conceptualized as an invention of nature (*Natura enim commenta est regem*, "Nature, after all, devised the idea of the king") and builds his praise of Nero relying on Vergil's description of the servile bees orbiting around the king and ready to die for him. It is significant that while addressing himself to Nero and constructing the parallel between the political and natural world, he employs *G.* 4, a text which "represents an attempt to engage in a constructive dialogue with Octavian on the potential courses available to him" (Nappa 2005: 1–2). Both Seneca and Vergil would have autocratic rulers as their primary addressee. Lucan reacts to Seneca's ambitious attempt to craft in *De Beneficiis* a new metaphysics of the Principate which blends ideas and techniques coming from kingship treatises, panegyrical orations, and philosophical disquisition.[33] He objects to the concept of a nation able to function properly only under a monarch. Therefore, at *BC* 2 he reverses Seneca's image of the bee-citizens offering their lives for a king (*Clem.* 1.4.1) and proposes that of Cato: a single man prepared to sacrifice his life for all citizens. As a responsible civil servant, Cato is awake and worried for the fate of the Republic (2.239–40). In dialogue with Brutus we see him reflecting on what he would like to accomplish for his nation, we hear about his wishes to receive the wounds of the whole war (309–11), to be the only one hit (*me solum invadite ferrum*, 315), and whose blood is going to be spilled (304–18). In his programmatic address to Nero at *De Clem.* 1.1, Seneca placed in front of the prince an idealized image of the prince himself for which Nero as a Stoic sage should rejoice (*te tibi ostenderem peruenturum ad uoluptatem maximam omnium*, "I give you a picture of yourself as someone who will attain the greatest pleasure of all") in the sheer awareness of behaving well and in accord with his own good conscience (*iuuat inspicere et circumire bonam conscientiam*), while many restless and powerless seek their destruction and that of others (*tum ... in hanc immensam multitudinem discordem, seditiosam, impotentem in perniciem alienam suamque*).[34] Lucan actualizes Seneca's image of virtue which Nero is invited to emulate with that of Cato who, in the act of speaking to Brutus, displays himself as a self-reflecting moral agent ready and happy to sacrifice himself for his country.

Lucan redefines Seneca's bees and can be considered another writer who uses the bee image in political discussion. Plato, for instance, had noticed that while the ruler of the bees is by birth equipped for his role, human rulers are not (*Pol.* 301e). Varro in his *De Re Rustica*, doubting the bees' capacity to rule themselves and featuring problems plaguing the hive (e.g., seditions, 3.16.18; runaway bees, 3.16.21), emphasized the control that a beekeeper must exert on his beehive (Carlson 2015: 93). Even Vergil depicted in detail a civil war among the bees (i.e., a fight between two bees for the control of the hive, *G.* 4.67–90) and brought his attention on the beekeeper. Lucan echoes them and in the *Bellum Civile* describes vulnerable bee-citizens protected by the beekeeper Cato.

Cato as a Beekeeper in *BC* 9

At *BC* 9.283–93, the bees are shown as lacking all the features that in the *Aeneid* are attributed to those occupied with building a nation, i.e., taking care of the reproductive cycle (*Aen.* 1.432), storing honey (1.432–3), and productively interacting with each other (1.433–4). Lucan's bees are forgetful of their brood (*effetas ceras*, 9.285), fly with selfish motivations (*sibi quaeque volat*, 9.287), and do not interact (*non miscent nexibus alas*, 9.286). Only after listening to Cato are they renewed and transformed, ready to care for their society and embrace war. Lucan's bees accept hard toil, reject a supreme ruler, and fight for the welfare of their households (9.289–93). They can do it thanks to Cato who, like a good beekeeper, stirs them to do what is proper. Vergil's focus on a domestic beehive (i.e., one which necessitates a beekeeper) "led him to emphasize the need for the management of an otherwise vulnerable and unstable society, and thus to highlight the absence of a benevolent higher power that could intervene to solve Rome's problems" (Morley 2007: 464). Lucan notices this aspect of Vergil's description and capitalizes on the idea of the virtuous beekeeper Cato (not a monarch or the gods) as the only one willing to intervene for the right reasons.

At *BC* 9.292–3, the narrator identifies Cato's voice (*voces Catonis*, 292) with the *Phrygii aeris sonus* (288) of the "shepherd on Monte Ibleo" (*in Hybleo ... pastor*, 291) who "is happy" (*gaudet*, 291) and confident (*securus*, 291) because through the production of honey he can guarantee the household welfare (*divitias servasse casas*, 292).³⁵ The word *pastor* for the beekeeper is supremely allusive. At *Aen.* 12.587, the noun *pastor* is applied by Vergil to a frustrated Aeneas about to attack Laurentum and similar to a beekeeper fumigating his bees constructing their beehive in an unsuitable place (587–9). Aristaeus, successfully producing new bees through the *bugonia*, is also called *pastor* at *G.* 4.312. Lucan's Cato, like Aristaeus, succeeds in bringing back to labor his bee-soldiers. The presence of the "pastor in the meadow" and of "the bees with their bloom-born labor and love of far-flung honey" brings to mind bucolic serenity and the accomplishments of the *senex Corycius* (116–48) who, through his hard work, is "first to collect honey from the honey comb" (*primus ... cogere pressis / mella favis*, 140–41) and transforms an unproductive field (125–30) into a spectacularly blooming orchard "equal in his opinion to the riches of kings" (*regum aequabat opes animis*, 132). Finally, *pastor* appears in Seneca's *Ep.* 34.1 describing a shepherd taking pleasure (*capit voluptatem*) in the growth of his flock. At *BC* 9.291, Cato, like Seneca's *pastor*, rejoices (*gaudet*, 291) in the return of the bees to work because he knows that it will be beneficial.

As Rolim de Moura has recently noticed, apiculture in Vergil's *Georgics* is considered through a politically charged language which is employed by Lucan for his own political goals: "In Virgil, the analogy with politics breaks down precisely due to the need of a beekeeper, which is the role Cato plays in Lucan's politics. In other words, Cato's speech has counteracted not only pure indiscipline but also the ideology of loyalty to warlord after whose death the soldiers are willing to disperse, like bees when their queen is lost" (Rolim de Moura 2010: 78). Lucan's Cato successfully fights the ideology of the civil war and responds to Seneca's *De Clementia*. Cato acting as a beekeeper is the protector and conscience of the state.

Conclusions

Lucan's characterization of Cato reveals an intense dialogue with the work of Seneca. Cato's political commitment and willingness to embrace civil war are at times kept in the background by Seneca, but they are brought into focus by Lucan who views Cato's fight as his last gift to the dying republic. Cato's beneficial and imitable behavior during the war reminds us of Seneca's treatment of the good benefactor of *De Beneficiis*. The contradictions which Seneca tried to lessen or harmonize through his spirit-empowering philosophy are dramatized by Lucan (e.g., in the dialogue between Brutus and Cato in *BC* 2) and explode in a world dominated by *nefas* and civil war. Even when Lucan objects to the *De Clementia*'s conceptual apparatus for the legitimization of sovereign *potestas* and *imperium*, his poem displays a profound re-elaboration of his uncle's ideas. Overall, the *Bellum Civile* and its Cato are not comprehensible without Seneca's composite, powerful, and lifelong meditation about freedom, death, politics, and the responsibilities of the good man.³⁶

Notes

1. Seneca's *Epistulae ad Lucilium* and Lucan's *Bellum Civile* are typically assigned to the years comprised between 61 and 65 CE. *De Beneficiis* could have been initiated as early as 56 CE. For the dating of these works, see Masters (1992: 216–47); Griffin (2013: 91–8); Marshall (2015: 33 and 41–2). Because of the unfeasibility of a more precise collocation, it is impossible to establish the direction of this influence, i.e., if Lucan is responding to his uncle or vice versa. See Roche in this volume for more on the interaction between Lucan's *BC* and Seneca's *Epistulae* and their relative dating.
2. Edwards (2007: 90–93). About *virtus*, cf. Cic., *Tusc.* 2.43. See McDonnell (2006: 12–141) for ties between *virtus* and *andreia* and its distinctively public value in Republican Rome.
3. The text of the *Epistulae* is that of Reynolds (1985), translation by Graver and Long.
4. For the legend of Cato, see Pecchiura (1965); Goar (1987); Edwards (2007: 1–5); Thorne (2010: 6–11). For Cato as a Stoic sage in Seneca, see Isnardi Parente (2000: 215–25) and also Griffin (2000: 545).
5. Cf. also Gowing (2005: 79), "In short, the memory of Cato Seneca most wishes to preserve is that of a moral *exemplum*, not as an exemplary opponent of absolutism."
6. Fantham (1982: 35) argues that *Ep.* 104 "does not suggest that Cato was right to join the Pompeian forces, or his decision necessary."
7. Bartsch (1997: 121). Cf. Martindale (1984: 74), who notices the inconsistent portrait of Cato in Seneca who seems uneasy with his involvement in the war at *Ep.* 14.12–13, *Ep.* 22.8, and *Ad Marc.* 20.6, but elsewhere seems more favorable (e.g., *Tranq.* 16.1, *Prov.* 2.9–12, *Const. Sap.* 2.1–2, *Ep.* 24.6–8, 71.8–10, 95.71, 104.29–33); see also Griffin (1992: 190–4).
8. See Canfora (2015: 198) and also (2000: 171).
9. Canfora (2000: 163) and (2015: 164, 170–1); cf. Sussman (1978: 26–33); identification of the precise timeframe covered by the work is not essential to my argument.
10. Arguments for political disengagement are developed by Seneca in his *De Otio* and *De Ira* 3.6.1–2; see (Thorne 2010: 136–45, 150–86) and George (1991: 249–50). Zientek (2018) for the generally negative connotation of the intratextual words related to *otium*.
11. See Thorne (2010: ch. 5, esp. 116) with good bibliography about the "Senecan voice of Brutus"; George (1991). Text of Lucan's *Bellum Civile* follows A. E. Housman's edition, English translation is by J. Wilson Joyce.
12. Cf. Sen., *Ep.* 107.11: *ducunt volentem fata, nolentem trahunt*, "the fates lead the willing man and drag the unwilling." Cato's position may indeed deviate from a normative Stoic acceptance of the will of the gods.
13. Fantham (1992: 134–6); Rudich (1997:122–3); Behr (2007: 151–3). Cf. Sen., *Ep.* 24.5.
14. The Latin text is Hosius (1914).
15. Griffin (2013: 46–47). Seneca's *De Beneficiis* "is the only surviving example of the category of works exclusively devoted to the subject" (Griffin 2013: 21). Benefits are also discussed in *Ep.* 81.
16. See Griffin (2003: 92); Coffee (2009: 9–39); Accardi (2015: 91–198). Cf. Chaumartin (1985: 313–29); Marino (2012: 127); Picone (2013: 29–38).
17. Cicero describes the *res publica* as the object of one's strongest allegiances (*Off.* 1.50–1) and locus for the fulfillment of human love (*Off.* 1.53–7).
18. Seneca had written a work *on Duties*, now lost.

19. *Oikeiôsis* begins in the bond between parent and child and is a key stage in humanity's moral development toward virtue; see Gloyn (2017: 6). For Reydam-Schils (2005: 81), Roman Stoicism's upgrade of the value of social relationships represents an original contribution to Stoic ethics.
20. See Letta (1997/98: 232 and 234), who specifies that in *Ben.* 7.16–20 the benefactor has turned himself into a tyrant, and pointed details (passion for the theatre and parties on boats) reveal the tyrant as Nero.
21. Cato's self-sacrifice cannot save Rome, yet Lucan wants the readers to ponder on "the model of the 'beneficial self-sacrifice' . . . that specifically confers its benefits upon others" (Thorne 2010: 170 and 180–1).
22. In 340 and 290 BCE, the ritual was enacted in Rome by the Decii (Liv. 8.9 and 10.28), who acquired great fame and saved Rome from defeat; see Leigh (1997: 131–5); McDonnell (2006: 200).
23. This attitude is a re-elaboration of Stoic parameters, a breach to an alleged Stoic orthodoxy.
24. The expression *facit aliquas partes* is repeated in *Ep.* 95.70.
25. On this episode, see Wilson (2002: 54–71); Fantuzzi (2012: 105 n.23).
26. Excellent analysis in Berno (2006: 55–77) and (2011: 233–53). On the horse as an image of the *sapiens* in Seneca, see Torre (1995: 371–8).
27. I am not concerned here with Seneca's theory of the soul (cf. *Ep.* 92.3–8; 71.27 and *Ira* 2.4.1), but simply noticing that in describing human inner tendencies, his *forma mentis* is conditioned by Platonic discourse.
28. Plutarch quotes Cicero's judgment that Cato seemed to be speaking in Plato's *Republic* and not the sewer of the Roman state, Plut., *Phoc.* 3.2; Stadter (2014: 313).
29. Cato's desert march is philosophically charged, but in it Cato also embodies the good Roman general: Leigh (2000: 100); Narducci (2001: 182–4).
30. In Africa, Cato speaks to his soldiers twice: after the mutiny at 9.256–83 and before the desert march at 9.379–406.
31. Dahlman (1970: 181–2); Roller (2001: 239–47); Morley (2007: 463–4); Braund (2009: 214); Starr (2012: 119–21). Cf. *Clem.* 1.19.2: another description of the King Bee. This treatise dates to 55–56 CE; see Marshall (2014: 41).
32. For the bees in *G.* 4, see: Dahlmann (1954); Wilkinson (1969); Leach (1977); Griffin (1979); Johnston (1980); Thomas (1982: 70–92); Starr (2012: 12–13).
33. Braund (2009: 23); Malaspina (2003: 148) and (2013: 9–77).
34. I am using the text of Braund (2009). On Seneca's royal political theory, see Stacey (2011) and Braund (2009: 64–76).
35. Ormsby (1970: 57).
36. For excellent reflections on Lucan's dependence on Seneca, see Castagna (2003).

References

Accardi, A. (2015), *Teoria e Prassi del beneficium da Cicerone a Seneca*, Palermo: Palumbo.
Ahl, F. (1976), *Lucan: An Introduction*, Cornell: Cornell University Press.
Barton, C. (2001), *Roman Honor: The Fire in the Bones*, Berkeley: University of California Press.

Bartsch, S. (1997), *Ideology in Cold Blood: A Reading of Lucan's Civil War*, Cambridge, MA: Cambridge University Press.
Behr, D. F. (2007), *Feeling History: Lucan, History, and the Poetics of Passion*, Columbus: Ohio State University Press.
Berno, F. (2006), "Il cavallo saggio e lo stolto Enea: due citazioni virgiliane in Seneca (*Epis.* 95.67-71; 56.12-14)," *AClass*, 49: 55-77.
Berno, F. (2011), "Seneca, Catone e due citazioni Virgiliane (Sen. *epis*. 95.67-71 e 104.31-32)," *SIFC*, 19 (2): 233-53.
Berno, F. (2014), "In Praise of Tubero's Pottery: A note on Seneca, *Ep.* 95.72-3 and 98.13," in M. Colish and J. Wildberger (eds.), *Seneca philosophus: Trends in classics, supplementary volumes 27*, 370-94, Berlin: De Gruyter.
Braund, S., ed. and trans. (2009), *Seneca: De Clementia*, Oxford: Oxford University Press.
Canfora, L. (2000), "Seneca e le guerre civili," in P. Parroni (ed.), *Seneca e il suo tempo*, 161-77, Rome: Salerno Editrice.
Canfora, L. (2015), *Augusto figlio di Dio*, Bari: Laterza.
Carlson, R. (2015), "The Honey Bee and Apian Imagery in Classical Literature," PhD diss., University of Washington, Seattle.
Castagna, L. (2003), "Lucano e Seneca: i limiti di una *aemulatio*," in I. Gualandri and G. Mazzoli (eds.), *Gli Annei: una famiglia nella storia e nella cultura della Roma imperiale, Atti del convegno internazionale di Milano, Maggio 2000*, 277-90, Como: Edizioni New Press.
Chaumartin, F.-R. (1985), *Le De Beneficiis de Sénèque: sa signification philosophique politique et sociale*, Lille: Société d'édition Les Belles Lettres.
Coffee, M. (2009), *The Commerce of War: Exchange and Social Order in Latin Epic,* Chicago: University of Chicago Press.
Dahlman, H. (1954), "Der Bienenstaat in Vergils *Georgica*," *Akademie der wissenschaftlichen und literatur, Abhandlungen*, 10: 547-62.
Edwards, C. (2007), *Death in Ancient Rome*, New Haven: Yale University Press.
Fantham, E., ed. (1982), *Lucan: De Bello Civili II*, Cambridge: Cambridge University Press.
Fantuzzi, M. (2012), *Achilles in Love: Intertextual Studies*, Oxford: Oxford University Press.
Feldherr, A. (1998), *Spectacle and Society in Livy's Histories*, Berkeley: University of California Press.
Fratantuono, L. (2015), "Lucan's Bees and the Ethnography of the *Pharsalia*," in P. Esposito and C. Walde (eds.), *Letture e Lettori di Lucano, Atti del Convegno Internazionale di studi, Fisciano 22-27 Marzo 2012*, 57-72, Pisa: ETS.
George, D. B. (1988), "Lucan's Caesar and οἰκείωσις Theory: The Stoic Fool," *TAPhA*, 118: 331-41.
George, D. B. (1991), "Lucan's Cato and Stoic Attitudes to the Republic," *ClAnt*, 10 (2): 237-58.
Gloyn, L. (2017), *The Ethics of the Family in Seneca*, Cambridge: Cambridge University Press.
Goar, R. J. (1987), *The Legend of Cato Uticensis from the First Century B.C. to the Fifth Century A.D.*, Brussels: Latomus.
Gowing, A. M. (2005), *Empire and Memory: The Representation of the Roman Republic in Imperial Culture*, Cambridge: Cambridge University Press.
Graver, M. and A. A. Long, eds. and trans. (2015), *Seneca. Letters on Ethics to Lucilius*, Chicago: University of Chicago Press.
Griffin, J. (1979), "The Fourth *Georgic*, Virgil and Rome," *G&R*, 26: 61-80.
Griffin, M. (1992), *Seneca: A Philosopher in Politics*, Oxford: Clarendon Press.
Griffin, M. (2000), "Seneca and Pliny," in C. Rowe and M. Schofield (eds.), *The Cambridge History of Greek and Roman Political Thought*, 532-58. Cambridge: Cambridge University Press.
Griffin, M. (2003), "*De Beneficiis* and Roman Society," *JRS*, 93: 92-113.
Griffin, M. (2013), *Seneca on Society: A Guide to De Beneficiis*, Oxford: Oxford University Press.
Hill, T. (2004), *Ambitiosa Mors: Suicide and Self in Roman Thought and Literature*, New York: Routledge.

Hosius, C., ed. (1914), *L. Annaei Senecae De Beneficiis Libri VII*, Leipzig: Teubner.
Housman, A. E., ed. (1927), *M. Annaei Lucani Belli Civilis Libri Decem*, Oxford: Oxford University Press.
Innocenti Pierini, R. (2014), "Freedom in Seneca: Some Reflections on the Relationship between Philosophy and Politics, Public and Private Life," in M. Colish and J. Wildberger (eds.), *Seneca philosophus. Trends in classics, supplementary volumes 27*, 167–88, Berlin: De Gruyter.
Isnardi Parente, M. (2000), "Socrate e Catone in Seneca: il filosofo e il politico," in P. Parroni (ed.), *Seneca e il suo tempo*, 215–25, Rome: Salerno Editrice.
Ker, J. (2009), "Outside and Inside: Senecan Strategies," in W. J. Dominik, J. Garthwaite, and P. Roche (eds.), *Writing Politics in Imperial Rome*, 249–73, Leiden: Brill.
Leach, E. W. (1977), "*Sedes Apibus*: From the *Georgics* to the *Aeneid*," *Vergilius*, 22: 2–16.
Leigh, M. (1997), *Lucan: Spectacle and Engagement*, Oxford: Clarendon University Press.
Leigh, M. (2000), "Lucan and the Libyan Tale," *JRS*, 90: 95–109.
Lentano, M. (2005), "Il dono e il debito: Verso un'antropologia del beneficio nella cultura romana," in A. A. Haltenhoff, A. Heil, and F.-H. Mutschler (eds.), *Römische Werte als Gegenstand der Altertumswissenschaft*, 125–42, Berlin: De Gruyter.
Letta, C. (1997–8), "Allusioni politiche e riflessioni sul principato nel 'De Beneficiis' di Seneca," *Limes*, 9–10: 227–44.
Malaspina, E. (2003), "La teoria politica del *De Clementia*: un inevitabile fallimento?," in E. Lo Cascio and A. De Vivo (eds.), *Seneca uomo politico e l'età di Claudio e Nerone, Atti del Convegno internazionale, Capri 25–27 Marzo 1999*, 139–57, Bari: Edipuglia.
Malaspina, E. (2009), *Lucio: Anneo Seneca. La Clemenza, Opere, Vol. V*, Milano: Utet.
Marino, R. (2012), "'Circolarità virtuosa' e 'virtù crudele' per una pragmatica relazionale nel *De beneficiis* di Seneca," *Minerva* 25: 125–47.
Marshall, C. W. (2015), "The Works of Seneca the Younger and his dates," in A. Heil and G. Damschen (eds.), *Brill's Companion to Seneca: Philosopher and Dramatist*, 33–44, Leiden: Brill.
Martindale, C. (1984), "The Politician Lucan," *G&R* 31 (1): 64–70.
Masters, J. (1992), *Poetry and Civil War in Lucan's Bellum Civile*, Cambridge: Cambridge University Press.
McDonnell, M. (2006), *Roman Manliness: "Virtus" and the Roman Republic*, Cambridge: Cambridge University Press.
Miles, G. (1980), *Virgil's Georgics: A New Interpretation*, Berkeley: University of California Press.
Morley, N. (2007), "Civil War and Succession Crisis in Roman Beekeeping," *Historia*, 56 (4): 462–70.
Nappa, C. (2005), *Reading after Actium: Vergil's Georgics, Octavian, and Rome*, Ann Arbor: University of Michigan Press.
Narducci, E. (2001), "Catone in Lucano (e alcune interpretazioni recenti)," *Athenaeum*, 89 (1): 171–86.
Ormsby, R. (1970), "The Literary Portrait of Cato Uticensis in Lucan's *Bellum Civile*," PhD diss., University of Washington, Seattle.
Pecchiura, P. (1965), *La figura di Catone Uticense nella letteratura latina*, Torino: Giappichelli.
Picone, G., ed. (2013), *Le regole del beneficio: commento tematico a Seneca, "De beneficiis I,"* Palermo: Palumbo.
Plass, P. (1995), *The Game of Death in Ancient Rome: Arena Sport and Political Suicide,* Madison: University of Wisconsin Press.
Reydam-Schils, G. (2005), *The Roman Stoics: Self, Responsibility, and Affection*, Chicago: University of Chicago Press.
Reynolds, L. D., ed. (1965), *Seneca: Ad Lucilium Epistulae Morales*, 2 vols, Oxford: Clarendon Press.
Rolim de Moura, A. (2010), "Cato in Libya (Lucan 9)," *Letras Clássicas*, 14: 63–91.

Roller, M. (2001), *Constructing Autocracy: Aristocrats and Emperors in Julio-Claudian Rome*, Princeton: Princeton University.
Rudich, V. (1993), *Political Dissidence under Nero: the Price of Dissimulation*, New York: Routledge.
Rudich, V. (1997), *Dissidence and Literature Under Nero: The Price of Rhetoricization*, London: Routledge.
Rudich, V. (2006), "Navigating the uncertain," *Arion*, 14 (1): 7–28.
Seo, J. M. (2013), *Exemplary Traits: Reading Characterization in Roman Poetry*, Oxford: Oxford University Press.
Stacey, P. (2011), "The Sovereign Person in Senecan Political Theory," *Republic of Letters*, 2 (2): 15-73.
Stadter, P. (2014), *Plutarch and his Roman Readers*, Oxford: Oxford University Press.
Starr, C. (2012), *The Empire of the Self: Self-Command and Political Speech in Seneca and Petronius*, Baltimore: Johns Hopkins University Press.
Stevenson, T. R. (1992), "The Ideal Benefactor and the Father Analogy in Greek and Roman Thought," *CQ*, 42: 421–36.
Sussman, L. A. (1978), *The Elder Seneca*, Leiden: Brill.
Syme, R. (1985), *Tacitus*, vols. I and II, Oxford: Oxford University Press.
Thomas, R. (1982), *Lands and Peoples in Roman Poetry: The Ethnographical Tradition*, Cambridge: Cambridge University Press.
Thorne, M. A. (2010), "Lucan's Cato the Defeat of Victory the Triumph of Memory," PhD dissertation, University of Iowa, Iowa City.
Tipping, B. (2011), "Terrible Manliness?: Lucan's Cato," in P. Asso (ed.), *Brill's Companion to Lucan*, 223–37, Leiden: Brill.
Torre, C. (1995), "Il cavallo immagine del *sapiens* in Seneca," *Maia*, 47: 371–78.
Wildberger, J. and M. Colish, eds. (2014), *Seneca philosophus*, Berlin: De Gruyter.
Wilkinson, L. P. (1969), *The Georgics of Virgil: A Critical Survey*, Cambridge: Cambridge University Press.
Wilson, D. (2002), *Ransom, Revenge and Heroic Identity in the Iliad*, Cambridge: Cambridge University Press.
Wilson Joyce, J., trans. (1993), *Lucan: Pharsalia*, Ithaca: Cornell University Press.
Zientek, L. (2018), "*Saeva quies* and Lucan's landscapes of anxiety," in D. Felton (ed.), *Landscapes of Dread in Classical Antiquity: Negative Emotions in Natural and Constructed Spaces*, 119–44, New York: Routledge.

PART IV
BACK TO THE FUTURE:
REPUBLIC AND EMPIRE

CHAPTER 9
LUCAN AND THE SPECTER OF SULLA IN JULIO-CLAUDIAN ROME
Julia Mebane

The fourth book of Lucan's *Bellum Civile* concludes on an ominous note. Looking back to the civil wars of the 80s BCE, the narrator remarks that the bloody power of Sulla, Marius, and Cinna lives on in the house of the Caesars.[1] This startling claim is couched in a condemnation of Curio's susceptibility to bribery, which is portrayed as the selling of Rome: *ius licet in iugulos nostros sibi fecerit ensis / Sulla potens Mariusque ferox et Cinna cruentus / Caesareaeque domus series, cui tanta potestas / concessa est? emere omnes, hic uendidit urbem* (Though powerful Sulla and fierce Marius and bloodthirsty Cinna and the line of the Caesarian house earned the right to use the sword against our throats, to whom was such great privilege granted? For they all bought the city, while he [Curio] sold it, 4.821–4).[2] Lucan constructs a historical trajectory of violence that begins with the generals of the 80s BCE and culminates in the Caesars of his own day.[3] Characterizing the prerogative to punish as the right to use the sword against citizen throats, the passage recalls 4.805–6: *has urbi miserae uestro de sanguine poenas / ferre datis, luitis iugulo sic arma, potentes* (With your blood, powerful ones, you force the miserable city to suffer these penalties, so you pay for war with your throat). Here it is not Rome's citizens but her generals who lose their necks, and synecdochally, their lives.[4] The repetition of *iugulum* exposes the self-destructive nature of internecine violence, in which those who wield the sword ultimately become victims of it.[5]

Although Lucan implicates Cinna, Marius, and Sulla in his reference to the *ius ensis*, he pays special attention to the last member of this list. As Asso (2009: *ad loc.* 822) notes, the chronology of the era is reversed so that Sulla comes first in the line of those who wield the sword. Lucan reinforces Sulla's centrality through his choice of nomenclature. Rather than refer to him by his famous agnomen *Felix*, Lucan calls him *potens* (4.822), the same adjective used to refer to the generals whose ambitions cost them their lives (4.806). He then employs a counterfactual that renders *felix* an attribute of Rome: *felix Roma quidem ciuisque habitura beatos, / si libertatis superis tam cura placeret / quam uindicta placet* (Rome could have been fortunate indeed, and have had happy citizens, if the gods had as great a concern for her liberty as they have for its vengeance, 4.807–9). By assimilating Sulla to the doomed *potentes* and assigning his agnomen to the strife-ridden Rome, Lucan locates the republican dictator within the paradigm of self-destruction. He does so despite the fact that the historical Sulla did not fall victim to civil war, relinquishing power and dying in retirement.[6] Revising Roman history to fit his narrative aims, Lucan suggests that this violent cycle began with the foundation of the city itself.[7] His reference to the blood penalties (*sanguine poenas*, 4.805) paid by Roman generals alludes to Romulus' words as he prepares to kill Remus in Ennius' *Annals*: *nam mi calido dabis sanguine poenas* ("You will pay the penalty to me with your warm blood," fr. 95 Skutsch).[8] Already encoded in Rome's origins is the right of the sword, which will be transferred from the despots of the 80s BCE to the generals of the 40s BCE to the Caesars of Lucan's own day. Sulla emerges as a key intermediary between these different periods of civic violence.

Lucan is hardly subtle in asserting that the conflict of the 80s shapes that of the 40s. He signals the programmatic role that Sulla and Marius will play in the epic in Book 1, when their shades are spotted breaking free of their graves: *e medio uisi consurgere Campo / tristia Sullani cecinere oracula manes, / tollentemque caput gelidas Anienis ad undas / agricolae fracto Marium fugere sepulchro* (Sulla's shade is seen rising from the middle of the Campus Martius and portending tragic oracles, and farmers flee Marius, who lifts his head in the icy waters of the Anio after abandoning his grave, 1.580–4).[9] The resurrection of Sulla and Marius foregrounds the repetition of civil war that is so central to Lucan's poetic project.[10] How their conflict prefigures and shapes that between Pompey and Caesar in the *Bellum Civile* has been the subject of much scholarly analysis.[11] Less often considered, however, is how Lucan's project of historical allusion functioned within a specifically Julio-Claudian context.[12] More than simply employing comparisons made standard in the late republic, Lucan responds to contemporary concerns over the prerogative to punish under the principate. This discourse employed analogies between Sulla and the *princeps* to criticize the arbitrary use of violence within the house of the Caesars. Lucan signals his engagement with it by depicting Sulla performing gruesome surgeries on the body politic. Drawing on medical imagery closely associated with the emperor Nero, Lucan invites his readers to consider what—if anything—distinguishes the despots of the 80s BCE from the *principes* of the Neronian present.

Sullan Lessons and the Civil War of 49 BCE

At first glance, it might seem less than intuitive that Sulla would serve as a cipher for the *princeps* in the *Bellum Civile*. By the time Lucan was writing, there was a well-established literary tradition analogizing Caesar to Marius and Pompey to Sulla. Such comparisons began early. As the nephew of Marius, Caesar exploited his connection to him by parading his *imago* in the funeral procession for his aunt Julia and erecting his victory trophies on the Capitolium (Plut., *Caes.* 5–6; see Tatum 2008: 29–35; Van der Blom 2010: 191). Sulla reportedly thought about killing Caesar as a young man because he saw "many Mariuses" in him (*nam Caesari multos Marios inesse*, Suet., *Div. Iul.* 2).[13] Pompey, in contrast, came of age and celebrated his first triumph as a commander under Sulla. He gained such prominence in Sulla's army that he acquired the nickname *adulescentulus carnifex* (the boy butcher, Val. Max. 6.2.8). Known for having told Sulla that more people worshipped the rising than the setting sun, Pompey too positioned himself as the successor of an elder general (Plut., *Pomp.* 14). Cicero's early speeches confirm the success of Caesar's and Pompey's attempts at self-fashioning; both are portrayed mimicking and then surpassing the feats of their chosen predecessors (*Prov. Cons.* 32; *Man.* 28, 30).[14] Such comparisons were initially adulatory, emphasizing the shared military prowess of two generations of Roman commanders.[15] As the republic veered toward civil war in the late 50s BCE, however, they took on a more sinister connotation.[16]

Cicero's civil war letters express concern that Caesar and Pompey will reproduce the crimes rather than accomplishments of their predecessors. Writing to Atticus in late 50 BCE, Cicero remarked that Caesar's victory would prove no better than those of Cinna and Sulla: *si boni victi sint, nec in caede principum clementiorem hunc fore quam Cinna fuerit nec moderatiorem quam Sulla in pecuniis locupletum* (If the good are defeated, that man will be neither more merciful than Cinna in the slaughter of leading men nor more moderate than Sulla in the plundering of the wealthy, *Att.* 7.7.7).[17] Yet he was hardly more enthused at the prospect of a Pompeian victory, observing, *genus illud Sullani regni iam pridem appetitur* (For a long time now he has been seeking that Sullan sort of despotism, *Att.* 8.11.2).[18] In response to rumors that Pompey had adopted the slogan *Sulla potuit: ego non potero?* (Sulla was able: will I not be able? *Att.* 9.10.2), Cicero invented the new verbs *sullaturio*, "to play the part of Sulla," and *proscripturio*, "to long to proscribe" (*Att.* 9.10.6). The same letter forges a close connection between the despots of the 80s and the indulgence of cruelty, a vice that Cicero sees reemerging in the current conflict between Caesar and Pompey: *at Sulla, at Marius, at Cinna recte. immo iure fortasse; sed quid eorum victoria crudelius, quid funestius? . . . huius belli genus fugi, et eo magis quod crudeliora etiam cogitari et parari videbam* (But one might say that Sulla, Marius, Cinna acted rightly. Legally, maybe; but what was crueler, what was deadlier, than their victory? . . . I avoided a war of that type, even more so because I saw that they were pondering and preparing even crueler things, *Att.* 9.10.3). Using the 80s as a frame for the conflict of 49 and portraying cruelty as the underbelly of victory, Cicero lays the rhetorical groundwork for Lucan's *Bellum Civile*.[19]

Within the *Bellum Civile*, Pompey's Sullan proclivities are a key theme of Caesar's speeches.[20] Addressing his troops before the Battle of Pharsalus, Caesar tells them, *cum duce Sullano gerimus ciuilia bella* (We wage civil war against a Sullan general, 7.307). His warning recalls an earlier passage from Book 1 in which he dwells on Pompey's Sullan tutelage at length: *nunc quoque, ne lassum teneat priuata senectus, / bella nefanda parat suetus ciuilibus armis / et docilis Sullam scelerum uicisse magistrum* (Now also, so that he does not spend his weary old age in retirement, he—accustomed to civil conflicts—prepares unspeakable wars and is easily taught to overcome Sulla, his teacher in crime, 1.324–6).[21] Whereas Sulla had at least given up power, Pompey will never let it go. Like a Hyrcanian tiger hunting cattle in the jungle, Caesar continues, his craving for blood is innate: *sic et Sullanum solito tibi lambere ferrum / durat, Magne, sitis. nullus semel ore receptus / pollutas patitur sanguis mansuescere fauces* (So also your thirst endures, Magnus, you who are accustomed to licking Sulla's sword. Blood, once it has been swallowed, never allows the tainted throat to become mild again, 1.330–2).[22] Even more damaging than Caesar's portrait of Pompey is Pompey's own endorsement of it. Declaring that his accomplishments to have made him more fortunate than Sulla Felix (*Sulla felicior*, 2.582), he celebrates surpassing his teacher. Only as his death looms in Book 8 does he realize his mistake: *actaque lauriferae damnat Sullana iuuentae* (He condemns the Sullan deeds of his laurel-crowned youth, 8.25). Sulla's tutelage made him a champion, he realizes, but in the doomed game of civil war.[23]

According to the logic of the parallel that Lucan sets up in the *Bellum Civile*, we might expect Pompey's death in Book 8 to put an end to Sulla's haunting presence in the epic. With the death of the student should come the end of the teacher's lessons. Yet just as resolution is denied to Pompey, whose body is half-burnt on a pyre and whose shade suddenly abandons its grave, so it is denied to the dictator who prefigures him.[24] Identifying the house of the Caesars as the new locus of the *ius ensis*, Lucan denies that Sulla ever returned to his burial on the Campus Martius. Such a claim becomes more legible when viewed in light of contemporary political discourse. For the *exemplum* of Sulla did not lie dormant between Cicero's civil war letters and the composition of the *Bellum Civile*.[25] Rather, it was activated at key moments from Octavian's rise to power to Nero's downfall to criticize the cruelty of Rome's rulers. Only by viewing Lucan in relation to this tradition do the ramifications of his historical typology come into full focus.

Sullan Cruelty and the House of the Caesars

By the time Lucan began writing the *Bellum Civile*, Sulla had become a paradigmatic tyrant in Roman political discourse. Catalyzed by late republican writers and given new life in the declamation schools, this posthumous image had little to do with the republican dictator himself.[26] It served instead to symbolize cruelty, a vice routinely linked to Sulla in the rhetorical exercises that Lucan would have studied as a youth.[27] Seneca the Elder records a speech by the Tiberian senator and orator Votienus Montanus in which the association already seems cliché: *ipse Montanus illum locum pulcherrime tractavit, quam multa populus Romanus in suis imperatoribus tulerit: in Gurgite luxuriam, in Manlio inpotentiam ... in Sulla crudelitatem* (Montanus himself discussed that topic—how much the Roman people have endured from its generals—very well: in Gurges, luxury, in Manlius, lack of moderation ... in Sulla, cruelty, Sen., *Contr.* 9.2.19). Julius Bassus articulated the same idea from the opposite direction; rather than stress Sulla's possession of cruelty, he notes his lack of clemency: *nemo sine vitio est: in Catone <deerat> moderatio, in Cicerone constantia, in Sulla clementia* (No one is without flaw; Cato lacked moderation, Cicero fortitude, and Sulla mercy, *Contr.* 2.4).[28] As "the example *par excellence* of *crudelitas*" (Bonner 1996: 277), Sulla took on an important role in Julio-Claudian political discourse. Used as a foil for the *princeps*, his memory became a locus for critical thinking about the nature and consequences of sole rule.[29]

The public persona of the *princeps* was crafted in implicit opposition to Sulla's *exemplum*. Whereas the republican dictator was defined by his cruelty, the Caesars stressed their clemency.[30] Augustus cited *clementia* as one of his four virtues on the *clupeus uirtutis* (*RG* 34.2) and crafted an iconography of *clementia* in art, architecture, and coinage (Dowling 2006: 126–68).[31] Tiberius did the same, issuing a series of coins advertising his *clementia* and endorsing the senate's construction of an *Ara Clementiae*.[32] Their efforts were reflected in texts like Velleius's *Historiae*, a history deeply loyal to the developing institution of the principate.[33] Velleius employs the term *clementia Caesaris* three times, applying it to both Julius Caesar (2.55) and Caesar Augustus (2.87, 2.100).[34] Dwelling on the clemency of father and son in their respective civil wars, he calls Augustus' victory at Actium *clementissima* (2.86). Their actions stand in contrast to those of Sulla, of whom Velleius writes, *imperio, quo priores ad vindicandam maximis periculis rem publicam olim usi erant, eo in inmodicae crudelitatis licentiam usus est* (He used the power, which previous dictators had formerly used to save the republic from the greatest of dangers, to give license to his unbridled cruelty, *Hist.* 2.28). Whereas Sulla used *imperium* to indulge his cruelty, the Caesars use it to express mercy. Locating the dictator far back in the annals of history, Velleius denies his relevance to contemporary politics.

Despite the efforts of Velleius, however, there are hints of an alternative mode of discourse in which Sulla and the Caesars were viewed in tandem rather than opposition. This line of critique may have already been developing under Julius Caesar, but Augustus' participation in the proscriptions of 43 provided a more immediate catalyst.[35] As Henderson (1998: 17) remarks, "When the triumviral proscriptions came in 43, it was christened a return, a 'son-of-Sulla' scenario." In the proscription edict preserved by Appian, the triumvirs promised to be more lenient than Sulla (4.2.10). Nevertheless, Juvenal reports that their actions earned them the nickname *Sullae discipuli tres* (the three students of Sulla, Juv. 2.28).[36] Even after securing sole rule, Augustus's Sullan past remained fraught.[37] Seneca the Elder preserves a speech in which Porcius Latro declares the return of Sullan bloodthirstiness under the triumvirs: *civilis sanguinis Sullana sitis in civitatem redit* (*Suas.* 6.3). Velleius resorts to special pleading to deny the connection, explaining, *furente deinde Antonio simulque Lepido . . . repugnante Caesare, sed frustra adversus duos, instauratum Sullani exempli malum, proscriptio* (Then Antony and Lepidus were raging simultaneously . . . Caesar disagreed, but opposed the two of them in vain. The horror of Sulla's example—proscription—was renewed, *Hist.* 2.66).[38] Even in as panegyrical a narrative as Velleius's *Historiae*, the name of Caesar Augustus sits uncomfortably close to that of Lucius Sulla. In the hands of writers less enthused about the principate, this proximity would be exploited to critical effect.

A collection of invective verses preserved in Suetonius's *Life of Tiberius* provides an early example of how Sulla's *exemplum* could be wielded as a rhetorical weapon against the *princeps*. According to Suetonius, the poem was circulated in response to Tiberius' cruelty: *multa praeterea specie gravitatis ac morum corrigendorum, sed et magis naturae optemperans, ita saeve et atrociter factitavit, ut nonnulli versiculis quoque et praesentia exprobrarent et futura denuntiarent mala* ("Moreover, he often acted so savagely and fiercely—under the pretext of severity and correcting public morals, but in fact indulging his nature—that some even used verses to both reproach present circumstances and warn of future evils," *Tib.* 59.1). Suetonius specifies the present and future as the relevant temporalities of the verses, but their critical force derives in part from their backward-looking gaze. Calling Tiberius *asper et immitis* ("a harsh and merciless man"), they compare him to Sulla and Marius (*Tib.* 59.1):

> fastidit vinum, quia iam sitit iste cruorem:
>   tam bibit hunc avide, quam bibit ante merum.
> aspice felicem sibi, non tibi, Romule, Sullam
>   et Marium, si vis, aspice, sed reducem ...

> That man shudders at wine, because he is now thirsty for blood; he drinks it as greedily as he used to drink undiluted wine. Look at Sulla, lucky for himself but not for you, Roman citizen, and look at Marius, if you wish, but after the return ...

The verses renew historical memory of the 80s BCE to cast Tiberius in the role of the bloodthirsty tyrant. Their imagery parallels Julio-Claudian portraits of Sulla, as when Seneca the Younger asks, *quis tamen umquam tyrannus tam avide humanum sanguinem bibit quam ille ...?* (Yet what tyrant ever drank human blood as greedily as he? *Clem.* 1.12.2).[39] Lucan will later evoke both of these images in Caesar's portrait of Pompey licking Sulla's sword (1.330–2). Here, however, it is the *princeps* who spills—and consumes—citizen blood. What Sulla accomplished through proscriptions, Tiberius accomplishes through punishments. With each penalty he exacts, the specter of the dictator creeps further into the house of the Caesars.

Tiberius' response to the verses reinforced rather than ameliorated the Sullan comparison.[40] Dismissing them as the opinion of those unhappy with his reforms, he reportedly replied, *oderint, dum probent* ("Let them hate me, provided that they respect me," Suet., *Tib.* 59.2). The remark was a gentler version of a famous line from Accius' *Atreus*: *oderint, dum metuant* (Let them hate, provided that they fear, *TRF* 203). The maxim had been considered the hallmark of the tyrant since the late republic, but came to be associated with Sulla specifically during the Julio-Claudian period.[41] Valerius Maximus prefaces his discussion of Sullan cruelty, for example, with a version of it: *ad summam, cum penes illam sit timeri, penes nos sit odisse* (In sum, if it is in her [cruelty's] power to be feared, let it be within ours to hate, 9.2. *praef.*). Seneca the Younger went so far as to assert (incorrectly) that it was a product of the Sullan era: *qualis illa dira et abominanda: 'oderint, dum metuant.' Sullano scias saeculo scriptam* (That severe and reprehensible phrase: 'Let them hate, provided that they fear.' You can tell it was written in the Sullan age, *Ira* 1.20.4).[42] Citing the maxim in his response to the verses, Tiberius validated their accusation of Sullan cruelty.[43]

Tacitus suggests that Sulla's *exemplum* only became more relevant in the transfer of power from Tiberius to Gaius. Using historical allusion to renew memory of the republican dictator, he reports that Tiberius upbraided Q. Sutorius Macro, the prefect of the praetorian guard, with an easily decipherable metaphor: *namque Macroni non abdita ambage occidentem ab eo deseri, orientem spectari exprobravit* (With an allusion hardly hidden, he reproached Macro for abandoning the setting sun and looking toward the rising one, *Ann.* 6.46).[44] Pompey gave Sulla the same warning when he began surpassing him: ἀλλ' ἐννοεῖν ἐκέλευσε τὸν Σύλλαν ὅτι τὸν ἥλιον ἀνατέλλοντα πλείονες ἢ δυόμενον προσκυνοῦσιν (But he urged Sulla to keep in mind that more people honored the rising than the setting sun, Plut., *Pomp.* 14). Applied to Tiberius and Gaius, it is the former who plays the role of Sulla and the latter who plays that of Pompey. Yet just as quickly as Tiberius assumes the character of Sulla, he casts it onto Gaius: *et Gaio Caesari, forte orto sermone L. Sullam inridenti, omnia Sullae vitia et nullam eiusdem virtutem habiturum praedixit* (And to Gaius Caesar, who happened to be mocking Lucius Sulla in an impromptu speech, he [Tiberius] predicted that he would have all of the vices of Sulla and none of his virtues, *Ann.* 6.46). Who was Gaius mocking? Perhaps it was Lucius Cornelius Sulla Felix, a descendant of the republican general and the consul of 33.[45] In his response, however, Tiberius links Gaius to the republican dictator, a man notorious for his jarring combination of virtues and vices (e.g., Vell. 2.17; Val. Max. 9.2.1). The effectiveness of Tiberius' witticism is nevertheless undercut by his (unintentional) identification with Sulla in the previous sentence. In Tacitus' construction of the scene, both Tiberius and Gaius participate in transforming the principate into a Sullan institution.

This anecdote may tell us more about Tacitus' view of Roman history than about Julio-Claudian political discourse. Nevertheless, Gaius invited contemporary comparison with Sulla. Suetonius hands down that he was even fonder than Tiberius of the maxim from Accius' *Atreus*: *tragicum illud subinde iactabat: oderint, dum metuant* (He was continually proclaiming that tragic phrase: Let them hate, provided that they fear, Suet., *Calig.* 30). In *De Ira*, Seneca portrays Gaius' punishments as an extension of Sulla's proscriptions. He begins by recounting the torture of Marius Gratidianus, a notorious act of Sullan cruelty: *L. Sulla praefringi crura, erui oculos, amputari linguam, manus iussit et, quasi totiens occideret quotiens vulnerabat, paulatim et per singulos artus laceravit* (Lucius Sulla ordered that his ankles be shattered, his eyes gouged out, his tongue and hands cut off, and, as if he could kill him as often as he wounded him, mangled him bit by bit and limb by limb, *Ira* 3.18.2).[46] He then poses a question: *quid antiqua perscrutor? modo C. Caesar Sex. Papinium cui pater erat consularis, Betilienum Bassum quaestorem suum, procuratoris sui filium, aliosque et senatores et equites Romanos uno die flagellis cecidit, torsit* (Why do I investigate ancient examples? Just recently Gaius Caesar whipped with the scourge and tortured Sextus Papinius, whose father was a consul, and Betilienus Bassus, his own quaestor and the son of his procurator, and other Romans—both senators and equites—in a single day, *Ira* 3.18.4).[47] Surpassing Sulla in the number of victims tortured in one day, Gaius' punishments prove even worse than Sulla's proscriptions. It is his use of violence against Roman citizens that enables the comparison.

Though not directly compared to Sulla in extant sources, Claudius too was represented within the paradigm of the bloodthirsty tyrant. In the *Apocolocyntosis*, Pedo Pompeius addresses him as *homo crudelissime* (13) before reciting the number of senators and equites that he murdered.[48] Imperial historians figured this cruelty as bloodthirstiness. Cassius Dio describes Claudius "satiating himself" (διεπίμπλατο, 60.13.4) on public executions and gladiatorial spectacles and "filling up on bloodshed and murder" (αἵματος καὶ φόνων ἀναπίμπλασθαι, 60.14.1). Suetonius also notes Claudius's penchant for watching executions and gladiatorial spectacles and attributes it to his bloodthirsty character: *saevum et sanguinarium natura fuisse, magnis minimisque apparuit rebus* (It was apparent from large and small matters that he was savage and bloodthirsty by nature, *Claud.* 34). Because Suetonius and Cassius Dio are typically thought to be independent of one another but to have used a common source, their shared portrait of Claudius may go back to contemporary discourse.[49] Either way, it is clear that a new language of political critique was developing under the Julio-Claudian principate. Merging the trope of the bloodthirsty tyrant with the historical *exemplum* of Sulla, it was used to criticize the use of violence as a tool of political control.

Seneca tries to insulate Nero from this line of rhetorical attack in the *De Clementia*, a treatise dedicated to the new *princeps* and devoted to the topic of mercy.[50] Within the text, Sulla serves as a negative *exemplum* in opposition to which Nero's rule is formulated. Urging Nero to avoid the example of the tyrant, Seneca writes, *tyrannus autem a rege factis distat, non nomine; nam et Dionysius maior iure meritoque praeferri multis regibus potest, et L. Sullam tyrannum appellari quid prohibet, cui occidendi finem fecit inopia hostium?* (A tyrant differs from a king in his deeds, not his name; for Dionysius the Elder can justly and deservedly be preferred to many kings, and what prohibits Lucius Sulla from being called a tyrant, to whom only a lack of enemies provided an end to slaughter? *Clem.* 1.12.1–2). Whereas Sulla took pleasure in the carnage of his fellow citizens, Nero's rule will be defined by an absence of bloodshed: *haec est, Caesar, clementia vera, quam tu praestas, quae non saevitiae paenitentia coepit, nullam habere maculam, numquam civilem sanguinem fudisse* (True clemency, Nero, is that which you show, which arises not from repentance for violence, which has no blemish, which has never shed citizen blood, *Clem.* 1.11).[51] Seneca addresses the *princeps* directly, but his audience extends to the Roman citizenry more broadly. Setting up Neronian mercy as the antithesis of Sullan cruelty, he assures readers that the specter of the dictator has finally departed from the *domus Augusta*.

Sullan Butchery and Neronian Medicine

In the *Bellum Civile*, Lucan challenges the neat divide that Seneca draws between Sulla and Nero in the *De Clementia*. Because the principate had become intertwined with Sullan despotism in complicated ways, Lucan's readers were primed to interpret his portrait of the 80s BCE in relation to imperial politics. As we saw above, Lucan invites them to do so when he remarks that the example of the 80s lives on in the house of the Caesars: *ius licet in iugulos nostros sibi fecerit ensis / Sulla potens Mariusque ferox et Cinna cruentus / Caesareaeque domus series* (Though powerful Sulla and fierce Marius and cruel Cinna and the line of the Caesarian house earned the right to use the sword against our throats, 4.821–3). This is not the only place that he blurs the boundary between Sullan despotism and Rome's current rulers. His portrait of Sulla in Book 2 is equally rich with contemporary resonance. Drawing on medical imagery closely associated with Nero, Lucan compares the "treatments" of Sulla to those of the *princeps*. In doing so, he asks what—if anything—distinguishes the proscriptions of the past from the punishments of the present.[52]

Lucan introduces Sulla's reign of terror in Book 2 through an extended medical metaphor.[53] He writes, *Sulla quoque inmensis accessit cladibus ultor. / ille quod exiguum restabat sanguinis urbi / hausit* (Then Sulla the avenger approached with vast destruction. He drained what little remained of the city's blood, 2.139–41).⁵⁴ Draining an already exsanguinated body of its blood, Sulla mimics the sacrifice of an old man shortly before: *paruum sed fessa senectus / sanguinis effudit iugulo* (But tired old age poured out a scanty amount of blood from the neck, 2.128–9). The repetition "assimilates the destruction of the community to that of the individual," easing the transition to a more explicit metaphor of the body politic (Fantham 1992: 140 *ad loc.*). Unsatisfied with bloodletting, Sulla moves on to the harsher treatment of amputating limbs: *dumque nimis iam putria membra recidit / excessit medicina modum, nimiumque secuta est, / qua morbi duxere, manus* (And while he severely cut away the putrid limbs, the medicine was excessive, and his hand pursued too far where the disease led, 2.141–3).⁵⁵ Analogies between healing remedies and statesmanship had been part of Roman political language since the late republic.⁵⁶ So had the refrain that one should try gentle treatments before bloodletting, amputation, and surgery.⁵⁷ Here, however, Lucan crafts a specific intertext with Seneca's *De Beneficiis*, which refers to *ingratus L. Sulla, qui patriam durioribus remediis, quam pericula erant, sanavit* (Ungrateful Lucius Sulla, who cured the country by remedies harsher than the dangers were, *Ben.* 5.16.3).⁵⁸ Employing the same metaphor in the *Bellum Civile*, Lucan invites his readers to consider Seneca's language of healing alongside his own.

Lucan reinforces the importance of his dialogue with Seneca by using the torture of Marius Gratidianus as an example of the amputations that Sulla performed on the body politic.⁵⁹ Just as Seneca does in *De Ira*, he details how each part of Marius' body was cut off (2.181–5):

auolsae cecidere manus exsectaque lingua
palpitat et muto uacuum ferit aera motu.
hic aures, alius spiramina naris aduncae
amputat; ille cauis euoluit sedibus orbes
ultimaque effodit spectatis lumina membris.

His torn-out arms fell down, and his cut-out tongue quivered and silently struck the air with silent motion. One man amputates the ears, another one the nostrils of the hooked nose: another unfolds the eyeballs from their hollow sockets, and finally tears out the eyes, after they have witnessed the limbs.

Quint (1993: 130) argues that the torture of Marius Gratidianus plays a programmatic role in the epic, symbolizing the destruction of the body politic in microcosm.⁶⁰ Seneca makes this explicit when he writes of Marius' torture, *indigna res publica quae in corpus suum pariter et hostium et vindicum gladios reciperet* (the republic was unworthy to receive into her body the swords of both enemies and protectors alike, *Ira* 3.18.2).⁶¹ Standing for Rome as a whole, Marius Gratidianus exemplifies what happens when the surgeon's hand pursues the disease of the body politic too far.

As we saw above, Seneca concludes his discussion of Marius Gratidianus by suggesting that Romans experienced worse punishments under Gaius. A primary aim of his political philosophy is to prevent Nero from performing similar "treatments" on Rome. In *De Clementia*, he does so by portraying Nero as an ideal physician to the body politic. Emphasizing the gentleness of his touch, he describes the *princeps* as *inclinatus ad mitiora, etiam, si ex usu est animadvertere, ostendens, quam invitus aspero remedio manus admoveat* (Inclined toward gentler ways even if it is necessary to punish, showing how unwilling he is to apply his hand to a harsh treatment, *Clem.* 1.13.4). Nero avoids bloodletting and surgery, Seneca explains, because he recognizes that he and the Roman citizenry are part of the same body: *Nam si, quod adhuc colligit, tu animus rei publicae tuae es, illa corpus tuum, vides, ut puto, quam necessaria sit clementia; tibi enim parcis, cum videris alteri parcere* (For if, and this is what has been suggested thus far, you are the mind of the polity and it is your body, you see, I think, how necessary mercy is; for you spare yourself, when you seem to spare another, *Clem.* 1.5.1). Nero is not only the physician to, but the animating life force of, the *res publica*. Performing amputations on the body politic is akin to removing his own limbs. His own self-interest, if nothing else, will prevent his remedies from becoming too extreme.

Even Seneca acknowledges, however, that gangrenous limbs sometimes need to be excised from the body politic. In these situations, Nero must be careful to restrain his hand from cutting too deep: *parcendum itaque est etiam improbandis civibus non aliter quam membris languentibus, et, si quando misso sanguine opus est, sustinenda est manus, ne ultra, quam necesse sit, incidat* (There must also be mercy even for corrupt citizens, as if they were feeble limbs, and, if bloodletting is ever required, the hand must be held back, so that it does not cut more deeply than is necessary, *Clem.* 1.5.1). If Seneca's description of sickly limbs, bloodletting, and a hand that cuts too deep sounds familiar, it is because all three of these elements play a role in the medical metaphor with which Lucan introduces Sulla's dictatorship: *ille quod exiguum restabat sanguinis urbi / hausit dumque nimis iam putria membra recidit / excessit medicina modum, nimiumque secuta est, / qua morbi duxere, manus* (He drained what little remained of the city's blood. And while he severely cut away the putrid limbs, the medicine was excessive, and his hand pursued too far where the disease led, 2.140–3). The resonance between Lucan's description of Sulla and Seneca's advice to Nero exposes the similar position that the two rulers occupy in the *res publica*. Each possesses the power of life and death over his fellow citizens; how he will use that power is figured as the choice between gentle and harsh remedies. Whether Nero employs diet and exercise over bloodletting and amputation is largely beside the point. What matters is that he—and he alone—gets to decide. It is his unchallenged possession of the prerogative to punish that renders him the inheritor of Sulla's legacy.

Viewed in relation to Julio-Claudian political language, the significance of the Roman elder's speech in Book 2 comes into clearer focus. Concluding his account of the horrors of the 80s BCE, he asks, *hisne salus rerum, felix his Sulla uocari, / his meruit tumulum medio sibi tollere Campo?* (For these reasons was Sulla called the salvation of the republic, for these reasons was he called Felix? For these reasons did he deserve to erect a tomb for himself in the middle of the Campus Martius? 2.221–2). Looking back to Sulla's abandonment of his grave in Book 1 and forward to Lucan's wordplay with the title *Felix* in Book 4, his question encapsulates the trajectory of Sulla's *exemplum* in the *Bellum Civile*. The warning that he offers next is thereby rendered all the more urgent: *haec rursus patienda manent, hoc ordine belli / ibitur, hic stabit ciuilibus exitus armis* (These things must be suffered again, through this sequence of war we will pass, this will be the result of civil war, 2.223–4).[62] His words apply not only to those who will experience the conflict between Caesar and Pompey, but also to those who will read Lucan under Nero.[63] As long as the specter of Sulla lurks in the house of the Caesars, Rome will remain trapped in its never-ending cycle of civil bloodshed.

Notes

1. Thanks are due to Laura Zientek and Mark Thorne for organizing the conference at which this paper was initially presented. Their feedback, as well as that of the referee and my fellow presenters, has greatly improved the paper.
2. Citations of Lucan follow Housman (1926). Translations are my own.
3. Roller (2001: 37) cites this passage as an example of how Lucan aims "to collapse the temporal distinction between the events narrated in the poem and the position from which they are narrated." Fratantuono (2012: 173) calls it "one of Lucan's most damning remarks about the principate."
4. The *potentes* addressed here include Curio, Caesar, and Pompey (Asso 2009: *ad loc.* 805–6).
5. Lintott (1971: 488) identifies "the suicide of old Rome" as the unifying theme of the poem.
6. Whether or not Julio-Claudian writers represent Sulla accurately is beyond the scope of the present investigation. For treatments of the historical Sulla, see Keaveney (2005); Santangelo (2007); Rosenblitt (2019). For issues of Sulla's reception, see Dowling (2000); Thein (2014); Eckert (2016a).
7. Lucan addresses the "original sin" of Romulus's fratricide at 1.93–7, on which see Fantham (2010: 214–18).
8. See Neel (2015: 46–8) on Ennius's treatment of the fratricide in relation to the later literary tradition.
9. I follow recent translators (Braund 1992; Fox 2012; Walters 2015) in interpreting *Sullani manes* as "the shade of Sulla" rather than "the corpses of those slain by Sulla," as Bagnani (1955) suggests.
10. See Dinter (2012: 119–54) and Masters (1992: 28–9) on repetition as a central theme of the epic.
11. Bartsch (1997: 55) writes, "Even the phenomenon of civil war itself, the struggle between Caesar and Pompey that is the subject of Lucan's poem, is not allowed to be unique, but is figured as the double or repetition of the earlier war of Sulla and Marius." See also Morford (1966); Fantham (1992: 28); Braund (1992: xxxiv); Henderson (1998: 181); Bernstein (2011: 275); Galtier (2016).
12. I follow Roller (2001: 6) in seeing the "dialogical, contested thinking-out and shaping of the principate" as a primary feature of Julio-Claudian literature.
13. A story also reported by Plut., *Caes.* 1.
14. See Gildenhard (2014: 264–5) on the parallels between Sulla and Pompey in the *Pro Lege Manilia*.

15. In *De Haruspicum Responso*, Cicero gives a sense of what positive memory of Sulla and Marius looked like: *Dissensit cum Mario, clarissimo civi, consul nobilissimus et fortissimus, L. Sulla* (Lucius Sulla, the noblest and boldest consul, fought with Marius, the most outstanding citizen).
16. For the late 50s as a period of crystallization for negative Sullan memory, see Laffi (1967); Hinard (1985: 91–4).
17. Grillo (2012: 78) compares this letter to Caesar's proclamations of mercy in his own *Bellum Civile*.
18. See also *Att.* 9.7.3; 9.14.2; 9.15.2; 10.7.1; 10.8.7.
19. Holliday (1969) addresses the relationship between the portrayals of Pompey in Cicero's letters and Lucan's *Bellum Civile*.
20. Lintott (1971: 498) locates Caesar's language in relation to Cicero's letters, as well as late republican invective and early imperial historiography. On the question of Lucan's sources, see Radicke (2004).
21. Roche (2009: *ad loc.* 326–31) compares Caesar's rhetoric to Cicero's civil war letters and Seneca's *De Clementia*.
22. Seidman (2017: 83–4) suggests that this metaphor sets up Lucan and Caesar in a contest "to represent the Roman past poetically."
23. Lucan calls civil war a game of fate at 6.8 (*placet alea fati*).
24. On Lucan's refusal to invest Pompey's death scene with closure, see Mebane (2016: 205–11); cf. Martin (2005); Easton (2011/2012). On the question of closure in the epic more broadly, see Masters (1992: 216–59); Stover (2008).
25. For Sulla as an *exemplum*, see Bloomer (1992: 50); van der Blom (2010: 240); Gildenhard (2014: 212). On the importance of *exempla* to Roman political culture, see Hölkeskamp (1996); Langlands (2018); Roller (2018).
26. Dowling (2000: 318) argues that it was during the Augustan period that "the presentation of Sulla as a cruel tyrant becomes more standardized and uniform."
27. "Giving Sulla advice" (*consilium dedimus Sullae*, Juv., *Sat.* 1.16) was a common *suasoria*, on which see Keane (2015: 27–8). Bonner (2010) discusses Lucan's relationship to the rhetorical schools.
28. Thein (2014: 166) argues that "the ancient reception of Sulla's clemency was for the most part negative," highlighting his cruelty as a civil war victor.
29. Henderson (1995: 125) writes, "Under figures such as 'Sulla', ruin of the Republic, Romans had been exchanging models for political thought, running over the same ground through a half dozen generations."
30. Huelsenbeck (2015: 49) argues, "There can hardly be a more positive demonstration of how different a ruler is from the tyrant Sulla than to exercise *misericordia*."
31. For Augustus' clemency and the development of the imperial virtues, see Wallace-Hadrill (1983); Griffin (2003a); Konstan (2005); Dowling (2006: 29–125). Braund (2009: 32) stresses the connection between clemency and sole rule, writing, "To put it bluntly, the self-restraint denoted by *clementia* was a concomitant of the monarchical power concentrated in the hands of the Roman *princeps*."
32. *RIC* 1.132. See Levick (1999: 64–5) on the coin type and altar.
33. In Syme's classic assessment, Velleius is "a typical government writer ... unswervingly loyal to Tiberius and to L. Aelius Seianus" (1939: 488). The work of Woodman (1983; 1987) has done much to establish his value.

34. On the *clementia Caesaris*, see Braund (2009: 34–8).
35. According to Ampius Balbus, Caesar had once said, *Sullam nescisse litteras, qui dictaturum deposuerit* (Sulla did not know his ABCs, when he laid down the dictatorship, attested at Suet., *Div. Iul.* 77).
36. Uden (2015: 256n27) speculates that this image was inspired by the *Philippic* 2.108.
37. Pliny the Elder reports that he was long hated for the proscriptions (*proscriptionis invidia*, 7.147), while Dio imagines Tiberius saying at Augustus's funeral oration, ἐν μηδενὶ τὸν Σύλλαν μιμησάμενος (He mimicked Sulla in no way, 56.38.1).
38. Gowing (2005: 48) argues that Velleius "perverts history just a bit" in order "to get around a very sticky problem."
39. Valerius Maximus similarly writes, *crudeliter totam urbem atque omnes Italiae partes civilis sanguinis fluminibus inundavit* (He cruelly flooded the whole city and all the parts of Italy with rivers of civil blood, 9.2.1).
40. Gunderson (2014: 141) argues that Suetonius depicts Tiberius as "an imperial failure of exemplarity ... the model emperor Augustus uses *exempla*, while Tiberius instead has *exempla* used against him."
41. Cicero cites a version of it to justify the assassination of Julius Caesar and "other tyrants" like Sulla (*Off.* 2.23–9). See Eckert (2016b) on its association with Sulla.
42. Manuwald (2011: 223) writes, "Seneca might have transferred conditions valid in his own time (and suitable to his argument) back to Accius' time and thus inferred a composition date."
43. Suetonius confirms the aptness of the comparison, writing, *dein vera plane certaque esse ipse fecit fidem* (He later proved them to be clearly true and accurate, *Tib.* 59.2).
44. See also Cass. Dio 58.28.4.
45. Commentators have not remarked upon the ambiguity of "L. Sulla" here. Woodman (2017: *ad loc.* 6.46) interprets Tiberius's and Gaius's exchange only in relation to the historical dictator, while Martin (2001: *ad loc.* 6.46.4) does not address the identity of "L. Sulla."
46. In addition to Lucan's narration of the event (on which see below), other versions can be found at [Q. Cic.] *Comm. Pet.* 10; Sall., *Hist.* 1.44M; Liv., *Per.* 88; Val. Max. 9.2.1; Asc. 84, 87, 89 (Clark); Flor., *Epit.* 2.9.26=3.21.26; Plut., *Sull.* 32.2. On the literary tradition, see Hinard (1984) and Marshall (1985).
47. Gloyn (2017: 162) argues that the anecdote about Gaius "demonstrates what happens when a family becomes concerned with power rather than virtue."
48. See Osgood (2011: 15) on Claudius's "remarkable cruelty."
49. On Cassius Dio's and Suetonius's shared sources, see Townend (1960) and Power (2012, esp. 431n4).
50. Seneca explains his choice of clemency as a subject in the opening line of the treatise: *scribere de clementia, Nero Caesar, institui, ut quodam modo speculi vice fungerer et te tibi ostenderem perventurum ad voluptatem maximam omnium* (I decided to write about clemency, Nero Caesar, so that I might in some way play the part of a mirror and show you to yourself as you are about to reach the greatest pleasure of all, *Clem.* 1.1.1). Through the metaphor of the mirror, Seneca provides Nero with a model of behavior to which he should aspire while also maintaining the fiction that he has already achieved the virtues about to be enumerated. See Rees (2012) on this distinctive type of didactic panegyric and Braund (2009: 1–91) for *De Clementia* in its historical and philosophical context.
51. Seneca's use of the phrase *civilem sanguinem* calls to mind Valerius Maximus, who uses it to describe Cinna's and Marius's actions: *L. Cinna et C. Marius hauserant quidem avidi*

civilem sanguinem (Lucius Cinna and Gaius Marius had indeed greedily drunk citizen blood, 2.7).

52. As Fantham (1992: *ad loc.* 139–65) points out, Lucan does not address the proscriptions as such, but rather focuses on the opportunities that they provided for personal revenge. By focusing on their cruelty rather than legality, he is better able to draw connections to the present.
53. On the body politic metaphor in the *Bellum Civile*, see Dinter (2012: 9–49); Mebane (2016).
54. Lucan's use of *ultor* looks forward both to Pompey, who represents his army as *ultores* (2.531), and to Brutus, who will become an *ultor* in the assassination of Caesar (5.207). The repetition of avengers in Roman history underscores the cycle of civil violence.
55. Tacitus makes a similar comment about Pompey: *gravior remediis quam delicta erant* (The remedies were more severe than the ills, *Ann.* 3.28.1). On Lucan's use of corporeal imagery, see McClellan in this volume.
56. Cicero promised to cure Rome of the Catilinarian Conspiracy (e.g., *Cat.* 1.31) and portrayed Pompey as a physician during his sole consulship: *sed quis non intellegit omnis tibi rei publicae partis aegras et labantis, ut eas his armis sanares et confirmares, esse commissas?* (But does anyone not understand that all the sick and withering parts of the republic have been entrusted to you so that you may heal and strengthen them with these weapons? *Mil.* 68).
57. In a letter to Atticus about Clodius, Cicero writes, *sed ego diaeta curare incipio, chirurgiae taedet* (But I am beginning to cure through diet; I am tired of surgery, *Att.* 4.3.3). See also *Att.* 2.1.6–7.
58. Griffin (2003b: *ad loc.* 16.3) notes the different uses of Sulla in *De Beneficiis*, *De Ira*, and *De Clementia*.
59. Fantham (1992: *ad loc.* 173–93) argues that Lucan "certainly knew his own uncle's account in *De ira* 3.18." Dinter (2012: 46–7) addresses how Lucan reworks the literary tradition more broadly.
60. Walters (2014: 116) argues that "Gratidianus was seen as a sort of stand-in for the Republic, and his mutilation was symbolic of the dismemberment of the Roman state."
61. Seneca's metaphor calls to mind the opening lines of the *Bellum Civile*, which describe *populumque potentem / in sua uictrici conuersum uiscera dextra* (a powerful population turned against its own innards by its conquering right hand, 1.2–3).
62. As Joseph notes in his discussion of this passage, "the principate itself emerges from the poem as a sort of repetition of perpetuation of civil war" (2012: 8).
63. See Henderson (1998: 181).

References

Asso, P. (2009), *A Commentary on Lucan: De Bello Civili IV*, Berlin: De Gruyter.
Bagnani, G. (1955), "*Sullani Manes* and Lucan's Rhetoric," *Phoenix*, 9: 27–31.
Bartsch, S. (1997), *Ideology in Cold Blood: A Reading of Lucan's Civil War*, Cambridge, MA: Harvard University Press.
Bernstein, N. (2011), "The Dead and Their Ghosts in the *Bellum Civile*: Lucan's Visions of History," in P. Asso (ed.), *Brill's Companion to Lucan*, 257–79, Leiden: Brill.
Blom, H. (2010), *Cicero's Role Models: The Political Strategy of a Newcomer*, Oxford: Oxford University Press.

Bloomer, W. (1992), *Valerius Maximus and the Rhetoric of the New Nobility*, Chapel Hill: University of North Carolina Press.
Bonner, S. (2010), "Lucan and the Declamation Schools," in C. Tesoriero (ed.), *Lucan*, 69–106, Oxford: Oxford University Press.
Braund, S. (1992), *Lucan: Civil War*, Oxford: Oxford University Press.
Braund, S. (2009), *Seneca: De Clementia*, Oxford: Oxford University Press.
Dinter, M. (2012), *Anatomizing Civil War: Studies in Lucan's Epic Technique*, Ann Arbor: University of Michigan Press.
Dowling, M. (2000), "The Clemency of Sulla," *Historia*, 49: 303–40.
Dowling, M. (2006), *Clemency and Cruelty in the Roman World*, Ann Arbor: University of Michigan Press.
Easton, S. (2011/2012), "Why Lucan's Pompey Is Better Off Dead," *CJ*, 107 (2): 212–23.
Eckert, A. (2016a), *Lucius Cornelius Sulla in der antiken Erinnerung: Jener Mörder, der sich Felix nannte*, Göttingen: De Gruyter.
Eckert, A. (2016b), "'There is no one who does not hate Sulla': Persuasion and Cultural Trama," in E. Sanders and M. Johncock (eds.), *Emotion and Persuasion in Classical Antiquity*, 133–47, Stuttgart: Franz Steiner Verlag.
Fantham, E. (1992), *Lucan: De Bello Civili Book II*, Cambridge: Cambridge University Press.
Fantham, E. (2010), "*Discordia Fratrum*: Aspects of Lucan's Conception of Civil War," in B. Breed, C. Damon, and A. Rossi (eds.), *Citizens of Discord: Rome and Its Civil Wars*, 207–20, Oxford: Oxford University Press.
Fox, M. (2012), *Lucan: Civil War*, New York: Penguin Books.
Fratantuono, L. (2012), *Madness Triumphant: A Reading of Lucan's* Pharsalia, Lanham: Lexington Books.
Galtier, F. (2016), "Le conflit entre Marius et Sylla: un souvenir traumatique dans la *Pharsale*," in F. Galtier and R. Poignault (eds.), *Présence de Lucain*, 17–31, Clermont–Ferrand: Centre de recherches A. Piganiol.
Gildenhard, I. (2014), *Cicero: On Pompey's Command (De Imperio), 27–49*, Cambridge: Open Book Publishers.
Gloyn, L. (2017), *The Ethics of the Family in Seneca*, Cambridge: Cambridge University Press.
Gowing, A. (2005), *Empire and Memory: The Representation of the Roman Republic in Imperial Culture*, Cambridge: Cambridge University Press.
Griffin, M. (2003a), "*Clementia* after Caesar: From Politics to Philosophy," in F. Cairns and E. Fantham (eds.), *Caesar against Liberty? Perspectives on His Autocracy*, 157–82, Cambridge: Francis Cairns.
Griffin, M. (2003b), *Seneca on Society: A Guide to De Beneficiis*, Oxford: Oxford University Press.
Grillo, L. (2012), *The Art of Caesar's Bellum Civile: Literature, Ideology, and Community*, Cambridge: Cambridge University Press.
Gunderson, E. (2014), "E.g. Augustus: *exemplum* in the *Augustus* and *Tiberius*," in T. Power and R. Gibson (eds.), *Suetonius the Biographer: Studies in the Roman Lives*, 130–45, Oxford: Oxford University Press.
Henderson, J. (1995), "Pump up the Volume: Juvenal, Satires 1.1.–21," *PCPhS*, 41: 101–37.
Henderson, J. (1998), *Fighting for Rome: Poets and Caesars, History, and Civil War*, Cambridge: Cambridge University Press.
Hinard, F. (1984), "La male mort," in Y. Thomas (ed.), *Du châtiment dans la cité: supplices corporels et peine de mort dans le monde antique*, 295–311, Rome: L'Ecole.
Hinard, F. (1985), *Les proscriptions de la Rome républicaine*, Paris: Boccard.
Hölkeskamp, K. (1996), "*Exempla* und *mos maiorum*. Überlegungen zum kollektiven Gedächtnis der Nobilität," in H.-J. Gehrke and A. Möller (eds.), *Vergangenheit und Lebenswelt: Soziale Kommunikation, Traditionsbildung und historisches Bewusstsein*, 301–38, Tübingen: Narr.

Holliday, V. (1962), *Pompey in Cicero's Correspondence and Lucan's Civil War*, The Hague: Mouton.
Housman, A. E. (1926), *M. Annaei Lvcani Belli civilis libri decem*, Cambridge, MA: Harvard University Press.
Huelsenbeck, B. (2015), "Shared Speech in the Collection of the Elder Seneca (*Contr.* 10.4): Towards a Study of Common Literary Passages as Community Interaction," in E. Amato, F. Citti, and B. Huelsenbeck (eds.), *Law and Ethics in Greek and Roman Declamation*, 35–62, Berlin: De Gruyter.
Joseph, T. (2012), *Tacitus the Epic Successor: Virgil, Lucan, and the Narrative of Civil War in the Histories*, Leiden: Brill.
Keane, C. (2015), *Juvenal and the Satiric Emotions*, Oxford: Oxford University Press.
Keaveney, A. (2005), *Sulla: The Last Republican*, 2nd edn, London: Routledge.
Konstan, D. (2005), "Clemency as a Virtue," *CPh*, 100 (4): 337–46.
Laffi, U. (1967), "Il mito di Silla," *Athenaeum*, 45: 255–77.
Langlands, R. (2018), *Exemplary Ethics in Ancient Rome*, Cambridge: Cambridge University Press.
Levick, B. (1999), *Tiberius the Politician*, 2nd edn, London: Routledge.
Lintott, A. (1971), "Lucan and the History of the Civil War," *CQ*, 21 (2): 488–505.
Manuwald, G. (2011), *Roman Republican Theatre*, Cambridge: Cambridge University Press.
Martin, P. (2005), "La tête de Pompée. Une relecture de Lucain," in F. Lestringant, B. Néraudau, D. Porte, and J.-C. Ternaux (eds.), *Liber amicorum: Mélanges sur la littérature antique et moderne à la mémoire de Jean-Pierre Néraudau*, 147–62, Paris: Honoré Champion Éditeur.
Masters, J. (1992), *Poetry and Civil War in Lucan's Bellum Civile*, Cambridge: Cambridge University Press.
Mebane, J. (2016), "Pompey's Head and the Body Politic in Lucan's *De Bello Civili*," *TAPhA*, 146 (1): 191–215.
Morford, M. (1966), "Lucan and the Marian Tradition," *Latomus*, 25 (1): 107–14.
Osgood, J. (2011), *Claudius Caesar: Image and Power in the Early Roman Empire*, Cambridge: Cambridge University Press.
Power, T. (2012), "Pyrrhus and Priam in Suetonius' *Tiberius*," *CQ*, 62 (1): 430–3.
Quint, D. (1993), *Epic and Empire: Politics and Generic Form from Virgil to Milton*, Princeton: Princeton University Press.
Radicke, J. (2004), *Lucans poetische Technik*, Leiden: Brill.
Rees, R. (2012), "The Modern History of Latin Panegyric," in R. Rees (ed.), *Latin Panegyric*, 3–48, Oxford: Oxford University Press.
Roche, P. (2009), *De Bello Civili Book 1*, Oxford: Oxford University Press.
Roller, M. (2001), *Constructing Autocracy: Aristocrats and Emperors in Julio-Claudian Rome*, Princeton: Princeton University Press.
Roller, M. (2018), *Models from the Past in Roman Culture: A World of Exempla*, Cambridge: Cambridge University Press.
Rosenblitt, J. (2019), *Rome after Sulla*, London: Bloomsbury.
Santangelo, F. (2007), *Sulla, the Elites, and the Empire: A Study of Roman Policies in Italy and the Greek East*, Leiden: Brill.
Stover, T. (2008), "Cato and the Intended Scope of Lucan's *Bellum Civile*," *CQ*, 58 (2): 571–80.
Syme, R. (1939), *The Roman Revolution*, Oxford: Oxford University Press.
Thein, A. (2014), "Reflecting on Sulla's Clemency," *Historia*, 63 (2): 166–86.
Townend, G. (1960), "The Sources of the Greek in Suetonius," *Hermes*, 88 (1): 98–120.
Uden, J. (2015), *The Invisible Satirist: Juvenal and Second-Century Rome*, Oxford: Oxford University Press.
Wallace-Hadrill, A. (1981), "The Emperor and His Virtues," *Historia*, 30 (3): 298–323.
Walters, B. (2014), "Reading Death and the Senses in Lucan and Lucretius," in S. Butler and A. Purves (eds.), *Synaesthesia and the Ancient Senses*, 115–26, London: Routledge.

Walters, B. (2015), *Lucan: Civil War*, Indianapolis: Hackett.
Woodman, A. (1977), *Velleius Paterculus: The Tiberian Narrative (2.94–131)*, Cambridge: Cambridge University Press.
Woodman, A. (1983), *Velleius Paterculus: The Caesarian and Augustan Narrative (2.41–93)*, Cambridge: Cambridge University Press.
Woodman, A. (2017), *The Annals of Tacitus: Books 5–6*, Cambridge: Cambridge University Press.

CHAPTER 10
RE-MEMBERING THE PALATINE IN LUCAN'S *BELLUM CIVILE*
Jesse Weiner

Introduction

Lucan presents the *Bellum Civile* as a monument and develops a tension between *memoria* and *oblivio* throughout the epic (Gowing 2005; Thorne 2011).[1] A struggle between often painful acts of remembrance and their consignment to oblivion plays out throughout the literary *monumentum*, especially in the poem's depictions of other monuments and their physical and hermeneutic instability. These dynamics are present in Lucan's brief but surprising treatment of a thoroughly Augustan monument: the Palatine Temple of Apollo. The Palatine Temple's presence in Lucan's Roman cityscape of 49 BCE—a full two decades before its dedication—marks a clear instance of temporal disjuncture. The rupture with competing versions of history represented by the temple has been earlier observed and discussed in Lucanian scholarship.[2] More remains to be said about this anachronism, however, especially as pertains to its politics and the ways in which it threatens to shift and obscure memory.

After briefly discussing monumentality in Lucan's Augustan predecessors and in the *Bellum Civile* more generally, I will argue that Lucan's Palatine Temple simultaneously functions as a locus of memory creation and of forgetting. The temple is at once a "mnemotope," a site around which collective memory is organized, determined, and performed, and a vehicle for "cultural repression" and the annihilation of "cultural memory."[3] This dual nature should not surprise us; civil wars produce fractured and divisive collective memories, to which recent controversies over the removal of Confederate statues in the United States stand as powerful reminders. "Like lightning rods," as Susan E. Alcock offers, these sorts of objects draw "energy to select versions of the past" (2002: 17). As a mnemotope, the Palatine monument is as unstable as the political situation Lucan depicts. What Augustus had built as a symbol of reconciliation, political legitimacy, and the restoration of the Republic, Lucan resets within the spatial and temporal landscape of Roman history to commemorate the civil war itself and the unconstitutional origins of Julio-Augustan *imperium*. Through the Palatine Temple, Lucan reconfigures the Roman cityscape to issue a literary *damnatio* of sorts against Augustus and, I suggest, to undermine the Apollonian pretensions of his Neronian present.

If any material object tends to be envisioned as permanent, it is a monument. Monuments are built to last, not only materially but also hermeneutically: they are commemorative objects crafted to convey accounts of history to posterity. As Kirk Savage puts it (1997: 4):

Public monuments are the most conservative of commemorative forms precisely because they are meant to last, unchanged, forever. While other things come and go, are lost and forgotten, the monument is supposed to remain a fixed point, stabilizing both the physical and the cognitive landscape. Monuments attempt to mold a landscape of collective memory, to conserve what is worth remembering and discard the rest.

Many of Lucan's literary predecessors, such as Vergil, Horace, Ovid, Livy, and Vitruvius, present numerous monuments as landmarks that "direct attention to specific places and events" and, in so doing, "[anchor] 'collective remembering' in material sites that that [serve] as rallying points for shared common memory and identity" (Osborne 2001: 50-1). "Geographical relics" and poetry share the power to determine and replicate memory for posterity (Hardie 1993: 17). The Augustan poets therefore present their own literary output as monumental in its own right and coterminous with the project of empire. Vergil, for example, joins the memory of two fallen heroes, Nisus and Euryalus, to the monuments of Rome, Roman political power, and the *Aeneid* itself as a monumental site of collective memory (9.446-9):

fortunati ambo! siquid mea carmina possunt,
nulla dies umquam memori vos eximet aevo,
dum domus Aeneae Capitoli immobile saxum
accolet imperiumque pater Romanus habebit.

Doubly fortunate! If my verses have any power, no day will ever erase you from the memory of time, so long as the house of Aeneas still inhabits the unmovable rock of the Capitoline and the Roman father holds empire.

Vergil's poem, the memories it produces (importantly, Nisus and Euryalus are Vergil's own invention), and the monumental "house of Aeneas" on the "unmovable rock of the Capitoline" will last as long as Roman *imperium* (Lowrie 2003: 59; Torres-Murciano 2009: 296-7). Vergil has earlier prophesied that this *imperium* is *sine fine* (*Aen.* 1.279), boundless, both spatially and temporally. Vergil's monuments and the social identities and memories they produce are affixed to Rome's imperial kismet. Horace's *Carm.* 3.30 provides the paradigm for this partnership, as Eleanor Winsor Leach observes, coupling its *monumentum aere perennius* with "the ritual life of the city" of Rome (1998: 66). Augustan literature tends to imagine Rome as the eternal city that would provide an unchanging showcase for its eternal monuments.[4]

Vergil frames the entire *Aeneid* as a monumental act of remembrance (1.7: *Musa, mihi causas memora*, "Muse, remember for me the causes"). However, as Aeneas reminds us in Carthage at the outset of his tale in *Aeneid* 2 (2.12-13: *quamquam animus meminisse horret luctuque refugit, / incipiam*, "Although my mind bristles to have remembered and recoiled in sorrow, I will begin"), "memory of landscape is not always associated with pleasure. It can be associated sometimes with loss, with pain, with social fracture and sense of belonging gone" (Taylor 2008: 2). This activity is quickly joined to place and landscape; deeply immersed in his memories, Aeneas tells us (2.27–30):

> iuvat ire et Dorica castra
> desertosque videre locos litusque relictum:
> hic Dolopum manus, hic saevus tendebat Achilles;
> classibus hic locus, hic acie certare solebant.

It was a joy to go to the Greek camps and to see the deserted places and the abandoned shore: here the warbands of the Greeks, here savage Achilles pitched their tents, here was the place for the fleet, here they were accustomed to fight in the battle line.

The repetitive *hic . . . hic* construction does more than add a sense of vividness to Aeneas' storytelling; Aeneas' memories are fundamentally joined to and organized around landscape and place.

It is against this backdrop that I situate Lucan and his presentation of monuments and memory production. Lucan, too, yokes landscape and monuments to politics and presents these mnemonic artifacts as symbiotic with imperial destiny. But, in contrast to hopeful presentations of *Roma aeterna* in the Augustan literary regime (Leigh 1997: 89–91), Lucan's *Bellum Civile* envisions a Rome at the breaking point, a *discors machina* on the verge of tearing itself apart, and this political instability is reflected in its material culture and shifting landscapes. For example, early in the proem Lucan yokes his painful topic of *bellum nefandum* (1.21) to Italy's crumbling monuments and decimated landscape (1.24–32).[5] Lucan depicts his monuments variously crumbling and falling into pieces on the one hand, while their meanings shift and are subject to reinterpretation and reinvention. Monuments, in Lucan's poem, occasion struggles over meaning, memory, and history. These struggles, too, are joined to politics and, in my reading, Lucan's poem in a sense prefigures W. E. B. Du Bois's warning about the official production of collective memory, that "the truth of history may be utterly distorted and contradicted and changed into any convenient fairy tale that the masters of men wish" (Du Bois 1935: 726; Blight 1994: 51). The *Bellum Civile* is a subversive project to rewrite imperial history, and Lucan couples his hostility to the Julio-Claudian principate and its versions of history with a systematic assault on the monuments with which those in power seek to legitimate, commemorate, control, and preserve the memory of their regimes.

The processes by which monuments experience violent destruction, decay, reclamation by nature, neglect, and hermeneutic inversion form a motif which runs throughout Lucan's poem. The mutable monuments presented in Lucan's epic are varied not only in their aspects and materials but also in the means by which they experience change, degradation, and rededication. For example, in Book 6, Caesar destroys monumental structures such as city walls and homes and repurposes the materials to build fortifications for war that rival the walls of Troy and Babylon, thereby weaponizing ruined monuments (6.32–51). Furthermore, the battle of Pharsalus threatens to unmake history and eradicate

Roman identity and memory (7.389–92). As an essential part of this process, the Italian *monimenta* of Veii, Gabii, and Cora will be annihilated by civil war and then consigned to decay through both time and neglect (7.392–9). Book 8 features an extended meditation on Pompey's gravestone, which Lucan doubly writes out of existence as stone and ash inwardly collapse on the one hand while its commemorative referent ("Here lies Pompey") disappears through custom and disbelief (867–72; of course, at another level the poem writes the stone *into* existence). And when Caesar tours the ruins of Troy in Book 9, time and decay have wrought such ruination on the site's *monimenta*, that "even the ruins have perished" (*etiam periere ruinae*, 9.969). Those monuments that still stand have been reclaimed by nature and its super-fecundity, as grasses, brambles, and thorn-brakes obscure manmade structures and render the monuments unrecognizable and, ultimately, uninterpretable. Caesar and his guide challenge each other with divergent readings of the site, none of which, in my reading, are narratologically endorsed or wholly censured by the poem (9.964–79; Weiner and Benz 2018). Lucan reminds us that, in the words of Charles Martindale, "what is constructed can also be deconstructed," and this is true of both monuments and history, neither of which "give us unmediated access to 'reality' or 'the truth'" (1993: 48).

Book 3 of the *Bellum Civile* features yet another monument, one more specifically tied to the Augustan principate and the means by which it commemorated and celebrated itself. It is also a monument that should not be there: the temple of Apollo Palatinus.

Caesar on the Palatine

Lucan's revisionist and anachronistic revaluation of the Palatine Temple of Apollo constitutes a bold attempt to wrest control of history and its monuments away from their makers. In its early imperial context, however, the monument had performed essential functions in Augustan narratives of legitimacy.

Aside from Lucan, our ancient literary sources suggest that Augustus (at the time Octavian Caesar, since he received the titles Augustus and Princeps in January, 27 BCE) vowed a temple to Apollo during his campaign against Sextus Pompey in 36 BCE and again to commemorate his victory at Actium in 31 BCE, which he attributed to Apollo's divine patronage.[6] Augustus followed through on his promise, and the temple to Apollo was dedicated in 28 BCE. For the location, Augustus famously chose a site adjacent to his own home on the Palatine Hill, thereby strengthening the association between himself and the god through spatial proximity, and Augustus later had the Sibylline Books moved to the temple. Suetonius ranks the building among the more impressive achievements of the Augustan building program (*Aug.* 29.1–3):

> publica opera plurima extruxit, e quibus vel praecipua: forum cum aede Martis Ultoris, templum Apollinis in Palatio, aedem Tonantis Iovis in Capitolio … templum Apollinis in ea parte Palatinae domus excitavit, quam fulmine ictam desiderari a deo haruspices pronuntiarant; addidit porticus cum bibliotheca Latina

Graecaque, quo loco iam senior saepe etiam senatum habuit decuriasque iudicum recognovit.

Augustus built many public works, from which these three certainly stand out as exceptional: his forum with the Temple of Mars the Avenger, the Palatine Temple of Apollo, and the Temple of Jupiter Tonans on the Capitoline Hill ... Augustus raised the Temple of Apollo in that part of his Palatine home, which the soothsayers pronounced were desired by the god, since it had been struck by lightning. He joined its portico with Greek and Latin libraries, where in old age he often held the senate and revised jury lists.

Charles L. Babcock notes that "this temple shared prominence on the Palatine with that of the Magna Mater and gave truly Roman status to the tutelary deity of Octavian by establishing him for the first time within the *pomerium*" (1967: 190). The temple therefore functioned simultaneously as a symbol of Augustus' proper religious reverence, his divine patronage, and the Augustan peace, albeit peace achieved through civil war (see Zanker 1987: 90–7; Syndikus 2006: 308). These dynamics are developed further in Propertius 4.6 (Günther 2006: 373–9). After celebrating Rome's victory at Actium through Apollo's loyalty (*vincit Roma fide Phoebi*, Prop. 4.6.57) and noting that "Apollo Actius gained a monument, since each of his arrows destroyed ten ships" (*Actius hinc traxit Phoebus monumenta, quod eius / una decem vicit missa sagitta ratis*, 67–8), Propertius writes (69–70):

bella satis cecini: citharam iam poscit Apollo
victor et ad placidos exuit arma choros.

I have sung enough of war: now victorious Apollo demands the lyre and sheds arms for peaceful dances.

This monument was central to the emperor's self-representation and the regime's attempt to control the memory of its divisive origins. The temple and the building program at large were part of a process by which Augustus "displaced competing versions of the past ... the image of the benign elder statesman and of his golden age of prosperity displaced the violence and lawlessness of Octavian, the teenage warlord" (Flower 2006: 116). The Palatine Temple associated the *princeps* and his victories with divine patronage and authority, and John F. Miller argues that the temple served as "the most visible and abiding expression of Augustus' affiliation with Apollo" (2009: 185). For Hans-Christian Günther, this monument is "*the* most representative building of the Augustan era," and the end of Propertius 4.6 "corresponds precisely to the 'Bildprogramm' of the temple on the Palatine with its accent on peace and devotion" (2006: 373–4, 378–9, my own emphasis; cf. Coutelle 2015: 739; Welch 2005: 106). Velleius, Josephus, Suetonius, and Cassius Dio rank it among Augustus' most impressive and important architectural achievements.[7] More germane to Lucan, his predecessors Vergil, Horace, Propertius, and Ovid each celebrate the temple in verse and thereby cement its status as a mnemotope around which Roman identity and Augustan memory collect.[8]

The reference to the monument in Lucan is so small it would be easy to miss. Two words identify the site: *Phoebea Palatia* (3.103). Lucan says nothing more on the building itself. Lucan's poetic predecessors give more expansive descriptions of the temple and its decorous ostentation. For example, Vergil's shield of Aeneas proleptically depicts "Augustus sitting on the snow-white threshold of radiant Apollo, receiving the gifts of foreign peoples on the god's behalf and attaching them to the lofty door-posts."[9] Propertius is even more elaborative, praising numerous pieces of the temple's luxurious statuary, its impressive marble columns, and its finely crafted ivory doors (2.31; Syndikus 2006: 308–9; Fantham 2012: 308–10). Elsewhere, Lucan's tendency is to meditate at length on his monuments and ruins, but here Lucan refuses to offer more than a name for this building and thereby distances himself from the Augustan poets, for whom the Palatine Temple functioned as mnemotope for self-association (Newman 1967: 19; Leigh 1997: 18–19).

It is surprising that we find the Palatine temple in Lucan at all. Early in *Bellum Civile* 3, Caesar enters Rome and convenes the Senate. Lucan plays fast and loose with his history, and the poet changes historical details to render Caesar's meeting with the Senate both unconstitutional and chronologically impossible (103–9):[10]

> Phoebea Palatia complet
> turba patrum nullo cogendi iure senatus
> e latebris educta suis; non consule sacrae
> fulserunt sedes, non, proxima lege potestas,
> praetor adest, vacuaeque loco cessere curules.
> omnia Caesar erat: privatae curia vocis
> testis adest.

Although there was no authority to call the Senate, a mob of senators were led out from their hiding places and they filled the Palatine Temple of Apollo; the sacred seats did not shine brilliantly with consuls, the praetor (next in power by law) was not present, and the empty chairs of office were removed from the place. Caesar was all of these: the senate was present to bear witness to the authority of a private voice.

Lucan has apparently taken at least two historical liberties with this episode. The first is that the poet chooses the chronologically impossible Palatine Temple of Apollo for the setting of the meeting. Elaine Fantham notes that it is a "deliberate anachronism that Lucan sets the meeting in the Palatine temple of Apollo constructed by Caesar's heir," a full two decades *after* the historical events Lucan describes.[11] Cassius Dio sets the meeting outside the Pomerium (41.15.2), and, irrespective of whether Dio is accurate, the Palatine Temple's presence in Rome two decades before its dedication is a clear instance of temporal disjuncture. Lucan's manipulations of history are hardly accidental products of haphazard historiography, and recent scholarship on Lucan and Latin poetry at large has rightly adopted the view that it is more productive to explore the possibility of interpreting, rather than removing or explaining away, such problems and inconsistencies (Masters 1992: 22; Roche 2005; O'Hara 2007).

I suggest that the significance behind the anachronism is intricately interwoven with Lucan's second deployment of poetic license in his treatment of the episode. Lucan emphatically stresses that the Senate met unconstitutionally, which contradicts other historical evidence. Cicero and Cassius Dio each name the two tribunes who convened the meeting and place at least two senators of consular rank at the event (Cic., *Att.* 9.19.2, 10.3a.2, *Fam.* 4.1.1; Cass. Dio 41.15.2; Fantham 1996: 140n7). Matthias Gelzer notes that the occasion may have "looked a sorry gathering," and yet "still, it had been legally summoned by the tribunes Antonius and Cassius" (Gelzer 1968: 208). The version presented by the *Bellum Civile*, however, is riddled with imagery and language to the contrary. *Nullo . . . iure, non . . . sacrae, non . . . lege* thrice issues the formulaic assertion (in each case the negative is separated from legal vocabulary by a single word)—reading almost as a magical incantation, willing it to be true—that what Caesar is doing violates the laws of Republican Rome. The *turba* at the temple recalls Propertius 2.31.4, in which *Danai femina turba senis* (the womanly mob of old Danaus) stands between the marble columns at the Palatine Temple (Ovid also notes this statuary at *Trist.* 3.1.61–2). This perhaps adds an extra layer of scorn to Lucan's condemnation by undermining the masculinity of those who rushed to recognize the authority of Caesar. Also, since the fifty daughters of Danaus notoriously murdered their husbands, the allusion introduces the menace of unlawful, disloyal, and sacrilegious violence into the meeting while foreshadowing Caesar's eventual assassination at the hands of the Senate. Despite the fact that there is a *turba* of senators filling (*complet*) the temple, Lucan complements his language of illegality with imagery of a vacant Senate House. The consuls are gone, the praetor is not present, and the *curules* are empty. This imagery of void is driven home with *vacuaeque loco*, giving the full impression of an empty space where one would once have found the senate. The passage constitutes a "negation antithesis," a technique by which Lucan employs "a list of negative statements that frustrate the expectations of the reader and highlights the inversion or suspension of natural order caused by civil war" (Roche 2009: 123; also Esposito 2004). The poet draws attention to the anachronism by filling a temple that should not exist with non-existent objects. The heavy alliteration in *vacuaeque loco cessere curules* emphasizes these poetics of void by evoking the sound of echoing within an empty chamber. "Caesar is all things" (*omnia Caesar erat*), filling and dominating the room and its vacated offices (Hardie 1993: 8; Henderson 2010: 474). *Omnia* here functions as an elision of individual Caesars; Caesar is all Caesars, an all-encompassing representation of imperial tyranny.

The paradoxical displacement, then, of this episode onto a temple built by Augustus to commemorate the military victories which cemented his regime—won in civil wars, no less—constitutes a re-membering of Roman cityscape and an ethical refashioning of Augustus' monument. Embedded within this mnemonic act is a reconstruction and reconfiguration of urban space and its architecture. Lucan takes a monument dedicated in 28 BCE and effectively inscribes a new date of construction upon it—or rather effaces the old one—and thereby removes credit from Augustus for its establishment, as well as the first emperor's agency in determining its meaning and controlling its message. In essence, we are reading a memory sanction, a literary *damnatio memoriae*. Even as it constitutes an erasure, *damnatio* is also an act of conjuring. At one level, Lucan strips explicit credit from Augustus for the monument. However, the temple cannot help but evoke the princeps for the poem's audience, though its altered context seeks to cast this memory into disgrace. It is not that Lucan destroys Augustus' monument. Rather, the *Bellum Civile* relocates and resets the temple in the temporal landscape of Roman history.[12]

Augustus' temple had been a symbol of continuity, since it paid homage to the ancient gods of the state under the guise of *religio*, through a classical monumental form. Now, Lucan rededicates the temple as a sign of the Julio-Claudian break with Rome's republican past and its traditions, locating the moment when the Senate lost constitutional legitimacy and Caesar assumed unlawful powers upon this very site. Suetonius and Josephus each report that, in his later years, Augustus the *pater patriae* was accustomed to convene the senate and conduct his official business of state in the Palatine Temple (Joseph. *War* 2.6.1; cf. Suet. *Aug.* 29.3, quoted above):

ἀθροίσαντος δὲ Καίσαρος τῶν συνέδριον ἐν τέλει Ῥωμαίων καὶ τῶν φίλων ἐν τῷ κατὰ τὸ Παλάτιον Ἀπόλλωνος ἱερῷ ...

Once Caesar [Augustus] had assembled a council of the principal Romans and his friends in the Palatine Temple of Apollo ...

Lucan thus receives a monument conceived and employed as a symbol of Augustan legitimacy and reforms it to commemorate the illegal (*nullo iure, non lege*) and immoral (*non sacrae*) origins of the regime. To this end, Caesar is called a "private citizen" (*privatae ... vocis*), emphasizing his lack of legitimate authority. To an extent, Lucan here responds to Vergil whose promise of a marble temple to the Sibyl in *Aeneid* 6 "cannot help," in the words of Alessandro Barchiesi, "but be only a specific hint toward the dedication of the Apollo Palatinus sanctuary by Octavian" (2005: 282), and Miller notes that "Vergil consistently imagines the Temple of Apollo as a thoroughly Augustan monument" (2009: 206).[13] However, whereas Vergil's *Aeneid* looks forward proleptically to celebrate Augustus' dedication of the temple, Lucan casts his gaze backwards to erase the emperor's name from the monument and turn the temple from a place of worship to the setting of a heinous, even treasonous, criminal act. In Vergil, Augustus receives the gifts of conquered nations at the Palatine Temple (*Aen.* 8.720–2); in Lucan the place is a site of Roman surrender to Caesar.

As Alcock observes (quoting Assmann), "'the past is modeled, invented, reinvented, and reconstructed by the present.' Forgetfulness is as pivotal to this process as remembrance" (2002: 16; cf. Assmann 1997: 9). Augustus had used his building program to help sell his regime as a repackaged Republic; Lucan hijacks these same monuments, inverting their authorially intended meanings to commemorate the violent, illegal, and sacrilegious end of the Republic and its *libertas*. For better or worse, the commemorative and ethical values of monuments are not unalterably affixed by the author or sculptor at the moment of creation, and Lucan's use of temporal paradox underscores his hermeneutic agenda: monuments do not simply commemorate the past for the present and future, nor is posterity the inactive recipient of antiquity.

The New Apollo

As Paul Roche has observed, "just as Augustus is the final cause and *telos* of the . . . *Aeneid*, Nero, for good or ill" similarly serves as the *telos* of the *Bellum Civile* (2005: 55). The Palatine Temple doubles as a symbol of both teleologies and, even as the *Bellum Civile* looks backwards to intervene in Vergil's Augustan narratives, Lucan's Palatine Temple operates simultaneously on a Neronian register. Over the course of his reign, Nero increasingly associated himself with Apollo, including Apollo Palatinus, to whom the emperor ultimately sacrificed in his triumph of 67 CE. The Palatine passage functions as part of a larger program within the *Bellum Civile* to undermine Nero's imperial associations with Apollo.

Nero followed Augustus in cultivating a close relationship between his regime and Apollo, both through public performances and the regime's iconography (Tucker 1983: 148–51; Champlin 2003a; 2003b: 112–44; Shotter 2008: 64). While Nero's sacrifice to Apollo Palatinus at his triumph in 67 clearly postdates Lucan, Nero had, palpably, promoted a triangulation between himself, Apollo, and Augustus as early as 59. Dio reports that at the Juvenalia of that year, Nero paid Augustiani to acclaim him with shouts of, "O glorious Caesar, O Apollo, O Augustus, another Pythian!"[14] In coinage of 64–5, Nero is depicted with a radiate crown and identified by inscription as "Augustus," while Apollo Citharoedus appears frequently in Neronian coinage between 62 and 65.[15] Lucan himself participates in Nero's Apollonian pretensions, since the *Bellum Civile* mentions Apollo more than any other deity.[16]

Even as Lucan resets the Palatine Temple in Rome's cityscape and timescape as a monument to commemorate the end of the Republic, the poet subtly undermines the piety behind Nero's own claims to be a new Apollo. Political use of Apollo and his Palatine Temple becomes a mark not of civic restoration but of violation, and Phoebus becomes a reminder of the principate's illegality rather than its legitimacy. The passage works in concert with Lucan's portrayal of Phoebus and his oracle, which, for all its violence, reads very much like a rape scene (cf. Ahl 1976: 125–7; O'Higgins 1988: 212–13; Hershkowitz 1998: 43–5). Frederick Ahl has read Lucan's depiction of the oracle at Delphi as anti-Neronian, since "Apollo's inspiration and prophetic utterances are no longer of any interest to man. His oracle is defunct, to all intents and purposes, revived briefly and disastrously" (1976: 48). In his extended reading of the scene alongside Vergil's Sibyl in *Aeneid* 6, Jamie Masters notes that the "struggle between prophetess and inspiring god, which amounts to a kind of spiritual rape, is a consistent element of the prophetic tradition; but surely Lucan is unique in the extent to which this violence is accentuated" (1992: 144; cf. Frankel 2010: 26–7). Lucan meditates upon the priestess Phemonoe's fear (*pavidam ... vatem*, 5.124; *metuens*, 5.128; *metus*, 5.142; *pavens*, 5.146; *conterrita virgo*, 5.161), and this fear is above all of entrusting herself to Apollo (*veritam se credere Phoebo*, 5.156). Despite the *virgo* Phemonoe's lack of consent (*haerentem dubiamque*, 5.145; *resistit*, 5.147; *confugit*, 5.162), Apollo and his priest each forces himself upon her. The priest "grabbed her and forced her to enter" the temple (*corripuit cogitque ... irrumpere*, 5.127). The divine "spirit thrust itself upon the *vates*" (*spiritus ingessit vati*, 5.165) and, "having at last mastered the Delphic breast more fully than ever before, Apollo penetrated her body" (*tandemque potitus / pectore Cirrhaeo non umquam plenior artus / Phoebados irrupit Paean*, 5.165–7). Dehumanized, Phemonoe is forced to bear Apollo's whip (*verbere*, 5.174), spurs (*stimulis*, 5.175), and controlling reins (*frenos*, 5.176). Henry Day notes that Phemonoe is "broken by Apollo" (2013: 99). In response, the suffering priestess "groaned and grunted loudly with panting breath, then a wretched wailing filled the vast cave" (*gemitus et anhelo clara meatu / murmura, tum maestus vastis ululatus in antris*, 5.191–2). When it is all over, "she falls, scarcely able to recover" (*vixque refecta cadit*, 5.224; Hardie 1993: 108).

Apollo becomes a "maleficent and eventually murderous deity," and the end of this violence is death (Masters 1992: 145). Lucan insists that "if the god enters her breast, the penalty (or reward) for receiving his power is an early death" (*nam, si qua deus sub pectora venit, / numinis aut poena est mors immatura recepti / aut pretium*, 5.116–18). Joseph Fontenrose notes that Lucan depicts a "reluctant Pythia forced to perform her office," whose fear and suffering manifests in "wild cries," "flight," "fainting," and "death," and that "Lucan attributes her behavior to Apollo's possession" (1978: 210; see also Masters 1992: 144). Like Phemonoe, Lucan is himself a *vates*, and Phoebus becomes a powerful foil for Nero especially in the god's final suppression of poetic voice: "Apollo suppressed the rest and bound her throat" (*cetera suppressit faucesque obstrinxit Apollo*, 5.197; see O'Higgins 1988: 213). If Nero is a new Apollo, the association is troubling and Apollo's violent subjugation of Phemonoe is, perhaps, evocative of Nero's violent treatment of his wives.

Together, Lucan's politically charged use of *Phoebea Palatia* at 3.103 and the Delphic episode invite the reader to revisit the famously ambiguous first invocation of Phoebus at 1.48—whatever the initial authorial intent of the proem.[17] After all, even if the proem had been conceived as sincere panegyric, the publication of the final seven books of the *Bellum Civile* cannot help but throw their shadow backwards over the introduction, especially in the wake of Lucan's *De Incendio Urbis*, presumed to have been composed in 64 after the great fire.[18] Lucan suggests that upon his apotheosis Nero might "mount Phoebus's flame bearing chariot and light up the world" (1.45–50):[19]

>   te, cum statione peracta
> astra petes serus, praelati regia caeli
> excipiet gaudente polo: seu sceptra tenere
> seu te flammigeros Phoebi conscendere currus
> telluremque nihil mutato sole timentem
> igne vago lustrare iuvet.

> When at last you [Nero] seek the stars once your watch has been completed, the palace of your chosen sky will welcome you with heaven rejoicing: whether it pleases you to hold the scepter or to mount Phoebus' flame-bearing chariot and to light up the world—fearing nothing from the changed sun—with roving fire.

As Stephen Hinds notes, "Lucan flatters the emperor by predicting for him a divine role which will neatly dovetail with his earthly self-image" (1987: 28). Suetonius, after all, tells us that at one point "Nero was judged to equal Apollo in song, and the Sun in driving a chariot" (*Apollinem cantu, Solem aurigando aequiperare existimaretur, Ner.* 53). However, the proem here links Nero not only to Phoebus but also to Phaethon, "the most spectacularly unsuccessful charioteer who ever rode," and Hinds suggests that *ipse vago* "acquires a worrisome connotation":

> If Nero is envisaged as steering the Sun's chariot 'with wandering flame', does that adjective *vagus* simply refer to the non-fixed position of the sun in the firmament (we are in the world of ancient astronomy, remember), or does it perhaps hint at the 'erratic' motion which is likely to characterize the chariot's course in the hands of this *Phaethon redivivus* (1987: 28)?[20]

Beyond Hinds' gloss of *vagus*, I suggest that *flammiger* (the word's earliest use in extant Latin literature) alludes to Ovid's *flammifer* at *Met.* 2.155, the very moment when Phaethon takes the reins on his disastrous chariot ride.[21] Nero and Phaethon become linked through this epic compound and, looking beyond Ovid's Phaethon, *flammifer* imports the specter of catastrophe into the passage. *Flammifer* is rare in extant Latin literature, and it is worth noting that its lone pre-Ovidian instance, found in Ennius, too, is ominous in its context: *flammiferam hanc vim quae me excruciat* ("this flame-bearing violence which tortures me," Enn., *Scen.* 29). In Lucan's Neronian present, Seneca describes an Erinys as *flammifera* (*Her. F.* 982). He also uses *flammifer* in the *Thyestes* to issue a dire prophesy that a celestial body will fall from the sky with apocalyptic consequences, reminiscent of *ekpyrosis*: *Leo flammiferis aestibus ardens / iterum e caelo cadet Herculeus* (The Herculean lion, burning with flame-bearing heat, will once more fall from the sky, 855–6).

Roche observes that this invocation of Phaethon occurs within a primary context of conflagration (2009: 153). Lucan's appeal for Nero to take Phoebus' reins is indeed swiftly followed by a lengthy simile in which the collapse of Rome into civil war is likened to cosmic dissolution, conflagration, and Stoic *ekpyrosis*.[22] The simile contains another reference to Phoebus, replete with disastrous consequences when one presumes to take the sun-god's place (72–80):

> nec se Roma ferens. sic, cum compage soluta
> saecula tot mundi suprema coegerit hora
> antiquum repetens iterum chaos, [omnia mixtis

sidera sideribus concurrent,] ignea pontum
astra petent, tellus extendere litora nolet
excutietque fretum, fratri contraria Phoebe
ibit et obliquum bigas agitare per orbem
indignata diem poscet sibi, totaque discors
machina divolsi turbabit foedera mundi.

Rome could not bear her own weight. Just as when the structure is dissolved the final hour closes out so many ages of the universe and again seeks ancient chaos, [all the constellations will rush together in confusion,] fiery stars will fall into the sea, the earth will refuse to spread its shores and will shake off the ocean, Phoebe will go against her brother and, disdaining to drive her chariot across the slanting sky, she will demand the day for herself, and the entire discordant machine will overthrow the laws of the universe torn asunder.

Here, too, we can read allusion to Ovid's Phaethon, since Lucan's *antiquum repetens iterum chaos* picks up Ovid's *in chaos antiquum* (*Met.* 2.299; Roche 2009: 153; Keith 2011: 121). If Rome is a scorched earth, what are we to make of Nero as a new Apollo and a new Phoebus? If Nero is to usurp the sun-god's chariot and light up the world, is he destined to crash and burn as a new Phaethon? As Suetonius reports of someone quoting to Nero from Greek tragedy, "when someone in casual conversation said, 'Upon my death let the earth be consumed by fire,' Nero answered, 'On the contrary, while I'm alive'" (*dicente quodam in sermone communi*: ἐμοῦ θανόντος γαῖα μειχθήτω πυρί, '*immo*,' *inquit*, 'ἐμοῦ ζῶντος*,'* Suet., *Ner.* 38.1).[23]

Set within this larger pattern of engagement with Apollo, Lucan's Palatine Temple anachronism becomes part of a program to undermine Nero's contemporary Apollonian pretensions. Through the temple on the Palatine Hill, Apollo becomes an emblem of the principate's illegal origins and the loss of *libertas* rather than the patron of a Republic restored. At Delphi, Apollo suppresses free expression and infringes upon *libertas* with brutal violence and so becomes an ugly figure for imperial association. Especially in the wake of the fire of 64 and the *De Incendio Urbis*, these scenes invite a reading of the proem in which the specters of *ekpyrosis* and Phaethon loom large. Nero may be destined to take the sun-god's place, but he may also be very bad at such a role and the consequences may be apocalyptic.

Conclusion

Lucan provokes an interpretive intervention from his audience and asks the reader to choose between competing, mutually exclusive accounts of Rome's past. As part of this project to redirect social memory, Lucan resets one of Rome's most visible Augustan mnemotopes into the pre-Augustan cityscape. The *Bellum Civile* emphasizes the relativism of history and memory through its conspicuous temporal inconsistencies; the

Palatine Temple of Apollo is certainly one pointed example of this, but it is by no means the only one. To the extent that Lucan exercises control over history and memory, he in turn discredits and dismantles Augustan monuments, and—at least to some extent—wrests hegemony over the past away from the Julio-Claudians. To accept Lucan's *Bellum Civile*—its versions of the past and its model of monumental commemoration—is to reconfigure the past and revalue Caesarian and Augustan versions of history and their commemorative symbols and artifacts. The dominion of the audience over monuments comes to the fore, as the *Bellum Civile* attempts to steal the Palatine Temple away from its maker. Much as Alois Riegl suggests of monuments' "historical value" (the hermeneutic value of which is determined by viewers and readers, rather than artists and authors), Lucan endeavors "to overthrow the supremacy of the creator as central to the significance" of both art and monuments, which subversively undermines not only the imperial victors of the Civil War but also the dominant aesthetic traditions of Rome (Riegl 1982; cf. Zerner 1976: 179).

As Margaret Drabble writes of Virginia Woolf's melancholy for a lost place, "the past lives on in art and memory, but it is not static: it shifts and changes as the present throws its shadow backwards" (Drabble 1979: 270, also quoted by Taylor 2008: 2). Written from the perspective of history's losers and striving against the monumentalizing accounts provided by the Augustan building program and its literary regime, the *Bellum Civile* bets its fortunes on the mutability of monuments, memory, and, with them, history. Lucan taps into the assumption that "social memory is manifestly a mighty force, but also a fugitive one. Memories overlap and compete; over time they change or are eradicated; people forget" (Alcock 2002: 1). Lucan, of course, fights an uphill battle in presenting his version of history and its monuments. As history would have it, Augustan monuments, the images they propagated, and the memories they determined generally proved more durable than those depicted in the *Bellum Civile*, though Lucan does succeed in putting forth a competing memory landscape and in imparting an enduring literary portrayal of Caesar. David Quint observes that "Lucan's capacity to overgo the *Aeneid* is impaired because he speaks from the side of the losers, contesting a vision of history upheld not only by Vergil's epic but by the reality of imperial power" (1993: 133).[24] But irrespective of whether Lucan successfully wins over his audience or merely shocks it out of its normative assumptions, the *Bellum Civile* calls attention to a discursive position in which it is readers and viewers who make monuments in the final analysis. In the wake of Riegl, David Bleich, Stanley Fish, and movements in reader response theory, many of us now take this point for granted.[25] But, in its Roman context, Lucan's conventionalist model of reception is quite radical. Lucan reminds us of the fickleness of collective memory and puts us on guard to the danger that, in our age of post-truths and fake news, history itself is, perhaps, at the mercy of architectural and rhetorical regimes. In this specific instance, the legality of Caesar's position and the integrity of the foundations upon which the principate was built are at stake. Lucan thereby creates an interpretive situation that is ethically, as well as hermeneutically, volatile.

Notes

1. I presented portions of this chapter on numerous occasions, including the 2016 Early Cultures Conference, "Feeling History," at the University of California, Irvine; "Lucan in His Contemporary Contexts" at Brigham Young University in 2017; and "Landscapes of War" at the 2017 Celtic Conference in Classics in Montréal. I am grateful for the thoughtful critiques I received on each occasion. Thanks are also due to this volume's editors and referees for their expert corrections and suggestions. Finally, this essay benefitted from Stephen Hinds and James I. Porter, who commented on early drafts of this material.
2. See, for example, Tucker (1983: 144); Fantham (1996); Radicke (2004: 240); Barchiesi (2005: 282); Nix (2008: 29).
3. Quotations are from Assmann (1995: 366), also discussed by Flower (2006: xix–xx). See also Assmann (1992); Assmann (1997); Brockmeier (2002); Bollig (2009: 19).
4. See also Ov., *Met.* 15.807–15, 871–9, which Boyle (2003: 10) reads in conversation with Horace's epilogue to book 3 of the *Odes*.
5. For the text of Lucan, I use David R. Shackleton Bailey's Teubner edition, reprinted as Shackleton Bailey (2009).
6. For a nuanced overview of the sources and the connections to Naulochus and Actium, see Lange (2009).
7. Josephus writes that the Palatine Temple was "a building which he [Augustus] had erected with wondrous ostentation" (κτίσμα δ' ἦν ἴδιον αὐτοῦ θαυμασίῳ πολυτελείᾳ κεκοσμημένον, *War* 2.6.1). Cf. Vell. Pat. 2.81.3.
8. Hor., *Carm* 1.31; Prop. 2.31, 4.6; Verg., *Aen.* 6.69, 8.720–2. Ov., *Trist.* 3.1.59–62 describes a "sublime, shining" temple, notable for its columns and statuary. On the Palatine in Augustan poetry, see especially Rea (2007).
9. *Aen.* 8.720–2: *ipse sedens niveo candentis limine Phoebi / dona recognoscit populorum aptatque superbis / postibus*.
10. On Lucan's willful manipulations of history, see Lintott (1971); Masters (1994).
11. Fantham (1996: 140). Fantham also observes that Lucan changes the episode to make the meeting unconstitutional. See also Radicke (2004: 240). Sarah A. Nix observes that "the temporal disjunction" represented by the temple "calls attention to the fictive nature of Caesarian claims in both a pre- and post-Augustan world" (2008: 292).
12. As John Henderson instructs, "'Since military history is primarily concerned with the claiming of space by force,' read the *Bellum Civile* as a Black Hole swallowing the coordinates of sense" (2010: 484, quoting Davis 1985: 56).
13. On the relation of this Lucan passage to Vergil, see especially Fantham (1996).
14. 62.20.4–5: καὶ ἦν ἀκούειν πως αὐτῶν λεγόντων 'ὁ καλὸς Καῖσαρ, ὁ Ἀπόλλων, ὁ Αὔγουστος, εἷς ὡς Πύθιος'. See also Tucker (1983: 150); Champlin (2003a: 276).
15. See, e.g., RIC Nero 121, 123, 205, 206, 207, 209, 211, 212, which depict Nero with a radiate crown and Apollo Citharoedus on the reverse. Cf. Champlin (2003b: 116–17): "Suetonius knew these coins and assumed, understandably, that they represented the statues of Nero in the dress of a citharode which the victorious emperor set up after his triumph of 67." Cf. Suet., *Ner.* 25.2.
16. Tucker (1983: 143) observes that "of all the pagan gods, Lucan's favorite appears to Phoebus." Inclusive of Apollo/Phoebus' various epithets, Tucker provides a chart detailing 123 mentions in the *Bellum Civile*.

17. While these lines present themselves as an encomium to Nero, they have also been read to satirize the emperor with subtle jokes about his squinty eyes, ample girth, and balding head. For overviews of these arguments, see Dewar (1994); Bartsch (1997: 173–4n64); O'Hara (2007: 134); Roche (2009); Penwill (2010); Ripoll (2010); Nellis (2011). Champlin (2003b: 114) takes Nero's apotheosis in Lucan seriously, reading the emperor as the poem's patron deity (cf. Grimal 1960), while Ahl (1976: 48) finds the passage subversive and less than flattering.
18. On *De Incendio Urbis*, see Rose (1966); Ahl (1971); McGann (1975); Ahl (1976: 352).
19. See Champlin (2003a: 282); Tucker (1983); Roche (2009). Dinter (2012: 14) notes that the sun, sometimes "Apollo" and more often "Phoebus" is "the most developed cosmic 'character'" in the *Bellum Civile*.
20. As Hinds notes (1987: 28), this connection to Phaethon "is not lost on the scholiast of the *Adnotationes*." Just as the seeming inconsistency of the encomium at large with the poem's later hostility toward Nero has provoked interpretive debates, so has this allusion. On this passage's full debt to Ovid's Phaethon episode, see Keith (2011: 118–20). Barrett, Fantham, and Yardley (2016: 263n56) accept that "unlike Phaethon, Nero's control of the chariot will be welcomed by all the gods," cf. Dewar (1994); Champlin (2003b: 134); Chaudhuri (2014: 168). Against this, O'Hara (2007: 134) notes that the allusion may be "uncomplimentary." Cf. Leigh (1997: 25); Roche (2009: 8–9, 153). Drawing from Seneca's *QNat*. and a painting of Phaethon in the *Domus Aurea*, Duret (1988) argues that Nero styled himself as Phaethon in his role of Apollo's successor, rather than failed usurper. Phaethon is named explicitly at Luc. 2.413 within a passage that has been argued to be anti-Neronian; Auhagen (1997).
21. Lucan uses *flammiger* again at 1.415 of the sun.
22. See Aymard (1951: 100); Getty (1955: 142); Lapidge (1979: 360–3). Sklenář (2003: 3–6) notes that Lucan nowhere suggests that, in a Stoic fashion, this apocalyptic conflagration "will be followed by a restoration of cosmic order." Cf. Johnson (1987: 17–18).
23. See also Champlin (2003b: 13). This anecdote is joined to Suetonius' accusation that Nero set fire to Rome in 64.
24. For an alternate view, see Roche (2005: 56), which challenges the notion that history and epics can have "winners" and "losers."
25. See, for example, Bleich (1978) and the essays in Fish (1980).

References

Ahl. F. M. (1971), "Lucan's *De Incendio Urbis, Epistulae ex Campania*, and Nero's Ban," *TAPhA*, 102: 1–27.
Ahl, F. M. (1976), *Lucan: An Introduction*, Ithaca: Cornell University Press.
Alcock, S. E. (2002), *Archaeologies of the Greek Past: Landscapes, Monuments, and Memories*, Cambridge: Cambridge University Press.
Assmann, J. (1992), *Das kulturelle Gedächtnis: Schrift, Erinnerung, und politische Identität in frühen Hochkulturen*, Munich: Verlag C. H. Beck.
Assmann, J. (1995), "Ancient Egyptian Antijudaism: A Case of Distorted Memory," in D. Schacter (ed.), *Memory Distortion: How Minds, Brains and Societies Reconstruct the Past*, 365–76, Cambridge, MA: Harvard University Press.
Assmann, J. (1997), *Moses the Egyptian: The Memory of Egypt in Western Monotheism*, Cambridge, MA: Harvard University Press.

Auhagen, A. (1997), "Nero—ein 'Phaethon' in Rom? Eine politische Deutung des Apennin-Exkurses in Lukans *Bellum Civile* (2, 396-438)," in T. Baier an F. Schimann (eds.), *Fabrica. Studien zur antiken Literatur und ihrer Rezeption*, 91-102, Stuttgart: Teubner.

Aymard, J. (1951), *Quelques séries de comparaisons chez Lucain*, Montpellier: C. Déhan.

Babcock, C. L. (1967), "Horace *Carm*. 1. 32 and the Dedication of the Temple of Apollo Palatinus," *CPh*, 62 (3): 189-94.

Barchiesi, A. (2005), "Learned Eyes: Poets, Viewers, Image Makers," in K. Galinsky (ed.), *The Cambridge Companion to the Age of Augustus*, 281-305, Cambridge: Cambridge University Press.

Barrett, A. A., E. Fantham, and J. C. Yardley, eds. (2016), *The Emperor Nero: A Guide to the Ancient Sources*, Princeton: Princeton University Press.

Bartsch, S. (1997), *Ideology in Cold Blood: A Reading of Lucan's* Civil War, Cambridge, MA: Harvard University Press.

Bleich, D. (1978), *Subjective Criticism*, Baltimore: The Johns Hopkins University Press.

Blight, D. W. (1994), "W.E.B. Du Bois and American Historical Memory," in G. Fabre and R. O'Meally (eds.), *History and Memory in African American Culture*, 45-71, New York: Oxford University Press.

Bollig, M. (2009), "Visions of Landscapes: An Introduction," in M. Bollig and O. Bubenzer (eds.), *African Landscapes: Interdisciplinary Approaches*, 1-38, New York: Springer.

Boyle, A. J. (2003), *Ovid and the Monuments: A Poet's Rome*, Bendigo, Vic.: Aureal.

Brockmeier, J. (2002), "Remembering and Forgetting: Narrative as Cultural Memory," *Culture & Psychology*, 8 (1): 15-43.

Champlin, E. (2003a), "Nero, Apollo, and the Poets," *Phoenix*, 57 (3/4): 276-83.

Champlin, E. (2003b), *Nero*, Cambridge, MA: The Belknap Press.

Chaudhuri, P. (2014), *The War with God: Theomachy in Roman Imperial Poetry*, Oxford: Oxford University Press.

Coutelle, E. (2015), *Properce, Élégies, livre IV*, Brussels: Latomus.

Davis, L. J. (1985), *Resisting Novels: Ideology and Fiction*, New York: Methuen.

Day, H. J. M. (2013), *Lucan and the Sublime: Power, Representation and Aesthetic Experience*, Cambridge: Cambridge University Press.

Dewar, M. (1994), "Laying it on with a Trowel: The Proem to Lucan and Related Texts," *CQ*, 44 (1): 199-211.

Dinter, M. T. (2012), *Anatomizing Civil War: Studies in Lucan's Epic Technique*, Ann Arbor: University of Michigan Press.

Drabble, M. (1979), *A Writer's Britain: Landscape in Literature*, London: Methuen.

Du Bois, W. E. B. (1935), *Black Reconstruction: An Essay toward the Part Which Black Folk Played in the Attempt to Reconstruct Democracy in America, 1860-1880*, New York: Harcourt, Brace and Company.

Duret, L. (1988), "Néron-Phaéthon ou la témérité sublime," *REL*, 66: 139-55.

Esposito, P. (2004), "Lucano e la 'negazione per antitesi'," in P. Esposito and E. M. Ariemma (eds.), *Lucano e la tradizione dell'epica Latina*, 39-67, Naples: Guida.

Fantham, E. (1996), "*Religio . . . dira loci*: Two Passages in Lucan *de Bello Civili* 3 and Their Relation to Vergil's Rome and Latium," *MD*, 37: 137-53.

Fantham, E. (2012), "Images of the City: Propertius' New-Old Rome," in E. Greene and T. Welch (eds.), *Propertius*, 302-19, Oxford: Oxford University Press.

Fish, S. (1980), *Is There a Text in This Class?: The Authority of Interpretive Communities*, Cambridge, MA: Harvard University Press.

Flower, H. I. (2006), *The Art of Forgetting: Disgrace & Oblivion in Roman Political Culture*, Chapel Hill: University of North Carolina Press.

Fontenrose, J. (1978), *The Delphic Oracle: Its Reponses and Operations with a Catalogue of Responses*, Berkeley: University of California Press.

Frankel, E. (2010), "Lucan as the Transmitter of Ancient Pathos," trans. L. Holford-Strevens, in C. Tesoriero (ed.), *Lucan*, 15–45, Oxford: Oxford University Press.
Gelzer, M. (1968), *Caesar: Politician and Statesman*, trans. P. Needham, Cambridge, MA: Harvard University Press.
Getty, R. J. (1955), *M. Annaei Lucani De Bello Civili Liber I*, Cambridge: Cambridge University Press.
Gowing, A. (2005), *Empire and Memory: The Representation of the Roman Republic in Imperial Culture*, Cambridge: Cambridge University Press.
Grimal, P. (1960), "L'Éloge de Néro au Pharsale: Est-il ironique?," *REL*, 38: 296–305.
Günther, H.-C. (2006), "The Fourth Book," in H.-C. Günther (ed.), *Brill's Companion to Propertius*, 353–96, Leiden: Brill.
Hardie, P. (1993), *The Epic Successors of Vergil: a study in the dynamics of a tradition*, Cambridge: Cambridge University Press.
Henderson, J. (2010), "Lucan/The Word at War," in C. Tesoriero (ed.), *Lucan*, 433–91, Oxford: Oxford University Press.
Hershkowitz, D. (1997), *The Madness of Epic: Reading Insanity from Homer to Statius*, Oxford: Clarendon Press.
Hinds, S. (1987), "Generalizing about Ovid," *Ramus*, 16 (1–2): 4–31.
Johnson, W. R. (1987), *Momentary Monsters: Lucan and His Heroes*, Ithaca: Cornell University Press.
Keith, A. (2011), "Ovid in Lucan: The Poetics of Instability," in P. Asso (ed.), *Brill's Companion to Lucan*, 111–32, Leiden: Brill.
Lange, C. H. (2009), *Res Publica Constituta: Apollo, Actium and the Accomplishment of the Triumviral Assignment*, Leiden: Brill.
Lapidge, M. (1979), "Lucan's Imagery of Cosmic Dissolution," *Hermes*, 107 (3): 344–70.
Leach, E. W. (1998), "Personal and Communal Memory in the Reading of Horace's *Odes*, Books 1–3," *Arethusa*, 31 (1): 43–74.
Leigh, M. (1997), *Lucan: Spectacle and Engagement*, Oxford: Oxford University Press.
Lintott, A. W. (1971), "Lucan and the History of the Civil War," *CQ*, 21 (2): 488–505.
Lowrie, M. (2003), "Rome: City and Empire," *CW*, 97 (1): 57–68.
Martindale, C. (1993), *Redeeming the Text: Latin poetry and the hermeneutics of reception*, Cambridge: Cambridge University Press.
Masters, J. (1992), *Poetry and Civil War in Lucan's Bellum Civile*, Cambridge: Cambridge University Press.
Masters, J. (1994), "Deceiving the reader: the political mission of Lucan *Bellum Civile* 7," in J. Elsner and J. Masters (eds.), *Reflections of Nero: Culture, History, and Representation*, 151–77, Chapel Hill: University of North Carolina Press.
McGann, M. J. (1975), "Lucan's *de Incendio Urbis*: The Evidence of Statius and Vacca," *TAPhA*, (105): 213–17.
Miller, J. F. (2009), *Apollo, Augustus, and the Poets*, Cambridge: Cambridge University Press.
Nelis, D. (2011), "Praising Nero (Lucan, *De Bello Civili* 1,33–66)," in G. Urso (ed.), *Dicere laudes: elogio, comunicazione, creazione del consenso*, 253–64, Pisa: Edizioni ETS.
Newman, J. K. (1967), *Augustus and the New Poetry*, Brussels: Latomus.
Nix, S. A. (2008), "Caesar as Jupiter in Lucan's *Bellum Civile*," *CJ*, 103 (3): 281–94.
O'Hara, J. J. (2007), *Inconsistency in Roman Epic: Studies in Catullus, Lucretius, Vergil, Ovid and Lucan*, Cambridge: Cambridge University Press.
O'Higgins, D. (1988), "Lucan as *Vates*," *ClAnt*, 7 (2): 208–26.
Osborne, B. S. (2001), "Landscapes, memory, monuments, and commemoration: putting identity in its place," *Canadian Ethnic Studies*, 33 (3): 39–77.
Penwill, J. (2010), "Damn with Great Praise?: The Imperial Encomia of Lucan and Silius," in A. Turner, J. K. O. Chong-Gossard, and F. Vervaet (eds.), *Private and Public Lies: The Discourse of Despotism in the Graeco-Roman World*, 211–30, Leiden: Brill.

Quint, D. (1993), *Epic and Empire: Politics and Generic Form from Vergil to Milton*, Princeton: Princeton University Press.

Radicke, J. (2004), *Lucans poetische Technik*, Leiden: Brill.

Rea, J. (2007), *Legendary Rome: Myth Monuments, and Memory on the Palatine and Capitoline*, London: Bloomsbury Academic.

Riegl, A. (1982), "The Modern Cult of Monuments: Its Character and Its Origin," trans. K. W. Forster and D. Ghirado, *Oppositions*, 25: 21–50.

Ripoll, F. (2010), "L'énigme du prologue et le sens de l'Histoire dans le *Bellum Ciuile* : une hypothèse interprétative," in O. Devillers and S. F. d'Espèrey (eds.), *Lucain en débat. Rhétorique, poétique et histoire*, 149–58, Bordeaux: Ausonius Éditions.

Roche, P. (2005), "Righting the Reader: Conflagration and Civil War in Lucan's *De Bello Civili*," *Scholia*, 14: 52–71.

Roche, P. (2009), *De Bello Ciuili: Book I*, Oxford: Oxford University Press.

Rose, K. F. C. (1966), "Problems in the chronology of Lucan's career," *TAPhA*, 97: 379–96.

Savage, K. (1997), *Standing Soldiers, Kneeling Slaves: Race, War, and Monument in Nineteenth-Century America*, Princeton: Princeton University Press.

Shackleton Bailey, D. R., ed. (2009), *Marcus Annaeus Lucanus: De bello civili libri X*, Berlin: De Gruyter.

Shotter, D. (2008), *Nero Caesar Augustus: Emperor of Rome*, London: Pearson.

Sklenář, R. (2003), *The Taste for Nothingness: A Study of* Virtus *and Related Themes in Lucan's* Bellum Civile, Ann Arbor: University of Michigan Press.

Syndikus, H. P. (2006), "The Second Book," trans. C. B. Brown, in H.-C. Günther (ed.), *Brill's Companion to Propertius*, 245–318, Leiden: Brill.

Taylor, K. (2008), "Landscape and Memory: cultural landscapes, intangible values and some thoughts on Asia," paper presented at the 16th ICOMOS General Assembly & International Symposium, Quebec, September 29 to October 4, 2008, https://www.researchgate.net/publication/242086790_Landscape_and_Memory_cultural_landscapes_intangible_values_and_some_thoughts_on_Asia (Accessed November 1, 2017).

Thorne, M. (2011), "*Memoria Redux*: Memory in Lucan," in P. Asso (ed.), *Brill's Companion to Lucan*, 363–82, Leiden: Brill.

Torres-Murciano, A. (2009), "Las secuelas del *Fortunati ambo* (Verg., *Aen*. IX 446–449): epopeya e imperio," *Emerita*, 77 (2): 295–315.

Tucker, R. A. (1983), "Lucan and Phoebus," *Latomus*, 42: 143–51.

Weiner, J. and T. Benz (2018), "Detroit and the Classical Sublime, or, In Defense of 'Ruin Porn,'" in D. Felton (ed.), *Landscapes of Dread in Classical Antiquity: Negative Emotion in Natural and Constructed Spaces*, 279–302, London: Routledge.

Welch, T. S. (2005), *The Elegiac Cityscape: Propertius and the Meaning of Roman Monuments*, Columbus: Ohio State University Press.

Zanker, P. (1987), *Augustus und die Macht der Bilder*, Munich: C. H. Beck.

Zerner, H. (1976), "Aloïs Riegl: Art, Value, and Historicism," *Daedalus*, 105 (1): 177–88.

CHAPTER 11
LUCAN'S NOSTALGIA AND THE INFECTION OF MEMORY
E. V. Mulhern

In the *Bellum Civile*, Lucan laments the death throes of Republican liberty.[1] A bitter poem, its pose of anger draws its power from the poet's ability to convey to his readers a vivid feeling of defiance followed by a sense of loss. But this promise of defiance struggles against Lucan's knowledge of the war's result. Michael André Bernstein calls this "backshadowing," the "retroactive foreshadowing in which the shared knowledge of the outcome of a series of events by narrator and listener is used to judge the participants in those events as though they too should have known what was to come" (1994: 16). For Bernstein, this strategy is common in treatments of historical apocalypses, and thus can apply to Lucan's approach to the civil wars, which is both generally and Stoically apocalyptic (e.g., the *ekpyrosis* at 1.72–80). Throughout the *BC*, moreover, there is a sense that even Lucan's supposed heroes Cato and Pompey are morally responsible for the outcomes of the war, and that both his characters and his audience are complicit in this disaster.

Despite this inevitable gloom, Lucan in some ways writes the *BC* as a nostalgic swansong for the Roman Republic. The word "nostalgia" did not exist in antiquity (for an historical overview of the term, see Illbruck 2012). Yet the Roman conception of history relies on an always implicit and often articulated assumption of decline; nostalgia, even if un-named, is certainly a category of thought. At least from the late Republic through the end of the western empire, Roman writers fondly imagine and claim to long for a humbler yet greater past, when life in the capital was traditional and predictable, and the empire secure and expanding. In fact, nostalgia always presents a paradox in its desire for the past: one cannot go home again, and one does not truly wish to. Even if impossible, however, nostalgia offers a space of rhetorical and psychic retrenchment that Roman authors find attractive and morally useful. The target of their nostalgia tends to be a synchronic—even achronic and eternal—*jeunesse dorée* of the Republic, the heyday of the citizen-farmer-soldier (Cairns 2002: 31). The historian Sallust, for example, places the last good age before the destruction of Carthage by Scipio Aemilianus in 146 BCE (*Cat.* 10.1), and this identification persists in Roman thought for centuries.

Lucan's focus of nostalgia, however, is that last rearguard action of principled Republicanism: the glorious failure of Cato. This location depends on an overvaluation of a past time and place, an overvaluation that suggests the subject has experienced displacement or trauma.[2] In this case, both distance and trauma divide Lucan from Pharsalus.[3] By the date of the *BC*'s composition, a century has passed since the defeat of Pompey, a century of continual blows to the citizen body and psyche. In response to those traumas—twenty years of civil war and proscriptions, followed by iteratively worse successors to Augustus—Lucan attempts to present a picture of a Republic untainted by contemporary ills. Throughout the *BC*, Lucan will lean on the assumed superiority of the heroic Roman past to emphasize present and recent disasters. His portrait of the past, however, presents problems for both poet and audience. Lucan does not remember the Republic, so he must rely on forms of collective memory. But collective memories are not universal (Walter 2004: 37), and Lucan's milieu is elite and self-consciously literary. Thus, though he decries the war and all its Caesarist consequences, he cannot avoid or erase his own courtly late Julio-Claudian zeitgeist. This often leads to backshadowing that undercuts his heroes, displaying their inability to measure up to his pristine standards. The tension of this tendency with his sentimental aims leads to the collapse of the nostalgic project. It seems that, even if he did manage to inspire his contemporaries to sincere action, or to bring Cato back, they would suffer the same defeats.

Lucan on the Past

Lucan's programmatic choices and statements attempt to establish a univalent relationship with the past. The generic choice of the hexameter history asserts antiquity and Republican *bona fides*, as Lucan eschews the mythological optimism of Vergil's *Aeneid* and retreats to Ennian historical epic.[4] Ancient opinion accepts Lucan's claims insofar as Servius considered that he had composed a history rather than an epic poem (Serv., *ad Aen.* 1.382). Yet claims of priority and rejection of received tradition introduce complications in Roman literary genealogy (Goldschmidt 2013: 40). Though Lucan's epic postdates and is set after Vergil's, it attempts to portray a time before Vergil's imperial frame existed. But Lucan does not, like Ennius, provide a first-hand account of any of his subject matter, nor does he have the contemporary's luxury of addressing his heroes as *invicte Scipio* (*Varia* 3, Vahlen). His knowledge is secondhand, his heroes lose the war, and his work cannot be a chronicle of Roman glory. In Lucan's day, the civil wars are still a fraught ideological battleground, on which Lucan attempts to fight by sidestepping Vergil and other such quasi-official Julio-Claudian accounts. But, as only one example, though Lucan rejects the *Götterapparat* of Vergil, he adopts the *Aeneid*'s attitude about the *vates* and his authoritative grasp of truth (Goldschmidt 2013: 57, discussed more fully below). Thus, even while Lucan attempts to appropriate the moral and historical authority of Ennius's age, he often conforms to post-Augustan poetic assumptions.

In parallel with this literary move, Lucan tries to evoke temporal nostalgia and erase historical developments by introducing characters from the remote and supposedly unambivalent past. After he explains the proximate causes of the civil war and places the blame on Pompey and Caesar, he explains how the Republic had already lost its way. He lists markers of contemporary decadence and highlights the disappearance of the citizen-soldier-farmer. For Lucan, ancient poverty is paradoxically fertile (*fecunda virorum / paupertas fugitur*, 1.165–6), as the recent scourge of *luxus* (1.162) cannot rear the salutary masculinity that once made Rome great (Gillespie forthcoming). He writes, "the lands, *once* tilled by the harsh plow of Camillus and bearing the *old* mattock of Curius, now extend far under unknown cultivators" (***quondam*** *duro sulcata Camilli / vomere et **antiquos** Curiorum passa ligones / longa sub ignotis extendere rura colonis*, 1.168–70, emphasis mine).[5] After these men and their exploits have passed into history, the rot sets in: "For when the world was conquered, Fortune brought excessive riches, and morals yielded to favorable circumstances, and enemy booty and plunder urged extravagance" (*namque, ut opes nimias mundo Fortuna subacto / intulit et rebus mores cessere secundis / praedaque et hostiles luxum suasere rapinae*, 1.160–2). Lucan chooses to present this pair together and undifferentiated to create a flattened vision of an ideal early Rome. He hammers on the passage of time and its concomitant moral decline, even telling us about the decline *before* he mentions the heroes, thereby immediately undermining them.

Focalizing this nostalgia through his characters, Lucan has Pompey emphasize temporal decline, twice listing great past Republicans (2.541–6, 7.346–60). First, Pompey again uses the unanswerable Camillus as a foil for Caesar: "Though fate wished to place you with the great Camillus and the Metelli, you are headed for Marius and Cinna" (*cum fata Camillis / te, Caesar, magnisque velint miscere Metellis, / ad Cinnas Mariosque venis*, 2.544–6). Additionally, by citing Catiline and Cethegus in the previous lines, the speaker points out the disjunction of his vicious contemporaries from their forebears. Pompey creates two moral centers of gravity: a virtuous cluster in the early Republic and a villainous band in the late. Similarly, as he attempts to raise the morale of his troops, he suggests that the ancient heroes should be marshalled among them: "if the fates should grant to *our times* Curius or the returning Camillus or the Decii vowing their fatal heads, here they would stand" (*si Curios **his** fata darent reducesque Camillos / **temporibus** Deciosque caput fatale voventes, / hinc starent*, 7.358–60, emphasis mine). He tries to collapse the distance between his own time and Camillus', while marking the disjunction with *his temporibus*. The contrary-to-fact subjunctives further emphasize the impossibility of this attempt.

Lucan also offers Lentulus, the senatorial hardliner, as an example of late Republican inadequacy. As the senate flees Rome in Book 5, Lentulus insists on their overseas legitimacy, saying, "When the Tarpeian rock burned with the torches of the Gauls, and Camillus lived at Veii—Rome was there" (*Tarpeia sede perusta / Gallorum facibus Veiosque habitante Camillo / illic Roma fuit*, 5.27–9). Lentulus attempts to use the name of Camillus to argue his point—wherever true Romans are, there is true Rome—but he flagrantly misunderstands Camillus' exemplary valence (Henderson 2000: 15). Camillus famously demanded the geographical centrality of Rome (Liv. 5.51); Veii can never be Rome, and neither can Dyrrhachium (arguing that Rome is nonetheless destabilized in this passage, see Bexley 2009: 463). Thus Lucan writes the last generation of the Republic, even those ostensibly on the right side, as people who do not understand their own past.

Finally, Erictho's reanimated corpse presents a personally observed account of these heroic Republican shades in their final home in the underworld: "I have seen weeping the Decii—father and son—with their souls dedicated to battle, and Camillus and Curius" (*vidi Decios natumque patremque, / lustrales bellis animas, flentemque Camillum et Curios*,

6.785–7). This is the same group again, and the type of group to be lifted from a handbook of exempla (Litchfield 1914). But this does not beg the question—Lucan is deliberately invoking an unambiguously glorious history to suggest that his current account is likewise inarguable. That he must reach back to the semi-legendary period of Roman history merely supports his argument. While old exempla tend to flatten, the accusations against the recent villains are more specific and anti-Republican, including late plots against the Republic and the Julian Marius: "Catiline exults with his chains torn and broken, and so does grim Marius and Cethegus exposed" (*abruptis Catilina minax fractisque catenis / exultat Mariique truces nudique Cethegi*, 6.793–4). He presents them not as Pompey's imagined heroes passing judgment on his contemporaries or a poet's hackneyed stock figures, but as the actual souls of the dead, whose authority is unquestioned.[6]

Yet, as Lucan revivifies the heroes of early Rome, his paean to the Roman age of glory subsides into an angry obituary, an admission that nostalgia cannot actually revive people or ideals, and a macabre proof of Fowler's observation that the processional instinct of the Romans manifests itself chiefly in triumphs and funerals (Fowler 2000: 96). Here the rituals merge, as the triumphators themselves are dead and the sole remaining triumph will be over the corpse of the Republic. The *pompa funebris*, particularly in its more triumphal aspects, should possess hortatory valence (Walter 2004: 90). Here, the only good man pleased in Hades is Lucius Brutus, looking forward to the great deed of his descendant: "I saw, alone rejoicing among the reverent shades, you, Brutus, the first consul after the kings were expelled" (*solum te, consul depulsis prime tyrannis, / Brute, pias inter gaudentem vidimus umbras*, 6.791–2). In one of the more temporally confused moments in a temporally confused scene, the corpse's account sweeps past Pharsalus to the Ides of March, placing on Sextus Pompey and the audience the weight of foreknowledge, or Bernstein's backshadowing. This is an inescapably Vergilian touch, echoing—albeit in harshly inverted terms—Anchises' catalogue of heroes in the underworld (Feeney 1986). In both the literal and literary senses, Lucan cannot escape his Caesarist present. Through the mediation of Lucan as *vates*, even the shades of ancient men know that Caesar will win this war, and Lucan must grapple with the Augustan account of Rome's past and future.

Lucan on the Inescapable Present

The poet admits early on that he will not achieve the destruction of Caesarism in perhaps the most famous line of the epic: *victrix causa deis placuit sed victa Catoni* (1.128). Here the poet again compresses time, but, instead of willing his heroes forward, he advances the war's result while explicating its causes. The care with which he sets up his plot suggests that he will offer a different outcome, in what, building on Bernstein, subsequent scholars call "sideshadowing." Sideshadowing is a common feature of classical epic, though it usually affirms teleological models (as in the *Punica*, for instance), a tendency which "derives from its self-conscious and explicit preoccupation with turning points and uncertainty" (Cowan 2010: 334). In just one other example, Lucan often makes this preoccupation explicit, as at 6.301, where "we are informed among other things that if the battle of Durrachium had turned out otherwise than it actually did, Rome would have been *felix ac libera regum*" (Due 1962: 101). Unlike Silius, who can write about Roman victories, Lucan invariably pulls the rug out from under his alternate history, undercutting any hope the audience may have acquired from counterfactuals the poet himself suggests. Perhaps all these foreclosing remarks—of which the Cato *sententia* is merely the most glaring example—are nihilistic concessions to an uncaring providence, as has been argued (Sklenář 1999: 293). I suggest instead that they mark a different vacuum: the inability of Cato or *Libertas* to emerge victorious and the concomitant inability of Lucan's nostalgic project to let them do so.

At Pharsalus, Lucan reminds the audience of the outcomes of the battle and its various aftermaths: the assassinations of Pompey and Caesar, the further wars, and all the blame that must be placed. The death of Pompey is adumbrated long before it occurs onstage, as the poet explains why Pompey flees the battlefield: "Or he wished to hide his death from Caesar's eyes. In vain, poor man: his father-in-law wishes to see his head wherever it may be offered" (*Caesaris aut oculis voluit subducere mortem / nequiquam, infelix: socero spectare volenti / praestandum est ubicumque caput*, 7.673–5). Lucan also repeatedly reminds us of Caesar's own death, commenting on the perverse preservation of his life at various stages within the poem. Erictho's poor soldier hints at the tyrannicide, but Lucan's narrator further remarks at the battle of Pharsalus, "Let him live, and let reign, so long as he falls as Brutus' victim" (*vivat et, ut Bruti procumbat victima, regnet*, 7.596). As Pompey dies, Lucan indignantly asks, "What will they call *this* crime, those who call Brutus' deed a sin?" (*scelus hoc quo nomine dicent / qui Bruti dixere nefas?*, 8.609–10). Finally, toward the end of the existing text, as Caesar is besieged in Alexandria, the narrator dedicates the dictator's future death to Pompey's shade: "Until patriotic swords meet in Caesar's guts, Pompey will be unavenged" (*dum patrii veniant in viscera Caesaris enses / Magnus inultus erit*, 10.528–9). At each branching point in the narrative, instead of opening up a real alternative, the outcome desired by the poet is foreclosed, and Lucan reminds the audience that the next branching will also end in disaster.

This logic of foreclosure comes all the way up to Lucan's own time, in the encomium to Nero: "But if fate could find no other way for Nero to come ... we will not complain at all, Gods; crimes and sins themselves please us, if they have this reward" (*quod si non aliam venturo fata Neroni / ... iam nihil, o superi, querimur; scelera ipsa nefasque / hac mercede placent*, 1.33, 37–8). The sincerity or irony of this passage is much debated (Mayer 1978; Dewar 1994; Kessler 2011), but neither is relevant here. Nero *is* emperor, and, living under the regime, Lucan's audience is aware and therefore complicit: they have accepted and are pleased by *scelera nefasque*. The plural of *querimur*, arguably merely poetic, may rather be a move to include Lucan's contemporaries. The inversion of time here is even more marked than the citation of Cato above. Only thirty-three lines into the epic, Lucan provides the ultimate result of the war, up to his own time. Every opening, every fleeting Republican moment of hope, will only accumulate toward this outcome. The audience is never truly in suspense, but Lucan constantly reminds them that he is offering only fantasy.

I now return to Cato, Lucan's arbiter of morality above and vehicle for the most sustained fantasy. He is Lucan's attempt to go home again, to recapture exactly the virtues of Curius and Camillus. Lucan enumerates these characteristics as he describes Cato after his remarriage to Marcia (2.348–90):

huic epulae vicisse famem, magnique penates
summovisse hiemem tecto, pretiosaque vestis
hirtam membra super Romani more Quiritis
induxisse togam, Veneris quoque maximus usus
progenies: urbi pater est urbique maritus,
iustitiae cultor, rigidi servator honesti,
in commune bonus ...

For this man, to conquer hunger was a feast, to keep the storm off with a roof was a great palace, to put a rough toga over his limbs like a Roman citizen was a precious robe, and children were the greatest purpose of sex: he was father and husband for the city, a cultivator of justice, a preserver of strict nobility, all for the common good ...

Cato the throwback thinks of his house only to keep off the rain, his meals only to get rid of his hunger. The toga, an essentially Roman garment, becomes still more anciently Romulan, as Lucan describes its style as *Romani more Quiritis*. Cato's toga is coarse and old-fashioned (*hirtam*), presumably like his great-grandfather's before him. Lucan suggests a foundational antiquity for Cato—he could share Romulus' hut as well as his toga. Not least, Cato fulfills the expectations for a perfect Roman by dedicating his entire life, including his family life, to the state: *urbi pater est urbique maritus*.[7] Lucan, through Cato, attempts to bring the unambiguous virtues of remote antiquity to his own day, freighting the past with such value that it inevitably collapses.

With Cato, Lucan compounds the levels of backshadowing: the poet knows that the Republican cause will be defeated and so does his audience, but he shows that even his characters know this.[8] Cato is conscious from the beginning that the task of restoring *libertas* to the *res publica* is beyond him, but he still will not abandon it before death: "Nor will I be torn away from you before I embrace your corpse, Roma; I will chase your name, Liberty, and your empty shade" (*non ante revellar / exanimem quam te complectar, Roma; tuumque / nomen, Libertas, et inanem persequar umbram*, 2.301–3). Cato also knows that after he fails, no one will be worthy to succeed him. As Seo has pointed out, although we lack the suicide of Cato in the poem, the shadow of it hangs over his own speeches and the failures of others in the poem to live up to his standard.[9] The "process of comparison, the reflexivity inherent in the Cato figure ... continues to operate as we view Cato himself—the danger is that he will disappoint no less than his imitators" (Seo 2011: 201). Cato's successes—like the *aristeia* of sorts in the African desert—are grotesque, and his glories are failures.[10]

In these contexts, Lucan is conscious of the toxic interplay of his need for the past to be worthy and his knowledge that it was not, and points a bitter, backshadowing finger at his own failed partisans. He tells us that Cato, however heroic, failed to preserve the Republic. His Cato tells us that he will fail to preserve the Republic. This outward, explicit knowledge of failure often manages to efface, for the reader, the extent to which Lucan's self-consciously nostalgic structure collapses in the face of Caesarism.

Lucan's Infected Memories

Even as Lucan dismembers the Caesarist and Augustan accounts of the civil wars, he is unable to disremember the ongoing Caesarism of the Neronian age. Lucan's portrait of the late Republic, for all its pose of angry priority, everywhere betrays its belatedness, the scar tissue of decades of Julio-Claudian rule. Lucan cannot revivify defunct attitudes and aesthetic conventions. Too much intervenes in his historical and poetic memory for him to be able to write a true account of the Republic.

Memory is never neutral, but necessarily selective and partial (on Roman approaches to memory, see Farrell 1997; Walter 2004; Galinsky 2016). Hedrick argues that "memory is by definition not just the knowledge of past; it is the knowledge of the past implicated with consciousness" (2016: 161). Lucan's sources (Pichon 1912; Radicke 2004) and surroundings, visible to us or not, have given him an extremely partial consciousness, carrying the flag for a lost cause: "Nothing rouses popular feeling more than a grievance unrectified" (Lowenthal 1994: 52). On the battlefield of memory, Lucan pits his literary-historical image of the Roman Republic against his present reality, yet his own statement on the bardic task admits the difficulty. As Caesar inspects the ruins of Troy, Lucan writes (9.980–6):

> O sacer et magnus vatum labor! omnia fato
> eripis et populis donas mortalibus aevum.
> invidia sacrae, Caesar, ne tangere famae;
> nam, si quid Latiis fas est promittere Musis,
> quantum Zmyrnaei durabunt vatis honores,
> venturi me teque legent; Pharsalia nostra
> vivet, et a nullo tenebris damnabimur aevo.

> O great and holy task of bards! You snatch all things from the fates and give eternity to mortals. Do not be infected by jealousy of this sacred fame, Caesar; for, if it is right to allow to the Latian Muses as much as the glories of Smyrna's bard endure, those to come will read me and you; my Pharsalia will live, and we will be condemned to darkness by no age.

Lucan attacks Caesar's arrogance and historical ignorance, suggesting that Caesar's deeds will crumble to dust like the tomb of Hector, which he can barely recognize. Lucan claims Homeric immortality for himself (*quantum Zmyrnaei durabunt vatis honores*), but the only name he mentions is that of Caesar. Explicitly moving the battle onto literary ground, Lucan writes that the future will *read* both Caesar and Lucan (*venturi me teque legent*). Lucan has already ceded the historical victory to his enemy, and, by including only Caesar's name, has also surrendered the aesthetic ground. Caesar is the man and Caesar's the account that he must attack (Thorne 2011: 366; Seidman 2017: *passim*). In Lucan's time, Caesar's deeds have not crumbled like the walls of Troy; indeed, his death merely allowed him to increase the tyranny he introduced (cf. Cic., *Ad Fam.* 14.10). Lucan cannot even escape his literary prison: as noted above, Lucan rejects the *Götterapparat* of Vergil but adopts Vergil's attitude about the *vates* and his authoritative grasp of truth (Goldschmidt 2013: 57), implicating himself in the Caesarist project. The vatic project of Lucan's *BC* tries to claim special knowledge beyond the merely historical—a better form of knowledge than Caesar's first-hand experience. Lucan claims here that he will offer an alternate history to Caesar's, but he never does.

Elsewhere Lucan again admits in his narrative voice that his entire poetic project is in vain on literary terms. He writes in an apostrophe to Pompey, "When these wars *are read*, hope and fear and doomed prayers will stir, and everyone, dumbfounded, will *read* these settled fates as if they were yet to come—and they will take your side, Magnus" (*cum bella* **legentur**, / *spesque metusque simul perituraque vota movebunt*, / *attonitique omnes veluti venientia fata*, / *non transmissa*, **legent**, *et adhuc tibi, Magne, favebunt*, 7.210–13, emphasis added). The *BC* is designed to move its audience, but even if they move in the desired direction, this cannot change the *transmissa fata*. They are not, for all the poet's efforts, *venientia*. These apostrophes tell us the literary result as well, and by their direct address invite special attention (see also Asso 2009).

In the exemplary mental framework of Roman memory, to mention Cato's name gives him and his ideals new life.[11] Lucan's aim throughout the poem, as argued by Thorne 2011, is to revive the *res publica*—or at least give it a fittingly impressive headstone—simply by remembering it. Lucan attempts to make *memoria* into *vita*, by perpetuating the "matrix of stories and values that made up the *mos maiorum*" (Thorne 2011: 369). But Lucan, in his twenties under Nero, has a short memory, and his account of the civil wars is not firsthand. He relies instead on cultural memory, in formal histories and in the literary milieu that swirls around him.[12] Lucan can and does read Caesar's *BC* with a critical eye, and refuses to accept its premises. To place Cato in the foreground, for example, is to reject the pre-Neronian literary heritage of Caesarism, and especially Caesar's own *De Bello Civili*, in which Cato is an irritating bit-part player. But even though Lucan can make narrative choices, memories are infectious: Lucan cannot escape living in a post-Caesar society, with all its cultural contagion. His conception of the late Republic is therefore fractured, tinged with a Julio-Claudian filter that changes both its specifics and its essence.

Even as the poet attempts to bring back the Republic, he can only write it in imperial terms. In Augustan poetry, Cato is at best ambivalent (as in Hor., *Carm.* 2.1.21–4), and largely absent (as in his brief notice in Verg., *Aen.* 8.670). In the intervening prose sources, Valerius Maximus' Tiberian Cato, for instance, is omnipresent and admirable, but his enemies are rarely named.[13] Seneca, in explicitly moralizing vein, often cites Cato as a virtuous *exemplum*, as at *Ep.* 97.10: "Every age will produce a Clodius, not every age will have a Cato" (*omne tempus Clodios, non omne Catones feret*). Thrasea Paetus evidently wrote a laudatory biography (Geiger 1979; Romm 2014: 158). Lucan, like his uncle and other contemporaries, develops this hagiographic portrait of Cato.[14] But then, veering away from Republican *bona fides*, Lucan suggests that Cato should be deified after his *aristeia* in Africa: "Behold the true father of your country, Rome, and most worthy of your altars, by whom no one would ever be ashamed to swear, and whom, if you still stood with your neck free, you would now one day be making into a god" (*ecce parens verus patriae, dignissimus aris / Roma, tuis, per quem numquam iurare pudebit, / et quem, si steteris umquam cervice soluta, / nunc, olim, factura deum es*, 9.601–4). Deification of mortals is antithetical to a free society, and for the Republic it was an alien custom of degenerate and servile Eastern powers. *Si steteris ... cervice soluta* is therefore contrafactual on multiple levels: Rome has been enslaved, and, if she had not been, the deification of Cato would be impossible and undesired. The title *parens patriae* itself, though a Republican possibility, suggests imperial practice.

In the opposite vein, Lucan visibly works against the official memory of Caesar by writing him as an elemental whirlwind of evil. He refutes Caesar's careful justifications of his invasion in his own *BC* 1 (constitutional irregularities, threats of violence against the tribunes, etc.). Caesar is a bloodthirsty monster in Lucan's introduction and throughout the poem (see Johnson 1987 *passim*). He ceases, for Lucan, to be either a Roman or a human being (1.146–50):

acer et indomitus, quo spes quoque ira vocasset,
ferre manum et numquam temerando parcere ferro,
successus urguere suos, instare favori
numinis, impellens quidquid sibi summa petenti
obstaret gaudensque viam fecisse ruina ...

Harsh and indomitable, wherever hope or rage called him, he brought his power and never spared his fearsome sword; he followed up his triumphs, battened on the favor of the gods, throwing down whatever stood in his way as he sought the heights, and rejoicing to make his way by ruin ...

Caesar's only motivation for the war is his own destructive ambition, and his inability to work within Republican bounds. As he meets the image of the pleading Roma at the Rubicon, he shows himself to be an enemy of the Republic and the Roman people, as she tells him: "Where further are you headed? Where, men, are you carrying my standards? If you come by law, if you are still citizens, this is as far as you may go" (*quo tenditis ultra? / quo fertis mea signa, viri? si iure venitis, / si cives, huc usque licet*, 1.190–2). As Caesar has rejected the weeping figure of his homeland, Lucan explicitly rejects Caesar, the Caesarean account of the war, and its Caesarean results. Yet, even for Julius Caesar to call the city *Roma* in this passage rather than *res publica* is an imperial expression (Feeney 1991: 294). Both Cato and the poet also call her Roma, which further shows us how trapped Lucan is within his own imperial contexts under the principate.

Again working consciously against the more palatable Augustan account, Lucan does not let Cleopatra's liaison with Caesar drop tactfully out of the record. Instead, he emphasizes it, placing Caesar's thirst for flesh in conjunction with his thirst for blood. He absolves Antony of responsibility, if not of wickedness: "Who would not forgive you for this insane love, Antony, since the harsh breast of Caesar drank those passions?" (*quis tibi vaesani veniam non donet amoris, / Antoni, durum cum Caesaris hauserit ignes / pectus?*, 10.70–2). But this is chiefly to emphasize his accusation of Caesar: "in the middle of his rage, in the midst of his madness, in a court haunted by the shade of Pompey, the adulterer, drenched in the blood of the Thessalian disaster, admits Venus to his cares, and mixes with war both illicit beds and illegitimate children" (*et in media rabie medioque furore / et Pompeianis habitata manibus aula / sanguine Thessalicae cladis perfusus adulter / admisit Venerem curis, et miscuit armis / illicitosque toros et non ex coniuge partus*, 10.72–6). Such conduct is unworthy of a Roman statesman-soldier at any period, but Lucan shows the specific fingerprints of the Augustan obsession with adultery and legitimacy. Lucan proliferates legalistic and moralistic terms about Caesar's own behavior—*adulter, illicitos, coniuge, pudor,* even *obscaena* (10.78). This reflects the particular concerns of Augustan moral legislation: the *lex Iulia de adulteriis coercendis*, which punished even male adulterers, or the *lex Papia Poppaea*, which encouraged aristocrats to offspring within marriage, to combat the fear of a barren aristocracy and its non-citizen liaisons. In a Neronian context, where the Julio-Claudian house is withering and Nero can produce no sons by his wives, these are a renewed concern.[15] His liaisons with freedmen, furthermore, shocked his biographers and historians (e.g., Suet., *Ner.* 29), and Lucan's flurry of affronted language perhaps reflects this attitude toward Nero's approach to marriage (Champlin 2003: 160–71).

As Lucan attempts to dismantle the legitimacy of *divus Julius* by recalling his many faults, he ends up judging them with the vitriol left by the Claudian and Neronian outrages as well as the vestiges of Augustan moralizing. His anachronistic standards for Caesar's affairs (famously tolerated and a source of public amusement in the dictator's own day), as well as the absurd suggestion of a *divus Cato*, override the realities of Republican structures.

Republican Matrons, Imperial Morals

This imperial framework dictates the characteristics not only of the male protagonists of the *BC*, but still more noticeably of the civil war's women, both wives and mistresses (for overviews of Lucan's women, see Finiello 2005; Sannicandro 2010; Mulhern 2017). The increased visibility of women in the early empire and the specific prescriptions and circumscriptions regarding their behavior influence the prominence and actions of Lucan's Roman wives. Even the physical appearance of the feminine borrows more from coins and other plastic arts of the principate than from Republican fashion or iconography. Roma at the Rubicon, in place of the helmet she has worn on coins for centuries, wears a turret crown on her streaming hair (*turrigero canos effundens vertice crines*, 1.188). This borrows from the Hellenistic practice of representing the Tyche of cities with mural crowns and the Julio-Claudian practice of representing imperial women in such garb.[16]

Rome now takes her visual cues from eastern cities, with their histories of kingship; empresses are abstracted into that Hellenistic image; Lucan's Roma, finally, is embodied resembling a member of the imperial family, dependent on the new reality of Roman kingship and the new imperial conception of the city.

Cornelia and Marcia are likewise enmeshed in imperial expectations. As Lucan's standard-bearers of old-fashioned Republican femininity, both women nevertheless find themselves acting out the provisions of later legislation. The poet does not invent these actions, but, in an historical epic, selectivity is instructive. The *lex Iulia de maritandis ordinibus* directs respectable aristocratic women to remarry soon after they are widowed, as the *BC*'s women do. Marcia comes straight from the pyre of Hortensius to remarry Cato: "a knock sounded at the doors, which the sacred Marcia burst through, mourning, having left behind the funeral-pyre of Hortensius" (*pulsatae sonuere fores, quas sancta relicto / Hortensi maerens irrupit Marcia busto*, 2.327–8). Later, the ghost of Julia Caesaris tells Pompey that his marriage to Cornelia came when the younger Crassus was not yet cold: "the concubine Cornelia—whom fate has damned always to drag her powerful husbands into disaster—has married you, straight from a glowing funeral-pyre" (*semperque potentis / detrahere in cladem fato damnata maritos / innupsit tepido paelex Cornelia busto*, 3.21–3). Lucan means for Julia to be jealous and derisive here, claiming special status as a *univira*. She compresses the timeline between her death and Pompey's remarriage for pathetic effect, and insults Cornelia with the inaccurate epithet *paelex*. The narrator, *pace* Caston (2011: 138), suggests no impropriety in either woman's conduct. In fact, Lucan paints both as exemplary matrons, doing their aristocratic Roman duty—by imperial standards.

Marcia, in her brief, programmatic, and improbable appearance in Book 2, further allows the poet to outline his other expectations for good Roman matrons. She has had three children with Cato before he marries her off to Hortensius: "When a *third* child paid the price of marriage, the fertile woman went to fill other families and mix twin houses by the blood of the mother" (*ubi conubii pretium mercesque soluta est / **tertia iam suboles**, alios fecunda penates / impletura datura geminas et sanguine matris / permixtura domos*, 2.330–3). Three is the salient number of children for the requirements of the aforementioned *lex Papia Poppaea*, and the repeated monetary terms *pretium* and *merces* suggest the financial provisions that law guarantees for those who fulfill its requirements. Marcia's fertility is explicitly in the service of the state; Cato divorced her to ensure the survival of another noble house, in line with the stated aims of Augustan family legislation. By remarrying her original husband, moreover, Marcia attempts to join Julia Caesaris in the august company of *univirae*. She asks that her gravestone say only that she was Cato's wife, erasing Hortensius from her life: "let them write 'Cato's Marcia' on my tomb" (*liceat tumulo scripsisse "Catonis / Marcia,"* 2.343–4).[17] Again, this memory-infection is historical as well as literary, for cult of the once-married woman was a pet project of early imperial women. Given legislation encouraging remarriage and the role of the inappositely twice-married Livia as model and patroness of relevant cults, this presents something of a paradox (Severy 2003). Marcia squares that circle for Lucan. She is *both* a dutiful matron—marrying (and divorcing) magistrates, producing as many children as they need—*and* a dramatically univiral paragon.

There is another angle to elite motherhood in the principate: the symbolic civic motherhood of the emperor's wife. The Julio-Claudian women are mothers both for and of the state—they must not only bear heirs but also appear as mothers for the whole empire. A central tenet of Julio-Claudian visual and religious propaganda is the slippage between the health of the imperial family and the health of the empire, and the emperor's wife plays a crucial role in this. As Kristina Milnor writes, imperial women "are able to take on real and important roles in the civic sphere, without compromising their perceived performance of 'traditional' domestic virtues" (Milnor 2005: 1). These domestic virtues include fertility, which explains the frequent portrayal of imperial women in the guise of Ceres.[18] That this fertility often ends up being misdirected or even tragic adds poignancy to Lucan's treatment of the subject in the person of Cornelia. After Pompey's death, she speaks in her husband's voice and, by appropriating all his sons to herself, also takes on the motherhood of the whole Republic. She says, "Receive, my *sons*, this civil war, and never, while any man of our race remains on the earth, let there be anywhere for Caesar to reign" (*excipite, o **nati**, bellum civile, nec umquam, / dum terris aliquis nostra de stirpe manebit, / Caesaribus regnare vacet*, 9.88–90, emphasis added). None of the men she addresses is actually her son. By *nostra stirps*, Cornelia means not her blood family but all the men left in Rome who count as true Romans. She assumes the role of mother to legitimize the cause; the Julio-Claudian line itself, by Nero's time, was legitimized *only* through the female line, which was "particularly evident in the case of Nero" (Mordine 2013: 107). In the act of promoting the cause of liberty, then, Lucan's Cornelia undermines herself by acting as if Pompey had been an emperor, and she already an emperor's wife.

For all its imperial baggage, Lucan's portrait of the preceding women is meant to be positive—at the end of the Republic, he maintains, Roman women were virtuous wives and mothers. Lucan emphasizes this primacy of the matron and mother as a contrast to Cleopatra, the paragon of threatening womanhood for the Julio-Claudians and beyond. The *BC*'s Cleopatra has moved on from the anonymous monster of the Augustan period outlined by Maria Wyke (1992). Lucan's introduction of her is compendious; she is accused of bribery and called both the "dishonor of Egypt" and the "Fury fatal to Latium" (*dedecus Aegypti, Latii feralis Erinys*, 10.59). In contrast to Vergil's depiction in particular, she does not come out and fight at Actium like a superhuman witch, though military and religious fears do persist: "She frightened the Capitol with her *sistrum* (if it is meet to say it), and sought Roman standards for unwarlike Canopus, and would have led triumphs at Pharos with Caesar captive" (*terruit illa suo, si fas, Capitolia sistro / et Romana petit imbelli signa Canopo / Caesare captivo Pharios ductura triumphos*, 10.63–5). The fear of *sistra* on the Capitoline (though a poetic exaggeration) may reflect the Augustan repression of the Isis-cult or Poppaea's involvement with the cult (Bricault 2015: 90). The fear of diluting the might of the Roman army (*Romana . . . signa*) with unwarlike Egypt (*imbelli . . . Canopo*) is a constant fear in the context of empire, and the picture of a woman leading an army could recall Agrippina's troublesome hold over the praetorians (e.g., Tac., *Ann.* 13.20.1 on the prefect Burrus' promotion).

Lucan's Cleopatra has further faults specific to the Neronian period, in addition to the standard perfumes and potions of the foreign temptress in Latin literature. Pothinus accuses her of paranoia and court intrigue in combination with promiscuity: "Whom among us—at least those of whom she is innocent—does Cleopatra believe is not harming her?" (*quem non e nobis credit Cleopatra nocentem / a quo casta fuit?*, 10.369– 70). Lucan implies here that Cleopatra buys loyalty and control in the court with her body and does not trust men who are not susceptible. Likewise, Agrippina's sexuality was treated as a cause for concern, including charges of incest, but most apposite here is that she "was also reputedly the lover of the freedman and imperial advisor Pallas," which was treated as an attempt "to control and maintain power through sexual manipulation" (Mordine 2013: 109). Both women exercise unacceptable (to the Roman mind) influence over the course of Roman history. Lucan's Cleopatra is even worse than Helen (10.60–2): she destroys a Republic and emasculates a Caesar (for the subversion of gender roles here, see Keith 2000: 55, 89). The dynastic concerns of the Julio-Claudians in general are probably at the forefront in Lucan's late apostrophe of Julia in this passage: "For shame! Forgetful of your Magnus, Julia, he has given you brothers from an obscene mother" (*pro pudor, oblitus Magni tibi, Iulia, fratres / obscaena de matre dedit*, 10.77–8). With the deaths of Julius Caesar and Julia Caesaris, a possible line of Republican statesmen is snuffed out, but this matters more if Lucan has already accepted the premise that Caesar has founded a dynasty. Lucan's anger that Cleopatra manages to destroy hopes of *legitimate* succession in the Julian family for another generation, taking Antony from Octavia as she took Caesar from Calpurnia, further builds on this assumption.

In a time when a series of manipulative, ambitious, or supposedly promiscuous imperial wives have threatened the health of the empire (or at least the emperor), this kind of concern about Cleopatra is especially germane. Suetonius is caustic about Claudius and his wives (*Claud*. 26), and we must expect that Lucan was privy to the prevailing gossip. Indeed, the Claudian context was presumably formative in Lucan's imagination growing up, and the parallel of Agrippina as a dual scourge to Claudius and Nero as Cleopatra was to Caesar and Antony may be at work here. For a woman to distract a Roman from his legitimate pursuits, to insist on her prerogatives and those of her own children (such as Agrippina's machinations on Britannicus' behalf) ahead of his previous duties, to introduce luxury and vice to the court—these are the fears of the Neronian age.

The *BC*'s Cleopatra assumes Agrippina's unwomanly claims to power and tendency toward dynastic disruption—the dark side of the power given to Livia as mother to the empire. In Lucan's contemporary context, women are literally king-makers and king-unmakers. Lucan seems to balk more at Cleopatra's foreignness than her gender: "There was a doubtful event near the Leucadian eddy, whether a woman—and not even one of ours!—should rule the world" (*Leucadioque fuit dubius sub gurgite casus, / an mundum ne nostra quidem matrona teneret*, 10.66–7). Yet even this grudging allowance of female power has its limits, and Lucan draws a more general moral for his Roman listeners. Any woman in such a position of power is troubling, and the name "Caesar" allows the audience to substitute identities. The poet accuses *Julius* Caesar, but Claudius' and Nero's *mésalliances* and misfortunes lurk just beneath the surface. Julia Caesaris is the only Julian to bear her gentilician name, perhaps reflecting the reliance of the dynasty on the female line—or worrying through her death in childbirth about the disasters brought through fertility or lack of it. Lucan's criteria for judging his women show the anxieties of his age.

The Specter of Caesarism

It is notoriously difficult to see past Augustan propaganda, as entire volumes have shown (e.g., Powell 1992; Galinsky 1996). Even if we are aware it is exerting its influence, it is nearly impossible to unpack. As only the most obvious example, though we know that Augustan literature had a vested interest in besmirching the character and abilities of the last Ptolemaic monarch, we have few satisfactory answers to our question: what *was* Cleopatra like? Outside the clear and well-explored boundaries of that particular political moment, it is even harder to unwind the tentacles of subsequent Julio-Claudian morals and aesthetics. The later literature of the principate reflects the social and political vicissitudes of the period, and, in its often obscure and adversarial tone, is trickier to read (Rudich 1997).

Lucan's revolutionary pose combined with his display of raw emotion asks the audience to take his sentimentality—nostalgia—at face value. He insists on the authenticity of his Cato's heroism and his Caesar's villainy. He marshals the ancient heroes of the Republic to his cause. The conflicts in the *BC* claim to be simple: the Republic against tyranny, honor against ambition, and so forth. But the poet cannot forget his history, and this infects the underlying structures of the poem. His Republican women resemble imperial matrons, and even his Cato labors under the weight of imperial standards. Though the aim of the *BC* may be to revive the memory of the Republic as a call to action against tyranny, Lucan often does not seem to work against the pressures of his contemporary imperial present. Sometimes, as with the encomium to Nero, he even emphasizes his own Julio-Claudian cage. For all the anger and vivacity of the epic, there is never a hope for Lucan's nostalgic project. From the beginning, he undercuts the rising action of the narrative by compressing the war and its aftermath in varying degrees. He, his characters, and his audience are all aware of the failure of the Republic. His own lifetime has infected his memories and the infection reaches back into his rewriting of the ostensibly pristine past. Even that past itself, however, is overloaded with value, and crumbles under his affective expectations of it.

As a coda: another layer to consider is our own inability to unlearn. It is impossible for us to read Lucan without knowing the manner of his death as well as that of Nero, his emperor, onetime friend, and fatal enemy. For this reason, the *BC* can read like a prescient and unusually well-crafted suicide note, both for Lucan and for the Julio-Claudian era. But we must read Lucan without this nearly automatic backshadowing, even if to "write history blind to the future is less difficult than to read it blind to the past that has intervened since the time of the narrative" (Bernstein 1994: 36). For us, the downfall of the Julio-Claudians and the epitaph written for them is obvious and inevitable. They deserve to be deconstructed and undercut, so Lucan has done so. Anti-Caesarism and anti-Neronianism seem to us straightforwardly related; resistance to each man parallel and with equivalent outcomes. Yet, however Lucan remembers the past, he cannot remember the future.

Notes

1. I owe a debt of gratitude to the patient and careful observations of Drs. Mark Thorne and Laura Zientek, who contributed many, many intriguing and enlightening comments and clarifications, as well as to the anonymous reviewers, whose input was invaluably constructive. To the original attendees of the Lucan+ conference at Brigham Young, I am thankful for the opportunity to take Lucan seriously on his own merits.
2. In Freudian terms, an *Überschätzung*. This chapter will not pursue Freudian readings of the *BC*, but see Walker (1996).
3. Literature on Lucan and trauma is rich and expanding, e.g., Walde (2011); Thorne (2016).
4. Vergil is not absent, but Vergilian echoes in Lucan are well documented elsewhere: Conte (1974); Ahl (1993); Hardie (1993); Albrecht (1999); Hömke (2010); Casali (2011), among many others.
5. The text of Lucan is Shackleton Bailey's Teubner of 2009. All translations are my own.
6. On who qualifies for such a list and how, particularly in the Neronian period, see Habinek (2000).
7. The adoption of Venus is a Caesarist touch, especially the respectable, rehabilitated Venus of the Julio-Claudians. The choice of both the dative and the word *urbs* rather than *patria* dissociates this from such titles as *parens* or *pater patriae*, adopted so often by the Julio-Claudians.
8. I pass over explicit instances of prophecy, such as Nigidius Figulus, Appius Claudius' trip to Delphi, and the maddened matron at the end of Book 1, where knowledge of future events is not surprising.
9. For the suicide's inclusion and other formal concerns, see especially Ahl (1968); Marti (1970); Colish (1985: 273); Stover (2008); Tracy (2011); for considerations of Stoic suicide under Nero in imitation of Cato and possibly in dialogue with Lucan, see Romm (2014: 159) and *passim*.
10. On Cato's heroism and the episode of the snakes, see Gorman (2001); Malamud (2003); Wick (2004: 29); Bexley (2010); Tipping (2011).
11. For treatments of exemplarity in various forms of Roman literature and performance, see Chaplin (2000); Walter (2004: 51–70); Tipping (2010); Langlands (2018); Roller (2018).
12. Assmann 1999 usefully outlines, especially, non-literary contributions to cultural memory.
13. Notably, Valerius generally talks about Cato's clothing (3.6.7), or studious nature (8.7.2), or even lack of luxury on campaign (4.3.12) rather than politics, though *libertas* (6.2.5) and his civic probity (2.10.8) do arise.
14. On Cato in particular as a model, and attitudes of largely Stoic intellectuals of the principate about the end of the Republic, see, e.g., Griffin (1986); George (1991); McGuire (1997); Wilkinson (2012).

15. As a small note, Nero's wives during Lucan's life, Octavia and Poppaea, have ill-omened names with respect to marital legislation.
16. Livia appears with a turret crown on a cameo in the Kunsthistorisches Museum in Vienna (AS IXa 95), as does a Tyche from Octavia's Corinthian temple at the Archaeological Museum in Corinth (S 1540). For the later women, Agrippina Maior appears as Roma and Agrippina Minor with a mural crown on the Gemma Claudia (Kunsthistorisches Museum, Vienna, AS IXa 63), and Wood, following others, identifies Messalina in a turreted crown in the Vatican (Museo Chiaramonti, 1814; Wood 1988: 423).
17. There exists a Propertian parallel in 1.11, where a woman composes her own epitaph to claim the role of the *univira* (Caston 2011: 138).
18. Livia in the statue now in the Louvre, inv. MR 259; Agrippina on the Sebasteion at Aphrodisias, crowning Nero.

References

Ahl, F. (1968), "Pharsalus and the *Pharsalia*," *C&M*, 29: 124–61.
Ahl, F. (1993), "Form Empowered: Lucan's *Pharsalia*," in A. J. Boyle (ed.), *Roman Epic*, 125–42, London: Routledge.
Albrecht, M. v. (1999), *Roman Epic: An Interpretative Introduction*, Leiden: Brill.
Assmann, J. (1999), *Das kulturelle Gedächtnis: Schrift, Erinnerung und politische Identität in frühen Hochkulturen*, Munich: Beck.
Asso, P. (2009), "The Intrusive Trope—Apostrophe in Lucan," in R. Ferri, J. M. Seo, and K. Volk (eds.), *Callida Musa: Papers on Latin Literature in Honor of R. Elaine Fantham*, 161–73, Pisa: Fabrizio Serra.
Bernstein, M. A. (1994), *Foregone Conclusions: Against Apocalyptic History*, Berkeley: University of California Press.
Bettini, M. (2000), "*mos, mores* und *mos maiorum*: Die Erfindung der 'Sittlichkeit' in der römischen Kultur," in M. Braun, A. Haltenhoff, and F.-H. Mutschler (eds.), *Moribus antiquis res stat Romana: Römische Werte und römische Literatur im 3. und 2. Jh. v. Chr.*, 303–52, Munich: Saur.
Bexley, E. M. (2009), "Replacing Rome: Geographic and Political Centrality in Lucan's *Pharsalia*," *CPh*, 104: 459–75.
Bexley, E. M. (2010), "The Myth of the Republic: Medusa and Cato in Lucan, *Pharsalia* 9," in N. Hömke and C. Reitz (eds.), *Lucan's Bellum Civile: Between Epic Tradition and Aesthetic Innovation*, 135–53, Berlin: De Gruyter.
Bricault, L. (2015), "The *Gens Isiaca* in Graeco-Roman Coinage," *NC*, 175: 83–102.
Cairns, F. (2002), "Propertius the Historian (3.3.1–12)?," in D. S. Levene and D. P. Nelis (eds.), *Clio and the Poets: Augustan Poetry and the Traditions of Ancient Historiography*, 25–44, Leiden: Brill.
Casali, S. (2011), "The *Bellum Civile* as an Anti-*Aeneid*," in P. Asso (ed.), *Brill's Companion to Lucan*, 81–109, Leiden: Brill.
Caston, R. R. (2011), "Lucan's Elegiac Moments," in P. Asso (ed.), *Brill's Companion to Lucan*, 133–52, Leiden: Brill.
Champlin, E. (2003), *Nero*, Cambridge, MA: Harvard University Press.
Chaplin, J. D. (2000), *Livy's Exemplary History*, Oxford: Oxford University Press.
Colish, M. L. (1985), *The Stoic Tradition from Antiquity to the Early Middle Ages I: Stoicism in Classical Latin Literature*, Leiden: Brill.

Conte, G. B. (1974), *Memoria dei poeti e sistema letterario: Catullo, Virgilio, Ovidio, Lucano*, Turin: Giulio Einaudi.
Cowan, R. (2010), "Virtual Epic: Counterfactuals, Sideshadowing, and the Poetics of Contingency in the *Punica*," in A. Augoustakis (ed.), *Brill's Companion to Silius Italicus*, 323–51, Leiden: Brill.
Delvigo, M. L. (2013), "*Per transitum tangit historiam*: Intersecting Developments of Roman Identity in Virgil," in J. Farrell and D. P. Nelis (eds.), *Augustan Poetry and the Roman Republic*, 19–39, Oxford: Oxford University Press.
Dewar, M. (1994), "Laying It on with a Trowel: The Proem to Lucan and Related Texts," *CQ*, 44: 199–211.
Due, O. S. (1962), "An Essay on Lucan," *C&M*, 23: 68–132.
Farrell, J. (1997), "The Phenomenology of Memory in Roman Culture," *CJ*, 92: 373–83.
Feeney, D. C. (1986), "History and Revelation in Vergil's Underworld," *PCPhS*, 32: 1–24.
Feeney, D. C. (1991), *The Gods in Epic: Poets and Critics of the Classical Tradition*, Oxford: Clarendon Press.
Finiello, C. (2005), "Der Bürgerkrieg: Reine Männersache? Keine Männersache! Erictho und die Frauengestalten im *Bellum Civile* Lucans," in C. Walde (ed.), *Lucan im 21. Jahrhundert*, 155–85, Munich: Saur.
Fowler, D. (2000), *Roman Constructions: Readings in Postmodern Latin*, Oxford: Oxford University Press.
Galinsky, K. (1996), *Augustan Culture: An Interpretive Introduction*, Princeton: Princeton University Press.
Galinsky, K., ed. (2016), *Memory in Ancient Rome and Early Christianity*, Oxford: Oxford University Press.
Geiger, J. (1979), "Munatius Rufus and Thrasea Paetus on Cato the Younger," *Athenaeum*, 57: 48–72.
George, D. B. (1991), "Lucan's Cato and Stoic Attitudes to the Republic," *ClAnt*, 10: 237–58.
Gillespie, C. C. (forthcoming), "Voiceless Grief: Domestic Disruption and the Failure of Fecundity in Lucan's *Bellum Civile*," in L. Fratantuono and C. Stark (eds.), *Blackwell Companion to Latin Epic, 14–96 CE*, West Sussex: Wiley Blackwell.
Goldschmidt, N. (2013), *Shaggy Crowns: Ennius'* Annales *and Virgil's* Aeneid, Oxford: Oxford University Press.
Gorman, V. B. (2001), "Lucan's Epic *Aristeia* and the Hero of the *Bellum Civile*," *CJ*, 96: 263–90.
Griffin, M. (1986), "Philosophy, Cato, and Roman Suicide: II," *G&R*, 33: 192–202.
Habinek, T. (2000), "Seneca's Renown: *Gloria, Claritudo*, and the Replication of the Roman Elite," *CA*, 19: 264–303.
Hardie, P. (1993), *The Epic Successors of Virgil: A Study in the Dynamics of a Tradition*, Cambridge: Cambridge University Press.
Hedrick Jr., C. W. (2016), "*Qualis Artifex Pereo*: The Generation of Roman Memories of Nero," in K. Galinsky (ed.), *Memory in Ancient Rome and Early Christianity*, 145–66, Oxford: Oxford University Press.
Henderson, J. (2000), "The Camillus Factory: *Per Astra ad Ardeam*," *Ramus*, 29: 1–26.
Illbruck, H. (2012), *Nostalgia: Origins and Ends of an Unenlightened Disease*, Evanston: Northwestern University Press.
Johnson, W. R. (1987), *Momentary Monsters: Lucan and His Heroes*, Ithaca: Cornell University Press.
Keith, A. M. (2012), *Engendering Rome: Women in Latin Epic*, Cambridge: Cambridge University Press.
Kessler, J. (2011), "The Irony of Assassination: On the Ideology of Lucan's Invocation to Nero," *SIFC*, 9: 129–44.

Langlands, R. (2018), *Exemplary Ethics in Ancient Rome*, Cambridge: Cambridge University Press.
Litchfield, H. W. (1914), "National *Exempla Virtutis* in Roman Literature," *HSPh*, 25: 1–71.
Lowenthal, D. (1994), "Identity, Heritage, and History," in J. R. Gillis (ed.), *Commemorations: The Politics of National Identity*, 41–57, Princeton: Princeton University Press.
Malamud, M. (2003), "Pompey's Head and Cato's Snakes," *CPh*, 98: 31–44.
Marti, B. M. (1970), "La structure de la *Pharsale*," in M. Durry (ed.), *Lucain: Sept exposés suivis de discussions*, 1–35, Geneva: Fondation Hardt.
Mayer, R. (1978), "On Lucan and Nero," *BICS*, 25: 85–8.
McGuire, D. T. (1997), *Acts of Silence: Civil War, Tyranny, and Suicide in the Flavian Epics*, Hildesheim: Olms-Wiedmann.
Milnor, K. (2005), *Gender, Domesticity, and the Age of Augustus: Inventing Private Life*, Oxford Studies in Classical Literature and Gender Theory, Oxford: Oxford University Press.
Mordine, M. J. (2013), "*Domus Neroniana*: The Imperial Household in the Age of Nero," in E. Buckley and M. T. Dinter (eds.), *A Companion to the Neronian Age*, 102–17, Chichester: Wiley-Blackwell.
Mulhern, E. V. (2017), "Roma(na) Matrona," *CJ*, 112 (4): 432–59.
Pichon, R. (1912), *Les sources de Lucain*, Paris: Leroux.
Powell, A., ed. (1992), *Roman Poetry and Propaganda in the Age of Augustus*, London: Bristol Classical Press.
Radicke, J. (2004), *Lucans poetische Technik: Studien zum historischen Epos*, Leiden: Brill.
Roller, M. B. (2018), *Models from the Past in Roman Culture: A World of* Exempla, Cambridge: Cambridge University Press.
Rudich, V. (1997), *Dissidence and Literature under Nero: The Price of Rhetoricization*, London: Routledge.
Sannicandro, L. (2010), *I personaggi femminili del Bellum Civile di Lucano*, Rahden: Leidorf.
Seidman, J. (2017), "A Poetic Caesar in Lucan's *Pharsalia*," *CJ*, 113 (1): 72–95.
Seo, J. M. (2011), "Lucan's Cato and the Poetics of Exemplarity," in P. Asso (ed.), *Brill's Companion to Lucan*, 199–221, Leiden: Brill.
Severy, B. (2003), *Augustus and the Family at the Birth of the Roman Empire*, New York: Routledge.
Shackleton Bailey, D. R., ed. (2009), *Marcus Annaeus Lucanus De Bello Civili Libri X*, Berlin: De Gruyter.
Sklenář, R. (1999), "Nihilistic Cosmology and Catonian Ethics in Lucan's *Bellum Civile*," *AJPh*, 120: 281–96.
Stover, T. (2008), "Cato and the Intended Scope of Lucan's *Bellum Civile*," *CQ*, 58: 571–80.
Thorne, M. (2011), "*Memoria Redux*: Memory in Lucan," in P. Asso (ed.), *Brill's Companion to Lucan*, 363–81, Leiden: Brill.
Thorne, M. (2016), "Speaking the Unspeakable: Engaging *Nefas* in Lucan and Rwanda 1994," in A. Ambühl (ed.), *Krieg der Sinne—Die Sinne im Krieg. Kriegsdarstellungen im Spannungsfeld zwischen antiker und moderner Kultur / War of the Senses—The Senses in War. Interactions and Tensions between Representations of War in Classical and Modern Culture = Thersites* 4, 77–119.
Tipping, B. (2010), *Exemplary Epic: Silius Italicus' Punica*, Oxford: Oxford University Press.
Tipping, B. (2011), "Terrible Manliness?: Lucan's Cato," in P. Asso (ed.), *Brill's Companion to Lucan*, 223–36, Leiden: Brill.
Tracy, J. (2011), "Internal Evidence for the Completeness of the *Bellum Civile*," in P. Asso (ed.), *Brill's Companion to Lucan*, 33–53, Leiden: Brill.
Walde, C. (2011), "Lucan's *Bellum Civile*: A Specimen of a Roman 'Literature of Trauma,'" in P. Asso (ed.), *Brill's Companion to Lucan*, 283–302, Leiden: Brill.
Walker, A. (1996), "Lucan's Legends of the Fall," *Ramus*, 25: 65–87.

Walter, U. (2004), Memoria *und* res publica: *zur Geschichtskultur im republikanischen Rom*, Frankfurt am Main: Verlag Antike.
Wick, C. (2004), *M. Annaeus Lucanus:* Bellum civile, *Liber IX: Einleitung, Text und Übersetzung*, Munich: Saur.
Wilkinson, S. (2012), *Republicanism during the Early Roman Empire*, London: Continuum International Publishing Group.
Wood, S. (1988), "*Memoriae Agrippinae*: Agrippina the Elder in Julio-Claudian Art and Propaganda," *American Journal of Archaeology*, 92: 409–26.
Wyke, M. (1992), "Augustan Cleopatras: Female Power and Poetic Authority," in A. Powell (ed.), *Roman Poetry and Propaganda in the Age of Augustus*, 98–140, London: Bristol Classical Press.

CHAPTER 12
LUCAN'S NERONIAN *RES PUBLICA RESTITUTA*
Andrew M. McClellan

Achille Mbembe has recently argued—expanding on Michel Foucault's concept of biopower and biopolitics—that modern terror states, through mass violence and the orchestrated denial of basic human rights, create "*death-worlds*, new and unique forms of social existence in which vast populations are subjected to conditions of life conferring upon them the status of *living dead*" (Mbembe 2003: 40).[1] Mbembe calls this "necropolitics" and its implementation "necropower." His focus is the postcolonial state, which has inherited the techniques of violence and power passed on from the initial abuses of colonization, but the argument largely extrapolates and globalizes the biopolitical state-of-exception of totalitarian internment camps, seen as the "central metaphor for sovereign and destructive violence" (Mbembe 2003: 12), which Hannah Arendt argues (building on Primo Levi's analyses) created a situation of living "outside of life and death" (1966: 444–7).[2] For Giorgio Agamben, the internment camp is a site which visited upon its politically divested detainees an unparalleled "absolute *conditio inhumana*" (1998: 95), which determined "not so much that [the detainee's] life is no longer life ... but, rather, that their death is not death" (2002: 70; cf. De Luna 2006: 207–10).[3] These inmates live beyond the threshold of life and "die" before their physical deaths. Under conditions of necropower, there exists a collapsing of formal definitions of law and structure, which leaves the ruling party in a position to define historical narrative and identity, right and wrong, good and evil, humanity and inhumanity, and life and death, without being subjected to scrutiny or requiring justification. The result is a muddying of social life which explodes any possibility of cogent history.

This might seem like an odd place to start, but I affix Mbembe's conception of necropolitics here at the beginning as a sort of lens for reading Lucan's metaphorical portrait of aristocratic life in contemporary Neronian Rome. There is little *physically* connecting Lucan and his wealthy, privileged contemporaries to the widespread victims of the horrors of the modern postcolonial state—and I do not in any way want to undersell this point. But the complaints of Lucan's indefatigable narrator (a "character" caught somewhere between the *real-life* Lucan and a clever authorial feint[4]), coupled with what I call the imagistic "deathscape" of Lucan's epic universe that he links etiologically/teleologically to the conditions of his own time, create a conceptual view of Neronian Rome that strikingly mirrors Mbembe's postcolonial death-world. My interests lie less in the actual living conditions of Lucan and his coterie in Nero's Rome than in the metaphorical language deployed to describe the sociopolitical circumstances created by decades of monarchical rule from Augustus to Nero.

More specifically, this chapter explores Lucan's interest in and utilization of body of state imagery, his vision of the symbolic death of Rome's *res publica*, and his devious engagement with Julio-Claudian rhetoric championing the principate as a "restoration," a rebirth of the old political system (*res publica restituta*). I take as a launch-pad for this examination the infamous necromancy of Lucan's wicked witch Erictho in *BC* 6, wherein these themes all converge most explicitly. We shall see that this idea of restoration has intimate associations with notions of *libertas* as it is construed in an imperial, Neronian context. What emerges from Lucan's complex picture of imperfect death and funeral ritual in his poem, I suggest, is a dark metaphor for both the state and the state of existence in Neronian Rome. Roman citizens living under the Caesars who have monopolized power, influence, and law, and who strive to control historical accuracy and memory and even life and death over subjects renders for them a life symbolically akin to Mbembian "living-death." Lucan's flashback to the war between Caesar and Pompey takes his audience back to the birth of this never-ending state of death.

It has always struck me as grimly delightful—and the epitome of Lucanian gallows humor—that the most graphic scene of corpse mistreatment in an epic full of corpse mistreatment elicits not corporeal obliteration but rather revivification. Such are the dark arts of Lucan's Thessalian witch Erictho, whose necromancy brings a dead Roman soldier back from death.[5] Erictho is a night-witch, an artisan and aesthetician of death and its associated rites, and she is, indisputably, the very best at her craft.[6] Among her many skills (6.520–69), it is her ability to revive the dead that is of most interest here (531–2).

Rumor of Erictho's abilities leads Sextus Pompey to her haunts, where he spies her on an escarpment casting spells (570–88). Sextus wishes to know the future on the eve of the climactic battle at Pharsalus (in the witch's backyard) that will pit the troops of his father, Pompey the Great, against Julius Caesar's renegade army. Erictho is happy to oblige and she lays out a plan of action for granting Sextus's request (619–23):

sed pronum, cum tanta nouae sit copia mortis,
Emathiis unum campis attollere corpus,
ut modo defuncti tepidique cadaueris ora
plena uoce sonent, nec membris sole perustis
auribus incertum feralis strideat umbra.

That's easy, when there's such an abundance of recent death,
to raise one body from the Emathian plain,
so that the mouth of a recently dead and warm corpse
can speak with a full voice, and no grim shade with limbs
burnt by the sun hiss faintly in our ears.[7]

It is no real surprise that a witch, for whom "every human death is put to use" (*hominum mors omnis in usu est*, 561), would resort to necromancy. And the fact that she is bursting with such confidence (*sed pronum*), outwardly at least, justifies Sextus's decision to enlist her aid against traditional (i.e., sanctioned) forms of divination, all of which we have seen fail over the course of the poem. What follows is an inversion of the *Aeneid*-style heroic *katabasis*: Erictho will draw the netherworld up to earth by conjuring the ghost of a dead Roman soldier to prophesy for Sextus. But in order to speak, this ghost will need a body. Erictho's skill is not simply in summoning *umbrae* from the realm of the dead, but in reanimating corpses as vessels for disembodied shades.

After scouring the corpse-strewn field for a suitable subject, Erictho drags the dead soldier to her workshop to prep the body for revivification. She cracks open the corpse's chest and pours in a vile witch's brew (667–84) before delivering a series of cacophonic howls (685–93), an incantation to the infernal gods (693–718), and finally a slew of rage-filled threats when the ghost initially balks at re-entering its old corporeal frame (719–49).

This does the trick. Once ghost and corpse are re-fused, the soldier bursts back to life. But Lucan immediately signals this re-charged vitality as degenerative or defective (755–9):[8]

> nec se tellure cadauer
> paulatim per membra leuat, terraque repulsum est
> erectumque semel. distento lumina rictu
> nudantur. nondum facies uiuentis in illo,
> iam morientis erat: remanet pallorque rigorque ...

> the corpse does not lift himself off of the ground
> piecemeal, limb by limb, but is repelled from the earth
> and set straight up in one motion. His eyes opened with perplexed
> stare: there was in him the appearance of someone not yet living,
> already dying: pallor and rigidity remain ...

The corpse-soldier is not quite dead *or* alive; it exists instead somewhere in between. Liminality is symptomatic of Lucan's Thessalian excursus: Erictho too hovers between life and death and is explicitly corpse-like in appearance, stained by a Thessalian landscape imbued with contradictions of time and space.[9] Her hovel is a fusion of upper and lower worlds (649–53), like Vergil's underworld entrance (*Aen.* 6.236–41) or Seneca's (*Thy.* 665–82). In each case, the blurring of boundaries and spatial confusion creates the impression that we have either descended below the world of the living or that Hell has come to us.[10] This liminal space suits Erictho. She lives in abandoned tombs like a corpse (*deserta ... busta / incolit*, Luc. 511–12); she is the "favorite" of the underworld gods (*grata deis Erebi*, 513). What's more, she *looks* like a corpse: *tenet ora profanae / foeda situ macies, caeloque ignota sereno / terribilis Stygio facies pallore grauatur*, 515–17 ("emaciation grips her unholy face filthy with decay, and unknown to the bright sky her terrible visage is heaped with Stygian pallor"). In Latin poetry, *pallor* indicates approaching death (e.g., Verg., *Aen.* 4.499, 8.709, 10.822, 12.221; Sen., *Ag.* 710). Erictho's *pallor* signifies her deathliness, but she is hardly "doomed"; rather, she exists *permanently* in a drawn-out state of dying. In this way, she mirrors the corpse-soldier whose *pallor* similarly defines the oddity of his liminal status (Luc. 6.776, 821). Both figures straddle two worlds (Korenjak 1996, *ad* 6.750–62).

Moments before battle breaks out the next day, Lucan describes the Pompeian soldiers' pallor-tinged faces, reprising the familiar poetic refrain of looming death: *multorum pallor in ore / mortis uenturae faciesque simillima fato*, 7.129–30 ("the pallor of impending death is on the faces of many, the appearance mirroring their fate"). The description is conspicuously heavy-handed; we do not need the final clause spelling out a well-worn poetic motif. But herein lies the joke. Erictho earlier described the Emathian plain as inundated with freshly slain soldiers (6.619), a source of derision among scholars who argue that Lucan has lost track of time in his narrative since the fighting has not begun yet in Thessaly. But the jumbled sequence of events here surely reflects the witch Erictho's skill in controlling and distorting time (cf. 6.461–65, 830).[11] Lucan's description of post-battle carnage in Book 7 memorably brings the events in Thessaly to a close, but, in a real sense, we have already seen this blood-soaked battlefield the night Erictho galvanized the corpse of a "Pompeian shade" (*Pompeiana . . . umbra*, 717). The battle of Pharsalus is framed by paired portraits of the plain strewn with *the same* corpses (6.619–41; 7.786–845). The soldiers' pallor, then, is both (traditionally) anticipatory—Lucan will describe their physical deaths in book 7—and also oddly *ex post facto*, or better, *post mortem*.

This bizarre, almost infectious warping of vitality on display in Thessaly offers the major takeaway from Lucan's necromantic excursus. The corpse-soldier's prophecy is an anti-climax (like other divinatory events in the poem); Sextus learns nothing intelligible and is promised the "surer prophet" of his spectral father in an event outside the scope of Lucan's poem (6.813–14). But the non-event of the prophecy throws the oddity of what we have just experienced into higher relief. Erictho does revivify a corpse, but there is clearly something *wrong* with it. This oddity is amplified when we discern that Erictho and the entire Pompeian army also take on the appearance of humans "not yet living, already dying" (758–9).

The perverted or corrupted state of life and death in Thessaly has larger implications for Lucan's poem and his metaphorical conception of living (and dying) in Nero's Rome. In what follows, I explore Lucan's interaction with earlier political discourse from the mid-first century BCE analogizing civil war to violence aimed at "state bodies."[12] Lucan's poem revives the war between Caesar and Pompey that dismembered the *res publica* more than a hundred years before Nero's ascension to the throne. The historical space here, and the inevitable rise of the principate out of the ashes of the earlier state, allows Lucan considerable room to toy with metaphorical language deployed during the Republic's collapse. The value of hindsight enables him to reimagine what has been exhumed from the tomb of the murdered *res publica* and to superimpose elements of Neronian Rome onto his depiction of its fall. Though the discussion will take us some ways away from Erictho and her corpse-soldier, I will eventually work back to both as a means of tying the various threads of my argument together.

From the epic's opening lines, Lucan signals his direct engagement with earlier literary metaphorizing that links civil war with corporeal violence. Civil war is "self-eviscerating," an analogy that functions as a constant refrain throughout the poem: *canimus populumque potentem / in sua uictrici conuersum uiscera dextra*, 1.1–2 ("we sing of a powerful people turning its victorious hand against its own viscera"). The image—and indeed Lucan's entire poem—replays and dramatizes in grand scale a climactic moment in the *Aeneid* that similarly construes civil war (the *same* civil war) in corporeal terms. Vergil, through the voice of Anchises, warns the pre-souls of Caesar and Pompey in the underworld against waging war with each other a thousand or so years in the future: *ne, pueri, ne tanta animis adsuescite bella / neu patriae ualidas in uiscera uertite uiris*, *Aen.* 6.832–3 ("no, my boys, don't habituate your spirits to *this* kind of warfare; don't turn your strength and vigor against the viscera of your own country").[13]

As Brian Walters (2011) has demonstrated most extensively, by the last few decades of the Republic, imagery of the body politic in various stages of decay was already a popular way of symbolizing the disruption of the Roman state as constant civil wars seemed bound to spawn further tyranny, despotism, and dissolution. Authors compared the state to a bloodless body (Cic., *Att.* 4.18.2 = SB 92.2), a body racked with plague or poison (Cic., *Att.* 2.1.7 = SB 21.7; Sall., *Cat.* 10.6, 11.3; cf. Cic., *Cat.* 1.31), a gangrenous body (Varro fr. 123 Riposati), and a body wounded or ripped to pieces (Cic., *Sest.* 17, *Phil.* 2.43; Sall., *Iug.* 41). As early as 59 BCE, Cicero could claim that the *res publica* was "dead" (*tota periit*, *Att.* 2.21.1 = SB 41.1),[14] and Suetonius records a quote attributed to Caesar by the Republican biographer Titus Ampius Balbus that "the *res publica* is nothing, just a name without a body or form" (*nihil esse rem publicam, appellationem modo sine corpore ac specie*, Suet., *Iul.* 77).

This organological imagery is crucial for Lucan's portrait of civil violence as he looks back on the collapse of the *res publica* from the imperial vantage point of Neronian Rome. In a reworking of a famous conceit (Cic., *Att.* 2.1.7 = SB 21; Sen., *Clem.* 1.5.1), for example, Lucan's Sulla is a mad surgeon cutting too deeply into the rotting limbs of the Roman state: *dumque nimis iam putria / membra recidit excessit medicina modum, nimiumque secuta est, / qua morbi duxere, manus* ("and while he hewed away limbs already now too rotten, his surgery crossed the line, and his hand followed too far where the sickness led," 2.141–3; see Fantham 1992: *ad* 2.140).[15] Later, Pompey fears the battle at Pharsalus will cause the Roman state body "wounds" (7.92–3), but the outcome is in fact much worse: *BC* 7 narrates the massacre of the *res publica* and the victory of Caesar(ism), shown triumphantly trampling through its *uiscera* (e.g., 7.578–85, 597–8, 697, 721–3).[16] And Cato, as he contemplates participation in the suicidal civil war, imagines himself as a father mourning the child-like Rome's smoldering "corpse" on a pyre (2.297–303). Cato's own metaphor anticipates his role as *laudator* in the (quasi-) funeral for Pompey in book 9, though here he imagines the corpse as physically present and not *in absentia* as Pompey had been, left half-burnt and headless on the Egyptian shoreline (8.708–11, 786–93). Lucan casts Pompey as the *res publica* incarnate, the poem's ill-stared synecdochic hero,[17] so Cato's metaphor has some resonant power here when we consider the inevitable fall of each.

The destruction of the Republic necessitates the destruction of *libertas*, "freedom"—a key feature of Republican aristocratic ideology—as Cato articulates explicitly: *tuumque /*

nomen, Libertas, et inanem persequar umbram ("and your name, Liberty, an empty shade even, I will pursue," 2.302–3). Cato's language echoes Lucan's description of Pompey as a "shadow of a great name" (*stat magni nominis umbra*, 1.135), the lexical cue linking Pompey with the (now) umbratic symbols that he and the *res publica* represented (Henderson 1998: 203; Thorne 2011: 377). Pompey, the *res publica*, and *libertas* are united by their deaths, but none of them receives a clean or clear requiem; they remain in an extended state of putrefaction. In the narrative present, Lucan expresses the wish to tear up Pompey's sham-tomb, recover his bones, and return his remains to Italy for *proper* burial (8.841–5).[18] Similarly, Pharsalus still holds the blood and bones of un-honored Roman soldiers, their remains now fodder for ploughshares (7.847–72). The poem symbolizes the death and mass funeral pomp for Rome's *res publica libera*, but the body politic (like Pompey's, like his soldiers' bodies at Pharsalus) is never buried but instead left rotting.

In this way, Lucan appropriates the self-eviscerating, cadaverous metaphorical language deployed during the last few decades of the Republic as part of his grand re-staging of the state's collapse. But while Republican rhetoric forms an important conceptual lens, Lucan also weaves into his poetic system Augustan and Julio-Claudian imperial ideology which sought to reformulate this imagery by claiming that the principate represented a "revitalization" of the *res publica* and (thus) *libertas*, and that power had been transferred back to the Senate (*res publica restituta*)—political propaganda akin to a Platonic or, more sinisterly, Kantian/Mbembian "noble lie" (γενναῖον ψεῦδος) overwriting foundational crimes (Plat., *Rep.* 414b–415d).[19] Augustus is explicit in the *Res Gestae* that his efforts to extinguish the civil wars precipitated nothing more than his reestablishment of the *res publica* and the transference of powers back to the senate and Roman people (*rem publicam ex mea potestate in senatus populique Romani arbitrium transtuli, RG* 34.1). Additional evidence supports early efforts to push this propagandistic party-line, e.g., *Laudatio Turiae* 2.25: *pacato orbe terrarum res[titut]a re publica* ("with the whole world pacified, the Republic restored"); *Fasti Praenestini* for January 13, 27 BCE: *corona quern[a uti super ianuam domus Imp. Caesaris] Augusti poner[etur senatus decreuit quod rem publicam] p. R. restitui[t]* ("the senate decreed that an oak crown should be placed above the door of the commander-in-chief Augustus Caesar because he restored the *res publica* to the Roman people"); an *aureus* dated to 28 BCE (BM 1995.4–1.1) shows a seated Octavian holding a scroll above the *scrinium*, with the legend: *leges et iura p.R. restituit* ("[Octavian] has restored the laws and rights to the Roman people"; Rich and Williams 1999); and *ILS* 81, a dedication to Octavian by SPQR, 29 BCE: *re publica conseruata* (the *res publica* preserved). The notion that Republican *libertas* came hand-in-hand with the restoration of the *res publica* is a point of emphasis. Looking back nearly sixty years, Augustus claims to have "set the *res publica* free" when he drove the oppressive faction of the "despot" Antony from Rome in 44 BCE (*rem publicam a dominatione factionis oppressam in libertatem uindicaui, RG* 1; see Roller 2001: 214–15); the *Fasti Amiternini* for August 1, 30 BCE regarding the Battle of Alexandria declare: *Feriae ex s.c. q(uod) e(o) d(ie) Imp. Caesar Diui f. rem p(ublicam) tristissim[o] periculo liberat* ("holiday by senatorial decree because on that day the commander-in-chief Caesar, son of the divine [Caesar], liberates the *res publica* from a most serious danger"; Rich and Williams 1999: 184–5); a *cistophorus* from 28 BCE (BM G.2207 = *RIC* 1² 476) identifies Octavian as *libertatis p.R. uindex* ("defender of freedom of the Roman people"; Rich and Williams 1999: 173–4, 185–8; Lange 2009: 182–3). In Mbembian terms, this is sovereignty exercising power outside (or in suspension) of the law, yet draped in the vocabulary and symbols of (Republican) political propriety.

This position of Republican "restoration"—delusive but powerful—continues well into the early principate, as authors like Velleius Paterculus and Valerius Maximus demonstrate most forcefully.[20] If Vitruvius could earlier elliptically imagine Augustus helping to guide a restored *res publica* through his advice and counsel (*praef.* 1), Velleius, for example, is much blunter: *prisca illa et antiqua rei publicae forma reuocata*, 2.89.4 ("that former and ancient form of the *res publica* was restored"). Ovid describes all of Rome's provinces being "restored to our people" on January 13, 27 BCE, perhaps on the same day Octavian was given the title "Augustus" (*redditaque est omnis populo prouincia nostro, Fast.* 1.589).[21] And Suetonius notes that Augustus restored the old Republican-era voting practices (*comitiorum quoque pristinum ius reduxit, Aug.* 40.2).

I suggest that the idea of "restoration" must be viewed within the matrix of body-political metaphors articulating the mutilation and/or death of the *res publica* in the decades before Augustus's rise to power. Julio-Claudian authors continue to describe the Roman state in corporeal terms, but now as a unified, healthy imperial political "body" secure in its position under the *princeps* (Squire 2015: 309–10 *et passim*). Augustan Rome for Ovid is a "large body of Empire" in which "no part risks falling to pieces" (*in tanto . . . / corpore pars nulla est quae labat imperii, Tr.* 2.231–2). Seneca describes Nero's Rome similarly at *Clem.* 2.2.1 (*omne imperii corpus*), and at *De ira* 2.31.7–8 (reworking Menenius Agrippa's fable of the "greedy belly," e.g., Liv. 2.32.8–12) he compares a functioning society to a harmonious human body (cf. Sen. *Clem.* 1.3.5). Ovid defines Augustus as "head-of-state" (*caput orbis, Tr.* 3.5.46), an image that Velleius (2.99) reconstitutes for Tiberius (*rei publicae lumen et caput*, "head and light of the *res publica*"), and which Seneca uses for Nero, through the recurrent foil of Augustus (*nam et illi uiribus opus est et huic capite*, "for that one [Augustus/Nero] needs strength and this one [the *res publica*] needs a head," *Clem.* 1.4.3; cf. 1.5.1, 2.2.1; see further discussion below).

More striking—and crucial for our purposes—is Velleius's description of the *Pax Augusta* in terms that blend the metaphorical state body imagery with the propaganda of Augustan "restoration": *sepultis . . . bellis ciuilibus coalescentibusque rei publicae membris, etiam coaluere quae tam longa armorum series laceraueret*, 2.90 ("after the civil wars were buried and the limbs of the *res publica* were growing back together again, even that which such a long string of wars had torn to pieces regrew"; cf. Val. Max. 2.8.7; Walters 2011: 183). Here "civil wars" are buried, but later, in a survey of Tiberius's accomplishments, it is the traditional republican values of justice, equity, and hard work that are "exhumed" by Tiberius and given back to the Roman state (*sepultaeque ac situ obsitae iustitia, aequitas, industria ciuitati redditae*, 2.126.2). Again, Velleius is explicit that it is the *res publica* that is being rejuvenated, not the creation of a new political system. And by appropriating the rhetorical/metaphorical language of Republican authors, he is able to turn the negative corporeal imagery on its head: the very *vitality* of the state depends upon and has been renewed by Augustus and his successor(s).

Lucan's poem savages this conceit in its own metaphorical terms.[22] The absurdity of the suggestion that Caesarism revived and restored the *res publica libera* gives Lucan the opportunity to retroject a perversion of the metaphor of the Republic's corporeality back into his conception of its "death" in the earlier civil wars. Velleius's corporeal model of *res publica restituta* is glowing in its appraisal of Caesarism; Lucan's is negative, warped, twisted. Many (perhaps Velleius among them) could no doubt justify the paradox of claiming a seamless continuity with the *res publica* through the establishment of an entirely new form of government by reminding themselves that monarchy—however it was articulated—had (seemingly) brought an end to decades of civil war, anticipating Tacitus' collocation of *pax et princeps* (*Ann.* 3.28.2). But for Lucan, Caesarism demanded "peace with a master"; Romans are "slaves" to *principes* (*cum domino pax ista uenit*, BC 1.670; cf. 1.669–72, 3.112–14, 145–7, 4.221–7, 577–9, 5.385–6; 7.442–7, 641–6, etc.). Lucan's poem metaphorically "revivifies" the slaughtered *res publica* in order to replay its bludgeoning death over again in hypertrophic detail.[23] And he chooses to re-stage the war between Caesar and Pompey because *this* (according to his narrator) was the conflict that instigated the present state of affairs in Neronian Rome, a world founded on the fiction of the Republic "reborn" and a return to Republican *libertas*.[24]

Lucan's most striking allegorical symbol for the Roman state from *res publica* to Empire is Erictho's reanimated, half-living, half-dying corpse-soldier. Much like Pompey's role as synecdoche for the *res publica*, Erictho's corpse-soldier functions as a metaphor for or symbol of the vicissitudes of the state. Charles Tesoriero argued similarly that the corpse-soldier symbolizes Rome's Republican "body politic," mutilated by Erictho in a microcosmic reflection of Caesar's treatment of Pompey's army at Pharsalus.[25] The Roman soldier is killed in Thessaly, but revivified into something bizarrely blurring the lines between life and death, as we have seen: *nondum facies uiuentis in illo / iam morientis erat*, 6.754–9 ("there was in him the appearance of someone not yet living, already dying"). If the Julio-Claudians have simply "restored" the traditional *res publica*, then like Erictho's corpse-soldier, the state is a grotesque distortion of true life; that is, it is a thing "not yet living, already dying." In the epic world of Lucan's narrator, life in this pseudo-Republican deathscape is a nightmare, a spectral world of half-life and slavery. With real *libertas* now long gone, a casualty of the atrocities visited upon Rome by Marius and Sulla, as Cato tells us (9.204–6), Lucan's contemporary Neronian audience share (bodily) their state's strange fate.

Lucan's focus on the death of *libertas* and the resultant state of imperial servitude is important here. Ulpian is most explicit when he tells us that Romans compared slavery—a functional and theoretical consequence of the loss of *libertas*[26]—with death (*seruitutem mortalitati fere comparamus*, Ulp., *Dig.* 50.17.209). But more valuable for our purposes is Lucan's uncle Seneca, whose late-Neronian *Epistulae* contain several discussions of slavery and death. In a famous account (*Ep.* 70.20–1), a German slave forced into the *uenatio* gladiator training school absconds to the lavatory, where he commits a gruesome suicide via *tersorium* (sponge-stick). The slave does this, we are told, as a means of attaining freedom from slavery, which is (worse than death) a fate akin to death-in-life. *Ep.* 77 spells this out in more direct terms. Seneca recalls a story about when Caligula was confronted by a chain gang slave on the Via Latina who begs for death. Caligula's response is cruel but telling: *nunc enim . . . uiuis?* ("are you really alive now?" 77.18).

The imagery here anticipates Orlando Patterson's (1982) formulation of the condition of slavery as a form of "social death," whereby the loss of freedom, power, autonomy, agency, identity (etc.) create for the slave a condition of death-in-life. Lucan's poem projects a macroscopic view of the metaphorical/philosophical implications of this grim harmony between slavery and death which squares with Mbembe's articulation of necropower as a form of sovereign domination tantamount to a broadly institutionalized master–slave dynamic. That is to say, for Lucan's narrator, Romans deprived of *libertas* as a result of tyrannical Caesarism are—like Seneca's deathly slaves—metaphorical "walking corpses" functioning in a sociopolitical space deprived of agency, definition, and boundaries, holding onto traditional titles/positions now utterly extrajudicial and stripped of function and influence (cf. O'Higgins 1988: 225). Like Erictho's grip on the functionality of the corpse-soldier, Caesar holds the body politic in a zombie-like state of existence.[27]

This is our narrator's frightening articulation of his present, since he projects the world of Neronian Rome onto the war between Caesar and Pompey, which functions as an etiology for the circumstances of his own time (Leigh 1997: 77–109). Despite our expectations, Pharsalus matched Caesar(ism) against *Libertas*, not Pompey: *sed par quod semper habemus, / Libertas et Caesar, erit* ("there will be that matched pair which we always have, Freedom and Caesar," 7.695–6); Caesar won (Ahl 1976: 25, 42–5, 55–6; Johnson 1987: 32, 122–3; 131–4, Quint 1993: 150–1). Caesar always wins, which is why there cannot exist both Caesar(s) and *libertas* at once (Gowing 2005: 95).

Like Lucan, Seneca is vociferous in championing the incompatibility of this collocation and he does so most often through the foil of Cato, similarly drawing on material from the end of the *res publica*. Consider (e.g.) *Ep.* 14.13 on Cato's decision to enter into a civil war in which *libertas* is already in ruins (*iam non agitur de libertate: olim pessum data est*), the aim now to determine who will be chosen as "master" (*dominus eligitur*; Gowing 2005: 77–9). The same imagery recurs elsewhere in Seneca's works, often with the breviloquent symbolism that *libertas* died with Cato: *neque enim Cato post libertatem uixit nec libertas post Catonem* ("for Cato did not outlive freedom, nor freedom Cato," *De const.* 2.2; cf. *Ep.* 24.7, 95.71; note Val. Max. 6.2.5). The fact that this incompatibility between Caesar(s) and *libertas* remains deeply relevant in Neronian Rome, and that both Lucan and Seneca conjure *exempla* from the end of the Republic to articulate it, is telling. It is why *BC*'s intruding apostrophic narrator is so conspicuously unobjective: Caesar's tyranny lives on in his successors (7.638–46):

maius ab hac acie quam quod sua saecula ferrent
uolnus habent populi; plus est quam uita salusque
quod perit: in totum mundi prosternimur aeuum.
uincitur his gladiis omnis quae seruiet aetas.

proxima quid suboles aut quid meruere nepotes
in regnum nasci? pauide num gessimus arma
teximus aut iugulos? alieni poena timoris
in nostra ceruice sedet. post proelia natis
si dominum, Fortuna, dabas, et bella dedisses.

From this battle the people suffer a wound greater
than their own time could bear; more than just life and safety
perished: we are cast down for the whole of eternity.
Every age which will be enslaved is defeated by *these* swords.
How did their children, their grandchildren after that deserve
to be born into despotism? Did we in fear bear arms
or guard our throats? The penalty of others' fear
rests on our necks. If you were going to give a master
to those born after battle, Fortuna, you should have also given us the fight.

Lucan manages, brilliantly—through a collapsing of temporal space[28] and (more generally) his incessant use of apostrophe[29]—to retroject not only the Julio-Claudian Caesars onto his protagonist Julius Caesar, but also his sociopolitically slavish, corpse-like aristocratic contemporaries back onto the players in the civil war that ultimately spawned them. Again, the target for this formulation is the Augustan/Julio-Claudian claim of *res publica restituta*. While Velleius and others project the erasure of the distinction between Republic and Empire in their work as a means of emphasizing the *good* of Caesarism as a revamped *res publica*, Lucan's efforts to erase the distinction highlight the utter fallaciousness of this position.

Lucan's intense and disruptive engagement with Vergil's scene of "future-history" in the underworld in *Aeneid* 6 adds additional metapoetic texture to this rewriting of Julio-Claudian propagandizing. As we have seen, Anchises admonishes the pre-souls of Caesar and Pompey, destined to unleash civil war on Rome in a future that Aeneas cannot possibly understand (*Aen.* 6.826–35). Lucan's epic breathes life into Vergil's phantoms and stages in grand scale Anchises' elliptical fears of Rome's self-destructive violence. Lucan has excised this scene from Vergil's textual body and "animated" it just as Erictho, the *uates* and internal poet-figure of Lucan's epic (O'Higgins 1998; Masters 1992: 205–15; Finiello 2005: 178–82), summons a Republican ghost from hell and re-incorporates it into a (metaphorical) *corpus*. Vergil's poem, which would ultimately become the textual "embodiment" of the Augustan propaganda machine, is, in Lucan's and Erictho's hands, a site for surgical probing. What emerges from this operation is as distorted as the political system that Vergil's poem was co-opted to champion.

Much of my discussion has focused on Lucan's engagement with pre-Neronian literary and sociopolitical material as part of a reorientation of metaphorical language in the context of his contemporary Rome. But it will be useful to look in a bit more detail at what Seneca does with similar imagery as a juxtaposition to Lucan's portrait in *BC*. I will focus on his magisterial praise-*cum*-protreptic *De Clementia* both for its imagistic treatment of the Roman state body and because, as a product of the early Neronian period (55–56 CE, following Braund 2009: 16–17), it offers a valuable foil for Lucan's writing near the *end* of Nero's reign. The driving conceptual paradigm of the treatise— addressed to the young emperor Nero—compares a seemingly symbiotic, interdependent relationship between the ruler and his people to the relationship of the mind (or head) to its body (1.3.5, 1.4.1, 1.4.3, 1.5.1, 1.14.3, 2.2.1, with Braund 2009: 58 and *ad loc.*). The analogy, as we have seen, is a common one. What is interesting is Seneca's articulation of this relationship in terms of a master–slave dynamic. The body is "slave" to the mind (*totum corpus animo deseruit*, 1.3.5); when an avaricious "master"-mind commands it, the body is compelled to act (*auarus dominus*, 1.3.5). The people, moreover, must be willing to "submit to the reins" (*ferre frenos*, 1.4.2)—stretching the metaphor to master– *animal*—and if the master–slave/animal dynamic breaks down for any reason, "the whole unified coherence of the greatest Empire will burst apart into many pieces"— the imagery is decidedly corporeal: physical, institutional, cosmic—bringing an end to the city's system of "obedience" and "domination" (*haec unitas et hic maximi imperii contextus in partes multas dissiliet, idemque huic urbi finis dominandi erit qui parendi fuerit*, 1.4.2). Rome's success, in other words, depends entirely upon the citizenry's enslavement to the *princeps*; without this, the state risks wholesale "bodily" dissolution.

That this master–slave dynamic appears as part of Seneca's larger elaborate *analogy* is important, and Susanna Braund is right to stress that by "reserving the language of domination and slavery for the comparison, Seneca keeps at arm's length the implication that the Roman people are Nero's slaves" (Braund 2009: 208). But that this language is deployed *at all* might strike us as somewhat jarring. If we keep reading, Seneca explicitly sets up the master–slave relationship as a negative paradigm for Nero's emulation in contrast, as Matthew Roller demonstrates, with the more positive model of the emperor's relationship with his subjects as that between father and child (father–child: 1.14.1-6; master–slave: 1.18.1–3; Roller 2001: 243–7). The firm but fair hand of the *paterfamilias* is preferable to the slave-owner's cruelty and antagonism toward his slaves—and of course Seneca has the interests of his aristocratic clique in mind. If the master–slave relationship is to be emphatically cast aside as inadvisable, why does Seneca deploy precisely this imagistic language in his initial overview of the role of the *princeps* (or *rex*) in the opening sections of the treatise?

The issue is further complicated by Seneca's contention that sovereignty is its own form of "slavery" (*ista ... seruitus est, non imperium*, 1.8.1; imagined as Nero's words), that the very conspicuousness of the *princeps* (as compared to the facelessness of the rabble) has a curtailing effect on his speech and actions; he is, in effect, held to a higher, even divine, standard (1.8.3). The master–slave dynamic is endemic in the relationship between ruler and subjects and, paradoxically, it works *both ways*. Seneca diagnoses a historical precedent for the present state of affairs: the master–slave relationship between the *princeps* and his subjects is ultimately a consequence of Augustus "wrapping himself around the *res publica*" (*olim enim ita se induit rei publicae Caesar*, 1.4.2), creating an *organic* entity, with Augustus as head and the *res publica* as body, that cannot survive with one part separated from the other (*seduci alterum non posset sine utriusque pernicie,*

1.4.2). The language here directly confronts Augustan and Julio-Claudian ideology of the *res publica restituta*, which, as we have seen, concomitantly championed the return of *libertas* (Stacey 2011: 31–2).[30] Like Lucan (and Velleius before him), Seneca pinpoints state-sponsored rhetoric refracted through the metaphorical language of stately bodies as a locus for contemporary socio-politics.

The role of *libertas* in this equation, however, is more complicated. There seems to be little room for "freedom" in Seneca's elaborate construction here. And we might simply conclude that—pre-empting Lucan—he sardonically deploys Augustan/Julio-Claudian propaganda to expose its own hypocrisy. We have already seen Seneca (like Lucan) directly challenge the compatibility of Caesarism and *libertas* in writing, perhaps before (*De const.* 2.2)[31] and certainly after (*Ep.* 14.13, 24.7, 95.71) the composition of *De Clementia*. Yet miraculously, Seneca claims Nero's Rome has attained "the happiest instantiation of the *res publica*, lacking nothing for the highest liberty except the license to be destroyed" (*laetissima forma rei publicae, cui ad summam libertatem nihil deest nisi pereundi licentia*, 1.1.8). Do we take this at face value? Is it fawning? Perhaps, more than anything, it is wishful thinking. Augustus reformed the state by permanently fusing *princeps* with *res publica* in a mutually interdependent, potentially mutually (self-)destructive organism. Seneca is clear that it is ultimately up to Nero to determine the fate of that state-body—will he model the behavior of the *paterfamilias* or the ruthless slave-owner? Lucan's poem, written around a decade after Seneca's *De Clementia*, shows us what could happen if the *princeps* makes the wrong choice.[32]

The corpse-soldier, as I have stressed, is the metaphorical embodiment of Lucan's dark worldview: the Republican body politic slain by civil war (in the deadly achronic Thessaly) only to be revived by the "Caesarian" Erictho, who controls its functioning like a master controls a slave. But Lucan's poem is inundated with characters like the corpse-soldier—like the liminal Erictho herself, like Pompey, the rotting trunk casting a shadow of its former efficacy (*BC* 1.140, fulfilled at 8.698, 722, etc.)—who occupy a space somewhere between living and dying as a product of the Caesarean/Neronian deathscape.

Recall how Marius Gratidianus is mutilated, covered with wounds, dismembered, but not given the final death-blow: the aim was "to spare the dying man death" (*pereuntis parcere morti* 2.180). Curio's troops die hemmed in, compressed, immobile, yet still *standing* (note the paradox at 4.787: *conpressum turba stetit omne cadauer*, "each corpse stood up squeezed together by the crowd," with Martindale 1976: 47; Chiesa 2005: 24–5), as the Numidians (and Lucan's audience) are denied the spectacularized epic *topos* of a corpse's clattering fall (4.777–87). Scaeva's *aristeia* ends with his body pin-cushioned with spears and arrows (6.191–206), half-blind (214–19), his comrades carrying his prostrate body away as if on a bier (250–9), and with Lucan's mock-eulogy of the fallen warrior (260–2), only to have the man mysteriously return alive to see off the poem (10.543–4). No one was a better shipman than Telo; the rough seas obeyed his ready hand. He was so skilled that even after multiple javelins pierced his heart, he managed to sail his vessel on (3.590–9). Nasidius is bitten by a Prester serpent whose poison causes his body to expand exponentially (9.790–804); his compatriots would have buried his corpse in a tomb were he not still, in death, expanding (*nondum stante modo crescens fugere cadauer*, 804). Tyrrhenus is struck in the head with a lead bullet, blinded, expecting death, only to realize his limbs still possess strength (3.709–15). He demands his comrades make him into a corpse-ballista and aim him in the direction of the enemy so he can rifle off darts mechanically with what life remains in his "corpse," exhorting himself (718–21):

> egere quod superest animae, Tyrrhene, per omnis
> bellorum casus. ingentem militis usum
> hoc habet ex magna defunctum parte cadauer:
> uiuentis feriere loco.

> Empty what's left of life, Tyrrhenus, through all
> misfortunes of war. There is a soldier's great usefulness
> in this corpse of yours, mostly dead now:
> it will be thrust out in place of a someone living.

These examples only scratch the surface.[33] Lucan's chief interest rests in an exploration of the fine line between life and death. He explores the dissolution of the lines demarcating "dead" and "alive" and expands the boundaries of this space into a new state of existence. Nicola Hömke suggests that Lucan places particular emphasis on human dying "as an independent phase of human existence" (Hömke 2010: 103–4; cf. Bartsch 1997: 17–29), arguing chiefly for aesthetic purposes. But this paints only part of the picture. These living corpses function as visceral analogues for Lucan's conception of an imperial slave-state, which concomitantly attacks imperial ideology hawking propaganda that monarchy was a "revived" *res publica libera*.

Lucan's contention that the loss of critical societal agency concomitant with a loss of *libertas*, rendering life akin to living-death, has resonances with Mbembe's portrait of the necropolitical death-world. For Mbembe, citizens of the postcolony subjected to the physical and psychological violence of necropower—akin to a master's power over slaves—are forced into a state of existence somewhere between life and death. In the postcolony, the stakes are high, and the horrific levels of violence on display in the locales that Mbembe analyzes across the globe fortify the metaphor with considerable visceral heft. Lucan's formulation is purely philosophical and rhetorical, but no less provocative in its deployment. He derives his elaborate metaphorical expression from earlier political imagery equating the "death" of the *res publica* with the concomitant "death" of *libertas*, yielding slave-like social death to citizens under the sovereign thumb. The metaphor is further fleshed out through a cynical reworking of the inherently corporeal Julio-Claudian ideology of *res publica restituta*. This narrative position functions as a powerful statement of imperial dissent. That Lucan would even write a historical epic detailing the civil wars and the rise of Caesarism flies in the face of Caesarian/Augustan/Vergilian attempts to overwrite or rewrite historical narrative, to "expurgate."[34] His writing also counters later historical narratives that may note the horrors of the civil wars but only in ways that highlight Caesar's or Octavian's role in squelching the violence and establishing peace. But that his poem not only articulates the brutalities, yet renders them so viscerally and historically present, makes the *Bellum Civile* a striking literary document.[35] Negotiating the space between life and death is symptomatic of Lucan's poetic portrait of living in a world disrupted by civil war, indeed of still living in that world.

Notes

1. Joy Connolly (2016) has independently also read Lucan through Mbembe's postcolonial lens, though to different ends. She argues that the grotesque violence and power of imperial Rome, as it is constructed in *BC*, unifies leaders and masses, similar to Mbembe's description of power-politics in Cameroon. Thanks to the editors, the anonymous press readers, and Susanna Braund for helpful comments on an earlier draft of this chapter. Thanks also to my fellow Lucanisti who attended the conference in Provo, and to Laura Zientek and Mark Thorne for their hospitality.

2. See also Bartsch (1997: 72). Cavarero (2009: 40–6) expands Arendt's argument that the camps were a site of horror in their ability (and aim) to destroy the unique individuality of occupants.

3. Cf. Simone Weil's comments on war's ability to render some humans "a hybrid of man and corpse," for whom there exists "a death that extends throughout a life, a life that death has frozen long before putting an end to it" (2003: 48–9). Weil's subject matter is the *Iliad*, but the horrors of war in Europe and the outbreak of World War II in particular help contextualize many of her dark observations.

4. Does the narrator's strident "Republicanism"—his rejection of Caesarism and longings for a pre-imperial Roman political system—reflect the historical Lucan's own views of Neronian political structure? The short answer is that we cannot be sure. Even though we know Lucan was forced to commit suicide in 65 CE as a result of his involvement in the so-called Pisonian Conspiracy aimed at overthrowing the emperor Nero, it is admittedly difficult to make arguments imposing biographical material onto Lucan's narratorial voice in his poem, even if the fact of his falling out with Nero seems to allow this analysis. The conspiracy itself aimed to replace Nero not with the old *res publica*, but with another, ideally more just, emperor (Piso). "Lucan-as-narrator" may be a sounder way to approach these issues, and this has been my approach throughout. For a range of interpretations of Lucan's "two voices," see esp. Martindale (1984); Feeney (1991: 276–83); Masters (1994); Ormand (1994); Leigh (1997); Bartsch (1997: 93–8); D'Alessandro Behr (2007); Asso (2009); Kimmerle (2015).

5. See my discussion of Erictho in McClellan (forthcoming), along with additional bibliography on this oft-analyzed episode.

6. For Erictho as a night-witch, see Gordon (1987: 239–40); Finiello (2005: 160–3); Tomassi Moreschini (2005: 149–50).

7. Translations throughout are my own.

8. See the important discussion in Tesoriero (2004: 191–2).

9. On Lucan's Thessalian landscape, see esp. Ambühl (2016).

10. On this point, see Feeney (1986); Masters (1992: 179–95); Hardie (1993: 76–7, 107–9). See also Korenjak (1996: *ad* 6.649f.), Arweiler (2006) on Thessaly subsuming elements of hell; cf. Dinter (2012: 69).

11. See, e.g., Duff (1928: 348 n1) and Håkanson (1979: 31); *contra* O'Higgins (1988: 218–19, 225–6), Arweiler (2006), Finiello (2005: 180), Fratantuono (2012: 249–50), Ambühl (2016: 307–8).

12. I have briefly discussed similar issues elsewhere (McClellan 2018: 63–6) in the context of Mary Shelley's reception of Lucan in her *Frankenstein*; I am grateful to be allowed space here for a more detailed analysis.
13. See succinctly Casali (2011: 85–6).
14. Cf. Cic., *Fam.* 4.5.4–5, 5.13; *Att.* 15.13a.1; *Phil.* 2 (*passim*), *Off.* 3.83 for a range of murder, mutilation, and dismemberment metaphors. See Walters 2011 for a thorough examination. On the Roman body politic in literature and sculpture (with an emphasis on the Augustan period), see now Squire (2015) with additional bibliography.
15. On Lucan's use of Sulla in the *BC*, see Mebane in this volume.
16. See Tesoriero (2004: 189); Gowing (2005: 92–4); Dinter (2012: 29–37); Galtier (2018: 359–61). On body imagery generally in Lucan, see Bartsch (1997: 10–47); Dinter (2012: 10–49).
17. See Hardie (1993: 4–5) for the concept; cf. Leigh (1997: 148–57) for more on Pompey in this role in the *BC*.
18. On Pompey's funeral in *BC* 8, see now McClellan (forthcoming: Chapter 3).
19. See Gowing (2005: 4–6), rightly, on *res publica* in the early imperial period as the Republic and not simply "the commonwealth." See Lange (2009: 181–90), who argues that the settlement of 28–27 BCE represents the fulfillment of the triumviral duties rather than that Octavian "restored" the *res publica*; similarly Woodman (1983: *ad* Vel. Pat. 2.89.4) with additional bibliography.
20. See esp. the captivating discussion in Gowing (2005: 28–66) on Velleius and Valerius Maximus.
21. The precise date is a bit hard to come by given the inconsistency of our sources; see Rich and Williams (1999: 191); Lange (2009: 187).
22. Cf. Quint (1993: 147): "The imperial regime ... claims to have unified into a closed form the history of which the human body is the instrument: the vicissitudes of the body in the *Pharsalia*, to the contrary, reflect the shapelessness of recent Roman history as the poem conceives it ... To portray history from the perspective of the lost republican cause and to counter the unifying historical fictions and narratives of imperial ideology, both bodies and poems must fall to pieces." See Bartsch (2010: 313–16) on Lucan as a sort of "anti-Velleius" (316) in his negative apostrophizing of the Roman imperial machine.
23. See similarly Walters (2011: 187–98).
24. On the destruction of *libertas* in the poem and its wider implications for Nero's Rome, see esp. Johnson (1987: 86–100); Quint (1993: 151–7); Bartsch (1997: 41–2) and (2010: 311–1); Galtier (2018: 359–71).
25. Tesoriero (2004: 191–2). Cf. Korenjak (1996: 29–30). Arweiler (2006) makes similar points, but ultimately sees Erictho herself as a symbol for the fragmentation or rupture ("Entzweiung") of the Roman state and a "condensation" of the poem ("Verdichtung des Textes").
26. Roller (2011: 228): "*libertas* means the same thing in all cases: it means 'the (desirable) condition of not being a slave.'" See further Roller (2001: Chapter 4) on the dynamics of the master-slave relationship—actual and metaphorical—in Julio-Claudian Rome.
27. See Tesoriero (2004: 201–7) for a detailed discussion of Erictho as a Caesar-figure in the poem: "Erichtho is Caesar unmasked: pure wickedness, selfish excess, a figure who views the civil war as a means to acquire personal power" (203). This association has implications as Lucan projects the Julio-Claudian "Caesars" more broadly back onto the historical figures in his poem.
28. See usefully Quint (1993: 149–51); Leigh (1997: 79–80); Rudich (1997: 148–9); Roller (2001: 37–8); Bartsch (2010: 311–12); Joseph (2017: 127–8).

29. Henderson (1998: 187); Bartsch (1997: 93–100). On apostrophe generally in *BC*, see esp. D'Alessandro Behr (2007); Asso (2009); Kimmerle (2015).
30. On Seneca's ambivalence toward Augustus and the Augustan regime, particularly in *De Clementia*, see esp. Rudich (1997: 59–66).
31. *De constantia sapientis* is notoriously difficult to date, but almost certainly falls between 47 and 64 CE. See Smith (2014: 121).
32. Note Gowing (2005: 100–1): "As his reign drew to a close, what Seneca feared in the *De Clementia* had in fact happened: Nero forgot himself, had become something that he initially was not. What he remembered—what he reinstantiated—was the Caesar Lucan had hoped to avert."
33. See Dinter (2012: 44–9) on the related phenomenon in the poem of the "automatism" of severed limbs.
34. E.g., Octavian destroyed documents relating to the triumvirs' actions in 36 BCE (App., *B Civ.* 5.132). He avoided elaboration of the civil wars in his *Res Gestae*, and Suetonius tells us that Claudius was coached by his mother Antonia and grandmother Livia not to present a "true and free account" of the time period between Caesar's murder and the end of the civil wars in his history of Augustus's reign (Suet., *Claud.* 41.2).
35. Cf. Thorne (2016) on the traumatic brutality of the Rwandan genocide as a comparative model for thinking about Lucan's attempt to render Roman civil war trauma into poetic form.

References

Agamben, G. (2002), *Remnants of Auschwitz: The Witness and the Archive*, trans. D. Heller-Roazen, New York: Zone Books.
Ambühl, A. (2016), "Thessaly as an Intertextual Landscape of Civil War in Latin Poetry," in J. McInerney and I. Sluiter (eds.), *Valuing Landscape in Classical Antiquity*, 297–322, Leiden: Brill.
Arendt, H. (1966), *The Origins of Totalitarianism*, New York: Harcourt, Brace & World.
Arweiler, A. (2006), "Erictho und die Figuren der Entzweiung—Vorüberlegungen zu einer Poetik der Emergenz in Lucans *Bellum civile*," *Dictynna*, 3: 3–71.
Asso, P. (2009), "The Intrusive Trope: Apostrophe in Lucan," *MD*, 61: 161–73.
Bartsch, S. (1997), *Ideology in Cold Blood: A Reading of Lucan's Civil War*, Cambridge, MA: Harvard University Press.
Bartsch, S. (2010), "Lucan and Historical Bias," in P. Asso (ed.), *Brill's Companion to Lucan*, 303–16, Leiden: Brill.
Braund, S. (2009), *Seneca: De Clementia*, Oxford: Oxford University Press.
Casali, S. (2011), "The *Bellum Civile* as an Anti-*Aeneid*," in P. Asso (ed.), *Brill's Companion to Lucan*, 81–110, Leiden: Brill.
Cavarero, A. (2009), *Horrorism: Naming Contemporary Violence*, trans. W. McCuaig, New York: Columbia University Press.
Chiesa, G. (2005), "La rappresentazione del corpo nel *Bellum civile* di Lucano," *Acme*, 58: 3–43.
Connolly, J. (2016), "A Theory of Violence in Lucan's *Bellum Civile*," in P. Mitsis and I. Ziogas (eds.), *Wordplay and Powerplay in Latin Poetry*, 273–97, Berlin: De Gruyter.
D'Alessandro Behr, F. (2007), *Feeling History: Lucan, Stoicism, and the Poetics of Passion*, Columbus: The Ohio State University Press.
De Luna, G. (2006), *Il corpo del nemico ucciso. Violenza e morte nella guerra contemporanea*, Turin: Einaudi.

Dinter, M. (2012), *Anatomizing Civil War: Studies in Lucan's Epic Technique*, Ann Arbor: University of Michigan Press.
Feeney, D. (1986), "History and Revelation in Vergil's Underworld," *PCPhS*, NS 32: 1–24.
Finiello, C. (2005), "Der Bürgerkrieg: Reine Männersache? Keine Männersache! Erictho und die Frauengestalten im Bellum Civile Lucans," in C. Walde (ed.), *Lucan im 21. Jahrhundert/Lucan in the 21st Century*, 155–85, Munich: De Gruyter.
Fratantuono, L. (2012), *Madness Triumphant: A Reading of Lucan*'s Pharsalia, Lanham: Lexington Books.
Galtier, F. (2018), *L'empreinte des morts: relations entre mort, mémoire et reconnaissance dans la "Pharsale" de Lucain*, Paris: Les Belles Lettres.
Gordon, R. (1987), "Lucan's Erictho," in M. Whitby, P. Hardie, and M. Whitby (eds.), *Homo Viator. Classical Essays for John Bramble*, 231–41, Bristol: Bristol Classical Press.
Gowing, A. (2005), *Empire and Memory: The Representation of the Roman Republic in Imperial Culture*, Cambridge: Cambridge University Press.
Håkanson L. (1979), "Textual Problems in Lucan's De bello ciuili," *PCPhS*, 205: 26–51.
Hardie, P. (1993), *The Epic Successors of Virgil: A Study in the Dynamics of a Tradition*, Cambridge: Cambridge University Press.
Henderson, J. (1998), *Fighting for Rome: Poets and Caesars, History and Civil War*, Cambridge: Cambridge University Press.
Hömke, N. (2010), "Bit by Bit towards Death: Lucan's Scaeva and the Aesthetisization of Dying," in N. Hömke and C. Reitz (eds.), *Lucan's "Bellum civile": Between Epic Tradition and Aesthetic Innovation*, 91–104, Berlin: De Gruyter.
Johnson, W. R. (1987), *Momentary Monsters: Lucan and His Heroes*, Ithaca: Cornell University Press.
Joseph, T. (2017), "Pharsalia as Rome's 'Day of Doom' in Lucan," *AJPh*, 138: 107–41.
Kimmerle, N. (2015), *Lucan und der Prinzipat. Inkonsistenz und unzuverlässiges Erzählen im Bellum Civile*, Berlin: De Gruyter.
Korenjak, M. (1996), *Die Ericthoszene in Lukans* Pharsalia: *Einleitung, Text, Übersetzung, Kommentar*, Frankfurt a. M: Peter Lang.
Lange, C. H. (2009), *Res Publica Constituta: Actium, Apollo, and the Accomplishment of the Triumviral Assignment*, Leiden: Brill.
Leigh, M. (1997), *Lucan: Spectacle and Engagement*, Oxford: Oxford University Press.
Martindale, C. A. (1976), "Paradox, hyperbole, and literary novelty in Lucan's De bello ciuili," *BICS*, 23: 45–54.
Martindale, C. (1984), "The Politician Lucan," *G&R*, 31: 64–79.
Masters, J. (1992), *Poetry and Civil War in Lucan's Bellum Civile*, Cambridge: Cambridge University Press.
Masters, J. (1994), "Deceiving the Reader: The Political Mission of Lucan's Bellum Civile," in J. Elsner and J. Masters (eds.), *Reflections of Nero: Culture, History, and Representation*, 151–77, Chapel Hill: University of North Carolina Press.
Mbembe, J.-A. (2003), "Necropolitics," trans. L. Meintjes, *Public Culture*, 15 (1): 11–40.
McClellan, A. M. (2018), "The Politics of Revivification in Lucan's Bellum Civile and Mary Shelley's *Frankenstein*," in J. Weiner, B. E. Stevens, and B. M. Rogers (eds.), *Frankenstein and its Classics: The Modern Prometheus from Antiquity to Science Fiction*, 59–75, London: Bloomsbury.
McClellan, A. M. (Forthcoming), *Abused Bodies in Roman Epic*, Cambridge: Cambridge University Press.
O'Higgins, D. (1988), "Lucan as *uates*," *ClAnt*, 7: 208–26.
Ormand, K. (1994), "Lucan's *auctor uix fidelis*," *ClAnt* 13: 38–55.
Patterson, O. (1982), *Slavery and Social Death: A comparative Study*, Cambridge, MA: Harvard University Press.

Quint, D. (1993), *Epic and Empire: Politics and Generic Form from Virgil to Milton*, Princeton: Princeton University Press.

Rich, J. W. and J. H. C. Williams (1999), "*Leges et Iura P.R. Restituit*: A New Aureus of Octavian and the Settlement of 28–27 BC," *NC*, 159: 169–213.

Roller, M. B. (2001), *Constructing Autocracy: Aristocrats and Emperors in Julio-Claudian Rome*, Princeton: Princeton University Press.

Rudich, V. (1997), *Dissidence and Literature Under Nero: The Price of Rhetoricization*, London: Routledge.

Smith, R. S. (2014), "*De constantia sapientis*," in G. Damschen and A. Heil (eds.), *Brill's Companion to Seneca*, 121–6, Leiden: Brill.

Squire, M. (2015), "*Corpus Imperii*: Verbal and Visual Figurations of the Roman 'Body Politic,'" *Word and Image*, 31: 305–30.

Stacey, P. (2011), "The Sovereign Person in Senecan Political Theory," *Republics of Letters: A Journal for the Study of Knowledge, Politics, and the Arts*, 2: 15–73.

Tesoriero, C. (2004), "The Middle in Lucan," in S. Kyriakidis and F. De Martino (eds.), *Middles in Latin Poetry*, 183–215, Bari: Levante.

Thorne, M. (2011), "*Memoria Redux*: Memory in Lucan," in P. Asso (ed.), *Brill's Companion to Lucan*, 363–81, Leiden: Brill.

Thorne, M. (2016), "Speaking the Unspeakable: Engaging *Nefas* in Lucan and Rwanda 1994," *Thersites*, 4: 77–119.

Tomassi Moreschini, C. O. (2005), "Lucan's Attitude towards Religion: Stoicism vs. Provincial Cults," in C. Walde (ed.), *Lucan im 21. Jahrhundert/Lucan in the 21st Century*, 130–54, Munich: De Gruyter.

Walters, B. C. (2011), "Metaphor, Violence, and the Death of the Roman Republic," PhD diss., Department of Classics, UCLA, Los Angeles.

Weil, S. (2003), *The Iliad, or the Poem of Force: A Critical Edition*, ed. and trans. by J. P. Holoka, New York: Peter Lang.

Woodman, A. J. (1983), *Velleius Paterculus: The Caesarian and Augustan Narrative (2.41–93)*, Cambridge: Cambridge University Press.

INDEX LOCORUM LUCANI ET SENECAE

Lucan		1.146–50	217	2.271–7	91
Bellum Civile		1.159	125 n.4	2.280	25
1.1–2	233	1.160–2	211	2.286–325	151
1.2	125 n.4	1.160–4	88 n.40	2.287	154
1.2–3	112, 186 n.61	1.165–6	210	2.289–95	115–16
1.8–24	112–13	1.168–70	211	2.292–3	125 n.3
1.10–30	124	1.181–2	86 n.25	2.293	154
1.11–12	124	1.188	218	2.297	154
1.12	116	1.190–2	217	2.297–303	233
1.19	113	1.274–9	91	2.297–305	154–5, 157, 158
1.19–20	122	1.324–6	175	2.297–316	157
1.21	193	1.330–2	175, 178	2.299	156
1.22	113	1.356–86	67 n.30	2.301–3	155, 214
1.24–9	113	1.415–16	101, 205 n.21	2.302–3	234
1.24–32	104, 193	1.498–504	92	2.304–18	164
1.33	213	1.580–4	174	2.314–15	25
1.33–66	19, 122	1.669–72	236	2.315	164
1.34–6	122	1.670	126 n.12, 236	2.323–5	160–1
1.37–8	213	1.678–88	114	2.327–8	219
1.38–43	104	1.682	163	2.330–3	219
1.44–5	122	2.2–3	98	2.343–4	219
1.45	6	2.7–11	94	2.348–90	214
1.45–50	122, 200–1	2.7–15	21	2.354–7	136
1.45–65	122	2.12–13	94	2.354–71	144 n.15
1.53–7	122	2.45–56	115	2.360–1	136, 144 n.17
1.62	210	2.48–52	115	2.372–3	136
1.66	2	2.68–133	124	2.379	136
1.66–182	113	2.71–2	86 n.25	2.380–3	144 n.14, 144 n.18
1.70–80	97–8	2.112	95		
1.70–82	37–8	2.113	95	2.382	105
1.71	92	2.114	94	2.384–91	137
1.72	38, 126 n.11, 127 n.35	2.115	95	2.390	114
		2.128–9	181	2.531	186 n.54
1.72–80	91, 92, 201, 209	2.139–41	181	2.541–6	211
		2.140–3	182, 233	2.571	95
1.73–80	113	2.141–3	181	2.582	175
1.74	40	2.157–9	126 n.7	2.632	116, 126 n.22
1.81	93, 126 n.11	2.180	240	2.633	116, 119
1.81–2	113	2.181–5	181	2.642–3	116, 126 n.5
1.83	125 n.4	2.214–18	126 n.21	2.824–5	80
1.84–6	114, 126 n.12	2.221–2	182	3.21–3	219
1.93–7	183 n.7	2.223–4	183	3.103	196, 200
1.106–7	126 n.17	2.234–325	115, 153	3.103–9	196
1.109	125 n.4	2.239–40	137, 163	3.108	7
1.128	212	2.240–1	136	3.112–14	23, 236
1.135	156, 234	2.266–7	154	3.118–21	25–6
1.140	240	2.267–73	115, 145 n.24	3.123–33	23

Index Locorum Lucani et Senecae

3.128	25	4.492–5	29	6.813–14	232		
3.134–40	23	4.496–7	29	6.821	232		
3.145–53	23–4	4.499	231	6.830	232		
3.145–7	236	4.500–2	29	7.5–6	101		
3.148–9	25	4.505–7	29	7.43	142		
3.149	25	4.512–14	29	7.52–5	54, 55		
3.154–68	43, 87 n.38	4.517–20	29	7.56–7	54		
3.155–68	115	4.570–9	28	7.58–61	55		
3.168	19	4.573–4	29	7.62–5	64		
3.169–297	116–17	4.577–9	236	7.62–7	54		
3.173	117	4.591–660	67 n.30	7.62–85	51		
3.174–5	126 n.19	4.777–87	240	7.63–4	63		
3.177	117, 126 n.20	4.805–9	173	7.65	57		
3.180	117, 126 n. 20	4.820	84	7.65–6	63		
3.197	117, 126 n.20	4.821–3	180	7.66	57		
3.199–200	117	4.821–4	173	7.67	55, 63		
3.202–3	117, 126 n.19	4.824	84	7.68	57		
3.205	117	5.27–9	211	7.68–85	55		
3.208–9	117	5.45–7	63	7.68–9	56, 65		
3.209–10	77	5.116–224	200	7.70	57		
3.210	117	5.122	87 n.31	7.73–4	56		
3.225	117	5.207	186 n.54	7.75	57		
3.236	117	5.385–6	236	7.77–8	56		
3.241–3	20	5.422–3	95	7.79–80	56, 57, 63		
3.246	117, 126 n.20	5.540–721	43	7.81	57		
3.256–63	117–18	6.8	184 n.23	7.84–5	56, 57, 64		
3.259–60	119	6.29	79	7.85–6	64		
3.264–6	118, 126 n.19	6.29–39	77–8	7.87–90	64		
3.271	117	6.32–51	193	7.91–2	65		
3.275	117	6.38	79	7.92–109	65		
3.277–9	117	6.147–8	125 n.3	7.92–3	233		
3.295	118	6.191–206	240	7.110–11	65		
3.303–55	67 n.30	6.214–19	240	7.113–23	65		
3.569	163	6.250–9	240	7.126–7	65		
3.590–9	240	6.260–2	240	7.129–30	232		
3.709–15	241	6.301	213	7.210–13	23, 216		
3.718–21	241	6.333–94	117	7.250	126 n.13		
4.50–105	86 n.20	6.396–9	77	7.251–382	114		
4.96–7	84	6.413–830	51	7.269–70	126 n.13		
4.110–20	99	6.429	87 n.31	7.278	126 n.13		
4.126	126 n.20	6.461–65	232	7.307	175		
4.221–7	236	6.511–17	231	7.346–60	211		
4.223–4	79	6.520–69	230	7.363	126 n.13		
4.223–7	76	6.570–88	230	7.385–459	120		
4.246	80	6.619	232	7.387–419	114, 126 n.5, 126 n.24		
4.295	76	6.619–23	230				
4.295–304	74–5, 85	6.619–41	232	7.389–92	194		
4.297	77	6.624–41	126 n.7	7.392–9	194		
4.297–8	79	6.629	87 n.31	7.405	121		
4.298	80	6.649–759	231	7.405–31	120		
4.476–520	26	6.717	232	7.407–59	124		
4.478–9	28	6.753–9	236	7.419–20	126 n.11, 126 n.24		
4.479–80	28	6.758–9	232				
4.480	28	6.776	232	7.420–5	114		
4.485–7	28	6.785–7	212	7.426	114		
4.488–93	29	6.791–4	212	7.427–30	121		

Index Locorum Lucani et Senecae

7.431	121	9.260	25	9.805–14	20
7.438	126 n.24	9.261	114	9.855–62	104
7.442–7	236	9.283–93	151, 164–5	9.889	144 n.18
7.443–4	121	9.291	145 n.21, 165	9.948–9	93
7.447	127 n.25	9.300–2	92	9.961–99	51
7.551	125 n.3	9.301–2	96	9.964–79	194
7.557	125 n.3	9.303	94	9.969	104, 194
7.578–85	233	9.303–4	92	9.980–6	215
7.596	213	9.303–11	93–4	9.998–9	104
7.597–8	233	9.303–18	91	10.59	220
7.599–616	51	9.305	95	10.60–2	221
7.638–46	237–8	9.311–18	101	10.66–7	221
7.640	19	9.313	92	10.70–6	218
7.641–6	236	9.315	95	10.77–8	221
7.645	114, 126 n.12	9.319–47	100	10.78	218
7.673–5	213	9.321	104	10.110–26	83
7.695	19	9.321–3	92	10.146–9	83
7.695–6	126 n.12, 237	9.324–47	93	10.147	125, 125 n.3
7.697	233	9.360–4	77	10.155–8	83
7.721–3	233	9.370–1	93	10.155–71	41
7.737–42	77	9.379–85	162	10.169	43
7.746–9	84	9.385	144 n.18	10.369–70	221
7.786–845	126 n.7, 232	9.387	161	10.528–9	213
7.847–72	234	9.394–5	161	10.543–4	240
8.25	176	9.394–406	144 n.14		
8.213–17	118–19	9.406–7	162	**Seneca**	
8.222–5	118–19	9.408	161	*Ad Marc.*	
8.229–30	126 n.5	9.411–13	120	1.3–4	154, 166 n.7
8.233–4	124	9.424–30	82–3	20.6	152
8.262–327	123	9.429–30	104		
8.266–7	125 n.3	9.431–44	96	*Ag.*	
8.269–71	124	9.436	97	487	99
8.290–4	119	9.438	21	710	231
8.299–302	124	9.438–45	97		
8.306–12	123	9.444–5	144 n.18, 162	*Apocol.*	
8.308	124	9.445–92	100	11.1–2	105
8.331–453	123	9.446–9	192	13	179
8.420–30	124	9.490–1	103		
8.423–6	124	9.492	103	*Ben.*	
8.609–10	213	9.498–510	144 n.14	1.4.2	156
8.698	240	9.505–9	139	1.6.1	155
8.708–11	233	9.509	137	2.12	157
8.722	240	9.527	21	2.20.2	8, 159
8.777–8	21	9.549	87 n.31	2.20.3	157
8.786–93	233	9.587–93	144 n.14	2.27.2	157
8.841–5	234	9.601–4	217	3.18.1	156
8.853	95	9.706	83	4.6.1	87 n.32
8.867–72	194	9.706–7	105	4.18.1	156
9.3	21	9.718–21	241	4.29.3	156
9.8	21	9.734	144 n.18	5.16.3	181
9.17–18	93	9.737–60	140	5.25.2	157
9.88–90	220	9.755	87 n.31	5.25.4–6	160
9.158–61	159	9.758–60	142	5.25.5	161
9.204–6	236	9.761–2	142	6.21.2	156
9.232–3	91	9.772	21	7.10.2–3	81
9.255–93	162–3	9.790–804	240–1	7.10.3–4	88 n.41

249

Index Locorum Lucani et Senecae

Ref.	Pages
7.10.9–10	88 n.41
3.15.4	155

Brev. Vit.

Ref.	Pages
14.2	145 n.26

Clem.

Ref.	Pages
1.1	164, 185 n.50
1.1.8	240
1.3.3	163
1.3.5	235, 239
1.4.1	163, 239
1.4.2	239–40
1.4.3	235, 239
1.5.1	182, 233, 235, 239
1.8.1	239
1.8.3	239
1.11	180
1.12.1–2	180
1.12.2	178
1.13.4	182
1.14.1–6	239
1.14.3	239
1.18.1–3	239
1.19.2	163, 167 n.31
2.2.1	235, 239
2.5.2	146 n.31
2.5.3	146 n.32

Constant.

Ref.	Pages
2.1–2	166 n.7
2.2	237, 240
3.1–2	141
3–4	144 n.9
10.3–4	145 n.26

Ep.

Ref.	Pages
5.1–6	145 n.28
9.3	138, 145 n.26
9.16	98
13.9	21
14	151, 154
14.3–4	152
14.11–14	153
14.12–13	152, 166 n.7
14.13	24, 240
16.5	22
17.7	21
21.4	61
21.9–10	143 n.2
22.8	166 n.7
24	151, 154
24.5	166 n.13
24.6–8	152, 153, 166 n.7
24.7	240
34.1	165
34.2	160
34.2–3	161
41.5	21
55.2	21
58.35	21
59.2	145 n.23
59.16	138, 145 n.24
66.18	141
66.49–53	144 n.7
66.51	21
67.7–9	151, 157–8
70.4	20
70.5–7	29
70.7–9	28
70.11	20, 28
70.12	28
70.13	29
70.20–1	236
70.22	29
70.26–7	29
71.8–10	166 n.7
71.18	160
71.22	152
71.27	167 n.27
71.33	144 n.8
73.9	157
74.17	144 n.8
76.9–10	27
76.20	27, 28
76.27	27
77.18	237
78.1–2	11 n.2
81	166 n.15
82.1–2	144 n.7
82.10–14	144 n.8
85.24	24
85.28	24, 25
85.27	21
88.29	24, 25
89.22	88 n.40
90.9–13	85 n.11
90.15	20
91	19
92.3–8	167 n.27
92.11	144 n.11
92.11–13	144 n.8
92.34	21
94.56	75
94.57	79
94.58	75
95.29–35	161
95.67–71	158
95.68	161
95.68–70	159–60
95.69–70	151, 153
95.70	167 n.24
95.71	166 n.7, 240
95.72	24
97	58
97.10	216
99.16	156
99.18	138
99.27	47 n.33
102.23	21
104.29–34	158, 166 n.7
104.30–2	151, 152, 153
104.31–2	158–9
107.11	166 n.12
115.11	81, 88 n.41
115.13	81
118.1–2	67 n.17
124.11	21

Helv.

Ref.	Pages
10.2	80, 82
19.2	11 n.2

Her. F.

Ref.	Pages
982	201

[*Her. O.*]

Ref.	Pages
1134	99

Ira

Ref.	Pages
1.1.1	147 n.44
1.20.4	178
2.4.1	167 n.27
2.14.1	160
2.20.3	47 n.33
2.31.7–8	235
3.2.6	147 n.44
3.6.1–2	166 n.10
3.18.2	179, 181
3.18.4	179
3.33.4	87 n.27

[*Oct.*]

Ref.	Pages
391	99
416–18	82
425	82
429	82
433	82
434	82

Phaedra

Ref.	Pages
527–8	81
540	81

Prov.

Ref.	Pages
2.2	145 n.26
2.9–12	166 n.7

2.10	153	3.27.1	86 n.20	832	99
3–4	144 n.7	4b.3.1–2	85 n.11	855–6	201
3.14	105	4b.5.4	21	1061–2	21
		5.15.1	78		
QNat		5.15.2	78–9	*Tranq.*	
1.17.6	80, 81,	5.15.3	79	6.2	160
	87 n.28	5.15.4	79, 81,	16.1	166 n.7
1.17.8	80		87 n.29		
1.17.10	80	6.12	101	*Tro.*	
2.1.4	21			521	86 n.25
2.45	94	*Thy.*			
2.53.1	21	336–403	27	*Vit. Beat.*	
2.59.3	145 n.26	348	27	12.4–13.3	143 n.2
3.15.3	87 n.27	365–8	27	21.1	135
3.27–30	126 n.20	665–82	231	22.4–5	144 n.8

GENERAL INDEX

Accius 177
Agrippina 4–5, 46 n.2, 82, 87 n.33, 220–1, 224 n.16, 224 n.18
Alexandria 41–3, 83–4, 213, 234
anachronism 191, 196–7, 202–3, 218
Annaei, house of the 3–4, 35, 75, 85 n.12
Apollo 101–2, 122, 194–6, 199–202, 205 n.19
    see also Palatine Temple of Apollo
apostrophe 55, 216, 221, 237–8
Appian 177, 244 n.34
Aristotle 67 n.28, 143 n.2
Arrian 66 n.2
Augustan poetry, see Horace; Ovid; Propertius; Tibullus; Vergil
Augustus 2, 5–7, 19, 86 n.16, 105, 120–2, 176–7, 185 n.37, 191, 194–9, 234–6, 239–40
Aulus, death of 138, 140–2, 146 n.37, 147 n.44
    see also snakebites
autocannibalism 140–2, 146 n.43, 147 n.44
autonomy, personal 24–5, 153, 237

backshadowing 209–10, 212, 214–15, 222
Bellum Civile 1–2, 5, 7, 51–2, 193–4
    composition 18–19, 127 n.41
    and nostalgia 209–10
    and Persius' *Satires* 33–4
    and rhetoric 63–4, 175–6
    shared characteristics with Seneca's *Epistulae* 19–29
    see also Lucan
bloodshed 65, 112, 116, 122, 164, 179, 180–3, 232–4
bloodthirstiness 58, 140–2, 173, 175, 177–80, 217–18
body imagery 33, 39–40, 42, 47 n.29, 126 n.7, 141, 181–2, 231, 233–6, 239
body politic 181–2, 186, 233–4, 236–7, 240
Brutus 25, 93, 115, 136, 145 n.24, 153–4, 160–2, 164, 166 n.11, 186 n.54, 212–13

Caesar, Julius
    in Cicero 57–61, 67 n.22, 175
    De bello civili 85 n.9
    historical 6, 9, 95, 157, 174–5, 177, 186 n.54, 233
    in Lucan 7, 19, 23–5, 28–9, 41–3, 55–7, 65, 77–9, 83–5, 92–3, 102, 104–6, 114, 118–19, 121, 125, 193–4, 196–8, 203, 212–13, 215–19, 237
Caesaris, Julia 219, 221–2
Caesarism 33, 124, 173–4, 212, 215–16, 222–3, 236–8, 240–1, 242 n.4
Caligula (Gaius) 3–5, 85 n.2, 178–9, 181, 237
Carrhae, Battle of 113, 120–1, 124
Cassius Dio 5–6, 46 n.20, 122, 179, 185 n.37, 185 n.44, 196–7
Cato the Younger
    in Lucan 151
        African march 93, 104–5, 124, 137–40, 152, 161–2
        as benefactor 153–7
        on civil war 25, 114–16, 154, 158, 233–4
        in memory 213–18, 222
        shipwrecked fleet 91–3, 100, 103, 105
        and Stoicism 126 n.16, 133, 135–42, 161
        suicide 105, 124, 153, 158, 214, 223 n.9
    in Seneca 25, 237
        as a fighter 158–61
        as a sage 152–3, 216
        suicide 24, 152–3
Cicero 7, 51–70, 102–3, 155–6, 161, 174–6, 233
    Acad. 144 n.8, 144 n.10, 185 n.57
    Arch. 66 n.2
    Att. 58– 62, 67 n.17, 67 n.19–23, 175, 184 n.18, 186 n.57, 197, 233
    Cat. 186 n.56, 233
    Div. 66 n.3
    De Fin. 7, 85 n.6, 135, 144 n.8, 144 n.10, 145 n.19, 146 n.29, 146 n.34
    De Natura Deorum 86 n.21, 102
    De Or. 67 n.28
    Fam. 51, 58, 61–2, 66 n.2–3, 197, 216, 243 n.14
    Man. 30, 175
    Mil. 186 n.56, 186 n.68
    Mur. 146 n.31
    Off. 86 n.21, 156, 166 n.17, 185 n.41, 243 n.14
    Phil. 233
    Prov. Cons. 175
    Sest. 233
    Tim. 94
    Tusc. 141, 145 n.23, 166 n.2
Cinna 173–5, 180, 211
civil wars, views of 79, 91, 104, 120–2, 152, 154, 193–4, 201, 210
    and the body politic 233–4, 236, 240
    and cosmic strife 98–100

General Index

and emperors as gods 122–3
as madness 100, 112–13
Claudius 3–6, 87 n.33, 105, 179–80, 221
clemency 176–7, 180
Cleopatra 41, 217, 220–2
closure 91, 99–100, 104–6
controversiae 4, 52–4, 61–2
  see also declamation; *suasoriae*
Cornelia 219–20
Cornutus 7–8, 33, 35, 40, 45 n.13, 46 n.20
corpse-soldier, see living dead
cosmology, see Stoicism, physics
Crassus 112–13, 116, 124, 219
cruelty 175–80, 237, 239
cultural memory 8–9, 191–4, 203, 210, 216
  see also mnemotopes
Curio 51–2, 67 n.29, 84, 173, 240

decay see ruin
declamation 4–5, 9, 41, 52–7, 61–5
  see also *controversiae*; *suasoriae*
Delphi 87 n.31, 199–200, 202
Diodorus Siculus 66 n.2, 87 n.26
Diogenes Laertius 94, 144 n.8, 144 n.11, 145 n.23,
  146 n.29, 146 n.32, 146 n.34
dismemberment 33, 40, 232, 240

ekpyrosis 37–41, 91–2, 98–9, 102–4, 201–2, 209
  see also ruin
emotions, see Stoicism
Ennius 174, 201
Epictetus 134, 143 n.2, 144 n.8–9, 145 n.29,
  146 n.29, 146 n.32, 146 n.38
Erictho 51, 87 n.31, 126 n.7, 211, 213, 230–2, 236–8,
  240
exaggeration 57, 78, 139, 220

Florus 86 n.16, 157, 185 n.46
funerals 27, 136, 154–6, 174, 212, 219, 230, 233–4

Gaius 24
Galen 146 n.36
geography 73, 75–7, 91–2, 100–1, 111, 113–19,
  124–5, 192
  see also mining; Pomponius Mela; Strabo; Syrtes

history, views of 193–4, 202–3, 209–10
Horace 34, 41, 47 n.30, 47 n.32, 91, 111, 120–3, 125,
  126 n.9, 127 n.25, 127 n.28–9, 127 n.35,
  127 n.39, 192, 195, 204 n.8, 216
hypallage 20
hyperbole 57
  see also exaggeration

identity 8–10, 113–16, 120, 123–5, 157, 192–5,
  229, 237

Iliad 67 n.32, 159
imperialism 111–15, 124
imperium 165, 177, 191–2, 239
interdiscursivity 34–5, 43–4, 203
intertextuality 17, 21, 34–6, 43, 45 n.11, 52, 84, 181

Josephus 5, 198, 204 n.7
Justinian 127 n.38
Juvenal 46 n.26, 147 n.43, 177, 184 n.27

landscape 73–4, 77–8, 95, 100, 103–4, 191–3, 231
Lentulus 123–4, 211
libertas 7, 19, 23–4, 76–7, 151, 153–6, 202, 213–14,
  230, 233–7
Libya 82, 100–1, 104–5, 106 n.8, 137–40, 152, 161
living dead 229–32, 236–7, 240–1
Livy 66 n.3, 85 n.9, 126 n.8, 155, 157, 167 n.22,
  185 n.46, 211, 235
Lucan
  biography 3–5, 36, 85 n.12, 242 n.4
  contemporary contexts 1–8, 17–21, 33–5, 74–6,
    138–9, 176–83, 221–2, 238–40
  and Persius 35–7
  satirical critique of Nero 33–6, 122, 200–1
  use of Cicero's letters 61–2, 175
  women depicted by 41, 136, 139–40, 211,
    213, 217–22, 230–2, 236–8, 240,
    243 n.27
  see also *Bellum Civile*
Lucretius 86 n.21, 87 n.36, 144 n.9
luxuria 79–83, 87 n.33, 210–11

Manilius 80, 127 n.38
Marcia 136, 139–40, 214, 219
Marcus Aurelius 144 n.8, 145 n.28
Marius 124, 173–5, 177–8, 180, 184 n.15,
  211–12, 236
Mbembe, Achille 229, 237, 241
memory, see cultural memory; mnemotopes
metaphor 65, 79, 93, 178, 229–33
  animal 158–65, 167, 239
  body politic 181–2, 233–41
  ekpyrosis 37–40, 92, 97–101, 201–2
  geographical 117–18
  medical 40, 180–2
  mining 74–6, 80, 84
mining 74–85, 86 n.17, 86 n.19
mnemotopes 191, 195–6, 202
monumentality 191–9, 203
Musonius Rufus 7–8, 46 n.23, 134, 144 n.7

nature 73–5, 78, 82, 97–106, 163, 193–4
necropolitics 229–30, 237, 241
Nero 2–9, 17–19, 41, 82, 143 n.6, 163–4, 174–6,
  180–2, 213, 242 n.4
  Apollonian pretensions 102, 199–202, 205 n.20

254

General Index

Lucan's critique of 33–6, 46 n.20
Parthian policy 111, 120–3
Neronian
  fears 7, 221–2
  literature 1–2, 33
  Rome 17, 19, 229–30, 232–40, 242 n.4

Ovid 1, 38, 192, 195
  Fasti 83, 87 n.34, 87 n.39, 235
  Metamorphoses 87 n.34, 97, 99, 147 n.43, 201–2, 204 n.4
  Tristia 19, 197, 204 n.8, 235

Palatine Temple of Apollo 191, 194–9, 202–3
Parthia 6, 124–5
  as *aliter mundus* 119–21, 123
  futility of Roman attitudes towards 123–5
  Nero's policy towards 6, 121–3
  rivers 117–19
  and Roman imperialism 111–16
Persius 8–9, 33–44
Petronius 41, 146 n.43
Phaethon 122, 201–2, 205 n.20
Pharsalus, battle of 51, 54–5, 63–5, 77, 84, 91, 102, 114, 116–18, 120–1, 124, 175, 193, 209, 213, 230, 232–4, 236
Philodemus 147 n.44
Pisonian conspiracy 5–6, 17, 36, 85 n.2, 124, 242 n.4
Plato 94, 160, 164, 234
Pliny the Elder 5, 73–4, 76, 78, 80, 84, 85 n.5, 86 n.19, 87 n.33–5, 87 n.39, 95, 185 n.37
Pliny the Younger 8, 85 n.2
Plutarch 62, 66 n.2–3, 144 n.10–11, 146 n.29, 167 n.28, 174, 178, 183 n.13, 185 n.46
Pompey
  in Cicero 57–63, 174–5
  death 67 n.33, 95, 162, 175–6, 220, 234
  in Lucan 51–2, 54–7, 63–5, 114–19, 123–4, 156, 174, 178, 211–13, 233–4
  in Seneca 152–3, 158–9
Pomponius Mela 77, 85 n.8, 86 n.23, 88 n.41, 92
Propertius 18, 127 n.39, 195–7, 204 n.8, 224 n.17

Quintilian 5, 54, 61, 63, 156

Republic, Roman 136–7, 152–8, 163, 175–8, 197–9, 209–22, 242 n.4
Res Gestae Divi Augusti 127 n.39, 176, 234
res publica 7, 152, 163, 181–2, 214, 216–17, 230–42
rhetorical strategies, *see controversiae*; declamation; *suasoriae*
rivers 77, 99, 117–19
  see also Parthia

Rome, *see* cultural memory; identity; imperialism; Neronian; Republic, Roman; ruin
ruin
  architectural 51, 103–4, 113–14, 215
  of body politic 64–5, 113, 233
  cosmic 38–9
  of *libertas* 24, 237
  monuments 193–4
  moral 41, 80
  ruina montium 76–9, 86 n.19
  see also ekpyrosis

Sallust 92, 106 n.4, 126 n.8, 185 n.46, 209, 233
Seneca the Elder 3, 9, 53, 58, 61–2, 153, 176–7
Seneca the Younger 3–4, 7–10, 17, 19–30, 238
  biography 3–4, 11 n.2, 85 n.12
  on *libertas* 240
  and Lucan's Cato 151–65
  on master-slave dynamics 239–40
  on medical metaphor 181–2
  on morality of mining 74, 78–84
  and Nero 180, 235
  on soldiers as bees 163–4
  and Stoicism 135, 138, 141
  on suicide 153
Sextus Empiricus 146 n.39
Silius Italicus 46 n.22
simile, *see* metaphor
slavery 24, 53, 86 n.17, 159, 236–41, 243 n.26
snakebites 20, 87 n.31, 138, 140–1, 146 n.33
  see also Aulus, death of
Spain 3, 75–6, 84, 85 n.8, 86 n.17
Statius 18, 46 n.22
Stobaeus 144 n.8, 144 n.11, 146 n.32
Stoicism 7–8, 26
  anti-Stoic *topoi* 140–2
  axiology of 24, 134–5, 144 n.10, 144 n.11, 153
  emotions 137–8
  ethics 7, 46 n.23, 74, 82, 85 n.6, 105
  oikeiōsis 145–6 n.29, 157, 167 n.19
  physics 23, 37–40, 73–5, 78–9, 82, 91, 94–5, 98–9, 101–2, 113, 117–18
  popular portrayals 133, 136–8
Strabo 77, 85 n.8, 85 n.10, 92, 127 n.38
suasoriae 3–4, 52–5, 57–8, 61–2, 64–5, 124, 153, 184 n.27
  see also controversiae; declamation
Suetonius 4–6, 17, 19, 35–6, 45 n.10, 87 n.30, 122, 127 n.31, 174, 177–9, 185 n.35, 185 n.43, 194, 201–2, 204 n.14–15, 218, 221, 233, 235, 244 n.34
suicide 3, 17, 20, 24, 26–9, 67 n.33, 104–5, 133, 142, 143 n.6, 152–4, 158, 214, 222, 236, 242 n.4
Sulla 9–10, 60, 173–83, 233, 236

255

General Index

Syrtes 104–5
   and closure 91, 99–100, 104
   as existing outside of temporal structures
      96–7, 103
   explanations of 91–104

Tacitus 4–6, 8, 17–8, 46 n.22, 87 n.30, 87 n.37,
      122, 146 n.31, 178–9, 186 n.55,
      220, 236
temporal dislocation 96–7, 191–2, 196, 198–9, 202,
      204 n.11, 210–2, 232, 237–8
   see also backshadowing
Thrasea Paetus 8, 134, 143 n.6, 216
Tibullus 18

Ulpian 236

Vacca 17
Valerius Flaccus 77
Valerius Maximus 174, 178–9, 185 n.39, 185 n.46,
      185 n.51, 223 n.13, 235, 237
Varro 164, 233
vates 200, 210–12, 216
Velleius Paterculus 177, 179, 204 n.7, 235
Vergil 1, 10, 34, 38, 155, 161, 210, 216, 220
   Aen. 20, 37, 46 n.22, 87 n.34, 125 n.3, 127 n.39,
      159, 164–5, 192–3, 198, 204 n.8–9, 231,
      233, 238
   G. 87 n.28, 97, 159–65, 167 n.32
Vitruvius 235

war, *see* civil wars, views of
women, *see* Agrippina; Lucan, women depicted by